Pentecostarion

Compiled and adapted from
approved sources
by
THE LITURGICAL COMMISSION
of
THE SISTERS OF THE ORDER OF ST. BASIL THE GREAT
Uniontown, Pennsylvania 15401

Pentecost
May 18, 1986

OUR HOLY FATHER AMONG THE SAINTS
BASIL THE GREAT

CONTENTS

For private use

Holy and Great Sunday of the Resurrection
Pascha

Resurrection Matins

The celebrant, fully vested in bright vestments and escorted by candle-bearers and servers, proceeds to the holy sepulcher, incenses the Plaschanitsa (Burial Shroud), and removes it from the sepulcher and carries it into the sanctuary, placing it upon the holy altar where it will remain until Ascension Day. During this ceremony, the people sing:

TROPARION

Tone 2 When You descended to death, O Immortal Life, * You destroyed the Abyss by the radiance of your divinity. * And when You raised the dead from the depths of the earth * all the heavenly powers cried out: * O Giver of life, Christ our God, glory to You!

The celebrant, carrying a handcross, and escorted by candle-bearers, servers, and appointed persons carrying the Holy Gospel Book and icon of the Resurrection, exits from the church followed by the faithful. They proceed once around the church, and where the custom exists, the bells are rung. During the procession, the faithful repeatedly sing the Troparion in Tone 6.

Tone 6 O Christ our Savior, * the angels in heaven sing the praises of your Resurrection; * make us, on earth, also worthy * to extol and glorify You with a pure heart.

The procession stops before the closed doors of the church where the celebrant incenses the Holy Gospel, the icon, and all the faithful. Then standing before the doors, the celebrant, holding the handcross in his left hand, signs the doors in the form of a cross with the censer three times. Candle-bearers stand at his right and left sides. The celebrant begins:

Priest: Glory to the holy, consubstantial, life-creating and undivided Trinity, always, now and ever and forever.

Response: Amen.

Then the priest sings the Troparion in special Tone 5:

Priest: Christ is risen from the dead! By death He conquered Death, and to those in the graves He granted life.

The faithful repeat the Troparion twice, and where the custom exists, the church bells are rung during the singing.

R. Christ is risen from the dead! By death He conquered Death, and to those in the graves He granted life. *(2 times)*

TROPARION WITH VERSICLES

The celebrant sings the following versicles, and to each one the people respond by singing: Christ is risen...

v. Let God arise and let his enemies be scattered, * and let those who hate Him flee from before His face.

Christ is risen...

v. As smoke vanishes, so let them vanish as wax melts before the fire.

Christ is risen...

v. So let the wicked perish at the presence of God, and let the righteous ones rejoice.

Christ is risen...

v. This is the day that the Lord has made, let us exalt and rejoice in it.

Christ is risen...

v. Glory be to the Father, and to the Son, and to the Holy Spirit, now and ever and forever. Amen.

Christ is risen...

Priest: Christ is risen from the dead! By death He conquered Death.

The doors are opened and the celebrant, preceded by candle-bearers enters the church followed by the faithful who sing:

R. And to those in the graves He granted life.

All the church bells are rung. Having entered the sanctuary, the celebrant, or deacon if one is assisting, begins the Litany of Peace.

LITANY OF PEACE

Deacon: In peace, let us pray to the Lord.

R. Lord, have mercy. *(after each petition)*

For peace from on high and for the salvation of our souls, let us pray to the Lord.

For peace in the whole world, for the well-being of the holy Churches of God and for the union of all, let us pray to the Lord.

For this holy Church and for all who enter it with faith, reverence, and the fear of God, let us pray to the Lord.

For our holy ecumenical Pontiff *(name)*, the Pope of Rome, let us pray to the Lord.

For our most reverend Archbishop and Metropolitan *(name)*, for our God-loving Bishop *(name)*, for the venerable priesthood, the diaconate in Christ, and all the clergy and the people, let us pray to the Lord.

For our civil authorities and all in the service of our country, let us pray to the Lord.

For this city, *(OR: for this village, OR: for this holy monastery)*, for every city and countryside, and for those living within them in faith, let us pray to the Lord.

For seasonable weather, for an abundance of the fruits of the earth, and for peaceful times, let us pray to the Lord.

For those who travel by sea, air, and land; for the sick, the suffering, the captive, and for their safety and salvation, let us pray to the Lord.

That we be delivered from all affliction, wrath, and need, let us pray to the Lord.

Protect us, save us, have mercy on us and preserve us, O God, by your grace.

Remembering our most holy, most pure, most blessed and glorious Lady, the Mother of God and ever-Virgin Mary with all the saints, let us commend ourselves and one another, and our whole life, to Christ our God.

R. To You, O Lord.

For to You is due all glory, honor, and worship, Father, Son, and Holy Spirit, now and ever and forever.

R. Amen.

RESURRECTION CANON

The celebrant begins the Canon of St. John Damascene, singing the first Irmos in each Ode. The faithful sing the remainder of each Ode while the celebrant incenses in the usual manner.

ODE 1

It is the day of Resurrection, * O people, let us be enlightened by it. * The Passover is the Lord's Passover, * since Christ, our God, has brought us from death to life * and from earth to heaven. * Therefore, we sing the hymn of victory.

***Refrain:* Christ is risen from the dead!**

Let us cleanse our senses * that we may see the risen Christ * in the glory of his Resurrection * and clearly hear

Him greeting us: * Rejoice! as we sing the hymn of victory.

Let the heavens properly rejoice, * and let the earth be glad, * and let the whole visible and invisible world celebrate; * for Christ, our everlasting joy is risen.

It is the day of Resurrection, * O people, let us be enlightened by it. * The Passover is the Lord's Passover, * since Christ, our God, has brought us from death to life * and from earth to heaven. * Therefore, we sing the hymn of victory.

LITANY

Again and again, in peace, let us pray to the Lord.

R. Lord, have mercy.

Protect us, save us, have mercy on us and preserve us, O God, by your grace.

R. Lord, have mercy.

Remembering our most holy, most pure, most blessed and glorious Lady, the Mother of God and ever-virgin Mary with all the saints, let us commend ourselves and one another, and our whole life to Christ our God.

R. To You, O Lord.

For You are the supreme ruler, and yours is the kingdom, the power, and the glory, Father, Son, and Holy Spirit, now and ever and forever.

R. Amen.

ODE 3

Come, let us partake of a new drink, * not miraculously produced from the barren rock, * but from the Fountain of Immortality, * springing up from the tomb of Christ. * In Him is our firm strength.

Refrain: **Christ is risen from the dead!**

Today all things are filled with light * earth and heaven and the world beneath. * Then let all creation celebrate * the Resurrection of Christ. * In Him is the firm foundation of all things.

I was buried yesterday with You, O Christ; * but today I rise, * resurrected with You. * Yesterday I crucified myself with You, O Savior. * Now glorify me with You in your kingdom.

Come, let us partake of a new drink, * not miraculously produced from the barren rock, * but from the Fountain of Immortality, * springing up from the tomb of Christ. * In Him is our firm strength.

LITANY

Again and again, in peace, let us pray to the Lord.

R. Lord, have mercy.

Protect us, save us, have mercy on us and preserve us, O God, by your grace.

R. Lord, have mercy.

Remembering our most holy, most pure, most blessed and glorious Lady, the Mother of God and ever-virgin Mary with all the saints, let us commend ourselves and one another, and our whole life to Christ our God.

R. To You, O Lord.

For You are our God, and we give glory to You, Father, Son, and Holy Spirit, now and ever and forever.

R. Amen.

HYPAKOE

The women with Mary, before the dawn, * found the stone rolled away from the tomb, * and they heard the angel say: * Why do you seek among the dead, as a mortal, the One who abides in everlasting light? * Behold the linens of burial. * Go in haste and proclaim to the world * that, having conquered Death, the Lord is risen; * for He is the Son of God, the Savior of mankind.

ODE 4

Let Habakkuk, * speaking in behalf of God, * stand with us at the divine watch; * let him show us the brilliant angel who proclaims: * Today salvation comes to the world; * for Christ, being almighty, is risen.

***Refrain:* Christ is risen from the dead!**

Christ had appeared as a man * when He was born of the Virgin. * As a mortal, he was called Lamb. * Being undefiled and without blemish, * He is our Passover; * and as true God, * He is proclaimed perfect.

Christ, our blessed crown, was sacrificed of his own will * like a yearling lamb for all of us, * and so became our cleansing Pasch. * From his tomb He shines on us again * as the splendid Sun of Righteousness.

David, ancestor of the Lord, * danced and made music before the Ark * which was only a symbol. * As God's holy people, * let us witness the symbol fulfilled * and rejoice in spirit; * for Christ, being almighty, is risen.

Let Habakkuk, * speaking in behalf of God, * stand with us at the divine watch; * let him show us the brilliant angel who proclaims: * Today salvation comes to the world; * for Christ, being almighty, is risen.

LITANY

Again and again, in peace, let us pray to the Lord.

R. Lord, have mercy.

Protect us, save us, have mercy on us and preserve us, O God, by your grace.

R. Lord, have mercy.

Remembering our most holy, most pure, most blessed and glorious Lady, the Mother of God and ever-virgin Mary with all the saints, let us commend ourselves and one another, and our whole life to Christ our God.

R. To You, O Lord.

For You are a gracious God, and You love mankind, and we give glory to You, Father, Son, and Holy Spirit, now and ever and forever.

R. Amen.

ODE 5

Let us rise at early dawn * and bring to our Master a hymn instead of myrrh; * and we shall see Christ, * the Sun of Righteousness * who enlightens the life of all.

***Refrain:* Christ is risen from the dead!**

When those bound by chains in the realm of Death * saw your boundless mercy, O Christ, * they hastened to the light with joy, * praising the Eternal Pasch.

Bearing torches let us meet the bridegroom, Christ, * as He comes forth from his tomb; * and let us greet, with joyful song, * the saving Pasch of God.

Let us rise at early dawn * and bring to our Master a hymn instead of myrrh; * and we shall see Christ, * the Sun of Righteousness * who enlightens the life of all.

LITANY

Again and again, in peace, let us pray to the Lord.

R. Lord, have mercy.

Protect us, save us, have mercy on us and preserve us, O God, by your grace.

R. Lord, have mercy.

Remembering our most holy, most pure, most blessed and glorious Lady, the Mother of God and ever-virgin Mary with all the saints, let us commend ourselves and one another, and our whole life to Christ our God.

R. To You, O Lord.

For sanctified and glorified is your all-honorable and majestic Name: the Father, and the Son, and the Holy Spirit, now and ever and forever.

R. Amen.

ODE 6

You have descended into the realm of Death, O Christ, * and have broken ancient bonds which held the captive. * You arose from the tomb on the third day * like Jonah from the whale.

Refrain: **Christ is risen from the dead!**

When You arose from the tomb, O Christ, * You preserved its seals intact, * just as in your holy birth * a virgin's vow was unbroken. * You opened to us the gates of Paradise.

O my Savior, being God, * willingly You offered yourself. * As a never consumed, yet living victim, * You gave yourself to the Father. * You arose from the tomb, * resurrecting Adam, the father of all.

You have descended into the realm of Death, O Christ, * and have broken ancient bonds which held the captive. * You arose from the tomb on the third day * like Jonah from the whale.

LITANY

Again and again, in peace, let us pray to the Lord.

R. Lord, have mercy.

Protect us, save us, have mercy on us and preserve us, O God, by your grace.

R. Lord, have mercy.

Remembering our most holy, most pure, most blessed and glorious Lady, the Mother of God and ever-virgin Mary with all the saints, let us commend ourselves and one another, and our whole life to Christ our God.

R. To You, O Lord.

For You are the King of peace and the Savior of our souls, and we give glory to You, Father, Son, and Holy Spirit, now and ever and forever.

R. Amen.

KONTAKION

Tone 8 Although You descended into the grave, O Immortal One, * You destroyed the power of Death. * You arose again as a victor, O Christ God. * You announced to the women bearing ointment: Rejoice! * You gave peace to your apostles * and resurrection to the fallen.

IKOS

Early in the morning before sunrise, as if it were already day, myrrh-bearing virgins were seeking the Sun, previously descended into the grave; and they cried out one to another: Come, O friends! Let us anoint with fragrant spices the life-giving and yet already buried body of Christ who has resurrected the fallen Adam. Let us hasten, as did the Magi, and adore Christ and bring our myrrh as a gift to Him who is wrapped not in swaddling clothes but in a shroud. Let us weep and exclaim: Arise, O Master, granting resurrection to the fallen!

Having beheld the Resurrection of Christ, * let us adore the holy Lord Jesus * who alone is sinless. * We bow to your Cross, O Christ, * and we praise and glorify your holy Resurrection. * You are our God * and besides You we recognize no other, * and we invoke your name. * Come, all you faithful, * and let us bow to the holy Resurrection of Christ, * since, through the Cross, * joy has come to all the world. * Ever praising the Lord, * let us extol his Resurrection, * since He, having endured the Crucifixion, * has destroyed Death by his death. *(3 times)*

Tone 8 Jesus is risen from the tomb, * as He foretold, * and granted us everlasting life * and great mercy.

ODE 7

God, who saved the three youths from the furnace, * has become man * and suffered as any mortal; * but his passion clothed his mortality * with the splendor of incorruption. * He is the only blessed One, God of our fathers, * and is worthy of all praise.

***Refrain:* Christ is risen from the dead!**

Pious women ran in tears to You, O Christ, bringing myrrh to You as dead; * but instead, they adored You in joy as the living God * and announced your mystical Passover to your disciples.

We celebrate the victory over Death, * the destruction of the deep Abyss, * and the birth of a new eternal life. * With joy, we praise the Author of all things, * the only Blessed One, God of our fathers, * for He is worthy of all praise.

This most splendid and saving night * is sacred and all-worthy of solemnity. * It heralds the bright day of Resurrection * on which the Eternal Light in the flesh, * has shown forth from the tomb to all.

God, who saved the three youths from the furnace, * has become man * and suffered as any mortal; * but his passion clothed his mortality * with the splendor of incorruption. * He is the only blessed One, God of our fathers, * and is worthy of all praise.

LITANY

Again and again, in peace, let us pray to the Lord.

R. Lord, have mercy.

Protect us, save us, have mercy on us and preserve us, O God, by your grace.

R. Lord, have mercy.

Remembering our most holy, most pure, most blessed and glorious Lady, the Mother of God and ever-virgin Mary with all the saints, let us commend ourselves and one another, and our whole life to Christ our God.

R. To You, O Lord.

For blessed and all-glorified is the majesty of your kingdom, Father, Son, and Holy Spirit, now and ever and forever.

R. Amen.

ODE 8

This is that chosen and holy day, * Feast of feasts, * most solemn day, * only king and lord of all Sabbaths, * on which we ever praise Christ.

***Refrain:* Christ is risen from the dead!**

Come, on this glorious day of Resurrection, * and partake of the fruit of the new vine, * the divine joy of Christ's kingdom, * ever praising Him, our God.

Lift up your eyes, O Zion, and behold. * See your children coming to you. * From the east, west, north, and south * they come to you like stars of light divine, * ever blessing Christ.

***Refrain:* O Most Holy Trinity, our God, glory be to You!**

O Almighty Father, Spirit, and Word, * three persons, yet one essence, * fullness of all being and divinity * we have been baptized in You, * and ever bless You.

This is that chosen and holy day, * Feast of feasts, * most

solemn day, * only king and lord of all Sabbaths, * on which we ever praise Christ.

LITANY

Again and again, in peace, let us pray to the Lord.

R. Lord, have mercy.

Protect us, save us, have mercy on us and preserve us, O God, by your grace.

R. Lord, have mercy.

Remembering our most holy, most pure, most blessed and glorious Lady, the Mother of God and ever-virgin Mary with all the saints, let us commend ourselves and one another, and our whole life to Christ our God.

R. To You, O Lord.

For blessed is your Name, and glorified is your kingdom, Father, Son, and Holy Spirit, now and ever and forever.

R. Amen.

ODE 9

Priest: Let us greatly extol the Theotokos and the Mother of Light in hymns!

The angel exclaimed to her, * full of grace: * Rejoice, O Pure Virgin; * again I say, rejoice! * Your Son is risen from the grave on the third day * and has raised the dead. * Let all nations rejoice!

Shine in splendor, * O new Jerusalem! * For the glory of the Lord * is risen upon you. * O Zion, sing with joy and rejoice! * And you, pure Mother of God, * rejoice in the resurrection of your Son.

***Refrain:* Christ is risen from the dead!**

How pleasingly divine and sweet * was your voice, O Christ, * when You promised, without fail, to remain with us * until the end of time. * We, the faithful, rejoice * in this firm foundation of hope.

O Christ, great and sacred Pasch, * Wisdom, Power, and Word of God, * grant that we be with You in your kingdom * on the never-ending day.

Shine in splendor, * O new Jerusalem! * For the glory of the Lord * is risen upon you. * O Zion, sing with joy and rejoice! * And you, pure Mother of God, * rejoice in the resurrection of your Son.

LITANY

Again and again, in peace, let us pray to the Lord.

R. Lord, have mercy.

Protect us, save us, have mercy on us and preserve us, O God, by your grace.

R. Lord, have mercy.

Remembering our most holy, most pure, most blessed and glorious Lady, the Mother of God and ever-virgin Mary with all the saints, let us commend ourselves and one another, and our whole life to Christ our God.

R. To You, O Lord.

For all the powers of heaven extol You, O Lord, and we give glory to You, Father, Son, and Holy Spirit, now and ever and forever.

R. Amen.

HYMN OF LIGHT

You, O King and Lord, * have fallen asleep * in the flesh as a mortal man, * but on the third day You arose again. * You have raised Adam * from his corruption and made Death powerless. * You are the Pasch of incorruption. * You are the salvation of the world. *(3 times)*

AT THE PRAISES

Tone 1 We praise your saving passion, O Christ! * We glorify your Resurrection!

You endured crucifixion; * You destroyed Death and rose from the dead. * Give peace to our lives, * O only almighty Lord.

You captured Hades, O Christ. * You raised us by your own Resurrection. * Make us worthy to praise and glorify You in purity of heart.

We glorify your divine humility; * we praise You, O Christ. * You were born of a virgin, * yet were not separated from the Father. * You became a mortal and suffered for us, * voluntarily enduring the Cross. * You rose from the tomb, * coming as from a bridal chamber to save the world. * O Lord, glory to You!

PASCHAL HYMNS

The faithful come to kiss the cross during these hymns.

Let God arise and let his enemies be scattered, and let those who hate Him flee from before his face.

Today the sacred Pasch is revealed to us, * holy and new Pasch, * the mystical Passover, * the venerable Passover, * the Pasch which is Christ the Redeemer, * spotless Pasch,

great Pasch, * the Pasch of the faithful, * the Pasch which is the key to the gates of Paradise, * the Pasch which sanctifies all the faithful.

As smoke vanishes, so let them vanish as wax melts before the fire.

O Women, * be the heralds of good news and tell what you saw; * tell of the vision and say to Zion: * Accept the good news of joy from us, * the news that Christ has risen. * Exalt and celebrate * and rejoice, O Jerusalem, * seeing Christ the King coming from the tomb * like a bridegroom.

So let the wicked perish at the presence of God, and let the righteous ones rejoice.

The myrrh-bearing women * arrived just before the dawn * at the tomb of the Giver of Life * and found an angel seated on the stone * who spoke these words to them: * Why do you seek the Living among the dead? * Why do you mourn the Incorruptible among those subject to decay? * Go, announce the good news * to his disciples.

This is the day that the Lord has made; let us exalt and rejoice in it.

Pasch so delightful, * Pasch of the Lord is the Pasch, * most honored Pasch now dawned on us. * It is the Pasch! * Therefore, let us joyfully embrace one another. * O Passover, save us from sorrow; * for today Christ has shown forth from the tomb * as from a bridal chamber * and filled the women with joy by saying: * Announce the good news * to my apostles.

Glory be to the Father, and to the Son, and to the Holy Spirit, now and ever and forever. Amen.

This is the Resurrection day. * Let us be enlightened by this Feast, * and let us embrace one another. * Let us call Brethren * even those who hate us, * and in the Resurrection * forgive everything; and let us sing:

Christ is risen from the dead! * By death He conquered Death, * and to those in the graves He granted life. *(3 times).*

After the veneration, the sermon of St. John Chrysostom may be read while the faithful remain standing.

LITANY OF SUPPLICATION

The deacon stands in his usual place and intones the Litany. If there is no deacon, the priest intones the Litany.

Deacon: Let us all say with our whole soul and with our

whole mind, let us say.

R. Lord, have mercy.

O Lord Almighty, God of our fathers, we pray You, hear and have mercy.

R. Lord, have mercy.

Have mercy on us, O God, according to your great mercy; we pray You, hear and have mercy.

R. Lord, have mercy. *(3)*

We also pray for our holy ecumenical Pontiff *(name)*, the Pope of Rome, and for our most reverend Archbishop and Metropolitan *(name)*, for our God-loving Bishop *(name)*, for those who serve and have served in this holy Church, for our spiritual guides, and for all our brothers and sisters in Christ.

R. Lord, have mercy. *(3)*

We also pray for our civil authorities and for all in the service of our country.

R. Lord, have mercy. *(3)*

We also pray for the people here present who await your great and abundant mercy, for those who have shown us mercy, and for all Christians of the true faith.

R. Lord, have mercy. *(3)*

Priest: For You are a merciful and gracious God, and we give glory to You, Father, Son, and Holy Spirit, now and ever and forever.

R. Amen.

SECOND LITANY OF SUPPLICATION

Deacon: Let us complete our morning prayers to the Lord.

R. Lord, have mercy.

Protect us, save us, have mercy on us and preserve us, O God, by your grace.

R. Lord, have mercy.

That this whole day may be perfect, holy, peaceful, and without sin, let us beseech the Lord.

R. Grant it, O Lord. *(after each following petition)*

For an angel of peace, a faithful guide, a guardian of our souls and bodies, let us beseech the Lord.

For the pardon and remission of our sins and offenses, let us beseech the Lord.

For what is good and beneficial to our souls, and for the peace of the whole world, let us beseech the Lord.

That we may spend the rest of our life in peace and repentance, let us beseech the Lord.

For a Christian, painless, unashamed, peaceful end of our life, and for a good account before the fearsome judgment-seat of Christ, let us beseech the Lord.

Remembering our most holy, most pure, most blessed and glorious Lady, the Mother of God and ever-Virgin Mary with all the saints, let us commend ourselves and one another, and our whole life, to Christ our God.

R. To You, O Lord.

Priest: For You, O God, are gracious and You love mankind, and we glorify You, Father, Son, and Holy Spirit, now and ever and forever.

R. Amen.

Priest: Peace † be with all!

R. And with your spirit.

Deacon: Bow your heads to the Lord.

R. To You, O Lord.

Priest: O holy Lord, You dwell on high and yet behold the things below; You look upon all creation with an all-encompassing eye: to You we bow in spirit and body, and to You we pray, O Holy of Holies. Extend your invisible hand from your holy dwelling place and bless all of us. If we have sinned willfully or not, now, because You are God, forgive us in your goodness and in your love for all people; and give us all your good things from the earth and from above. For it is yours to be merciful and to save us, O Christ our God; and to You we give glory, Father, Son, and Holy Spirit, now and ever and forever.

R. Amen.

DISMISSAL

Deacon: Wisdom!

R. Give the blessing!

Priest: Blessed is the One-Who-Is, blessed is Christ our God, always, now and ever and forever.

R. Amen. O God, strengthen the true faith, forever and ever.

Priest: O most holy Mother of God, save us!

R. Shine in splendor, O new Jerusalem; for the glory of the is risen upon you. O Zion, sing with joy and rejoice. And you, pure Mother of God, rejoice in the resurrection of your Son.

Priest: Glory be to You, O Christ, our God, our hope; glory be to You!

R. Christ is risen from the dead! By death He conquered Death, and to those in the graves He granted life. Lord, have mercy. Lord, have mercy. Lord, have mercy. Give the blessing!

Priest: May Christ our true God, risen from the dead, ***(Bright Week only:*** *by death conquering Death and granting life to those in the graves,)* have mercy on us and save us through the prayers of His most pure Mother and all the saints, for He is gracious and loves mankind.

R. Amen.

Sunday Evening Vespers

The celebrant, fully vested in bright vestments, stands before the Holy Altar and begins with: "Blessed is our God..." immediately the Paschal Troparion is sung three times.

Christ is risen from the dead! * By death He conquered Death, * and to those in the graves He granted life.

TROPARION WITH VERSICLES

The celebrant sings the following versicles, and to each one the people respond by singing: Christ is risen...

v. Let God arise and let his enemies be scattered, * and let those who hate Him flee from before His face.

Christ is risen...

v. As smoke vanishes, so let them vanish as wax melts before the fire.

Christ is risen...

v. So let the wicked perish at the presence of God, and let the righteous ones rejoice.

Christ is risen...

v. This is the day that the Lord has made, let us exalt and rejoice in it.

Christ is risen...

v. Glory be to the Father, and to the Son, and to the Holy Spirit, now and ever and forever. Amen.

Christ is risen...

LITANY OF PEACE

The deacon stands in his usual place and intones the Litany. If there is no deacon, the priest intones the Litany before the closed royal doors.

Deacon: In peace, let us pray to the Lord.

R. Lord, have mercy. *(after each petition)*

For peace from on high and for the salvation of our souls, let us pray to the Lord.

For peace in the whole world, for the well-being of the holy Churches of God and for the union of all, let us pray to the Lord.

For this holy Church and for all who enter it with faith, reverence, and the fear of God, let us pray to the Lord.

For our holy ecumenical Pontiff *(name)*, the Pope of Rome, let us pray to the Lord.

For our most reverend Archbishop and Metropolitan *(name)*, for our God-loving Bishop *(name)*, for the venerable priesthood, the diaconate in Christ, and all the clergy and the people, let us pray to the Lord.

For our civil authorities and all in the service of our country, let us pray to the Lord.

For this *city,(OR: for this village, OR: for this holy monastery)*, for every city and countryside, and for those living within them in faith, let us pray to the Lord.

For seasonable weather, for an abundance of the fruits of the earth, and for peaceful times, let us pray to the Lord.

For those who travel by sea, air, and land; for the sick, the suffering, the captive, and for their safety and salvation, let us pray to the Lord.

That we be delivered from all affliction, wrath, and need, let us pray to the Lord.

Protect us, save us, have mercy on us and preserve us, O God, by your grace.

Remembering our most holy, most pure, most blessed and glorious Lady, the Mother of God and ever-Virgin Mary with all the saints, let us commend ourselves and one another, and our whole life, to Christ our God.

R. To You, O Lord.

Priest: For to You is due all glory, honor, and worship,

Father, Son, and Holy Spirit, now and ever and forever.

R. Amen.

AT PSALM 140

Tone 2 Come, let us adore God the Word, * who was born of the Father before all ages, * and was incarnate of the Virgin Mary; * for of his own free will He suffered the Cross * and submitted himself to burial, * and arose from the dead to save me, a sinful one.

Christ our Savior cancelled the decree that was written against us * by nailing it to the Cross, * and He abolished the dominion of Death. * Let us glorify his Resurrection on the third day.

Let us, together with the archangels, sing of Christ's Resurrection; * for He is the Redeemer and Savior of our souls. * He will come again in awesome glory and mighty power * to judge the world which He has fashioned.

Although You died and were buried, * the angel yet declared You as Master. * He said to the women: Come and see where the Lord was placed; * for He is risen as He foretold, * because He is almighty. * Therefore, we worship You, the only immortal One, * and we beseech You to have mercy on us, O Giver of life.

O Christ, You have abolished the curse of the tree by your Cross; * You have destroyed the power of Death by your burial, * and You enlightened the human race by your Resurrection. * Therefore, we cry out to You: * O God and Benefactor, glory to You!

O Lord, the gates of Death opened before You in fear, * and the gatekeepers of Hades were filled with dread at the sight of You. * You smashed the gates of brass and crushed the posts of iron. * Then You burst our chains asunder * and led us out from the darkness, * away from the shadow of death.

Glory be: Let us all come and prostrate ourselves in the house of the Lord, * singing this hymn of salvation: * O Christ, You were crucified on the tree and rose from the dead, * and You now abide in the bosom of the Father. * Please cleanse us of our sins.

Now and ever: At the coming of grace, O Virgin, * the shadow of the law passed away. * For, as the bush, though burning, was not consumed, * You, though giving birth, still remained a virgin. * In place of the pillar of fire, the Sun of Righteousness shone forth. * Instead of Moses, Christ, the salvation of our souls, appeared.

GREAT PROKEIMENON

Tone 7 What God is great as our God? You are the God who works wonders!

v. You showed your power among the peoples. Your strong arm redeemed your people.

v. I said: Now I begin, and this is the will of the Most High.

v. I remember the deeds of the Lord. I remember your wonders of old.

GOSPEL

Deacon: O that we be deemed worthy of hearing the Holy Gospel, in peace let us pray to the Lord, our God.

R. Lord, have mercy. *(3 times)*

Deacon: Wisdom! Let us stand and listen to a reading of the Holy Gospel.

Priest: Peace † be with all!

R. And with your spirit.

Deacon: A reading of the Holy Gospel according to Saint John.

R. Glory be to You, O Lord; glory be to You!

Deacon: Let us be attentive! *(Reads John 20: 19 - 25)*

R. Glory be to You, O Lord; glory be to You!

APOSTICHA

Tone 2 Your Resurrection, O Christ our Savior, * has enlightened the whole universe; * and, through it, You call back to yourself all creation. * Almighty God, glory to You!

PASCHAL HYMNS

Let God arise and let his enemies be scattered, and let those who hate Him flee from before his face.

Today the sacred Pasch is revealed to us, * holy and new Pasch, * the mystical Passover, * the venerable Passover, * the Pasch which is Christ the Redeemer, * spotless Pasch, great Pasch, * the Pasch of the faithful, * the Pasch which is the key to the gates of Paradise, * the Pasch which sanctifies all the faithful.

As smoke vanishes, so let them vanish as wax melts before the fire.

O Women, * be the heralds of good news and tell what you saw; * tell of the vision and say to Zion: * Accept the good news of joy from us, * the news that Christ has risen. * Exalt and celebrate * and rejoice, O Jerusalem, * seeing Christ the King coming from the tomb * like a bridegroom.

So let the wicked perish at the presence of God, and let the righteous ones rejoice.

The myrrh-bearing women * arrived just before the dawn * at the tomb of the Giver of Life * and found an angel seated on the stone * who spoke these words to them: * Why do you seek the Living among the dead? * Why do you mourn the Incorruptible among those subject to decay? * Go, announce the good news * to his disciples.

This is the day that the Lord has made; let us exalt and rejoice in it.

Pasch so delightful, * Pasch of the Lord is the Pasch, * most honored Pasch now dawned on us. * It is the Pasch! * Therefore, let us joyfully embrace one another. * O Passover, save us from sorrow; * for today Christ has shown forth from the tomb * as from a bridal chamber * and filled the women with joy by saying: * Announce the good news * to my apostles.

Glory be to the Father, and to the Son, and to the Holy Spirit, now and ever and forever. Amen.

This is the Resurrection day. * Let us be enlightened by this Feast, * and let us embrace one another. * Let us call Brethren * even those who hate us, * and in the Resurrection * forgive everything; and let us sing:

Christ is risen from the dead! * By death He conquered Death, * and to those in the graves He granted life.

LITANY OF SUPPLICATION

SECOND LITANY OF SUPPLICATION

DISMISSAL

Deacon: Wisdom!

R. Give the blessing!

Priest: Blessed is the One-Who-Is, blessed is Christ our God, always, now and ever and forever.

R. Amen. O God, strengthen the true faith, forever and ever.

Priest: O most holy Mother of God, save us.

R. Shine in splendor, O new Jerusalem; for the glory of the Lord is risen upon you. O Zion, sing with joy and rejoice; and you, pure Mother of God, rejoice in the resurrection of your Son.

Priest: Glory be to You, O Christ, our God, our hope; glory be to You!

R. Christ is risen from the dead! By death He conquered Death, and to those in the graves He granted life. Lord, have mercy. Lord, have mercy. Lord, have mercy. Give the blessing!

Priest: May Christ our true God, risen from the dead, ***(Bright Week only:** by death conquering Death and granting life to those in the graves,)* have mercy on us and save us through the prayers of His most pure Mother and all the saints, for He is gracious and loves mankind.

R. Amen.

Monday Matins

Everything is the same as Paschal Matins except there is no procession and the Small Litany is taken only after the Third, Sixth, and Ninth Odes.

AT THE PRAISES

Tone 2 All creation and everything that breathes glorifies You, O Lord; * for by the Cross You abolished Death * that You might manifest to the world your Resurrection from the dead. * For You alone are the Lover of Mankind.

What do the Pharisees now say? * How was it that the guardian soldiers lost the King whom they were guarding? * Why was it that the stone could not retain the Rock of life? * Therefore, either you must deliver to us Him who was buried. * or worship with us Him who is risen, and say: * Glory to your bountiful mercies, our Savior, glory to You!

Rejoice, O nations, and be glad; * for the angel sat on the stone of the grave, * and gave us the good news, saying: * Christ the Savior of the world is risen from the dead. * He has filled the world with fragrant aroma. * Rejoice, O nations, and be glad.

At your conception, O Lord God, * an angel said to her who is full of grace: Rejoice! * At your Resurrection an angel rolled away the stone * from the door of your glorious tomb. * The first angel spoke with signs of joy instead of sorrow, * and the latter brought us the good news * of a Lord who gives life instead of death. * Therefore, we shout to You, O Benefactor of all, * glory to You, O Lord!

PASCHAL HYMNS

Let God arise and let his enemies be scattered, and let those who hate Him flee from before his face.

Today the sacred Pasch is revealed to us, * holy and new Pasch, * the mystical Passover, * the venerable Passover, * the Pasch which is Christ the Redeemer, * spotless Pasch, great Pasch, * the Pasch of the faithful, * the Pasch which is the key to the gates of Paradise, * the Pasch which sanctifies all the faithful.

As smoke vanishes, so let them vanish as wax melts before the fire.

O Women, * be the heralds of good news and tell what you saw; * tell of the vision and say to Zion: * Accept the good news of joy from us, * the news that Christ has risen. * Exalt and celebrate * and rejoice, O Jerusalem, * seeing Christ the King coming from the tomb * like a bridegroom.

So let the wicked perish at the presence of God, and let the righteous ones rejoice.

The myrrh-bearing women * arrived just before the dawn * at the tomb of the Giver of Life * and found an angel seated on the stone * who spoke these words to them: * Why do you seek the Living among the dead? * Why do you mourn the Incorruptible among those subject to decay? * Go, announce the good news * to his disciples.

This is the day that the Lord has made; let us exalt and rejoice in it.

Pasch so delightful, * Pasch of the Lord is the Pasch, * most honored Pasch now dawned on us. * It is the Pasch! * Therefore, let us joyfully embrace one another. * O Passover, save us from sorrow; * for today Christ has shown forth from the tomb * as from a bridal chamber * and filled the women with joy by saying: * Announce the good news * to my apostles.

Glory be to the Father, and to the Son, and to the Holy Spirit, now and ever and forever. Amen.

This is the Resurrection day. * Let us be enlightened by this Feast, * and let us embrace one another. * Let us call Brethren * even those who hate us, * and in the Resurrection * forgive everything; and let us sing:

Christ is risen from the dead! * By death He conquered Death, * and to those in the graves He granted life.

Monday Evening Vespers

The celebrant, fully vested in bright vestments, stands before the Holy Altar and begins with: "Blessed is our God..." immediately the Paschal Troparion is sung three times.

Christ is risen from the dead! * By death He conquered Death, * and to those in the graves He granted life.

TROPARION WITH VERSICLES

The celebrant sings the following versicles, and to each one the people respond by singing: Christ is risen...

v. Let God arise and let his enemies be scattered, * and let those who hate Him flee from before His face.

Christ is risen...

v. As smoke vanishes, so let them vanish as wax melts before the fire.

Christ is risen...

v. So let the wicked perish at the presence of God, and let the righteous ones rejoice.

Christ is risen...

v. This is the day that the Lord has made, let us exalt and rejoice in it.

Christ is risen...

v. Glory be to the Father, and to the Son, and to the Holy Spirit, now and ever and forever. Amen.

Christ is risen...

LITANY OF PEACE

AT PSALM 140

Tone 3 By your Cross, O Christ our Savior, * the power of Death has been vanquished * and the deceit of the devil has been destroyed. * Therefore, the human race, saved by faith, * offers You hymns of praise forever.

O Lord, all creation has been enlightened by your Resurrection, * and Paradise has been reopened; * therefore, all creation extols You * and offers You hymns of praise forever.

I glorify the power of the Father, Son, and Holy Spirit; * and I praise the dominion of the undivided Divinity, * the consubstantial Trinity, * who reigns forever and ever.

We adore your precious Cross, O Christ, * and with hymns of praise we glorify your Resurrection; * for by your wounds we have all been healed.

Let us sing the praises of the Savior, * who was incarnate of the Virgin; * for He was crucified for our sake, * and on the third day He arose from the dead, * granting us his great mercy.

Christ descended into Hades and announced to those confined there: * Take courage, for today I have conquered Death. * I am the Resurrection, the One who will set you free. * I have shattered the gates of the realm of Death.

Glory be: O Christ our God, we unworthily stand in your most pure temple, * and offer to You our evening hymns. * From the depths of our souls we cry out to You: * O Lover of Mankind, who has enlightened the world * by your resurrection on the third day, * deliver your people from the hands of your enemies.

Now and ever: O most honorable Virgin, we are filled with awe * when we consider that you gave birth to Christ who is both God and man. * O immaculate Lady, without knowing man, * you gave birth in the flesh to a Son without a human father. * This Son, from all eternity, was begotten by God the Father without a mother, * and when He took on our human nature, * He did not undergo any change. * Nothing was added to his divine nature, nor was it divided. * The properties of both his divine and human nature remained intact. * We therefore entreat you, O blessed Virgin, * to save the souls of those who, in true faith, * acknowledge you as the Mother of God.

GREAT PROKEIMENON

Tone 7 But our God is in the heavens; He does whatever He wills.

- ***v.*** When Israel came forth from Egypt, Jacob's sons from an alien people.
- ***v.*** The sea fled at the sight; the Jordan turned back on its course.
- ***v.*** Why was it, sea, that you fled; that you turned back, Jordan, on your course?

APOSTICHA

Tone 3 O Christ, who darkened the sun by your passion * and enlightened all creation by your Resurrection, * accept our evening prayer, for You indeed love all people.

PASCHAL HYMNS

Let God arise and let his enemies be scattered, and let those who hate Him flee from before his face.

Today the sacred Pasch is revealed to us, * holy and new Pasch, * the mystical Passover, * the venerable Passover, * the Pasch which is Christ the Redeemer, * spotless Pasch, great Pasch, * the Pasch of the faithful, * the Pasch which is the key to the gates of Paradise, * the Pasch which sanctifies all the faithful.

As smoke vanishes, so let them vanish as wax melts before the fire.

O Women, * be the heralds of good news and tell what you saw; * tell of the vision and say to Zion: * Accept the good news of joy from us, * the news that Christ has risen. * Exalt and celebrate * and rejoice, O Jerusalem, * seeing Christ the King coming from the tomb * like a bridegroom.

So let the wicked perish at the presence of God, and let the righteous ones rejoice.

The myrrh-bearing women * arrived just before the dawn * at the tomb of the Giver of Life * and found an angel seated on the stone * who spoke these words to them: * Why do you seek the Living among the dead? * Why do you mourn the Incorruptible among those subject to decay? * Go, announce the good news * to his disciples.

This is the day that the Lord has made; let us exalt and rejoice in it.

Pasch so delightful, * Pasch of the Lord is the Pasch, * most honored Pasch now dawned on us. * It is the Pasch! * Therefore, let us joyfully embrace one another. * O Passover, save us from sorrow; * for today Christ has shown forth from the tomb * as from a bridal chamber * and filled the women with joy by saying: * Announce the good news * to my apostles.

Glory be to the Father, and to the Son, and to the Holy Spirit, now and ever and forever. Amen.

This is the Resurrection day. * Let us be enlightened by this Feast, * and let us embrace one another. * Let us call Brethren * even those who hate us, * and in the Resurrection * forgive everything; and let us sing:

Christ is risen from the dead! * By death He conquered Death, * and to those in the graves He granted life.

Tuesday Matins

Everything is the same as Paschal Matins except there is no procession and the Small Litany is taken only after the Third, Sixth, and Ninth Odes.

AT THE PRAISES

Tone 3 Come together all you nations * and understand the might of this awesome mystery! * Our Savior, the Word from the beginning, * has suffered crucifixion and burial for us of his own will. * On the third day He rose again to save us all. * Let us bow down in worship to Him.

The soldiers that guarded You, O Lord, * related all the wonders which had come to pass; * but the vain assembly of the Sanhedrin filled their hands with bribes, * thinking they could hide your Resurrection * which is glorified through all the world. * Have mercy on us.

All creation was filled with joy * when it received the news of your Resurrection. * When Mary Magdalene went to your tomb, * she found an angel in shining garments sitting on the stone. * He said: Why do you seek the Living among the dead? * He is not here; He is risen as He said. * He goes before you to Galilee.

O Master, the Lover of Mankind, * in your light we see light. * For You have risen from the dead, * granting salvation to the human race. * Let all creation glorify You; * have mercy on us, O sinless One.

PASCHAL HYMNS

Let God arise and let his enemies be scattered, and let those who hate Him flee from before his face.

Today the sacred Pasch is revealed to us, * holy and new Pasch, * the mystical Passover, * the venerable Passover, * the Pasch which is Christ the Redeemer, * spotless Pasch, great Pasch, * the Pasch of the faithful, * the Pasch which is the key to the gates of Paradise, * the Pasch which sanctifies all the faithful.

As smoke vanishes, so let them vanish as wax melts before the fire.

O Women, * be the heralds of good news and tell what you saw; * tell of the vision and say to Zion: * Accept the good news of joy from us, * the news that Christ has risen. * Exalt and celebrate * and rejoice, O Jerusalem, * seeing Christ the King coming from the tomb * like a bridegroom.

So let the wicked perish at the presence of God, and let the righteous ones rejoice.

The myrrh-bearing women * arrived just before the dawn * at the tomb of the Giver of Life * and found an angel seated on the stone * who spoke these words to them: * Why do you seek the Living among the dead? * Why do you mourn the Incorruptible among those subject to decay? * Go, announce the good news * to his disciples.

This is the day that the Lord has made; let us exalt and rejoice in it.

Pasch so delightful, * Pasch of the Lord is the Pasch, * most honored Pasch now dawned on us. * It is the Pasch! * Therefore, let us joyfully embrace one another. * O Passover, save us from sorrow; * for today Christ has shown forth from the tomb * as from a bridal chamber * and filled the women with joy by saying: * Announce the good news * to my apostles.

Glory be to the Father, and to the Son, and to the Holy Spirit, now and ever and forever. Amen.

This is the Resurrection day. * Let us be enlightened by this Feast, * and let us embrace one another. * Let us call Brethren * even those who hate us, * and in the Resurrection * forgive everything; and let us sing:

Christ is risen from the dead! * By death He conquered Death, * and to those in the graves He granted life.

Tuesday Evening Vespers

The celebrant, fully vested in bright vestments, stands before the Holy Altar and begins with: "Blessed is our God..." immediately the Paschal Troparion is sung three times.

Christ is risen from the dead! * By death He conquered Death, * and to those in the graves He granted life.

TROPARION WITH VERSICLES

The celebrant sings the following versicles, and to each one the people respond by singing: Christ is risen...

v. Let God arise and let his enemies be scattered, * and let those who hate Him flee from before His face.

Christ is risen...

v. As smoke vanishes, so let them vanish as wax melts before the fire.

Christ is risen...

v. So let the wicked perish at the presence of God, and let the righteous ones rejoice.

Christ is risen...

v. This is the day that the Lord has made, let us exalt and rejoice in it.

Christ is risen...

v. Glory be to the Father, and to the Son, and to the Holy Spirit, now and ever and forever. Amen.

Christ is risen...

LITANY OF PEACE

AT PSALM 140

Tone 4 We never cease to adore your life-giving Cross, O Christ our God, * and we glorify your Resurrection on the third day. * For You, almighty One, have thereby restored the corrupted nature of all * and reopened the way to heaven, * since You alone are gracious and You love all people.

O Savior, You have absolved the penalty of disobedience, * committed through the tree of Eden, * by willingly being nailed to the tree of the Cross. * As almighty God, You descended into Hades * and broke asunder the bonds of Death. * We, therefore, venerate your Resurrection from the dead * and joyfully cry out to You: * Almighty Lord, glory to You!

O Lord, You have battered down the gates of Hades, * and by your death You have dissolved the realm of Death. * You have freed the human race from corruption, * bestowing life, incorruption, and your great mercy upon the world.

Come, all you people, * let us sing the praises of our Savior's Resurrection on the third day. * For we have thereby been delivered from the invincible bonds of Hades,* and we have received incorruption, together with eternal life. * Therefore, we cry out to You * after your crucifixion, burial, and resurrection: * Save us by your Resurrection, for You love all people.

O Savior, with the angels we sing the praises of your Resurrection on the third day. * For the very ends of the universe have thereby been enlightened, * and we have been saved from the deceit of the Enemy. * Therefore, we cry out to You, * almighty Savior, Giver of Life, and Lover of Mankind: * Save us by your Resurrection.

O Christ our God, You have demolished the brazen gates of Hades. * You have broken asunder the bonds of death * and lifted up the fallen human race. * Therefore, we cry out with one accord: * O Lord, who arose from the dead, glory to You!

Glory be: O Lord, your birth from the Father is timeless and eternal; * your incarnation from the Virgin is beyond the understanding of all * and beyond the expression of our words. * Your descent into Hades and victory over Death * caused Satan and his angels to tremble with fear. * Your Resurrection on the third day * brought to all people incorruption and great mercy.

Now and ever: O Mother of God, David the Prophet and Forefather of Christ, foretold in song * the great things that would happen to you. * He revealed that you would be a queen, * standing at the right hand of God; * and that you would be the Mother of Life and intercessor for the world. * He prophesied that God, in his good will toward all, * would become incarnate of you without a human father. * Thus He would restore his image within us * which had become disfigured by our passions. * He would seek out the lost sheep that was trapped in the hills; * He would lift it upon his shoulder and carry it to his Father * who would place it in the midst of his heavenly hosts. * In like manner, Christ will save the world because of his great and abundant mercy.

GREAT PROKEIMENON

Tone 8 I cry aloud to God, cry aloud to God that He may hear me.

v. In the day of my distress I sought the Lord.

v. My soul refused to be consoled.

v. Your ways, O God, are holy.

APOSTICHA

Tone 4 In being lifted upon the Cross, O Lord, * You abolished the curse which we had inherited from our ancestors. * By going down into Hades, * You freed from eternal captivity those imprisoned there * and granted incorruption to the human race. * We, therefore, praise your life-giving and redeeming Resurrection.

PASCHAL HYMNS

Let God arise and let his enemies be scattered, and let those who hate Him flee from before his face.

Today the sacred Pasch is revealed to us, * holy and new Pasch, * the mystical Passover, * the venerable Passover, * the Pasch which is Christ the Redeemer, * spotless Pasch, great Pasch, * the Pasch of the faithful, * the Pasch which is the key to the gates of Paradise, * the Pasch which sanctifies all the faithful.

As smoke vanishes, so let them vanish as wax melts before the fire.

O Women, * be the heralds of good news and tell what you saw; * tell of the vision and say to Zion: * Accept the good news of joy from us, * the news that Christ has risen. * Exalt and celebrate * and rejoice, O Jerusalem, * seeing Christ the King coming from the tomb * like a bridegroom.

So let the wicked perish at the presence of God, and let the righteous ones rejoice.

The myrrh-bearing women * arrived just before the dawn * at the tomb of the Giver of Life * and found an angel seated on the stone * who spoke these words to them: * Why do you seek the Living among the dead? * Why do you mourn the Incorruptible among those subject to decay? * Go, announce the good news * to his disciples.

This is the day that the Lord has made; let us exalt and rejoice in it.

Pasch so delightful, * Pasch of the Lord is the Pasch, * most honored Pasch now dawned on us. * It is the Pasch! * Therefore, let us joyfully embrace one another. * O Passover, save us from sorrow; * for today Christ has shown forth from the tomb * as from a bridal chamber * and filled the women with joy by saying: * Announce the good news * to my apostles.

Glory be to the Father, and to the Son, and to the Holy Spirit, now and ever and forever. Amen.

This is the Resurrection day. * Let us be enlightened by this Feast, * and let us embrace one another. * Let us call Brethren * even those who hate us, * and in the Resurrection * forgive everything; and let us sing:

Christ is risen from the dead! * By death He conquered Death, * and to those in the graves He granted life.

Wednesday Matins

Everything is the same as Paschal Matins except there is no procession and the Small Litany is taken only after the Third, Sixth, and Ninth Odes.

AT THE PRAISES

Tone 4 You suffered death on the Cross, * and You arose from the dead. * We glorify your holy Resurrection, O almighty Lord.

By your Cross You delivered us from the ancient curse, O Christ; * by your death You have utterly destroyed the Devil who tyrannized the human race; * by your Resurrection You have filled the whole world with joy. * Therefore, we cry out to You: * O Lord who rose from the dead, glory to You!

By your Cross lead us to your truth, O Christ our Savior; * deliver us from the snares of the Enemy. * You are risen from the dead; * now raise us up from our fall into sin. * Stretch forth your hand to us, O Lord, * through the prayers of your saints.

O only Son and Word of God, * You were not separated from the bosom of the Father * when You came to earth out of love for us * and became a man without undergoing change. * In the flesh You suffered death on the Cross * even though You are beyond all suffering in your divinity. * You rose from the dead, granting immortality to the human race, * for You alone, O Lord, are almighty.

PASCHAL HYMNS

Let God arise and let his enemies be scattered, and let those who hate Him flee from before his face.

Today the sacred Pasch is revealed to us, * holy and new Pasch, * the mystical Passover, * the venerable Passover, * the Pasch which is Christ the Redeemer, * spotless Pasch,

great Pasch, * the Pasch of the faithful, * the Pasch which is the key to the gates of Paradise, * the Pasch which sanctifies all the faithful.

As smoke vanishes, so let them vanish as wax melts before the fire.

O Women, * be the heralds of good news and tell what you saw; * tell of the vision and say to Zion: * Accept the good news of joy from us, * the news that Christ has risen. * Exalt and celebrate * and rejoice, O Jerusalem, * seeing Christ the King coming from the tomb * like a bridegroom.

So let the wicked perish at the presence of God, and let the righteous ones rejoice.

The myrrh-bearing women * arrived just before the dawn * at the tomb of the Giver of Life * and found an angel seated on the stone * who spoke these words to them: * Why do you seek the Living among the dead? * Why do you mourn the Incorruptible among those subject to decay? * Go, announce the good news * to his disciples.

This is the day that the Lord has made; let us exalt and rejoice in it.

Pasch so delightful, * Pasch of the Lord is the Pasch, * most honored Pasch now dawned on us. * It is the Pasch! * Therefore, let us joyfully embrace one another. * O Passover, save us from sorrow; * for today Christ has shown forth from the tomb * as from a bridal chamber * and filled the women with joy by saying: * Announce the good news * to my apostles.

Glory be to the Father, and to the Son, and to the Holy Spirit, now and ever and forever. Amen.

This is the Resurrection day. * Let us be enlightened by this Feast, * and let us embrace one another. * Let us call Brethren * even those who hate us, * and in the Resurrection * forgive everything; and let us sing:

Christ is risen from the dead! * By death He conquered Death, * and to those in the graves He granted life.

Wednesday Evening Vespers

The celebrant, fully vested in bright vestments, stands before the Holy Altar and begins with: "Blessed is our God..." immediately the Paschal Troparion is sung three times.

Christ is risen from the dead! * By death He conquered Death, * and to those in the graves He granted life.

TROPARION WITH VERSICLES

The celebrant sings the following versicles, and to each one the people respond by singing: Christ is risen...

v. Let God arise and let his enemies be scattered, * and let those who hate Him flee from before His face.

Christ is risen...

v. As smoke vanishes, so let them vanish as wax melts before the fire.

Christ is risen...

v. So let the wicked perish at the presence of God, and let the righteous ones rejoice.

Christ is risen...

v. This is the day that the Lord has made, let us exalt and rejoice in it.

Christ is risen...

v. Glory be to the Father, and to the Son, and to the Holy Spirit, now and ever and forever. Amen.

Christ is risen...

LITANY OF PEACE

AT PSALM 140

***Tone* 5** With your precious Cross, O Christ, * You have put the Devil to shame. * With your Resurrection You have deadened the sting of sin * and have saved us from the gates of Death. * We, therefore, glorify You, O only-begotten Son of God.

O Christ who granted resurrection to all people, * You were led like a lamb to the slaughter. * Then the princes of Hades were struck with terror * as they saw the gates of their tearful domain being lifted up; * for Christ, the King of Glory, entered therein * and exclaimed to those in chains: Go forth from here! * and to those in darkness: Go forth into the light!

What a great wonder! * The Creator of invisible beings suffered in the flesh for all people * and rose from the dead as immortal. * Come, therefore, all you nations and adore Him; * for through his compassion we have been freed from the snares of the Devil, * and we have learned to praise the one God in three persons.

We offer to You our evening worship, * O Light whom the darkness of night can never extinguish. * For in these latter days your radiance has appeared to the world, * shining in your flesh as light reflected from a mirror. * Your brilliance has descended even to the depths of Hades and dissolved its gloom. * O Lord, Giver of Light, glory to You, * for You have shown the radiance of your Resurrection to all the nations.

Let us glorify Christ, the author of our salvation, * for by his resurrection from the dead * the world has been delivered from the deception of Satan. * The choirs of angels rejoice as the treachery of evil spirits vanishes. * Fallen Adam arises, and the Devil is vanquished.

Those who guarded the tomb of Christ * were told by the evil men who hired them: * Take this silver and keep silent. * Tell no one of the Resurrection of Christ; * rather tell everyone that while you were sleeping his body was stolen. * But who has ever heard of a body being stolen, * a body which had already been anointed? * Why would anyone take a body from the grave naked * and leave the burial shroud in the tomb? * Do not deceive yourselves, O people of Judea. * Study the teachings of the Prophets, * and you will come to understand that Jesus Christ is almighty God * and truly the Savior of the world.

Glory be: O Lord our Savior, * who subjected hell and conquered Death, * and enlightened the world through your precious Cross, * have mercy on us.

Now and ever: The passing of the Israelites through the Red Sea * was already a foreshadowing of the virgin-birth. * On that occasion, Moses parted the waters; * at the Incarnation, Gabriel announced the miracle of God's union with Mary. * In ancient times, the Israelites passed through the depths of the sea * without being drenched by the waters; * now the Virgin has given birth to Christ without seed. * After the Israelites passed through the sea, it remained impassable; * after the birth of Emmanuel, the immaculate Virgin remains forever incorrupt. * O God, who exists from all eternity, and yet appeared as man, * have mercy on us.

GREAT PROKEIMENON

Tone 7 O God, listen to my prayer, do not hide from my pleading.

v. Attend to me and reply.

v. For they bring down evil upon me.

v. As for me, I will cry to God, and the Lord will save me, evening, morning, and at noon.

APOSTICHA

Tone 5 O Christ our Savior, * we lift up our voices in song to glorify You. * For, in your love for all people, * You became incarnate without leaving heaven; * You accepted the Cross and Death; * You cast down the gates of Hades; * and on the third day You arose from the dead * for the salvation of our souls.

PASCHAL HYMNS

Let God arise and let his enemies be scattered, and let those who hate Him flee from before his face.

Today the sacred Pasch is revealed to us, * holy and new Pasch, * the mystical Passover, * the venerable Passover, * the Pasch which is Christ the Redeemer, * spotless Pasch, great Pasch, * the Pasch of the faithful, * the Pasch which is the key to the gates of Paradise, * the Pasch which sanctifies all the faithful.

As smoke vanishes, so let them vanish as wax melts before the fire.

O Women, * be the heralds of good news and tell what you saw; * tell of the vision and say to Zion: * Accept the good news of joy from us, * the news that Christ has risen. * Exalt and celebrate * and rejoice, O Jerusalem, * seeing Christ the King coming from the tomb * like a bridegroom.

So let the wicked perish at the presence of God, and let the righteous ones rejoice.

The myrrh-bearing women * arrived just before the dawn * at the tomb of the Giver of Life * and found an angel seated on the stone * who spoke these words to them: * Why do you seek the Living among the dead? * Why do you mourn the Incorruptible among those subject to decay? * Go, announce the good news * to his disciples.

This is the day that the Lord has made; let us exalt and rejoice in it.

Pasch so delightful, * Pasch of the Lord is the Pasch, * most honored Pasch now dawned on us. * It is the Pasch! * Therefore, let us joyfully embrace one another. * O Passover, save us from sorrow; * for today Christ has shown forth from the tomb * as from a bridal chamber * and filled the women with joy by saying: * Announce the good news * to my apostles.

Glory be to the Father, and to the Son, and to the Holy Spirit, now and ever and forever. Amen.

This is the Resurrection day. * Let us be enlightened by this Feast, * and let us embrace one another. * Let us call Brethren * even those who hate us, * and in the Resurrection * forgive everything; and let us sing:

Christ is risen from the dead! * By death He conquered Death, * and to those in the graves He granted life.

Thursday Matins

Everything is the same as Paschal Matins except there is no procession and the Small Litany is taken only after the Third, Sixth, and Ninth Odes.

AT THE PRAISES

Tone 5 You came forth from the grave, O Lord, * which had been sealed by the transgressors of the law, * just as You were born of the Theotokos. * For the bodiless angels did not know how You were incarnate. * Likewise, the guardian soldiers did not see the moment of your Resurrection, * for these two marvels were concealed from the curious minds * but were revealed to those who worshiped the mystery in faith. * Therefore, grant joy and great mercy to us who offer You praise.

O Lord, You demolished the gates of everlasting damnation, * and You broke asunder the chains of the grave. * You rose from the tomb leaving your wrappings in the grave * in testimony of your three-day burial; * and leaving the guards watching at the tomb, * You preceded your disciples into Galilee. * Great is your mercy, O Lord, whom the whole world cannot contain. * O Savior, have mercy upon us.

O Lord, who suffered for us, * the women hastened to your tomb to behold You. * When they arrived, they saw an angel sitting on the stone of the grave. * He said to them: The Lord is risen! * Go and tell the disciples that the Savior of our souls is risen from the dead.

O Lord and Savior, * You came into the midst of your disciples though the doors were closed * just as You came out of the sealed tomb, * showing the sufferings of the flesh which You accepted; * for You submitted to suffering patiently since You are of the seed of David. * But since You are the Son of God, You saved the world. * Great is your mercy, O Lord, whom the whole world cannot contain. * O Savior, have mercy on us.

PASCHAL HYMNS

Let God arise and let his enemies be scattered, and let those who hate Him flee from before his face.

Today the sacred Pasch is revealed to us, * holy and new Pasch, * the mystical Passover, * the venerable Passover, * the Pasch which is Christ the Redeemer, * spotless Pasch, great Pasch, * the Pasch of the faithful, * the Pasch which is the key to the gates of Paradise, * the Pasch which sanctifies all the faithful.

As smoke vanishes, so let them vanish as wax melts before the fire.

O Women, * be the heralds of good news and tell what you saw; * tell of the vision and say to Zion: * Accept the good news of joy from us, * the news that Christ has risen. * Exalt and celebrate * and rejoice, O Jerusalem, * seeing Christ the King coming from the tomb * like a bridegroom.

So let the wicked perish at the presence of God, and let the righteous ones rejoice.

The myrrh-bearing women * arrived just before the dawn * at the tomb of the Giver of Life * and found an angel seated on the stone * who spoke these words to them: * Why do you seek the Living among the dead? * Why do you mourn the Incorruptible among those subject to decay? * Go, announce the good news * to his disciples.

This is the day that the Lord has made; let us exalt and rejoice in it.

Pasch so delightful, * Pasch of the Lord is the Pasch, * most honored Pasch now dawned on us. * It is the Pasch! * Therefore, let us joyfully embrace one another. * O Passover, save us from sorrow; * for today Christ has shown forth from the tomb * as from a bridal chamber * and filled the women with joy by saying: * Announce the good news * to my apostles.

Glory be to the Father, and to the Son, and to the Holy Spirit, now and ever and forever. Amen.

This is the Resurrection day. * Let us be enlightened by this Feast, * and let us embrace one another. * Let us call Brethren * even those who hate us, * and in the Resurrection * forgive everything; and let us sing:

Christ is risen from the dead! * By death He conquered Death, * and to those in the graves He granted life.

Thursday Evening Vespers

The celebrant, fully vested in bright vestments, stands before the Holy Altar and begins with: "Blessed is our God..." immediately the Paschal Troparion is sung three times.

Christ is risen from the dead! * By death He conquered Death, * and to those in the graves He granted life.

TROPARION WITH VERSICLES

The celebrant sings the following versicles, and to each one the people respond by singing: Christ is risen...

v. Let God arise and let his enemies be scattered, * and let those who hate Him flee from before His face.

Christ is risen...

v. As smoke vanishes, so let them vanish as wax melts before the fire.

Christ is risen...

v. So let the wicked perish at the presence of God, and let the righteous ones rejoice.

Christ is risen...

v. This is the day that the Lord has made, let us exalt and rejoice in it.

Christ is risen...

v. Glory be to the Father, and to the Son, and to the Holy Spirit, now and ever and forever. Amen.

Christ is risen...

LITANY OF PEACE

AT PSALM 140

Tone 6 O Christ, You won the victory over Hades; * You ascended the Cross so that You might raise up with yourself * all those who dwelt in the darkness of Death. * Almighty Savior, You are free from Death * and bestow life by your divine light. * We, therefore, beseech You to have mercy on us.

Today Christ has conquered Death. * He has risen from the grave as He had foretold, * bestowing great joy upon the world. * Therefore, let us all lift up our voices and sing: * O Fount of Life, O Light whom no one can approach, * almighty Savior, have mercy on us.

O Lord, where can we sinners flee from You, * for You are present in all creation? * You are present in heaven, for it is your dwelling place. * Your power prevails in Hades where You conquered Death. * O Master, your sustaining hand touches even the depths of the sea. * Where, then, can we take refuge except in You? * We, therefore, prostrate ourselves before You and pray: * O Lord, risen from the dead, have mercy on us.

We exalt in your Cross, O Christ, * and we sing the glory of your Resurrection. * For You are our God, and we have no other Lord but You.

Glory to your might, O Lord, * for You have conquered the power of Death. * You have renewed us through your Cross, * granting us life and incorruption.

We forever bless the Lord and praise his Resurrection, * for by suffering crucifixion, * He has destroyed Death by his death.

Glory be: By your death and burial, O Lord, * You broke asunder the bonds of Hades; * and by your resurrection from the dead, * You enlightened the whole world. * We, therefore, exclaim: Glory to You, O Lord!

Now and ever: Who would not bless you, most holy Virgin? * Who would not praise the most pure manner in which you gave birth? * For the only-begotten Son, who eternally proceeds from the Father, came forth from you. * He took flesh from you in a manner that is beyond understanding. * He, who by nature is God, took on our nature for our sake. * Yet He did not become divided into two persons; * rather, He remained one person with two distinct and unconfused natures. * O most pure Lady, we implore you: * Beseech your Son and God to have mercy on our souls.

GREAT PROKEIMENON

Tone 7 I love You, Lord, my strength, my rock, my fortress, my Savior.

v. My God is the rock where I take refuge; my shield, my mighty help, my stronghold.

v. The Lord is worthy of all praise; when I call I am saved from my foes.

v. From his temple He heard my voice; my cry came to his ears.

APOSTICHA

Tone 6 O Christ our Savior, * the angels in heaven sing the praises of your Resurrection; * make us, on earth, also worthy * to extol and glorify You with a pure heart.

PASCHAL HYMNS

Let God arise and let his enemies be scattered, and let those who hate Him flee from before his face.

Today the sacred Pasch is revealed to us, * holy and new Pasch, * the mystical Passover, * the venerable Passover, * the Pasch which is Christ the Redeemer, * spotless Pasch, great Pasch, * the Pasch of the faithful, * the Pasch which is the key to the gates of Paradise, * the Pasch which sanctifies all the faithful.

As smoke vanishes, so let them vanish as wax melts before the fire.

O Women, * be the heralds of good news and tell what you saw; * tell of the vision and say to Zion: * Accept the good news of joy from us, * the news that Christ has risen. * Exalt and celebrate * and rejoice, O Jerusalem, * seeing Christ the King coming from the tomb * like a bridegroom.

So let the wicked perish at the presence of God, and let the righteous ones rejoice.

The myrrh-bearing women * arrived just before the dawn * at the tomb of the Giver of Life * and found an angel seated on the stone * who spoke these words to them: * Why do you seek the Living among the dead? * Why do you mourn the Incorruptible among those subject to decay? * Go, announce the good news * to his disciples.

This is the day that the Lord has made; let us exalt and rejoice in it.

Pasch so delightful, * Pasch of the Lord is the Pasch, *

most honored Pasch now dawned on us. * It is the Pasch! * Therefore, let us joyfully embrace one another. * O Passover, save us from sorrow; * for today Christ has shown forth from the tomb * as from a bridal chamber * and filled the women with joy by saying: * Announce the good news * to my apostles.

Glory be to the Father, and to the Son, and to the Holy Spirit, now and ever and forever. Amen.

This is the Resurrection day. * Let us be enlightened by this Feast, * and let us embrace one another. * Let us call Brethren * even those who hate us, * and in the Resurrection * forgive everything; and let us sing:

Christ is risen from the dead! * By death He conquered Death, * and to those in the graves He granted life.

Friday Matins

Everything is the same as Paschal Matins except there is no procession and the Small Litany is taken only after the Third, Sixth, and Ninth Odes.

AT THE PRAISES

Tone 6 Your Cross, O Lord, is life and resurrection to your people, * and we place our hope in it. * Therefore, we sing to You: * O our risen God, have mercy on us.

Your burial, O Master, opened Paradise to the human race. * Delivered from Death, we now sing to You: * O our risen God, have mercy on us.

With the Father and the Spirit, * let us glorify Christ risen from the dead. * Let us cry to Him with a full voice: * You are our life and resurrection; have mercy on us.

You rose from the tomb on the third day, * as it was written, O Christ, * and raised our ancestors with You. * Therefore, the human race glorifies You * and praises your holy Resurrection.

PASCHAL HYMNS

Let God arise and let his enemies be scattered, and let those who hate Him flee from before his face.

Today the sacred Pasch is revealed to us, * holy and new Pasch, * the mystical Passover, * the venerable Passover, * the Pasch which is Christ the Redeemer, * spotless Pasch,

great Pasch, * the Pasch of the faithful, * the Pasch which is the key to the gates of Paradise, * the Pasch which sanctifies all the faithful.

As smoke vanishes, so let them vanish as wax melts before the fire.

O Women, * be the heralds of good news and tell what you saw; * tell of the vision and say to Zion: * Accept the good news of joy from us, * the news that Christ has risen. * Exalt and celebrate * and rejoice, O Jerusalem, * seeing Christ the King coming from the tomb * like a bridegroom.

So let the wicked perish at the presence of God, and let the righteous ones rejoice.

The myrrh-bearing women * arrived just before the dawn * at the tomb of the Giver of Life * and found an angel seated on the stone * who spoke these words to them: * Why do you seek the Living among the dead? * Why do you mourn the Incorruptible among those subject to decay? * Go, announce the good news * to his disciples.

This is the day that the Lord has made; let us exalt and rejoice in it.

Pasch so delightful, * Pasch of the Lord is the Pasch, * most honored Pasch now dawned on us. * It is the Pasch! * Therefore, let us joyfully embrace one another. * O Passover, save us from sorrow; * for today Christ has shown forth from the tomb * as from a bridal chamber * and filled the women with joy by saying: * Announce the good news * to my apostles.

Glory be to the Father, and to the Son, and to the Holy Spirit, now and ever and forever. Amen.

This is the Resurrection day. * Let us be enlightened by this Feast, * and let us embrace one another. * Let us call Brethren * even those who hate us, * and in the Resurrection * forgive everything; and let us sing:

Christ is risen from the dead! * By death He conquered Death, * and to those in the graves He granted life.

Friday Evening Vespers

The celebrant, fully vested in bright vestments, stands before the Holy Altar and begins with: "Blessed is our God..." immediately the Paschal Troparion is sung three times.

Christ is risen from the dead! * By death He conquered Death, * and to those in the graves He granted life.

TROPARION WITH VERSICLES

The celebrant sings the following versicles, and to each one the people respond by singing: Christ is risen...

v. Let God arise and let his enemies be scattered, * and let those who hate Him flee from before His face.

Christ is risen...

v. As smoke vanishes, so let them vanish as wax melts before the fire.

Christ is risen...

v. So let the wicked perish at the presence of God, and let the righteous ones rejoice.

Christ is risen...

v. This is the day that the Lord has made, let us exalt and rejoice in it.

Christ is risen...

v. Glory be to the Father, and to the Son, and to the Holy Spirit, now and ever and forever. Amen.

Christ is risen...

LITANY OF PEACE

AT PSALM 140

Tone 8 O Christ, during this spiritual service, * we sing to You these evening prayers, * commemorating the mercy You have shown us * by your Resurrection.

O Lord, O Lord, do not cast us away from your face; * but in your kindness have mercy on us * through your Resurrection.

Rejoice, O holy Zion, * the Mother of Churches and the dwelling place of God; * for you were the first to receive the forgiveness of sins * through the Resurrection.

Christ the Word was begotten by God the Father before all ages; * yet in these latter times, * He freely willed to take flesh from the Virgin who did not know man. * By his death on the Cross and his Resurrection, * He saved the human race from the ancient curse of death.

O Christ, we glorify your Resurrection; * for by rising from the dead * You freed the race of Adam from the sufferings of Hades, * and as God You granted eternal life * and great mercy to the world.

Glory to You, O Christ our Savior, * the only-begotten Son of God; * for You were nailed to the Cross, * and then arose from the dead on the third day.

Glory be: We glorify You, O Lord; * for of your own free will You suffered crucifixion for our salvation. * Almighty Savior, we worship You. * We implore You not to cast us away from your face; * but hear our prayer and save us by your Resurrection, * for You truly love all people.

Now and ever: In his love for the human race, * the King of heaven appeared on earth and dwelt among us. * For He took flesh from the pure Virgin, * and, being thus incarnate, He came forth from her. * The only Son of God remained one person, * but He now possessed two natures. * For this reason, we profess that He is truly perfect God and perfect man. * Therefore, we beseech You, O Virgin Mother, * implore Christ, whom we proclaim as God, * to have mercy on our souls.

GREAT PROKEIMENON

Tone 8 For You, O God, hear my prayer, grant me the heritage of those who fear You.

v. From the end of the earth I call: my heart is faint.

v. Let me hide in the shelter of your wings.

v. So I will always praise your name.

APOSTICHA

Tone 8 O Jesus, You descended from heaven * so that You might ascend the Cross. * O immortal Life, You came to die. * You are the true light to those who live in darkness, * and You are the resurrection of the fallen. * Therefore, O Savior of all, we glorify You.

PASCHAL HYMNS

Let God arise and let his enemies be scattered, and let those who hate Him flee from before his face.

Today the sacred Pasch is revealed to us, * holy and new

Pasch, * the mystical Passover, * the venerable Passover, * the Pasch which is Christ the Redeemer, * spotless Pasch, great Pasch, * the Pasch of the faithful, * the Pasch which is the key to the gates of Paradise, * the Pasch which sanctifies all the faithful.

As smoke vanishes, so let them vanish as wax melts before the fire.

O Women, * be the heralds of good news and tell what you saw; * tell of the vision and say to Zion: * Accept the good news of joy from us, * the news that Christ has risen. * Exalt and celebrate * and rejoice, O Jerusalem, * seeing Christ the King coming from the tomb * like a bridegroom.

So let the wicked perish at the presence of God, and let the righteous ones rejoice.

The myrrh-bearing women * arrived just before the dawn * at the tomb of the Giver of Life * and found an angel seated on the stone * who spoke these words to them: * Why do you seek the Living among the dead? * Why do you mourn the Incorruptible among those subject to decay? * Go, announce the good news * to his disciples.

This is the day that the Lord has made; let us exalt and rejoice in it.

Pasch so delightful, * Pasch of the Lord is the Pasch, * most honored Pasch now dawned on us. * It is the Pasch! * Therefore, let us joyfully embrace one another. * O Passover, save us from sorrow; * for today Christ has shown forth from the tomb * as from a bridal chamber * and filled the women with joy by saying: * Announce the good news * to my apostles.

Glory be to the Father, and to the Son, and to the Holy Spirit, now and ever and forever. Amen.

This is the Resurrection day. * Let us be enlightened by this Feast, * and let us embrace one another. * Let us call Brethren * even those who hate us, * and in the Resurrection * forgive everything; and let us sing:

Christ is risen from the dead! * By death He conquered Death, * and to those in the graves He granted life.

Saturday Matins

Everything is the same as Paschal Matins except there is no procession and the Small Litany is taken only after the Third, Sixth, and Ninth Odes.

AT THE PRAISES

Tone 8 O Lord, though You stood in judgment before the throne of Pilate, * You did not vacate your heavenly throne where You sit with the Father. * You arose from the dead, * releasing the world from the bondage of the Enemy; * for You are compassionate and the Lover of Mankind.

You gave us your Cross, O Lord, as a weapon against Satan, * who fears and trembles since he is unable to behold its power. * For it raised the dead and triumphed over Death. * Therefore, we worship your burial and your holy Resurrection.

You were placed in a grave like the dead, O Lord; * the soldiers guarded You as a slumbering King; * and as a Treasure of life, they sealed You. * But You arose and granted incorruptibility to our souls.

The angel proclaimed your Resurrection, O Lord, * and filled the guards with fear; * but to the women he cried out, saying: * Why do you seek the Living among the dead? * Truly He is risen as God * and grants life to the whole world.

PASCHAL HYMNS

Let God arise and let his enemies be scattered, and let those who hate Him flee from before his face.

Today the sacred Pasch is revealed to us, * holy and new Pasch, * the mystical Passover, * the venerable Passover, * the Pasch which is Christ the Redeemer, * spotless Pasch, great Pasch, * the Pasch of the faithful, * the Pasch which is the key to the gates of Paradise, * the Pasch which sanctifies all the faithful.

As smoke vanishes, so let them vanish as wax melts before the fire.

O Women, * be the heralds of good news and tell what you saw; * tell of the vision and say to Zion: * Accept the good news of joy from us, * the news that Christ has risen. * Exalt and celebrate * and rejoice, O Jerusalem, * seeing Christ the King coming from the tomb * like a bridegroom.

So let the wicked perish at the presence of God, and let the righteous ones rejoice.

The myrrh-bearing women * arrived just before the dawn * at the tomb of the Giver of Life * and found an angel seated on the stone * who spoke these words to them: * Why do you seek the Living among the dead? * Why do you mourn the Incorruptible among those subject to decay? * Go, announce the good news * to his disciples.

This is the day that the Lord has made; let us exalt and rejoice in it.

Pasch so delightful, * Pasch of the Lord is the Pasch, * most honored Pasch now dawned on us. * It is the Pasch! * Therefore, let us joyfully embrace one another. * O Passover, save us from sorrow; * for today Christ has shown forth from the tomb * as from a bridal chamber * and filled the women with joy by saying: * Announce the good news * to my apostles.

Glory be to the Father, and to the Son, and to the Holy Spirit, now and ever and forever. Amen.

This is the Resurrection day. * Let us be enlightened by this Feast, * and let us embrace one another. * Let us call Brethren * even those who hate us, * and in the Resurrection * forgive everything; and let us sing:

Christ is risen from the dead! * By death He conquered Death, * and to those in the graves He granted life.

Thomas Sunday

Vespers

AT PSALM 140

Tone 1 When the doors were closed and the disciples were gathered together, * You suddenly appeared in their midst, O Jesus our Almighty God. * You granted them peace and filled them with the Holy Spirit; * You commanded them to wait and not depart from Jerusalem * until they were clothed with power from on high. * Therefore, we cry to You, O Lord: * Glory to You, our Light, our Resurrection, and our Peace. *(2 times)*

Eight days after your Resurrection, O Lord, * You appeared to your disciples in the room where they were gathered; * You greeted them, saying: Peace be with you! * Then You showed your hands and side to the doubting disciple. * He, therefore, cried out in an act of faith: * My Lord and my God, glory to You! *(2 times)*

Even though the doors were closed, You came to your disciples, O Christ, * and Thomas, called the Twin, was not with them. * Therefore, he did not believe what they told him. * You did not deem him unworthy for his lack of faith, * but in your goodness, You confirmed his faith * by showing him your pure side * and the wounds in your hands and feet. * He touched them, and when he saw You, * he confessed You to be neither an abstract God nor merely human; * and he cried out: My Lord and my God, glory to You! *(2 times)*

On the eighth day the Savior came to the doubting disciples. * He granted them peace and said to Thomas: * O Apostle, come and touch my hands which were pierced by nails. * How wonderful is this doubt of Thomas! * It brought the hearts of believers to the knowledge of God. * Therefore, he cried out with fear: * My Lord and my God, glory to You! *(2 times)*

Tone 2 After your Resurrection, O Lord, * You appeared in the midst of your disciples and granted them peace * as they gathered together behind closed doors. * And Thomas was convinced after seeing your hands and side; * therefore, he confessed that You are Lord and God, * and Savior of those who place their trust in You. * O Lover of Mankind, glory to You!

Although the doors were closed, Jesus appeared to his disciples. * He took away their fear and granted them peace. * Then He called Thomas and said to him: * Why did you doubt my Resurrection from the dead? * Place your hand in my side; * see my hands and my feet. * Through your lack of faith everyone will come to know of my passion and my Resurrection, * and they will cry out with you: * My Lord and my God, glory to You!

Tone 6 **Glory be...now and ever:** Although the doors were locked, You appeared to your disciples, O Christ; * but through providence, Thomas was not with them. * For he said: I will not believe until I see the Lord, * until I see the side from which the blood and water of our baptism came forth, * until I see the wound by which He healed all people from the great wound, * and I see that He is not a pure spirit, but a person made of flesh and bones. * Therefore, O Lord, who trampled Death and made Thomas firm in his belief, * O Lord, glory to You!

PROKEIMENON

Of the day

AT THE LITIJA

Tone 4 Manifesting the brightness of your divinity, * You appeared even though the doors were closed, O Lord. * Standing in the midst of your disciples, * You uncovered your side * and showed them the wounds of your hands and feet, * delivering them from the sadness that had overcome them. * You spoke to them clearly and said: * As you see, my friends, I have assumed flesh; * I am not a pure spirit. * You spoke to the disciple who had doubted * and asked him to touch your wounds, saying: * Explore my wounds and doubt no longer. * The disciple touched You with his hand * and discovered both your divinity and humanity; * filled with fear, he cried out in faith: * My Lord and my God, glory to You!

Tone 8 Touch my side with your hand, O Thomas; * feel the traces of the nails, * be no longer unbelieving, but believing, said Christ. * When Thomas touched the Lord, he cried out in a loud voice: * You are my Lord and my God; glory to You!

Tone 8 **Glory be...now and ever:** Although the doors were closed and the disciples reunited, * the Savior appeared in the place where they were gathered. * Standing in the midst of them, He said to Thomas: * Come and touch my wounds and see the marks of the nails; * do not persist in your unbelief, * but with faith, proclaim my Resurrection from the dead.

APOSTICHA

Tone 4 O marvelous wonder! * The lack of faith gave birth to a certainty of faith; * for Thomas said: Unless I see, I will not believe! * Therefore, when he touched your side, * he acknowledged that You were the Incarnate Son of God, * and he knew that You truly suffered in the flesh; * and thus he proclaimed your resurrection from the dead, saying: * My Lord and my God, glory to You!

O praise the Lord, Jerusalem! Zion, praise your God!

O marvelous wonder! * For grass has touched the fire and was not burned. * Thomas placed his hand into the fiery side of the Savior, * and he was not consumed by touching Him. * Truly, his soul was changed from doubt to faith, * and he exclaimed from the depth of his spirit: * You are my Master and my God who arose from the dead. * O Lord, glory to You!

He has strengthened the bars of your gates; He has blessed the children within you.

O marvelous wonder! * John leaned on the bosom of the Word, * and Thomas was made worthy to touch his side. * The first discovered the depth of theology, * and the other was privileged to announce the plan of salvation; * for he clearly revealed the mystery of his Resurrection, saying: * My Lord and my God, glory to You!

Tone 5 **Glory be...now and ever:** How great is your infinite compassion, O Lover of Mankind; * for because of your long-suffering You were struck by your enemies; * You were touched by an apostle * and deeply pierced by those who denied You. * How did You become incarnate? * How were You crucified, O Sinless One? * Teach us to cry out as Thomas: * My Lord and my God, glory to You!

TROPARION

Tone 7 Though the tomb had been sealed, * from the tomb You arose, O Life and Christ our God. * Though the door had been locked, * You appeared among the disciples, O Resurrection of all; * and thus You restored an upright spirit for us * according to your great mercy. *(3 times)*

Sunday Matins

SESSIONAL HYMN I

Tone 1 The disciples were in hiding out of fear of the Jews, * and they gathered in the upper room in Zion. * You stood in their midst, O Lord of goodness; * and though the doors were closed, You appeared and filled them with joy. * You showed them your hands and the wound of your side, * saying to the doubting disciple: * Stretch forth your hand and know that it is I who have suffered for you.

Glory be...now and ever: *(Repeat the above)*

SESSIONAL HYMN II

Tone 1 Although the doors were closed, O Christ, * You appeared to your disciples as the Life of all. * You showed them your hands, your feet, and your side, * to strengthen their faith in your Resurrection from the grave. * But Thomas was not with them and so he said: * If I do not see with my own eyes * I will not be convinced by your words.

Glory be...now and ever: *(Repeat the above)*

POLYELEOS

EXALTATION

We extol You, * O Life-giving Christ, * because You descended into Hades for our sake, * and You resurrected all with You.

v. The Lord is king, with majesty enrobed.

v. For He bursts the gates of bronze and shatters the iron bars.

v. He led them forth from darkness and gloom and broke their chains to pieces.

v. The Lord arose as though from sleep, and He smote their enemies.

v. Let God arise, and let his enemies be scattered.

v. This is the day the Lord has made. Let us rejoice and be glad in it.

v. **Glory be...now and ever...**

Alleluia! Alleluia! Alleluia! Glory be to You, O God! *(3 times)*

SESSIONAL HYMN

Tone 1 When the Lord rose from the grave * and appeared to his disciples in a marvelous manner, He said: * O Thomas, having seen my side and the marks of the nails, * why do you doubt my Resurrection? * Thomas, called the Twin, answered the Creator: * You are truly my Lord and my God.

GRADUAL HYMNS

Tone 4 My sinful desires have encircled me, * from my youth they have oppressed me; * but You, O Savior, will come to aid me. * You will protect me and save me.

May the enemies of Zion be confounded by the Lord; * may they be as grass which withers, * which is dried up by the fire.

Glory be...now and ever: Every spirit lives by the grace of the Holy Spirit, * and is raised up in all purity; * it is mystically enlightened by the one God in three Persons.

PROKEIMENON

Tone 4 O praise the Lord, Jerusalem! Zion, praise your God!

v. He has strengthened the bars of your gates; He has blessed the children within you.

GOSPEL

Matthew 28: 16 - 20

Having beheld the Resurrection of Christ, * let us adore the holy Lord Jesus * who alone is sinless. * We bow to your Cross, O Christ, * and we praise and glorify your holy Resurrection. * You are our God * and besides You we recognize no other, * and we invoke your name. * Come, all you faithful, * and let us bow to the holy Resurrection of Christ, * since, through the Cross, * joy has come to all the world. * Ever praising the Lord, * let us extol his Resurrection, * since He, having endured the Crucifixion, * has destroyed Death by his death.

(3 times)

AFTER PSALM 50

Glory be: Through the intercession of the apostles, O Merciful One, remit our many sins.

Now and ever: Through the intercession of the Mother of God, O Merciful One, remit our many sins.

Tone 6

Have mercy on me, God, in your kindness. In your compassion blot out my offense.

Jesus is risen from the tomb, * as He foretold, * and granted us everlasting life * and great mercy.

CANON

ODE 1

Tone 1 Let us sing a hymn of victory, all you people, * to the One who delivered the people of Israel * from the harsh servitude of Pharoah; * for He is covered with glory.

Refrain: **Glory to your holy Resurrection, O Lord!**

Today is the springtime of our souls, * because Christ is risen as a sun from the tomb on the third day. * He has dispelled the dark winter of our sins; * let us sing to Him, for He is covered with glory.

This present hour which is Queen of all the others, * makes a cortege for the brilliant day, the King of days. * It delights the newly elected people of the Church, * who sing unceasingly to the resurrected Christ.

Glory be...now and ever: O Christ, neither the gates of death, nor the seals of the tomb, * nor the bars of the gates could hold You back; * but resurrected from the dead, * You appeared before your friends, O Master, * giving them the peace that surpasses all understanding.

It is the day of Resurrection; * O people, let us be enlightened by it. * The Passover is the Lord's Passover, * since Christ, our God, has brought us from death to life * and from earth to heaven. * Therefore, we sing the hymn of victory.

ODE 3

Tone 1 O Christ, strengthen me on the unshakable rock of your commandments. * Enlighten me in the brightness of your face, * for there is no one holy but You, O Lord.

Refrain: **Glory to your holy Resurrection, O Lord!**

O Christ, by your Cross * You renewed us from an ancient condition; * You led us from death to immortality, * ordaining us to lead a new life in You.

O Christ, You were enclosed in the tomb * by the limits of your flesh, * You are the One whom nothing can contain. * You resurrected and even though the doors were closed, * You appeared to your disciples, O Lord almighty.

Glory be...now and ever: O Christ, as a witness to your glorious Resurrection, * You showed to your disciples * the wounds You freely bore for us.

Come, let us partake of a new drink, * not miraculously produced from the barren rock, * but from the Fountain of

Immortality, * springing up from the tomb of Christ. * In Him is our firm strength.

HYPAKOE

Tone 6 As You appeared to your disciples * and gave them your peace, * come also to us, O God our Savior, and save us.

ODE 4

Tone 1 Awesome is the mystery of your work of salvation, O Christ. * The prophet Habakkuk saw it from afar * as he penetrated the divine secrets. * He said: O Lover of Mankind, * You have come for the salvation of your people.

Refrain: **Glory to your holy Resurrection, O Lord!**

By tasting the gall, Christ has redeemed the gluttony of old. * Now He allows our first father to partake * of his illumination and his peaceful communion.

You were pleased to be known, * O Christ and Lover of Mankind. * That is why You directed Thomas to that knowledge * by offering your side to be examined by his doubt. * Thus You strengthened the world * in the faith in your Resurrection on the third day.

Having richly drawn from the inexhaustible treasury of your pierced side * which was pierced by the lance of the soldiers, * Thomas filled the world with the wisdom and knowledge of God.

Glory be...now and ever: With our hymns we praise your blessed tongue, O Thomas. * It was the first to reverently announce * the Source of our life, Jesus our Lord and our God, * by the touch which filled you with grace and truth.

Let Habakkuk, * speaking in behalf of God, * stand with us at the divine watch; * let him show us the brilliant angel who proclaims: * Today, salvation comes to the world; * for Christ, being almighty, is risen.

ODE 5

Tone 1 In this night vigil, we sing to You, O Christ, * equal to the Father in eternity * and the Savior of our souls; * grant peace to the world, O Lord and Lover of Mankind.

Refrain: **Glory to your holy Resurrection, O Lord!**

You appeared to your disheartened friends, O Savior, * and your presence dispelled the sadness of their hearts. *

You made them leap for joy by your holy Resurrection.

It is truly proper to rejoice with you, O Thomas, * for the boldness of your action; * you had the courage to touch the side * which blazed with the fire of the divinity.

Glory be...now and ever: O Lord, You have shown us * how the doubt of Thomas could lead us to faith; * in your wisdom You indeed foresee all that is for our good, * O Christ, the Lover of Mankind.

Let us rise at early dawn * and bring to our Master a hymn instead of myrrh; * and we shall see Christ, * the Sun of Righteousness * who enlightens the life of all.

ODE 6

Tone 1 You have saved your prophet from the sea monster, O Lover of Mankind; * now I beseech You: * draw me out of the abyss of my sins.

Refrain: **Glory to your holy Resurrection, O Lord!**

You did not let Thomas sink into the abyss of unbelief, * but You extended your hands, * O Lord, so that he could examine them.

Our Savior has said: * By touching Me you will see * that I am made of flesh and bones. * It is I, and I have not changed.

Glory be...now and ever: Thomas, who was not present at your first appearance, O Lord, * then touched your side, * and in faith he acknowledged You.

You have descended into the realm of Death, O Christ, * and have broken ancient bonds which held the captive. * You arose from the tomb on the third day * like Jonah from the whale.

KONTAKION

Tone 8 Thomas placed his restless hand * into your life-giving side, O Christ our God; * and since You entered, although the doors were locked, * he cried to You with the other apostles: * You are my Lord and my God.

IKOS

Who stopped the hand of the disciple from being melted when he approached the fiery side of the Savior? Who gave him such boldness, to be able to touch this blazing door? Surely it was the One who was touched, for if He had not given this power to a hand made of clay, how could it have touched the wounds which shook both heaven and earth? And Thomas received the grace to touch Christ and shout out to Him: You are my Lord and my God.

ODE 7

Tone 1 The people, called together at the sound of the instruments, * had to worship the idols of the tyrant; * but as their fathers before them, * the young men, singing hymns of Zion with David, * resisted the order of the tyrant and changed the flames into fresh dew. * They sang the hymn of praise: * Blessed are You, O our God and the God of our fathers.

Refrain: **Glory to your holy Resurrection, O Lord!**

O first of days and lord of days! * This is the day whose brightness brings joy * to the new people chosen by God. * It bears the sign of eternity * and completes the octave of the time to come. * O Lord worthy of all praise, * blessed are You, O our God and the God of our fathers.

By his unusual impudence, * Thomas the twin made us profit from his doubts of faith. * By his unbelief he dispelled the ignorance and darkness for the world. * For himself he wove a crown of immortality, * saying to Christ: You are the Lord; to You belong praise and great glory. * Blessed are You, O our God and the God of our fathers.

It is not in vain that Thomas doubted, * that he did not immediately admit your Resurrection. * He acted in such a way * that the Resurrection is an indisputable belief * to all the nations on earth. * By his doubt he strengthens the faith of all * and teaches us to say: * You are the Lord; to You belong praise and great glory. * Blessed are You, O our God and the God of our fathers.

Glory be...now and ever: Timidly Thomas placed his hand into your life-giving side. * There he perceived the double energy of the two natures * united in You without confusion, O Christ the Savior. * In faith he cries out: * You are the Lord; to You belong praise and great glory. * Blessed are You, O our God and the God of our fathers.

God, who saved the three youths from the furnace, * has become man * and suffered as any mortal; * but his passion clothed his mortality * with the splendor of incorruption. * He is the only blessed One, God of our fathers, * and is worthy of all praise.

ODE 8

Tone 1 He who protected the youths in the flaming furnace * and who came down to them in the form of an angel,* He is the Lord. * Sing to Him and exalt Him throughout the ages.

Refrain: **Glory to your holy Resurrection, O Lord!**

Even though he longed to see You, * Thomas began by not believing; * but when he was favored with the sight of You, * he called You Lord and God, * You the Master whom we praise and exalt throughout the ages.

Let us bless the Lord, Father, Son, and Holy Spirit.

He who endured the unbelief of Thomas, * showing him his life-giving side * and yielding to the examination by his hand, * He is the Lord. * Sing to Him and exalt Him throughout all ages.

Now and ever: The precious treasure which you concealed * was revealed for us, O Thomas. * With a tongue inspired by God * and confessing his divinity, you have said: * Praise Christ and exalt Him throughout all ages.

Let us praise, bless, and worship the Lord, singing and exalting Him above all forever.

This is that chosen and holy day, * Feast of feasts, * most solemn day, * only king and lord of all Sabbaths, * on which we ever praise Christ.

MAGNIFICAT

ODE 9

Tone 1 O most radiant Lamp, O God-bearer, * you are the brilliant glory of the Lord * and are exalted above all creatures; * with our hymns we extol you.

Refrain: **Glory to your holy Resurrection, O Lord!**

On this most bright day, * filled with the light of your grace, O Christ, * You appeared to your disciples in all your beauty and goodness; * with our hymns we extol You.

Your side was examined and touched by a mortal hand, * yet it was not burned by your divinity; * with our hymns we extol You.

Glory be...now and ever: O Christ, You rose from the tomb, and You are our God. * Though we have not seen your Resurrection with our own eyes, * yet we eagerly believe in You, * and with our hymns we extol You.

Shine in splendor, * O new Jerusalem! * For the glory of the Lord is risen upon you. * O Zion, sing with joy and rejoice! * And you, pure Mother of God, * rejoice in the Resurrection of your Son.

HYMN OF LIGHT

Tone 3 O Thomas, do not refuse to believe in Me, * for I was wounded for your sake. * Examine my wounds with your hand; * be of one mind with the other disciples * and proclaim that I am the living God.

Tone 3 **Glory be...now and ever:** Today the fragrance of Spring arises, * and the new creation rejoices. * Today the locks are pulled from the door of the disbelief of Thomas, * and the nails of doubt are broken by the presence of the Lord. * In an act of faith the Apostle confesses: * You are indeed my Lord and my God.

AT THE PRAISES

Tone 1 After your wondrous Resurrection, * O Lord and source of Life, * You entered even though the doors were locked, * just as You did not break the seals of the tomb. * You filled your glorious disciples with joy, * and in your goodness, You gave them your Spirit of Truth. *(2 times)*

When You appeared to your disciples, O Lord, * Thomas, who was called the Twin, was not with them. * Thus he did not believe in your Resurrection, * and he said to those who saw You: * Unless I place my finger into his side * and into the marks of the nails, * I will not believe that He is risen.

O Thomas, touch Me as you wish, * extend your hand and realize that I am flesh and bones; * know that I truly have a human body, said Christ. * Do not persist in your unbelief, but now believe. * And Thomas responded: You are my Lord and my God! * Glory to your holy Resurrection!

Tone 6 **Glory be:** Eight days after your Resurrection, * O only Son and Word of God, * You appeared to your disciples through locked doors * and granted them your peace. * To the unbelieving disciple You showed the marks of your passion, saying: * Reach out and examine my hands, feet, and the wound of my side. * He was convinced and cried out to You: * My Lord and my God, glory to You!

Tone 2 **Now and ever:** You are truly most blessed, O virgin Mother of God. * Through the One who was incarnate of you, * Hades was chained, Adam revived, the curse wiped out, * Eve set free, Death put to death, * and we ourselves were brought back to life. * That is why we cry out in praise: * Blessed are You, O Christ our God, * who finds in this your good pleasure. Glory to You!

AFTER THE DISMISSAL

Gospel Stanza Number 1

Tone 1 **Glory be...now and ever:** The Lord appeared to his disciples * who had hastened to the mountain for his ascension from here below, * and they bowed before Him. * They learned of his universal power * and were sent to all the peoples of the earth * to announce his Resurrection from the dead * and his return from earth to heaven. * He also promised to be with them always, * and his word is truth; * for He is Christ our God, the Savior of our souls.

Sunday Evening Vespers

AT PSALM 140

Tone 1 After your wondrous Resurrection, O Lord and Source of Life, * You entered even though the doors were locked, * just as You did not break the seals of the tomb. * You filled your glorious disciples with joy, * and in your goodness, You gave them your Spirit of Truth.

When You appeared to your disciples, O Lord, * Thomas, who was called the Twin, was not with them. * Thus he did not believe in your Resurrection, * and he said to those who saw You: * Unless I place my finger into his side * and into the marks of the nails, * I will not believe that He is risen.

O Thomas, touch Me as you wish; * extend your hand and realize that I am flesh and bones; * know that I truly have a human body, said Christ. * Do not persist in your unbelief, but now believe. * And Thomas responded: You are my Lord and my God! * Glory to your holy Resurrection!

Three Stichera from the Saint of the day

Tone 1 **Glory be...now and ever:** When the doors were closed and the disciples were gathered together, * You suddenly appeared in their midst, O Jesus our Almighty God. * You granted them peace and filled them with the Holy Spirit; * You commanded them to wait and not depart from Jerusalem * until they were clothed with power from on high. * Therefore, we cry to You, O Lord: * Glory to You, our Light, our Resurrection, and our Peace.

GREAT PROKEIMENON

Tone 7 What God is great as our God? You are the God who works wonders!

v. You showed your power among the peoples. Your strong arm redeemed your people.

v. I said: Now I begin, and this is the will of the Most High.

v. I remember the deeds of the Lord. I remember your wonders of old.

APOSTICHA

Tone 1 Accept our evening prayer, O holy Lord, * and grant us forgiveness of sins, * for You alone manifested the Resurrection to the world.

I have lifted up my eyes to You enthroned in heaven. Behold, as the eyes of servants are on the hands of their masters, as the eyes of a maid are on the hands of her mistress, so are our eyes on the Lord our God until He has mercy on us.

My sins are like a great gulf, O Savior, * and I am sinking hopelessly because of them. * Give me your hand as You did to Peter. * Save me, O God, and have mercy on me.

Have mercy on us, O Lord, have mercy on us; for we have been filled with shame; our soul is all too full of the mockery of the rich, of the contempt of the proud.

Through the prayers of all the saints and the Mother of God, * give us your peace, O God, and have mercy on us; * for You alone are generous.

Tone 1 **Glory be...now and ever:** Eight days after your Resurrection, O Lord, * You appeared to your disciples in the room where they were gathered; * You greeted them, saying: Peace be with you! * Then You showed your hands and side to the doubting disciple. * He, therefore, cried out in an act of faith: * My Lord and my God, glory to You!

TROPARIA

Of the Saint

Tone 7 **Glory be...now and ever:** Though the tomb had been sealed, * from the tomb You arose, O Life and Christ our God. * Though the door had been locked, * You appeared among the disciples, O Resurrection of all; * and thus You restored an upright spirit for us * according to your great mercy.

Monday Matins

SESSIONAL HYMN I

Tone 1 The soldiers guarding your tomb, O Savior, * became as dead men at the lightning flash of the angel * who appeared to announce your Resurrection to the women. * We glorify You, for You have cleansed us from corruption. * We fall down before You, for You rose from the tomb, our only God.

Lord, do not reprove me in your anger; punish me not in your rage.

In sin my mother conceived me, * and like the Prodigal I dare not lift up my eyes towards heaven; * but your love gives me confidence, and I cry out to You: * Spare me and save me, O God.

Their span extends through all the earth, their words to the utmost bounds of the world.

O Lord, You are the glory of those who struggle and the crown of the victors; * You are the adornment of the glorious martyrs. * By their constancy in battle they have put the impious to flight, * and by the power of God they received victory from heaven. * Through their prayers, O Lord, grant us your great mercy.

Glory be...now and ever: O wonder of wonders! * Creation exalts with joy as it sees you, O Full of Grace; * without seed you conceived and gave birth in a manner beyond words * to the One whom even the angels cannot contemplate. * O Virgin Mother of God, * intercede with Him for the salvation of our souls.

SESSIONAL HYMN II

Tone 1 Thomas dared to touch with his hand * the side of Him who is untouchable; * yet his hand was not consumed by fire. * He diligently probed the wounds, * crying out concerning Him whose side was pierced for us: * You are my Lord and my God, who has endured the passion.

Glory be...now and ever: *(Repeat the above)*

Having beheld the Resurrection of Christ...

CANON

HYMN OF LIGHT

Tone 3 O Thomas, do not refuse to believe in Me, * for I was wounded for your sake. * Examine my wounds with your hand; * be of one mind with the other disciples * and proclaim that I am the living God.

Tone 3 **Glory be...now and ever:** Today the fragrance of Spring arises, * and the new creation rejoices. * Today the locks are pulled from the door of the disbelief of Thomas, * and the nails of doubt are broken by the presence of the Lord. * In an act of faith the Apostle confesses: * You are indeed my Lord and my God.

AT THE PRAISES

Tone 1 We praise your saving passion, O Christ! * We glorify your Resurrection! *(2 times)*

Remember, O soul, * that judgment in another world awaits you! * Everything hidden will then be revealed to all! * Do not forget here those things which are yet to come, * but prepare yourself, crying to the Judge: * Save me, O God, and have mercy on me!

O come, all you faithful, * let us honor Christ's champions in hymns and spiritual songs! * They enlighten the universe and proclaim the faith! * They are ever-flowing fountains, gushing healing for the faithful! * Through their prayers, O Christ our God, * grant peace to your world * and great mercy to our souls.

Tone 1 **Glory be...now and ever:** Even though the doors were closed, You came to your disciples, O Christ, * and Thomas, called the Twin, was not with them. * Therefore, he did not believe what they told him. * You did not deem him unworthy for his lack of faith, * but in your goodness, You confirmed his faith * by showing him your pure side * and the wounds in your hands and feet. * He touched them, and when he saw You, * he confessed You to be neither an abstract God nor merely human; * and he cried out: My Lord and my God, glory to You!

APOSTICHA

Tone 2 With lips newly purified, * let mortals join angels and sing * to Him who rose on the third day from the tomb; * He raised the world with himself.

O praise the Lord, Jerusalem! Zion, praise your God!

You were seen, O Savior, by your apostles * though the

doors were locked. * Through them we are renewed by the Holy Spirit.

He has strengthened the bars of your gates; He has blessed the children within you.

We see You, O King of all, * not with these earthly eyes, * but with hearts aflame with desire. * We believe in You, our God, * and with our songs we extol You.

Tone 1 **Glory be...now and ever:** On the eighth day the Savior came to the doubting disciples. * He granted them peace and said to Thomas: * O Apostle, come and touch my hands which were pierced by nails. * How wonderful is this doubt of Thomas! * It brought the hearts of believers to the knowledge of God. * Therefore, he cried out with fear: * My Lord and my God, glory to You!

Monday Evening Vespers

AT PSALM 140

Tone 4 Risen from the tomb, O Almighty Lord, * You came to your friends through closed doors. * To Thomas You showed the wounds of the nails * and your side which was pierced by a lance, * strengthening and confirming him, O Word, * in believing that in your compassion * You endured the saving passion.

The Lord said to Thomas, the Twin: * Do not be faithless, but believing, * because of my great humility and boundless self-emptying. * I am truly He who suffered * and rose again from the tomb on the third day. * I have robbed the treasury of Hades * giving life to the dead of all ages.

Thomas was amazed as he beheld You; * He cried: You are my Lord and my God! * I believe, O Lover of Mankind, that You are the One * who suffered and so healed our passions. * I fall down before your majesty, * and I proclaim to the world your awesome and saving Resurrection.

Three Stichera from the Saint of the day

Tone 1 **Glory be...now and ever:** On the eighth day the Savior came to the doubting disciples. * He granted them peace and said to Thomas: * O Apostle, come and touch my hands which were pierced by nails. * How wonderful is this doubt of Thomas! * It brought the hearts of believers to the knowledge of God. * Therefore, he cried out with fear: * My Lord and my God, glory to You!

APOSTICHA

Tone 1 O you people, walk around Zion and encompass her. * And there give glory to Him who is risen from the dead. * For He is our God who delivers us from our sins.

I have lifted up my eyes to You enthroned in heaven. Behold, as the eyes of servants are on the hands of their masters, as the eyes of a maid are on the hands of her mistress, so are our eyes on the Lord our God until He has mercy on us.

O Savior, by my sinful thoughts and evil deeds, * I have brought judgment on myself. * Grant me the grace of conversion, O God, * so that I may call out to You: * Save me, O gracious Benefactor, and have mercy on me.

Have mercy on us, O Lord, have mercy on us; for we have been filled with shame; our soul is all too full of the mockery of the rich, of the contempt of the proud.

O Saints, your confession of faith in the arena * destroyed the strength of devils and set us free from delusion. * When you were beheaded you cried out: * O Lord, may the sacrifice of our souls be acceptable in your sight; * for in our love for You, the Lover of Mankind, * we have despised this temporal life.

Tone 2 **Glory be...now and ever:** After your Resurrection, O Lord, * You appeared in the midst of your disciples and granted them peace * as they gathered together behind closed doors. * And Thomas was convinced after seeing your hands and side; * therefore, he confessed that You are Lord and God, * and Savior of those who place their trust in You. * O Lover of Mankind, glory to You!

TROPARIA

Of the Saint

Tone 7 **Glory be...now and ever:** Though the tomb had been sealed, * from the tomb You arose, O Life and Christ our God. * Though the door had been locked, * You appeared among the disciples, O Resurrection of all; * and thus You restored an upright spirit for us * according to your great mercy.

Tuesday Matins

SESSIONAL HYMN I

Tone 1 The women who came to your tomb early in the morning * trembled at the sight of the angel. * The tomb shone with life, * and they were struck with astonishment. * Therefore, they returned to the apostles, proclaiming the Resurrection. * Christ, who alone is mighty and powerful, * has despoiled Hades and raised all those held in corruption. * He has released us from the fear of condemnation * by the power of the Cross.

Lord, do not reprove me in your anger; punish me not in your rage.

If the just are saved only with difficulty, * how shall I prove myself, sinner that I am? * I have borne neither the burden nor the heat of the day; * but count me with those who came at the eleventh hour * and save me, O Lord.

Their span extends through all the earth, their words to the utmost bounds of the world.

As good soldiers in the faith, * fearless and without reproach before the tyrants, * you boldly walked towards Christ carrying his precious Cross upon yourselves. * After completing the course of your struggles, you received victory from on high. * Glory to Him who strengthened you! * Glory to Him who crowned you! * Glory to Him who heals us through you!

Glory be...now and ever: Come, O faithful, let us venerate the holy Mother of God; * let us bow before her for she is our unshakable rampart. * She can speak in our behalf to the Son whom she conceived. * Through her prayers we can be saved from death * and from the punishment that threatens our souls.

SESSIONAL HYMN II

Tone 5 Let us all worthily glorify in song * the memory of Christ's Apostle. * Through him our faith is wondrously confirmed, * for he diligently examined the marks of the nails. * He proclaimed the faith to the world, * and he begs the Savior to have mercy on our souls.

Glory be...now and ever: *(Repeat the above)*

Having beheld the Resurrection of Christ...

CANON

HYMN OF LIGHT

Tone 3 O Thomas, do not refuse to believe in Me, * for I was wounded for your sake. * Examine my wounds with your hand; * be of one mind with the other disciples * and proclaim that I am the living God.

Tone 3 **Glory be...now and ever:** Today the fragrance of Spring arises, * and the new creation rejoices. * Today the locks are pulled from the door of the disbelief of Thomas, * and the nails of doubt are broken by the presence of the Lord. * In an act of faith the Apostle confesses: * You are indeed my Lord and my God.

AT THE PRAISES

Tone 1 You endured crucifixion; * You destroyed Death and rose from the dead. * Give peace to our lives, * O only almighty Lord. *(2 times)*

Do not cast me away, O my Savior! * I am imprisoned in sins and laziness. * Raise up my mind to thoughts of repentance. * Make me an industrious worker in your vineyard. * Though I ask to be hired at the eleventh hour, * grant me your great mercy!

The ranks of the great King's army * resisted the lawless demands of the tyrant. * Bravely they despised their tortures. * They trampled down every deceiver. * Now they have won their crowns * and pray the Savior to grant us peace and great mercy.

Tone 2 **Glory be...now and ever:** Although the doors were closed, Jesus appeared to his disciples. * He took away their fear and granted them peace. * Then He called Thomas and said to him: * Why did you doubt my Resurrection from the dead? * Place your hand in my side; * see my hands and my feet. * Through your lack of faith everyone will come to know of my passion and my Resurrection, * and they will cry out with you: * My Lord and my God, glory to You!

APOSTICHA

Tone 2 O faithful, join the angels' choir * singing ceaseless praises to Christ who is risen * from his three days in the tomb. * He has raised the world with himself.

Their span extends through all the earth, their words to the utmost bounds of the world.

Thomas returned to the faith * by probing your opened

side, O compassionate One. * Through him we have come to know * that You are our Lord and our God!

The heavens proclaim the glory of God, and the firmament shows forth the work of his hands.

O our Redeemer, give peace to your people. * By your rising from the tomb, * You have raised the world from Hades, * O all-powerful Lord!

Tone 6 **Glory be...now and ever:** Although the doors were locked, You appeared to your disciples, O Christ; * but through providence, Thomas was not with them. * For he said: I will not believe until I see the Lord, * until I see the side from which the blood and water of our baptism came forth, * until I see the wound by which He healed all people from the great wound, * and I see that He is not a pure spirit, but a person made of flesh and bones. * Therefore, O Lord, who trampled Death and made Thomas firm in his belief, * O Lord, glory to You!

Tuesday Evening Vespers

AT PSALM 140

Tone 1 The Lover of Mankind rose from the dead on the third day. * He said to Thomas: See and feel the wounds in my hands and feet; * know Me as the changeless God * who accepted your earthly image and suffered in it.

Thomas the Twin was amazed; * seeing the wounds on the hands and feet, * he marvelled at the miracle and touched the side of the Lord. * Then he proclaimed to the pagans * your rising from the tomb on the third day.

I receive great joy, O my Savior, * seeing your Resurrection confirmed by positive facts * which Thomas had a chance to touch. * So I proclaim You as truly God and truly man.

Three Stichera from the Saint of the day

Tone 4 **Glory be...now and ever:** Manifesting the brightness of your divinity, * You appeared even though the doors were closed, O Lord. * Standing in the midst of your disciples, * You uncovered your side * and showed them the wounds of your hands and feet, * delivering them from the sadness that had overcome them. * You spoke to them clearly and said: * As you see, my friends, I have assumed flesh; * I am not a pure spirit. * You spoke to the disciple who had doubted * and asked him to touch your wounds, saying: * Explore my wounds and doubt no longer. * The disciple touched You with his hand * and discovered both your divinity and humanity; * filled with fear, he cried out in faith: * My Lord and my God, glory to You!

APOSTICHA

Tone 1 The Cross was planted upon the place of the skull; * and from the everlasting spring that flowed from the side of the Savior, * it brought forth for us the Flower of immortality.

I have lifted up my eyes to You enthroned in heaven. Behold, as the eyes of servants are on the hands of their masters, as the eyes of a maid are on the hands of her mistress, so are our eyes on the Lord our God until He has mercy on us.

Come you people, praise and worship Christ. * Glorify his Resurrection from the dead; * for He is our God who has delivered the world * from the deceit of the Enemy.

Have mercy on us, O Lord, have mercy on us; for we have been filled with shame; our soul is all too full of the mockery of the rich, of the contempt of the proud.

How beautiful is the manner of your exchange, O Saints; * for you have given your blood and received heaven. * Truly, you have done well! * You have obtained immortality by forsaking corruptible things. * Making a single choir with the angels, * you sing unceasingly the praises of the consubstantial Trinity.

Tone 8 **Glory be...now and ever:** Touch my side with your hand, O Thomas; * feel the traces of the nails, * be no longer unbelieving, but believing, said Christ. * When Thomas had been touched by the finger of the Lord, * He cried out in a loud voice: * You are my Lord and my God; glory to You!

TROPARIA

Of the Saint

Tone 7 **Glory be...now and ever:** Though the tomb had been sealed, * from the tomb You arose, O Life and Christ our God. * Though the door had been locked, * You appeared among the disciples, O Resurrection of all; * and thus You restored an upright spirit for us * according to your great mercy.

Wednesday Matins

SESSIONAL HYMN I

Tone 1 By your crucifixion, O Christ, * the curse of the tyrant was abolished, * and by your suffering, the power of evil was overthrown, * for it was not an angel nor a human but You yourself who did save us. * O Lord, glory to You!

Exalt the Lord our God; bow down before Zion, his footstool. He, the Lord, is holy.

Isaac was led up the mountain as a sacrifice; * Jonah descended into the deep. * Both were images of your passion, O Savior: * the first was bound for the slaughter, * the other prefigured your death * and your wondrous rising to life. * O Lord, glory to You!

God is to be feared in his holy place. He is the Lord, the God of Israel.

By the sufferings your saints endured for You * be moved with compassion, O our God, and heal all our sorrows; * we pray to You, O Lord and Lover of Mankind.

Glory be...now and ever: O Virgin, we are assured of your protection * and delivered from all danger through your prayers. * We are always defended by the Cross of your Son, * and we, the faithful, extol you.

SESSIONAL HYMN II

Tone 1 Thomas dared to touch with his hand * the side of Him who is untouchable; * yet his hand was not consumed by fire. * He diligently probed the wounds, * crying out concerning Him whose side was pierced for us: * You are my Lord and my God, who has endured the passion.

Glory be...now and ever: *(Repeat the above)*

Having beheld the Resurrection of Christ...

CANON

HYMN OF LIGHT

Tone 3 O Thomas, do not refuse to believe in Me, * for I was wounded for your sake. * Examine my wounds with your hand; * be of one mind with the other disciples * and proclaim that I am the living God.

Tone 3 **Glory be...now and ever:** Today the fragrance of Spring arises, * and the new creation rejoices. * Today the locks are pulled from the door of the disbelief of Thomas, * and the nails of doubt are broken by the presence of the Lord. * In an act of faith the Apostle confesses: * You are indeed my Lord and my God.

AT THE PRAISES

Tone 1 You have given life to us, O Savior, * by being nailed to the Cross. * To You is due a hymn of praise, O Master! *(2 times)*

You captured Hades, O Christ. * You raised us by your own Resurrection. * Make us worthy to praise and glorify You in purity of heart.

Neither tribulation, prison, nor hunger, * persecutions, scourgings, nor wild beasts' fury, * the sword, or the threat of fire * could separate you blessed martyrs from God. * In your desire for Him, * your suffering bodies had become alien to you; * wishing to escape, you scorned the coming of death. * Therefore, you worthily receive the reward of your combat, * becoming heirs of the heavenly kingdom. * You have boldness before God, the Lover of Mankind. * Beg Him to grant peace to the world * and great mercy to our souls.

Tone 8 **Glory be...now and ever:** Although the doors were closed and the disciples reunited, * the Savior appeared in the place where they were gathered. * Standing in the midst of them, He said to Thomas: * Come and touch my wounds and see the marks of the nails; * do not persist in your unbelief, * but with faith, proclaim my Resurrection from the dead.

APOSTICHA

Tone 2 Behold, a new wonder! * Strange is the mystery. * The hand of the Apostle, * only chaff before the fire, * is not burned by touching God.

Their span extends through all the earth, their words to the utmost bounds of the world.

Come, O faithful, * hasten to purify your hands from defilement * and from the stains of passion, * that you may embrace the Master's side.

The heavens proclaim the glory of God, and the firmament shows forth the work of his hands.

Surrender all your perceptions, O my soul, * and grant the divine wisdom. * This is the will of Christ: * to complete your sanctification.

Tone 2 **Glory be...now and ever:** You have renewed the earth. * You have restored the leaves of the trees. * You have opened the flowers of spring. * Now restore my soul by the increase of virtue.

Wednesday Evening Vespers

AT PSALM 140

Tone 2 Without leaving the Father's bosom, O Christ * You did appear on earth in the flesh. * In your compassion You accepted the passion and death * to rise again on the third day. * You came through closed doors as the Almighty One. * Thomas rejoiced when he felt your divine side * and glorified You as Lord and Creator.

You were nailed upon the Cross and your side was pierced by a lance; * You tasted gall, O Christ, and endured death; * and You were placed in the tomb as one dead. * But, as God You destroyed the bonds of Hades, * resurrecting those dead from all ages. * Therefore, You appeared to your disciples; * by your wounds You confirmed your Resurrection.

The Passover is our present feast: * a mystical Passover, the Passover of God; * a Passover of salvation, * a Passover leading us to immortal life; * this Passover drives all sorrow away. * This Passover is the disciples' gift of joy. * Therefore, Thomas cried: * You are the Lord and my God, * who has conquered the kingdom of Hades.

Three Stichera from the Saint of the day

Tone 4 **Glory be...now and ever:** O marvelous wonder! * The lack of faith gave birth to a certainty of faith; * for Thomas said: Unless I see, I will not believe! * Therefore, when he touched your side, * he acknowledged that You were the Incarnate Son of God, * and he knew that You truly suffered in the flesh; * and thus he proclaimed your resurrection from the dead, saying: * My Lord and my God, glory to You!

APOSTICHA

Tone 1 O Christ, by your passion we have been freed from suffering; * and by your Resurrection we have been delivered from corruption. * O Lord, glory to You!

I have lifted up my eyes to You enthroned in heaven. Behold, as the eyes of servants are on the hands of their masters, as the eyes of a maid are on the hands of her mistress, so are our eyes on the Lord our God until He has mercy on us.

O Lyre of the apostles, * whose many strings were moved by the Holy Spirit, * you destroyed the hateful devils; * and, proclaiming the one God, * you delivered the people from the delusion of idols * and taught them to worship the consubstantial Trinity.

Have mercy on us, O Lord, have mercy on us; for we have been filled with shame; our soul is all too full of the mockery of the rich, of the contempt of the proud.

O Martyrs, worthy of praise, * though the earth may not have covered you, heaven received you, * opening to you the gates of Paradise, where you dwell, * delighting in the Tree of Life. * Beseech Christ to grant our souls peace and great mercy.

Tone 4 **Glory be...now and ever:** O marvelous wonder! * For grass has touched the fire and was not burned. * Thomas placed his hand into the fiery side of the Savior, * and he was not consumed by touching Him. * Truly, his soul was changed from doubt to faith, * and he exclaimed from the depth of his spirit: * You are my Master and my God who arose from the dead. * O Lord, glory to You!

TROPARIA

Of the Saint

Tone 7 **Glory be...now and ever:** Though the tomb had been sealed, * from the tomb You arose, O Life and Christ our God. * Though the door had been locked, * You appeared among the disciples, O Resurrection of all; * and thus You restored an upright spirit for us * according to your great mercy.

Thursday Matins

SESSIONAL HYMN I

Tone 1 The Life of all was nailed to the Cross, * the immortal Lord was numbered among the dead. * He is our Savior who rose on the third day, * raising Adam from corruption. * The heavenly powers cry aloud to You, O Giver of Life: * Glory to your Resurrection! * Glory to your condescension, * O Lover of Mankind!

Their span extends through all the earth, their words to the utmost bounds of the world.

O wise Apostles who have caught the whole world in your net, * you haved received the love of God. * Intercede for us who now sing: * O Lord, save your Christian people and preserve us from all danger * through the prayers of your apostles.

God is to be feared in his holy place. He is the Lord, the God of Israel.

Let us all entreat the martyrs of Christ * who intercede for our salvation. * Let us all go to meet them in faith * that we may find grace and healing through these guardians of the faith * for they dispel the demons.

Glory be...now and ever: O Virgin, the prophets clearly announced you as the Mother of God, * and the divine apostles have proclaimed you to the world as the object of our faith. * We, therefore, reverently venerate you and sing to you with one heart, * and we always preserve for you the name of Theotokos.

SESSIONAL HYMN II

Tone 1 The Word said to the doubting Thomas: * Now that you see my side, disbelieve in Me no longer; * feel with your finger; explore with your hand. * Recognize the marks of the wounds and proclaim to the world * my life-giving Resurrection from the tomb.

Glory be...now and ever: *(Repeat the above)*

Having beheld the Resurrection of Christ...

CANON

HYMN OF LIGHT

Tone 3 O Thomas, do not refuse to believe in Me, * for I was wounded for your sake. * Examine my wounds with your hand; * be of one mind with the other disciples * and proclaim that I am the living God.

Tone 3 **Glory be...now and ever:** Today the fragrance of Spring arises, * and the new creation rejoices. * Today the locks are pulled from the door of the disbelief of Thomas, * and the nails of doubt are broken by the presence of the Lord. * In an act of faith the Apostle confesses: * You are indeed my Lord and my God.

AT THE PRAISES

Tone 1 We glorify your divine humility; * we praise You, O Christ. * You were born of a virgin, * yet were not separated from the Father. * You became a mortal and suffered for us, * voluntarily enduring the Cross. * You rose from the tomb, * coming as from a bridal chamber to save the world. * O Lord, glory to You! *(2 times)*

Let us praise with one accord, as is proper, * Peter and Paul, Luke, Matthew, Mark, and John, * Andrew, Thomas, Bartholomew, and Simon the Canaanite, * James, Philip, and the whole company of the disciples.

Rejoice in the Lord, you holy Martyrs! * You have fought the good fight. * You resisted emperors and you conquered tyrants. * You did not fear fire and sword. * While your bodies were devoured by wild beasts, * you sent up hymns to Christ, joining with the angels. * You have received heavenly crowns. * Beg Him to grant peace to the world * and great mercy to our souls.

Tone 4 **Glory be...now and ever:** O marvelous wonder! * John leaned on the bosom of the Word, * and Thomas was made worthy to touch his side. * The first discovered the depth of theology, * and the other was privileged to announce the plan of salvation; * for he clearly revealed the mystery of his Resurrection, saying: * My Lord and my God, glory to You!

APOSTICHA

Tone 2 Let sorrow now pass away. * I have calmed the tempest of your souls. * I have banished the Enemy, * and for those who believe in Me, * I have made the spiritual spring to bloom.

Their span extends through all the earth, their words to the utmost bounds of the world.

You were seen by your apostles, O Savior, * though the doors were locked. * Through them we are renewed by the Holy Spirit.

The heavens proclaim the glory of God, and the firmament shows forth the work of his hands.

We see You, O King of all, * not with these earthly eyes, * but with hearts aflame with desire. * We believe in You, our God, * and with our songs we exalt You!

Tone 6 **Glory be...now and ever:** Eight days after your Resurrection, * O only Son and Word of God, * You appeared to your disciples through locked doors * and granted them your peace. * To the unbelieving disciple You showed the marks of your passion, saying: * Reach out and examine my hands, feet, and the wound of my side. * He was convinced and cried out to You: * My Lord and my God, glory to You!

Thursday Evening Vespers

AT PSALM 140

Tone 1 Clothed in robes of righteousness, whiter than snow * let us rejoice in the present Paschal feast * on which Christ, the Sun of Righteousness, shone from the dead, * filling us with joy that knows no end.

This feast is the queen and sovereign of feasts; * this is truly the day which the Lord has made! * Let us rejoice in its mystery, O People, * as David sang of old, * for behold, Christ has come through locked doors, * granting peace to his disciples.

The unbelief of Thomas * strengthens our faith in the Resurrection of the Word; * He is both God and Man. * He rose from the black depths of Hades. * Thomas probed the wounds on his hands and feet with eager hands, * that all the world might believe.

Three Stichera from the Saint of the day

Tone 2 **Glory be...now and ever:** Although the doors were closed, Jesus appeared to his disciples. * He took away their fear and granted them peace. * Then He called Thomas and said to him: * Why did you doubt my Resurrection from the dead? * Place your hand in my side; * see my hands and my feet. * Through your lack of faith everyone will come to know of my passion and my Resurrection, * and they will cry out with you: * My Lord and my God, glory to You!

APOSTICHA

Tone 1 The precious Cross of the Savior * is our unshakable wall; * for all of us, who have put our hope in it, are saved.

> **I have lifted up my eyes to You enthroned in heaven. Behold, as the eyes of servants are on the hands of their masters, as the eyes of a maid are on the hands of her mistress, so are our eyes on the Lord our God until He has mercy on us.**

Accept our evening prayer, O holy Lord, * and grant us

forgiveness of sins, * for You alone manifested the Resurrection to the world.

Have mercy on us, O Lord, have mercy on us; for we have been filled with shame; our soul is all too full of the mockery of the rich, of the contempt of the proud.

Through the prayers of all the saints, O Lord, * and of the Mother of God, * grant us your peace and have mercy on us, * for You alone are the God of tenderness.

Tone 8 **Glory be...now and ever:** Touch my side with your hand, O Thomas; * feel the traces of the nails, * be no longer unbelieving, but believing, said Christ. * When Thomas touched the Lord, he cried out in a loud voice: * You are my Lord and my God; glory to You!

TROPARIA

Of the Saint

Tone 7 **Glory be...now and ever:** Though the tomb had been sealed, * from the tomb You arose, O Life and Christ our God. * Though the door had been locked, * You appeared among the disciples, O Resurrection of all; * and thus You restored an upright spirit for us * according to your great mercy.

Friday Matins

SESSIONAL HYMN I

Tone 1 We bow before the wood of your Cross, O Lover of Mankind! * You were nailed to it, O Life of all. * You opened the gates of Paradise to the thief * who came to You in faith, O Savior. * He was made worthy of joy by confessing: Remember me, O Lord. * Receive us as You received him as we cry: * We have all sinned; * in your compassion do not turn us away.

Exalt the Lord our God; bow down before Zion, his footstool. He, the Lord, is holy.

The soldiers guarding your tomb, O Savior, * became as dead men at the lightning flash of the angel * who appeared to announce your Resurrection to the women. * We glorify You, for You have cleansed us from corruption. * We fall down before You, for You rose from the tomb, our only God.

God is to be feared in his holy place. He is the Lord, the God of Israel.

O Lord, You are the glory of those who struggle and the

crown of the victors; * You are the adornment of the glorious martyrs. * By their constancy in battle they have put the impious to flight, * and by the power of God they received victory from heaven. * Through their prayers, O Lord, grant us your great mercy.

Glory be...now and ever: The Mother saw her Lamb and Shepherd * hanging lifeless on the Cross; * she wept, and sighing as a mother she said: * How shall I bear your ineffable condescension and voluntary passion, * O my Son and Lord of all goodness?

SESSIONAL HYMN II

Tone 1 Blessed are you, for you touched the wounds of Him * who by his opened side healed the festering sores of Adam, * granting immortality to us who believe in Him. * Blessed are you, for by your good confession * you bore witness to the apostles' proclamation of his Resurrection.

Glory be...now and ever: *(Repeat the above)*

Having beheld the Resurrection of Christ...

CANON

HYMN OF LIGHT

Tone 3 O Thomas, do not refuse to believe in Me, * for I was wounded for your sake. * Examine my wounds with your hand; * be of one mind with the other disciples * and proclaim that I am the living God.

Tone 3 **Glory be...now and ever:** Today the fragrance of Spring arises, * and the new creation rejoices. * Today the locks are pulled from the door of the disbelief of Thomas, * and the nails of doubt are broken by the presence of the Lord. * In an act of faith the Apostle confesses: * You are indeed my Lord and my God.

AT THE PRAISES

Tone 1 By your Cross, O Christ, * You have fashioned one fold and one Church * for the assembly of angels and those on earth. * O Lord, glory to You! *(2 times)*

We praise your saving passion, O Christ! * We glorify your Resurrection!

O come, all you faithful, * let us honor Christ's champions in hymns and spiritual songs! * They enlighten the universe and proclaim the faith! * They are ever-flowing fountains, gushing healing for the faithful! * Through their prayers, O Christ our God, * grant peace to your world * and great mercy to our souls.

Tone 8 **Glory be...now and ever:** Although the doors were closed and the disciples reunited, * the Savior appeared in the place where they were gathered. * Standing in the midst of them, He said to Thomas: * Come and touch my wounds and see the marks of the nails; * do not persist in your unbelief, * but with faith, proclaim my Resurrection from the dead.

APOSTICHA

Tone 4 You were crucified, opening Paradise for all. * You raised the dead with yourself, O our Life. * You have destroyed Death by your power. * You have joined things of heaven to those of earth. * You have filled the choir of apostles with your words of peace * in your boundless compassion, O Word of God.

Their span extends through all the earth, their words to the utmost bounds of the world.

The curse has been banished. * Immortal Life has come forth. * The ancient chains are broken. * Let heaven rejoice; let the earth and everything in it be glad. * Christ is risen and Death is withered away. * This day is bright with good cheer, * for through the locked doors * the Lord and Giver of Life enters.

The heavens proclaim the glory of God, and the firmament shows forth the work of his hands.

This is the day which the Lord has made. * Let us rejoice and be glad. * The Giver of Life is risen and Hades is wailing. * O choir of apostles, hear the joyful news. * O unbeliever Thomas, feel the Master's side. * Feel and proclaim his two natures.

Tone 8 **Glory be...now and ever:** Touch my side with your hand, O Thomas; * feel the traces of the nails, * be no longer unbelieving, but believing, said Christ. * When Thomas touched the Lord, he cried out in a loud voice: * You are my Lord and my God; glory to You!

Friday Evening Vespers

AT PSALM 140

Tone 1 When the doors were closed and the disciples were gathered together * You suddenly appeared in their midst, O Jesus our Almighty God. * You granted them peace and filled them with the Holy Spirit; * You commanded them to wait and not depart from Jerusalem * until they were clothed with power from on high. * Therefore, we cry to You, O Lord: * Glory to You, our Light, our Resurrection, and our Peace.

Eight days after your Resurrection, O Lord, * You appeared to your disciples in the room where they were gathered; * You greeted them, saying: Peace be with you! * Then You showed your hands and side to the doubting disciple. * He, therefore, cried out in an act of faith: * My Lord and my God, glory to You!

Even though the doors were closed, You came to your disciples, O Christ, * and Thomas, called the Twin, was not with them. * Therefore, he did not believe what they told him. * You did not deem him unworthy for his lack of faith, * but in your goodness, You confirmed his faith * by showing him your pure side * and the wounds in your hands and feet. * He touched them, and when he saw You, * he confessed You to be neither an abstract God nor merely human; * and he cried out: My Lord and my God, glory to You!

Three Stichera from the Saint of the day

Tone 6 **Glory be:** Although the doors were locked, You appeared to your disciples, O Christ; * but through providence, Thomas was not with them. * For he said: I will not believe until I see the Lord, * until I see the side from which the blood and water of our baptism came forth, * until I see the wound by which He healed all people from the great wound, * and I see that He is not a pure spirit, but a person made of flesh and bones. * Therefore, O Lord, who trampled Death and made Thomas firm in his belief, * O Lord, glory to You!

Tone 1 **Now and ever:** Let us praise the Virgin Mary * who, although born of our humanity, gave birth to the Lord of all. * The angels extol her in song; * for she is the glory of the whole world, * the gateway to heaven, and the adornment of the faithful. * As the Mother of God, she is heaven itself and the very temple of God. * She broke down the wall of enmity between the human race and God * thereby bringing us peace and opening the gates of the Kingdom. * Let us, therefore, cling to her as the anchor of our faith; * and our Lord, who was born of her, will be our protector. * Take courage then, O people of God, * for the Almighty himself will defeat your enemies.

APOSTICHA

Tone 1 Accept our evening prayer, O holy Lord, * and grant us forgiveness of sins, * for You alone manifested the Resurrection to the world.

The Lord reigns, He is clothed in majesty.

O you people, walk around Zion and encompass her. * And there give glory to Him who is risen from the dead. * For He is our God who delivers us from our sins.

For He has made the world firm, which shall not be moved.

Come you people, praise and worship Christ. * Glorify his Resurrection from the dead; * for He is our God who has delivered the world * from the deceit of the Enemy.

Holiness befits your house, O Lord, for length of days.

O Christ, by your passion we have been freed from suffering; * and by your Resurrection we have been delivered from corruption. * O Lord, glory to You!

Tone 5 **Glory be...now and ever:** How great is your infinite compassion, O Lover of Mankind; * for because of your long-suffering You were struck by your enemies; * You were touched by an Apostle * and deeply pierced by those who denied You. * How did You become incarnate? * How were You crucified, O Sinless One? * Teach us to cry out as Thomas: * My Lord and my God, glory to You!

TROPARIA

Of the Saint

Tone 7 **Glory be...now and ever:** Though the tomb had been sealed, * from the tomb You arose, O Life and Christ our God. * Though the door had been locked, * You appeared among the disciples, O Resurrection of all; * and thus You restored an upright spirit for us * according to your great mercy.

Saturday Matins

SESSIONAL HYMN I

Tone 1 The soldiers guarding your tomb, O Savior, * became as dead men at the lightning flash of the angel * who appeared to announce your Resurrection to the women. * We glorify You, for You have cleansed us from corruption. * We fall down before You, for You rose from the tomb, our only God.

Glory be: The women who came to your tomb early in the morning * trembled at the sight of the angel. * The tomb shone with life, and they were struck with astonishment. * Therefore, they returned to the apostles, proclaiming the Resurrection. * Christ, who alone is mighty and powerful, * has despoiled Hades and raised all those held in corruption. * He has released us from the fear of condemnation * by the power of the Cross.

Now and ever: O Holy Tabernacle, when Gabriel cried out to you: * Rejoice O Virgin, full of grace, * the Lord of all became incarnate of you, * as the righteous David had foretold. * In bearing your Creator, you have shown yourself to surpass the vastness of the heavens. * We, therefore, cry out: Glory to Him who dwelt in you! * Glory to Him who came forth from you! * Glory to Him who has set us free through your life-giving birth!

SESSIONAL HYMN II

Tone 1 The disciples were in hiding out of fear of the Jews, * and they gathered in the upper room in Zion. * You stood in their midst, O Lord of goodness; * and though the doors were closed, You appeared and filled them with joy. * You showed them your hands and the wound of your side, * saying to the doubting disciple: * Stretch forth your hand and know that it is I who have suffered for you.

Glory be...now and ever: *(Repeat the above)*

Having beheld the Resurrection of Christ...

CANON

HYMN OF LIGHT

Tone 3 O Thomas, do not refuse to believe in Me, * for I was wounded for your sake. * Examine my wounds with your hand; * be of one mind with the other disciples * and proclaim that I am the living God.

Tone 3 **Glory be...now and ever:** Today the fragrance of Spring arises, * and the new creation rejoices. * Today the locks are pulled from the door of the disbelief of Thomas, * and the nails of doubt are broken by the presence of the Lord. * In an act of faith the Apostle confesses: * You are indeed my Lord and my God.

AT THE PRAISES

Tone 1 We praise your saving passion, O Christ! * We glorify your Resurrection!

You endured crucifixion; * You destroyed Death and rose from the dead. * Give peace to our lives, * O only almighty Lord.

You captured Hades, O Christ. * You raised us by your own Resurrection. * Make us worthy to praise and glorify You in purity of heart.

We glorify your divine humility; * we praise You, O Christ. * You were born of a virgin, * yet were not separated from the Father. * You became a mortal and suffered for us, * voluntarily enduring the Cross. * You rose from the tomb, * coming as from a bridal chamber to save the world. * O Lord, glory to You!

Tone 6 **Glory be...now and ever:** Eight days after your Resurrection, * O only Son and Word of God, * You appeared to your disciples through locked doors * and granted them your peace. * To the unbelieving disciple You showed the marks of your passion, saying: * Reach out and examine my hands, feet, and the wound of my side. * He was convinced and cried out to You: * My Lord and my God, glory to You!

APOSTICHA

Tone 1 After your wondrous Resurrection, O Lord and Source of Life, * You entered even though the doors were locked, * just as You did not break the seals of the tomb. * You filled your glorious disciples with joy, * and in your goodness, You gave them your Spirit of Truth.

O praise the Lord, Jerusalem! Zion, praise your God!

When You appeared to your disciples, O Lord, * Thomas, who was called the Twin, was not with them. * Thus he did not believe in your Resurrection, * and he said to those who saw You: * Unless I place my finger into his side * and into the marks of the nails, * I will not believe that He is risen.

He has strengthened the bars of your gates; He has blessed the children within you.

O Thomas, touch Me as you wish, * extend your hand and realize that I am flesh and bones; * know that I truly have a human body, said Christ. * Do not persist in your unbelief, but now believe. * And Thomas responded: You are my Lord and my God! * Glory to your holy Resurrection!

Tone 1 **Glory be...now and ever:** On the eighth day the Savior came to the doubting disciples. * He granted them peace and said to Thomas: * O Apostle, come and touch my hands which were pierced by nails. * How wonderful is this doubt of Thomas! * It brought the hearts of believers to the knowledge of God. * Therefore, he cried out with fear: * My Lord and my God, glory to You!

Sunday of the Myrrh-Bearing Women

Vespers

AT PSALM 140

Tone 2 Come, let us adore God the Word, * who was born of the Father before all ages * and was incarnate of the Virgin Mary; * for of his own free will He suffered the Cross * and submitted himself to burial, * and arose from the dead to save me, a sinful one.

Christ our Savior cancelled the decree that was written against us * by nailing it to the Cross; * and He abolished the dominion of Death. * Let us glorify his Resurrection on the third day.

Let us, together with the archangels, sing of Christ's Resurrection; * for He is the Redeemer and Savior of our souls. * He will come again in awesome glory and mighty power * to judge the world which He has fashioned.

Although You died and were buried, * the angel yet declared You as Master. * He said to the women: Come and see where the Lord was placed; * for He is risen as He foretold, * because He is almighty. * Therefore, we worship You, the only Immortal One, * and we beseech You to have mercy on us, O Giver of Life.

O Christ, You have abolished the curse of the tree by your Cross; * You have destroyed the power of Death by your burial, * and You enlightened the human race by your Resurrection. * Therefore, we cry out to You: * O God and Benefactor, glory to You!

O Lord, the gates of Death opened before You in fear, * and the gatekeepers of Hades were filled with dread at the sight of You. * You smashed the gates of brass and crushed the posts of iron. * Then You burst our chains asunder * and led us out from the darkness, away from the shadow of death.

Let us all come and prostrate ourselves in the house of the Lord, * singing this hymn of salvation: * O Christ, You were crucified on the tree and rose from the dead; * and You now abide in the bosom of the Father. * Please cleanse us of our sins.

Early at dawn, the myrrh-bearing women arose, * and, carrying spices, they came to the tomb of the Lord; * and not finding what they expected, * the pious women pondered the removal of the stone. * They spoke to one another, saying: * Where are the seals of the grave? * Where is the guard which Pilate sent with great care? * And behold, a radiant angel appeared and proclaimed to them: * Why do you tearfully seek the Living One who gives life to all mortal flesh? * Christ our God has risen from the dead. * He is the Almighty One * who grants to all enlightenment, eternal life, and great mercy.

Why do you sprinkle your myrrh with tears, O women disciples? * The stone is rolled away, and the tomb is empty; * behold, Life has triumphed over Death. * The seals give brilliant witness: * that the guards of the godless have watched in vain, * that mortal nature has been saved by the flesh of God, * and that Hades is in mourning. * Hasten in joy, proclaiming to the apostles, * that Christ, the conqueror of Death, is the first-born of the dead. * He shall go before you into Galilee.

The myrrh-bearing women, O Christ, rose up early and hastened to your tomb, * seeking to anoint your most pure body. * But when the glad tidings were brought to them by the words of the angel, * they hastened to the apostles as messengers of joy. * The Leader of our salvation has risen and conquered Death. * He grants the world eternal life and great mercy.

Tone 6 **Glory be:** The myrrh-bearing women, O Savior, came to your grave; * and they saw that it was empty * but did not find your most pure body. * Therefore, they cried out with tears and said: * Who has robbed us of our hope? * Who has taken away a naked and anointed corpse, * the only consolation to his Mother? * How could they bury the One who trampled down Hades? * But in your own power, O Lord, * arise after three days as You said * and grant great mercy to our souls.

Tone 2 **Now and ever:** At the coming of grace, O Virgin, * the shadow of the Law passed away. * For, as the bush, though burning, was not consumed, * You, though giving birth, still remained a virgin. * In place of the pillar of fire, the Sun of Righteousness shone forth. * Instead of Moses, Christ, the salvation of our souls, appeared.

AT THE LITIJA

Tone 1 Why have you come to the tomb, O myrrh-bearing women? * Why do you seek the Living One among the dead? * Have faith, for the Lord is risen, said the angel.

With fear, the women came to the tomb eager to anoint your body, * and when they did not find it, they looked anxiously one to the other; * for they were not aware of the Resurrection. * Then an angel appeared to them and said: * Christ is risen! He grants us his great mercy.

Mary Magdalene and the other Mary came to the tomb seeking the Lord * and saw an angel as radiant as light sitting upon the stone. * He said to them: Why do you seek the Living One among the dead? * He is risen as He said, * and you shall find Him in Galilee. * To Him let us bow down and sing: * O Lord, risen from the dead, glory to You!

Tone 6 **Glory be:** Joseph asked for the body of Jesus. * He placed it in his own new tomb. * It was fitting for the Lord to come forth from the tomb * as from a bridal chamber. * You destroyed the dominion of Death. * You opened the gates of Paradise to the human race. * Glory to You, O Lord!

Tone 6 **Now and ever:** Christ the Lord, our Creator and Redeemer, * came forth from your womb, O most pure Virgin. * He clothed himself in our human flesh * to set us free from the original curse of Adam. * Therefore, O Mary, we praise you, without ceasing, * as the true Virgin Mother of God, * and we sing with the angels: * Rejoice, O Lady, advocate, protector, and salvation of our souls.

APOSTICHA

Tone 2 Your Resurrection, O Christ our Savior, * has enlightened the whole universe; * and, through it, You call back to yourself all creation. * Almighty God, glory to You!

PASCHAL HYMNS

Let God arise and let his enemies be scattered, and let those who hate Him flee from before his face.

Today the sacred Pasch is revealed to us, * holy and new Pasch, * the mystical Passover, * the venerable Passover, * the Pasch which is Christ the Redeemer, * spotless Pasch, great Pasch, * the Pasch of the faithful, * the Pasch which is the key to the gates of Paradise, * the Pasch which sanctifies all the faithful.

As smoke vanishes, so let them vanish as wax melts before the fire.

O Women, * be the heralds of good news and tell what you saw; * tell of the vision and say to Zion: * Accept the good news of joy from us, * the news that Christ has risen. * Exalt and celebrate * and rejoice, O Jerusalem, * seeing Christ the King coming from the tomb * like a bridegroom.

So let the wicked perish at the presence of God, and let the righteous ones rejoice.

The myrrh-bearing women * arrived just before the dawn * at the tomb of the Giver of Life * and found an angel seated on the stone * who spoke these words to them: * Why do you seek the Living among the dead? * Why do you mourn the Incorruptible among those subject to decay? * Go, announce the good news * to his disciples.

This is the day that the Lord has made; let us exalt and rejoice in it.

Pasch so delightful, * Pasch of the Lord is the Pasch, * most honored Pasch now dawned on us. * It is the Pasch! * Therefore, let us joyfully embrace one another. * O Passover, save us from sorrow; * for today Christ has shown forth from the tomb * as from a bridal chamber * and filled the women with joy by saying: * Announce the good news * to my apostles.

Tone 5 **Glory be:** O Lord, who clothes yourself with light as with a garment, * Joseph and Nicodemus took You down from the Cross, * and seeing You without life, without a garment, and without a grave, * in their compassion they wept and lamented: * Woe is me, most sweet Jesus. * The sun was covered with darkness * when it saw You suspended upon the Cross. * The earth quaked with fear, * and the veil of the Temple was torn in two. * I see that You willingly endured death for my sake. * How then shall I bury You, O my God? * With what linens shall I cover You? * With what hands shall I touch your most pure body? * What hymns shall I sing at your death? * Therefore, O compassionate Lord, I glorify your passion, * and I praise your burial and your resurrection, crying out: * O Lord, glory to You!

Tone 5 **Now and ever:** This is the Resurrection Day. * Let us be enlightened by this Feast, * and let us embrace one another. * Let us call Brethren * even those who hate us, * and in the Resurrection, * forgive everything; and let us sing: * Christ is risen from the dead! * By death He conquered Death, * and to those in the graves He granted life.

TROPARIA

Tone 2 When You descended to death, O Immortal Life, * You destroyed the Abyss by the radiance of your divinity. * And when You raised the dead from the depths of the earth, * all the heavenly powers cried out: * O Giver of life, Christ our God, glory to You!

***Tone 2* Glory be:** The noble Joseph took down your most pure body from the Cross. * He wrapped it in a clean shroud, * and with fragrant spices laid it in burial in a new tomb. * But You arose in three days, O Lord, * bestowing great mercy upon the world.

***Tone 2* Now and ever:** The angel stood by the tomb and cried out to the women bringing ointment: * Ointments are for the dead, * but Christ has shown himself not subject to corruption. * So now cry out: The Lord has risen, * bestowing great mercy upon the world.

Sunday Matins

SESSIONAL HYMN I

Tone 2 You did not prevent the sealing of the stone at your tomb, * and by your Resurrection You bestowed on all the rock of fidelity. * O Lord, glory to You!

Arise then, Lord, lift up your hand. O God, do not forget the poor!

You did not leave the bosom of the Father, * yet for our salvation You accepted the tomb and the Resurrection. * O Lord, glory to You!

Glory be...now and ever: O Mother of God, the mysteries which surround you are exceedingly glorious, * and beyond the power of understanding. * For you retained the seal of purity, * and your virginity remained inviolate; * yet you are acknowledged, without doubt, * to be the Mother who gave birth to the true God. * We beg you, therefore, to entreat Him to save our souls.

SESSIONAL HYMN II

Tone 2 The myrrh-bearing women arrived early in the morning * and seeing the tomb of the Lord empty, they ran to the apostles and said: * The Mighty One has broken the strength of Death * and has delivered all those held in the bonds of Hades. * Announce with confidence that Christ our God is truly risen * and grants great mercy to us.

I will praise You, Lord, with all my heart; I will recount all your wonders.

The women prepared myrrh to anoint You * and secretly came to your tomb early in the morning. * They feared the boldness of the Jews, * and they expected the soldiers to be keeping guard. * But their weakness triumphed over manly strength * for tenderness finds favor with God. * And so they cry out: Arise, O Lord, * protect us and save us for the love of your name.

Glory be...now and ever: We praise you, O Mother of God * for you are covered with glory more than any other. * Death has been put to death and Hades trampled underfoot * by the Cross of your Son. * He raised us from death granting us eternal life. * Paradise is again offered for us to enjoy as before. * Therefore, in thanksgiving we glorify the love and power of Christ our God.

HYPAKOE

The women went to the tomb after your passion * to anoint your body, O Christ our God. * They saw the angels and were astonished; * for they heard them crying with a loud voice: * The Lord is risen and grants great mercy to the world.

GRADUAL HYMNS

Antiphon I

I lift the eyes of my heart to the heavens; * I lift them up, O Lord. * Save me by the brightness of your light.

O Christ, have mercy upon us, * for we have sinned against You in every hour. * Before the end, give us the grace to return to You.

Glory be...now and ever: The Holy Spirit has sovereignty over all creation; * He is its sanctification and movement. * For He is God, of one substance with the Father and the Son.

Antiphon II

Without the help of the Lord who is among us, * no one could be saved from the Enemy who wishes our death.

My enemies roar against me like lions; * do not deliver your servant to their teeth.

Glory be...now and ever: To the Holy Spirit is dominion and honor; * for, as God, He gives strength to every creature, * preserving them in the Father and through the Son.

Antiphon III

Those who put their trust in the Lord are like Mount Zion; * they shall never be shaken by the attacks of the Enemy.

Those who live according to the ways of God * do not stretch their hands toward evil; * for Christ does not let his heritage fall under the sword of the impious.

Glory be...now and ever: The Holy Spirit is the fount of all wisdom. * Through Him grace is given to the apostles; * through Him the martyrs are crowned in their struggles; * and through Him the prophets receive their vision.

PROKEIMENON

Tone 2 Lord, rise up in your anger, rise against the fury of my foes; my God, awake! You will give judgment.

v. Lord God, I take refuge in You. From my pursuer save me and rescue me.

GOSPEL

Mark 16: 9 - 20

Having beheld the Resurrection of Christ, * let us adore the holy Lord Jesus * who alone is sinless. * We bow to your Cross, O Christ, * and we praise and glorify your holy Resurrection. * You are our God * and besides You we recognize no other, * and we invoke your name. * Come, all you faithful, * and let us bow to the holy Resurrection of Christ, * since, through the Cross, * joy has come to all the world. * Ever praising the Lord, * let us extol his Resurrection, * since He, having endured the Crucifixion, * has destroyed Death by his death.

(3 times)

CANON

The CANON OF THE RESURRECTION may be sung first with each Ode of the Canon; the versicle "Christ is risen from the dead" is sung with the Canon of the Resurrection.

ODE 1

Tone 1 You destroyed the boundaries of death, O Immaculate Virgin, * when You gave birth to Christ, the eternal Life, * who today is risen from the tomb * and enlightens the whole world.

Refrain: **Most holy Mother of God, save us!**

Seeing your Son and our God risen, * O Full of Grace and immaculate One, * you rejoice together with the apostles, O Mother of God; * you were the first to receive the proclamation of salvation * as the beginning of all joy.

Tone 2 O my soul, sing the song of Moses: * The Lord is my help and my protection; * He has saved me. * He is my God, and I will glorify Him.

Refrain: **Glory to your holy Resurrection, O Lord!**

You suffered bodily on the Cross, * O divinity beyond all suffering, * and your side was pierced, * opening a stream of blood and water to the world. * You are our God and we glorify You.

I venerate your crucifixion; I glorify your burial; * I praise and adore your Resurrection, * and I cry out to You, O Lord of goodness: * You are our God and we glorify You.

You have tasted the bitter gall, * O Lord in whom the Church finds its sweetness. * From your side which was pierced with the lance * You gushed forth our immortality. * You are our God and we glorify You.

O Savior who raised the dead, * You yourself were numbered among the dead; * You tasted death even though your body did not undergo corruption in the grave. * You are our God and we glorify You.

Zion rejoices and may heaven exalt in joy with us; * for Christ is risen, raising the dead who now sing: * You are our God and we glorify You.

Joseph wrapped your most pure body in a white shroud, O Christ, * and he placed You in a new tomb, O Savior, * even though as God You raise the dead.

Hastening early in the morning, * the holy myrrh-bearers have seen Christ; * they proclaimed to the disciples: * Christ is truly risen; * come with us and sing praise to Him.

Glory be: Most Holy Trinity, unique divinity, * without beginning or end, Father, Son, and Holy Spirit, * grant salvation to the world. * You are our God and we glorify You.

Now and ever: In your womb, O most pure Virgin, * you brought an end to the ancient curse. * You blossomed forth our blessing by giving birth to your Child. * He is God even though He bears our flesh.

It is the day of Resurrection; * O people, let us be enlightened by it. * The Passover is the Lord's Passover, * since Christ, our God, has brought us from death to life * and from earth to heaven. * Therefore, we sing the hymn of victory.

ODE 3

Tone 1 I returned today to life that knows no sunset, * by the goodness of Him born of you, O immaculate Virgin; * make his glory shine to the ends of the world.

Refrain: **Most holy Mother of God, save us!**

The God whom you brought into the world in the flesh, O immaculate Virgin, * is risen from the dead as He foretold. * Dance and celebrate and extol Him as God.

Tone 2 Make the sterile desert of my spirit * fertile and fruitful, O Lord, * for in your goodness * You look after the growth of all good.

Refrain: **Glory to your holy Resurrection, O Lord!**

On the Cross, O Jesus my Savior, You stretched out your hands pierced with nails * to gather all your scattered people * and to lead them to the knowledge of God.

The people said to Pilate: * Release Barabbas the criminal * and raise up this just One; * crucify the sinless Lord.

When You were placed on the Cross, O Christ, * the earth shook, light became dark, * and many of the dead came forth from the grave * venerating your power, O Lord.

Standing near your Cross, O Lord Jesus, * your Mother cried out sighing: * Alas, O my Son, where is the Lamb of God now going, * the One who was immolated for the salvation of all?

Bowing before your Cross and tomb, * I praise your passion and the nails of your hands, * together with the lance that pierced your side; * and I worship your holy Resurrection.

Resurrected, You despoiled our Enemy; * Adam and Eve were both freed, * escaping the chains of death by your holy Resurrection.

When You resurrected, O Christ, * the bars and gates of Hades were shattered; * the chains of Death were broken, * terrified by your power, O Lord.

May Joseph come and stand among us, saying: * He is

risen, the God whom I carried, * Jesus the Redeemer, * who in his love raised up Adam.

May the Twelve rejoice with us, * with the myrrh-bearing women, with Joseph and the disciples of Christ, * and with the holy women who followed Jesus.

Glory be: Together with the Father, I also praise the Son, * and I sing praise to the Spirit of truth. * I adore the unique nature distinguished in three persons * and united in one essence.

Now and ever: O blessed One of the root of Jesse! * O holy Virgin, for our sake you gave birth in the flesh * to the flowering rod who is Christ.

Come, let us partake of a new drink, * not miraculously produced from the barren rock, * but from the Fountain of Immortality, * springing up from the tomb of Christ. * In Him is our firm strength.

SESSIONAL HYMN

Tone 2 With zeal the holy women brought myrrh to your tomb, O Savior, * and their souls were filled with joy by a resplendent angel. * They proclaimed You as the God of the universe, * and they cried joyfully to the disciples: * He is risen, our Lord and our Life.

Glory be...now and ever: The choir of your disciples joined the myrrh-bearers with joy; * together with them we all celebrate this feast and glorify your holy Resurrection. * Through their prayers, O Lord and Lover of Mankind, we pray to You: * Grant great mercy to your people.

ODE 4

Tone 1 O immaculate Virgin, * He who made Adam your first father, * was made a man from your womb; * and by his death He destroyed the Death caused by sin, * and today He makes the divine brilliance of his holy Resurrection shine on you.

Refrain: **Most holy Mother of God, save us!**

The Messiah to whom you gave birth, * you behold today even more beautiful, O holy Virgin; * for He rises in glory from among the dead, * brilliant with beauty and grace and purity; * with the apostles, you glorify the Lord today in joy * for the salvation of the human race.

Tone 2 Seeing the Virgin give you birth, the Prophet proclaimed aloud: * I heard your voice O Lord, and I was filled with fear; * for You came forth from Teman, O Christ, * from the holy and overshadowed mountain.

Refrain: **Glory to your holy Resurrection, O Lord!**

By your Cross You have despoiled the dens of Hades, * awakening the dead and crushing the dominion of Death. * We praise your burial, bowing down with all the children of Adam, * and we worship your holy Resurrection.

You wished to ascend your Cross, O Savior, * and save us from the curse of old because of your mercy. * Deliver me also from the bond of my passions, * for You can do whatever You will.

You have nailed the ancient curse on the Cross, * and by the blood flowing from your wounds, * You made your blessing flow over me. * Deliver me also from the bond of my passions, * for You can do whatever You will.

Seeing You, O Savior, * Hades was irritated in its infernal depths, * since it was forced to give up those that it formerly had swallowed, * all the dead of whom it is now deprived.

Despite the seals placed on the tomb and the soldiers put on guard, * the Lord is risen as He said, * delivering me from the bond of my passions, * for He can do whatever He wills.

Risen from the dead, You despoiled Hades and gave life to the dead; * by your Resurrection You opened to me the well-springs of immortality. * Deliver me also from the bond of my passions, * for You can do whatever You will.

May the evildoers be ashamed, for Christ is risen, * awakening the dead and crying out to them: * Take courage, for I have conquered the world. * Believe in Him or remain silent, * all those who reject the Resurrection.

When You resurrected from the grave You said to the myrrh-bearers: Rejoice! * You sent them to proclaim your Resurrection to your apostles. * Deliver me also from the bond of passions, O Lord, * for You can do whatever You will.

Let us honor Joseph, a supporter of godliness, * a member of the Council, and a disciple of the Lord. * Let us also praise the myrrh-bearers and the apostles. * With all of them, O faithful, * let us joyfully celebrate the Resurrection of the Savior.

Glory be: Who is able to express * the indivisible glory of the supreme Divinity? * For it is one by nature, the consubstantial Trinity, * and is praised as three persons without beginning.

Now and ever: O Mother of God and most pure Virgin, * implore without ceasing the One who dwelt in your womb * and to whom you gave birth without seed, * that He deliver me from the bond of my passions, * for you can aid us as you wish.

Let Habakkuk, * speaking in behalf of God, * stand with us at the divine watch; * let him show us the brilliant angel who proclaims: * Today, salvation comes to the world; * for Christ, being almighty, is risen.

ODE 5

Tone 1 Divinely illumined by the life-giving rays * of the Resurrection of your Son, * O Mother of God and Virgin immaculate, * the assembly of the faithful shines in beauty.

Refrain: **Most holy Mother of God, save us!**

O King of glory, * when You became incarnate, your mother's virginity remained, and You did not break the seals of the tomb. * All creation rejoices when it sees your holy Resurrection.

Tone 2 Driving away the darkness of my soul * by the light of your divine commandments; * enlighten me, O God and Savior, * for You are the only King of peace.

Refrain: **Glory to your holy Resurrection, O Lord!**

Stripping me of the ancient garment * that had been woven for me by the power of iniquity, * You have clothed me, O Lord, * in the garment of immortality.

Alas, my sin has sewn me a garment of fig leaves; * for I have followed the advice of the Serpent * and not kept your commandment, O Savior.

My soul has been wounded by sin * and injured by the robbers of thought. * But Christ has come through Mary, * and He will heal me by pouring on the ointment of his mercy.

Standing near the Cross of the Redeemer, * the all-pure Mother of God cried out maternally and sighed: * You now leave me all alone, O my Son and my God!

With the weapon of your Cross, * You have destroyed the

Serpent, that prince of evildoers; * and by your Resurrection, O Lord, * You have broken the sting of death.

O Death, where is your sting? * Where is the victory of Hades? * Rejoice, Adam, for Death is abolished * by the life of Him who is risen from the dead.

The myrrh-bearing women came to the tomb of Him * who carried life even to Hades, * and they heard the good news of the Resurrection of Christ.

Celebrating today the memory * of the holy myrrh-bearing women and of all your disciples, * O Lord, we praise You in your radiant Resurrection.

All the faithful, let us praise, as is fitting, * the noble Joseph of Arimathea * who took the body of Christ down from the Cross * and piously gave Him a respectful burial.

Glory be: I worship You in three persons, O my God; * I bow before the Father, the Son, and the most Holy Spirit, * confessing the unity of the three persons.

Now and ever: We the faithful honor you with our hymns, * for you surpassed nature in giving birth without seed to Christ, * our only Lord who has himself renewed my corrupted nature.

Let us rise at early dawn * and bring to our Master a hymn instead of myrrh; * and we shall see Christ, * the Sun of Righteousness * who enlightens the life of all.

ODE 6

Tone 1 O Virgin Mother of God, * those who were once subjected to death * and to the corruption of the grave, * are now raised to immortal and eternal life * by Him who was incarnate from your womb.

Refrain: **Most holy Mother of God, save us!**

O immaculate Virgin, * He who wondrously dwelt in your womb and became flesh, * descended into the depths of the earth, * and rising from the tomb, * raised with Him all human nature.

Tone 2 O God and Savior, I am sinking in the abyss of sin; * I am immersed in the ocean of this life; * but as Jonah came forth from the whale, * draw me from the gulf of my passions and save me, O Lord.

Refrain: **Glory to your holy Resurrection, O Lord!**

Take courage! Hades is put to death, * for by his death on

the Cross Christ has turned the sword against it. * It is now deprived of its spoils * and has lost all the dead which it had seized.

Hades is despoiled! Take courage, O people! * The tombs are opened. * Awaken! Christ calls you forth from Hades; * He has come to redeem the human race from the grave and death.

The Source of life said to Hades: * I have now come to reclaim the dead * which you had formerly swallowed up. * For He is God who has come to redeem the human race from the grave and death.

Christ is risen, destroying our Enemy; * breaking the bonds, He has delivered the human race. * In his tenderness He has raised up Adam, our first father, * by extending his hand as the God of goodness.

Having wrapped You in a shroud, O Christ, * the noble Joseph placed you in a tomb. * With precious ointments he anointed the destroyed temple of your most pure body, * and then he rolled a stone over the entrance to the tomb.

Why do you hasten, O myrrh-bearers? * Why are you carrying myrrh to the living God? * Christ is risen as He said. * Wipe away your tears * and from now on change your tears into joy.

Glory be: O faithful, let us praise the unique Trinity; * let us glorify the Father and the Son, * together with the Spirit who is consubstantial with the Father * and dwells with Him from the beginning, * divinity sharing the same eternity.

Now and ever: Without sowing nor laboring, O pure Virgin, * as a true vine you have conceived the Grape of immortality * whose juice flows forth for us * as a fount of eternal joy.

You have descended into the realm of Death, O Christ, * and have broken ancient bonds which held the captive; * You arose from the tomb on the third day * like Jonah from the whale.

KONTAKION

Tone 2 By your Resurrection, O Christ our God, * You told the women bringing ointment to rejoice; * and You stilled the weeping of Eve, the first mother. * You instructed the women to announce to your apostles: * The Savior has risen from the tomb.

IKOS

Coming near to your tomb, O Savior, the myrrh-bearers hesitated, saying to each other: Who will roll the stone away from the tomb for us? They looked and saw that it had been rolled away. Startled by the sight of the radiant angel, they were seized with fear and wanted to flee, but the young man cried out to them: Do not be afraid! The One whom you seek is risen; come and see the place where the body of Jesus lay. Hasten to his disciples and proclaim to them: The Savior is risen from the tomb!

ODE 7

Tone 1 O Virgin immaculate, * today your Son destroyed Death, * giving eternal life to all mortals from all ages, * for He is the God of our fathers, * and to Him alone belong blessing and glory.

Refrain: **Most holy Mother of God, save us!**

O Full of Grace, * He who reigns over all creation * became incarnate and dwelt in your womb, * having suffered death by the Cross; * as God all-powerful He is risen, * making us rise with Him.

Tone 2 Inspired by the Cherubim, the youths in the furnace sang: * Blessed are You, O our God; * You have declared the just sentence. * It is for our faults that You treat us so. * To You belong glory and eternal praise.

Refrain: **Glory to your holy Resurrection, O Lord!**

Wishing to save the work of your hands * from wandering astray, O God of goodness, * You endured being nailed to a cross * to restore in your flesh, O Savior, * the image that was broken by our passions. * Destroying Hades, You raised up the dead with You.

Raised upon the Cross, O God of tenderness, * You called all people back to You according to your promise. * In truth, O Lord, You deigned to suffer death for our sins; * even to the Thief You opened the gates of Paradise, O Savior.

You raised the destroyed temple of your body * from the grave on the third day according to your promise, * so that You might truly manifest the glory * that You share with us in faith; * You freed the prisoners which Hades formerly held captive.

What do the stricken guards now say? * How was He stolen whom they were not able to guard? * If they did not see Him raised up, how can they say that his body was stolen? * The empty tomb together with the shroud and wrappings are witnesses to this.

Who is this dead One whom you guard? * Why do you seal the stone for fear that someone might steal Him? * Behold now the tomb and the seals: * How is He risen if He is not the Lord God? * Rather believe the departed just ones * who have appeared to many after their resurrection.

Glory be: With the Father we also glorify the Son and the Holy Spirit, * crying out with an unceasing voice: * O Holy Trinity, have mercy on us! * In your love, save us, O Divinity, * glorified in three persons forever.

Now and ever: How have you held as an infant in your womb, O immaculate Virgin, * the God whom the angels in heaven adore? * According to the wisdom of his good will, * He dwelt there to save all the children of Adam * and to repeal the bitter condemnation * that was reaped from the forbidden tree.

God, who saved the three youths from the furnace, * has become man * and suffered as any mortal; * but his passion clothed his mortality * with the splendor of incorruption. * He is the only blessed One, God of our fathers, * and is worthy of all praise.

ODE 8

Tone 8 The Creator came into this world * from you, O Virgin Mother of God; * destroying the jail of Hades, * He gave resurrection to us mortals; * and we also bless Christ forever.

Refrain: **Most holy Mother of God, save us!**

Destroying all power of Death * on the day of his Resurrection, O Virgin, * your Son and the all-powerful God * made us partakers of his glory and divinity. * We also bless Christ forever.

Tone 2 Let us sing a hymn of blessing * to Him who prefigured the wondrous mystery of the Virgin to Moses * through the burning bush on Sinai; * to Him is due great glory forever!

Refrain: **Glory to your holy Resurrection, O Lord!**

The rays of the sun were hidden in fear * when they saw the sufferings of Christ. * The dead rose up and the mountains trembled; * the earth shook in fright * and Hades was deprived of its spoils.

In days of old the thrice-blessed youths * raised their hands in the furnace. * Thus they prefigured the image of your precious Cross * on which You, O Jesus Christ, * shattered the power of the Enemy.

The arguments of the unbelievers are nothing but lies! * For the soldiers saw nothing in their sleep. * Who rolled away the stone from the tomb? * It was none other than Christ who is risen * and has raised all the dead with Him.

Who dried up the sterile fig tree? * Who healed the paralyzed hand? * Who fed the multitude in the desert? * It was none other than Christ our God * who raised all the dead with Him.

Who gave sight to the blind? * Who healed the lepers and the lame? * Who made the people cross the Red Sea as if on dry land? * It was none other than Christ our God * who raised all the dead with Him.

Who raised from the tomb the man who was dead four days? * Who raised the dead son of a widowed mother? * Who freed the paralytic from his mat? * It was none other than Christ our God * who raised all the dead with Him.

The rock itself is a witness * together with the tomb that was guarded by the soldiers; * even the seals placed on the tomb say: * Christ is truly risen! He lives forever!

Christ is truly risen; * Hades is empty, the Serpent is crushed, and Adam returned to grace. * Despite the doubts of the impious, * the entire human race is saved by Christ.

Let us bless the Lord, Father, Son, and Holy Spirit.

Together with the Father * we also glorify the Son and the Holy Spirit as one God, the Holy Trinity, * and we sing this hymn: * Holy, holy, holy are You, O Lord, forever.

Now and ever: O Virgin, you carried the bread of heaven and the wheat of eternity in your womb. * Without change or mixture, * you kneaded Him from the dough of humanity and gave birth to Him; * having two natures, * He is the only Christ and our God.

Let us praise, bless, and worship the Lord, singing and exalting Him above all forever.

This is that chosen and holy day, * Feast of feasts, * most solemn day, * only king and lord of all Sabbaths, * on which we ever praise Christ.

OMIT MAGNIFICAT

ODE 9

Tone 1 O Virgin, with one voice we, the faithful, extol you: * Rejoice, door of the Lord; rejoice, spiritual city; * rejoice, for you made the light of your Son shine upon us * on the day of his Resurrection.

Refrain: **Most holy Mother of God, save us!**

O immaculate One, full of grace, * exalt and dance in joy, O divine door of brightness; * for Jesus rested in the tomb * and rose in glory more brilliant than the sun; * and He enlightens the whole human race.

Tone 2 O only Mother of God, * who in a marvelous manner conceived the Word * who eternally came forth from the Father, * we the faithful extol you.

Refrain: **Glory to your holy Resurrection, O Lord!**

On the Cross the Good Thief recognized You as God, * and You made him an inhabitant of the heavenly Paradise when he said: * Remember me, O almighty Savior.

For us You were insulted by the faithless and lawless impious ones, * even though You were the One who wrote the tablets of the Law * for your servant Moses on Mount Sinai.

For us, O Savior, You drank vinegar and gall, * even though You were the One * who gave your body and precious blood * as the nourishment for eternal life.

A sword pierced your life-giving side, O Christ, * bringing forth blood and water * as a source of eternal life for the world.

You were numbered among the dead, * even though You give life to us who were placed in the tomb. * You emptied the tombs when You conquered Hades and raised up Adam.

You are risen, O Jesus, * and the Enemy is in chains; * both Hades and the tombs are emptied, * and the dead rise up to adore You, O Lord.

Who would steal a dead body, especially a naked one? * This is no myth: * Christ is risen breaking down the gates and bolts of Hades.

Glory to You, O Christ, Savior and Source of life; * You have made light dawn upon the darkness of error, * illuminating the whole world by your Resurrection.

Let us praise Joseph, the noble counsellor; * together with the myrrh-bearers and the disciples of the Lord, * he attests to the Resurrection of Christ.

O faithful, let us praise Joseph of Arimathea, * together with Nicodemus and the ointment-bearing women; for they said: * The Lord is truly risen!

Glory be: O eternal Father and uncreated Son, * sharing the same throne wih the Spirit, * You are the only true God, * in the triple unity of nature and the trinity of persons.

Now and ever: Jesse rejoices and David exalts! * Behold, here is the Virgin who, as a branch planted by God, * has given birth to Christ the eternal Flower.

Shine in splendor, * O new Jerusalem! * For the glory of the Lord * is risen upon you. * O Zion, sing with joy and rejoice! * And you, pure Mother of God, * rejoice in the Resurrection of your Son.

HYMN OF LIGHT

Tone 2 You, O King and Lord, * have fallen asleep * in the flesh as a mortal man, * but on the third day You arose again. * You have raised Adam * from his corruption and made Death powerless. * You are the Pasch of incorruption. * You are the salvation of the world.

***Tone 2* Glory be...now and ever:** O myrrh-bearing women, listen to the news that brings joy: * I have put Hades, that cruel tyrant, to flight; * I have made the world rise from the depths of the tomb; * hasten to my friends, the disciples, and quickly bring this good news to them. * For it is my will that the work of my hands shines with joy * because in days of old it gave birth to sorrow.

AT THE PRAISES

Tone 2 All creation and everything that breathes glorifies You, O Lord; * for by the Cross You abolished Death * that You might manifest to the world your Resurrection from the dead. * For You alone are the Lover of Mankind.

What do the Pharisees now say? * How was it that the guardian soldiers lost the King whom they were guarding? * Why was it that the stone could not retain the Rock of Life? * Therefore, either you must deliver to us Him who was buried * or worship with us Him who is risen and say: * Glory to your bountiful mercies, our Savior, glory to You!

Rejoice, O nations and be glad; * for the angel sat on the stone of the grave * and gave us the good news, saying: * Christ the Savior of the world is risen from the dead. * He has filled the world with fragrant aroma. * Rejoice, O nations, and be glad.

At your conception, O Lord God, * an angel said to her who is full of grace: Rejoice! * At your Resurrection an angel rolled away the stone * from the door of your glorious tomb. * The first angel spoke with signs of joy instead of sorrow, * and the latter brought us the good news * of a Lord who gives life instead of death. * Therefore, we shout to You, O Benefactor of all, * glory to You, O Lord!

The women brought spices mixed with tears to your tomb, * but their words became full of joy * when they said: The Lord is risen!

Let the nations and people praise Christ our God * who suffered crucifixion willingly for our sakes, * and remained in the tomb for three days. * Let them worship his Resurrection from the dead, * by which all the ends of the earth were enlightened.

O Christ, You were crucified and buried as You willed. * You held Death captive and resurrected in glory as Lord and God, * who granted the world life eternal and great mercy.

O transgressors of the Law, * when you sealed the stone, * you did in truth magnify the miracle for us as the guards know; * especially since you persuaded them to say * on the day of his resurrection from the tomb: * While we slept the disciples came and stole Him away. * For who would steal a corpse, especially a naked one? * He truly arose in his divine power * leaving his shroud in the grave; * without breaking the seals He has trampled down Death, * and He has given to the human race life eternal and great mercy.

Tone 2 **Glory be:** The companions of Mary were bearing their ointments * and wondering how they would carry out their plan; * but they saw the stone removed * and a divine messenger appeared to them, * and he gave peace to their troubled souls. * For he said that the Lord Jesus is risen. * Take the good news to his disciples and messengers, * so that they may go ahead to Galilee * where they will see Him risen from the dead. * He is the Lord and Giver of life.

Tone 2 **Now and ever:** You are truly most blessed, O virgin Mother of God. * Through the One who was incarnate of you, * Hades was chained, Adam revived, the curse wiped out, * Eve set free, Death put to death, * and we ourselves were brought back to life. * That is why we cry out in praise: * Blessed are You, O Christ our God, * who finds in this your good pleasure; glory to You!

AFTER THE DISMISSAL

Gospel Stanza Number 2

Tone 2 **Glory be...now and ever:** They who were with Mary came and brought ointments, * but they wondered how they would achieve their goal. * However, they saw that the stone had already been rolled away, * and a divine angel appeared and gave peace to their troubled souls. * He said: The Lord Jesus has risen. * Therefore, proclaim to his disciples * that they should hasten to Galilee and behold Him risen from the dead; * for He is the Lord, the Giver of life.

Sunday Evening Vespers

AT PSALM 140

Tone 5 Your hands were pierced with nails on the tree of the Cross, * and You destroyed the curse that came through the forbidden tree. * By your divine power You raised from the dead * those who were in the tombs from all ages. * Therefore, we praise your divine power and sing to You: * O Divine Pasch! O Jesus all-powerful! * You are our Life and Light from the Father! * Because of this, heaven and earth rejoice, * singing triumphant hymns to You, * O Word of God, O Christ our Sustainer; * You grant great mercy to the world.

Is the Life still resting among the dead? * Is our Unsetting Sun still beneath the earth? * asked the myrrh-bearing women as they sighed: * Come, let us hasten and look within the tomb of the Holy One. * There they saw a radiant angel, and they were afraid. * However, he changed their sorrow into joy, saying: * The Giver of Life has risen; * fear not, O friends of God, * the Lord reigns and grants great mercy to the world.

Before the sun was up, a group of women sought the true Sun, * whom they believed had set in the tomb. * To these myrrh-bearers, the radiant angel appeared and said: * The resplendent Light enlightens those who sleep in the darkness. * Go and announce to the radiant disciples * that sorrow is now changed into joy. * With a confident heart and clapping of hands, cry out with joy: * The Pasch of joy now saves us. * Christ is risen and grants great mercy to the world.

Three Stichera from the Saint of the day

Tone 1 **Glory be...now and ever:** Why have you come to the tomb, O myrrh-bearing women? * Why do you seek the Living One among the dead? * Have faith, for the Lord is risen, said the angel.

APOSTICHA

Tone 2 Come, let us adore God the Word, * who was born of the Father before all ages * and was incarnate of the Virgin Mary; * for of his own free will He suffered the Cross * and submitted himself to burial * and arose from the dead to save me, a sinful one.

I have lifted up my eyes to You enthroned in heaven. Behold, as the eyes of servants are on the hands of their masters, as the eyes of a maid are on the hands of her mistress, so are our eyes on the Lord our God until He has mercy on us.

I cry out to You, O Christ my Savior, * with the voice of the Publican. * Be merciful to me as You were to him, * and have mercy on me, O God.

Have mercy on us, O Lord, have mercy on us; for we have been filled with shame; our soul is all too full of the mockery of the rich, of the contempt of the proud.

Since you did not love earthly delights, O Martyrs, * you were worthy of the blessings of heaven, * and now you abide with the angels. * O Lord, through their prayers, have mercy on us and save us.

Tone 1 **Glory be...now and ever:** With fear, the women came to the tomb eager to anoint your body, * and when they did not find it, they looked anxiously one to the other; * for they were not aware of the Resurrection. * Then an angel appeared to them and said: * Christ is risen! He grants us his great mercy.

TROPARIA

Tone 2 The noble Joseph took down your most pure

body from the Cross. * He wrapped it in a clean shroud, * and with fragrant spices laid it in burial in a new tomb. * But You arose in three days, O Lord, * bestowing great mercy upon the world.

Glory be: *Of the Saint*

Tone 2 **Now and ever:** The angel stood by the tomb and cried out to the women bringing ointment: * Ointments are for the dead, * but Christ has shown himself not subject to corruption. * So now cry out: The Lord has risen, * bestowing great mercy upon the world.

Monday Matins

SESSIONAL HYMN I

Tone 1 You did not prevent the sealing of the stone at your tomb, * and by your Resurrection You bestowed on all the rock of fidelity. * O Lord, glory to You!

Lord, do not reprove me in your anger; punish me not in your rage.

O Lord who robes the heavens with clouds, * in this world You yourself were the garment of the martyrs. * They endured the punishment of the impious * and destroyed the lies of the false gods. * Through their intercession deliver us from the invisible Enemy * and save us, O God our Savior.

Their span extends through all the earth, their words to the utmost bounds of the world.

My sins have overwhelmed me like the waves of the sea, * and as a small boat on the ocean I am swept away by the surge of iniquity. * Lead me to the harbor of peace, O Lord, * and save me by bringing me back to You.

Glory be...now and ever: O Mother of God, fount of mercy, * deem us worthy of compassion. * Look upon a sinful people; * as always show your power; * for, placing our trust in you, * we cry out to you: Rejoice! * as once did Gabriel, the prince of angels.

SESSIONAL HYMN II

Tone 2 In their fervor the women brought myrrh to your tomb, O Savior. * A radiant angel brought joy to their souls. * They proclaimed You as the God of all, crying to the apostles: * Truly the Life of all is risen from the tomb.

Glory be...now and ever: *(Repeat the above)*

Having beheld the Resurrection of Christ...

CANON

HYMN OF LIGHT

Tone 2 You, O King and Lord, * have fallen asleep * in the flesh as a mortal man, * but on the third day You arose again. * You have raised Adam * from his corruption and made Death powerless. * You are the Pasch of incorruption. * You are the salvation of the world.

Tone 2 **Glory be...now and ever:** O myrrh-bearing women, listen to the news that brings joy: * I have put Hades, that cruel tyrant, to flight; * I have made the world rise from the depths of the tomb; * hasten to my friends, the disciples, and quickly bring this good news to them. * For it is my will that the work of my hands shines with joy * because in days of old it gave birth to sorrow.

AT THE PRAISES

Tone 2 All creation and everything that breathes glorifies You, O Lord; * for by the Cross You abolished Death * that You might manifest to the world your Resurrection from the dead. * For You alone are the Lover of Mankind. *(2 times)*

When I consider my foolish deeds * I take refuge in your compassion; * as the publican, the prodigal, * and the sinful woman, * I bow down to You. * Before condemning me, O my God, * spare me and save me in your goodness.

Having suffered death for Christ, * O victorious Witnesses of the Lord, * in heaven you have placed your soul into the hands of God, * and your relics are carried through the whole world. * Priests and kings bow before them, * and all the nations cry out in joy: * Precious in the eyes of the Lord is the death of his friends.

Tone 1 **Glory be...now and ever:** Mary Magdalene and the other Mary came to the tomb seeking the Lord * and saw an angel as radiant as light sitting upon the stone. * He said to them: Why do you seek the Living One among the dead? * He is risen as He said, * and you shall find Him in Galilee. * To Him let us bow down and sing: * O Lord, risen from the dead, glory to You!

APOSTICHA

Tone 6 Praise Christ with psalms, O peoples; * sing to him in joy! * A great Passover has shone forth for us! * Christ, the Giver of life, is risen from the tomb. * He is the Redeemer of all creation.

O Lord, you once favored your land and revived the fortunes of Jacob.

You said to the myrrh-bearers: Rejoice! * You changed Eve's curse into joy. * You did arise and send your disciples * to proclaim your third-day Resurrection from the tomb.

Mercy and faithfulness have met; justice and peace have embraced.

Christ, our great and holy Passover, * has risen upon us. * Come, let every soul be illumined; * behold, a most radiant day has dawned for us. * Let us rejoice and be glad.

Tone 2 **Glory be...now and ever:** The women brought spices mixed with tears to your tomb, * but their words became full of joy * when they said: The Lord is risen!

Monday Evening Vespers

AT PSALM 140

Tone 2 The myrrh-bearers came at dawn, bearing spices, * seeking You, O Christ, the Life of all. * They wept in their desire to see You. * Instead, they heard a young man shout from inside the tomb: * Stop your lamentations. * Rejoice in your salvation. * Proclaim to all that the Lord is risen.

O noble Joseph, * you took Christ the King down from the Cross. * He who sits on the cherubic throne was borne on your shoulders. * O blessed hands; O happy eyes which gazed upon his face; * most honorable arms that carried God the Word to the tomb; * You laid the Light of the world to rest beneath the earth. * May your memory be eternal.

The feast of the myrrh-bearers and blessed Joseph * is a fountain of the life of Paradise for us. * It waters the earth with showers of grace. * It pours rivers of resurrection joy on us. * The assembly of the faithful celebrates and sings: * Glory to You, O Lord! * You have given resurrection to the universe.

Three Stichera from the Saint of the day

Tone 2 **Glory be...now and ever:** The myrrh-bearing women, O Christ, rose up early and hastened to your tomb, * seeking to anoint your most pure body. * But when the glad tidings were brought to them by the words of the angel, * they hastened to the apostles as messengers of joy. * The Leader of our salvation has risen and conquered Death. * He grants the world eternal life and great mercy.

APOSTICHA

Tone 2 Christ our Savior cancelled the decree that was written against us, * by nailing it to the Cross; * and He abolished the dominion of Death. * Let us glorify his Resurrection on the third day.

I have lifted up my eyes to You enthroned in heaven. Behold, as the eyes of servants are on the hands of their masters, as the eyes of a maid are on the hands of her mistress, so are our eyes on the Lord our God until He has mercy on us.

I cry out to You, O Christ my Savior, * with the voice of the Publican. * Be merciful to me as You were to him, * and have mercy on me, O God.

Have mercy on us, O Lord, have mercy on us; for we have been filled with shame; our soul is all too full of the mockery of the rich, of the contempt of the proud.

Through the prayers of the holy martyrs * and their songs of praise to Christ, * all error has come to an end, * and all people are saved by faith.

Tone 2 **Glory be...now and ever:** Why do you sprinkle your myrrh with tears, O women disciples? * The stone is rolled away, and the tomb is empty; * behold, Life has triumphed over Death. * The seals give brilliant witness: * that the guards of the godless have watched in vain, * that mortal nature has been saved by the flesh of God, * and that Hades is in mourning. * Hasten in joy, proclaiming to the apostles, * that Christ, the conqueror of Death, is the firstborn of the dead. * He shall go before you into Galilee.

TROPARIA

Tone 2 When You descended to death, O Immortal Life, * You destroyed the Abyss by the radiance of your divinity. * And when You raised the dead from the depths of the earth, * all the heavenly powers cried out: * O Giver of life, Christ our God, glory to You!

Glory be: *Of the Saint*

Tone 2 **Now and ever:** The angel stood by the tomb and cried out to the women bringing ointment: * Ointments are for the dead, * but Christ has shown himself not subject to corruption. * So now cry out: The Lord has risen, * bestowing great mercy upon the world.

Tuesday Matins

SESSIONAL HYMN I

Tone 2 You accepted burial and rose for the salvation of all * without leaving the Father's pure bosom in heaven; * glory to You, O Lord!

Lord, do not reprove me in your anger; punish me not in your rage.

I am the sterile tree, O Lord; * I have not borne the fruit of repentance. * I fear the axe and the unquenchable fire. * That is why I pray You before the end, save me, O Lord, * and lead me back to You.

Their span extends through all the earth, their words to the utmost bounds of the world.

You have made your martyrs shine brighter than gold; * you have glorified your saints in your goodness. * By their prayers, O Christ our God and Lover of Mankind, * give peace to our life and accept our prayers as incense, * for You repose among the saints.

Glory be...now and ever: You surpassed nature and its laws; * you have united virginity to your divine birth-giving. * You alone have conceived the One who is beyond time and who was begotten before you; * we extol you, O Mother of God.

SESSIONAL HYMN II

Tone 2 The myrrh-bearers came early to the tomb. * When they found it empty, they said to the apostles; * The power of corruption has ended; * the prisoners of Hades are released. * Proclaim boldly that Christ is risen, * granting great mercy to the world.

Glory be...now and ever: *(Repeat the above)*

Having beheld the Resurrection of Christ...

CANON

HYMN OF LIGHT

Tone 2 You, O King and Lord, * have fallen asleep * in the flesh as a mortal man, * but on the third day You arose again. * You have raised Adam * from his corruption and made Death powerless. * You are the Pasch of incorruption. * You are the salvation of the world.

***Tone 2* Glory be...now and ever:** O myrrh-bearing women, listen to the news that brings joy: * I have put Hades, that cruel tyrant, to flight; * I have made the world rise from the depths of the tomb; * hasten to my friends, the disciples, and quickly bring this good news to them. * For it is my will that the work of my hands shines with joy * because in days of old it gave birth to sorrow.

AT THE PRAISES

Tone 2 What do the Pharisees now say? * How was it that the guardian soldiers lost the King whom they were guarding? * Why was it that the stone could not retain the Rock of Life? * Therefore, either you must deliver to us Him who was buried * or worship with us Him who is risen and say: * Glory to your bountiful mercies, our Savior, glory to You! *(2 times)*

O Lord born of a Virgin, * do not look at my sins, * but purify my heart and make it a temple of the Holy Spirit. * Do not reject me far from your sight; * for with You is the abundance of salvation.

Having taken the Cross of Christ as an invincible trophy * the holy martyrs have destroyed the power of the Demon. * Now having been crowned in heaven, * they have become our protectors * who intercede unceasingly for us.

***Tone 2* Glory be...now and ever:** Early at dawn, the myrrh-bearing women arose, * and, carrying spices, they came to the tomb of the Lord; * and not finding what they expected, * the pious women pondered the removal of the stone. * They spoke to one another, saying: * Where are the seals of the grave? * Where is the guard which Pilate sent with great care? * And behold, a radiant angel appeared and proclaimed to them: * Why do you tearfully seek the Living One who gives life to all mortal flesh? * Christ our God has risen from the dead. * He is the Almighty One * who grants to all enlightenment, eternal life, and great mercy.

APOSTICHA

Tone 2 Today the Sun of threefold splendor shines brightly on earth; * destroying the gloom of evil passions. * Christ is risen enlightening the apostolic choir. * Those who had bound themselves by faith and love to Him rejoice. * Joseph of Arimathea is glad, * and the memory of the honorable myrrh-bearers shines as a splendid crown; * they are the women first to praise and glorify the divine Resurrection.

O Lord, you once favored your land and revived the fortunes of Jacob.

Joseph, you carried on your shoulders * the Son who sits at the right hand of the Father; * you anointed the inexhaustible sweetness with myrrh; * you buried the Resurrection of the world in your tomb. * You concealed behind a stone * the One who wraps himself with light as his cloak. * We praise his radiant passion and resurrection in song.

Mercy and faithfulness have met; justice and peace have embraced.

The ranks of angels shuddered in fear * when they saw you, O Joseph, burying Christ. * The universe blesses you. * We faithful, as we marvel at his Resurrection, * are inspired to fervently honor both you and the myrrh-bearers. * We cry to you ceaselessly: * Pray with them that we may be saved * and deliver us from dangers and afflictions.

Tone 1 **Glory be...now and ever:** With fear, the women came to the tomb eager to anoint your body, * and when they did not find it, they looked anxiously one to the other; * for they were not aware of the Resurrection. * Then an angel appeared to them and said: * Christ is risen! He grants us his great mercy.

Tuesday Evening Vespers

AT PSALM 140

Tone 2 The myrrh-bearing women had stood before the tomb; * they mourned for Christ when they saw the stone had suddenly been rolled away. * They were utterly confused by its removal, * but when they heard the angel's words confirming the Resurrection * of Him who was numbered among the dead for us, * the women disciples of Christ rejoiced.

The myrrh-bearing women disciples of Christ * fulfilled the command of the angel robed in white. * He said to them: Hades has been despoiled. * The King who died is risen to save us all. * He will provide his disciples with everlasting joy.

The women disciples of Christ, * forsaking their streams of tears, * brought the joyful message to his apostolic witnesses; * informing them of the resurrection of the Word from the tomb: * We demand that you listen to our wonderful news. * Rejoice, the end of sorrow has come!

Three Stichera from the Saint of the day

Tone 6 **Glory be...now and ever:** The myrrh-bearing women, O Savior, came to your grave, * and they saw that it was empty * but did not find your most pure body. * Therefore, they cried out with tears and said: * Who has robbed us of our Hope? * Who has taken away a naked and anointed corpse, * the only consolation to his Mother? * How could they bury the One who trampled down Hades? * But in your own power, O Lord, * arise after three days as You said * and grant great mercy to our souls.

APOSTICHA

Tone 2 O Christ the Savior, * save me by the power of the Cross. * And have mercy on me, * O God, who saved Peter in the sea.

> **I have lifted up my eyes to You enthroned in heaven. Behold, as the eyes of servants are on the hands of their masters, as the eyes of a maid are on the hands of her mistress, so are our eyes on the Lord our God until He has mercy on us.**

Let us, together with the archangels, sing of Christ's Resurrection; * for He is the Redeemer and Savior of our souls. * He will come again in awesome glory and mighty power * to judge the world which He has fashioned.

> **Have mercy on us, O Lord, have mercy on us; for we have been filled with shame; our soul is all too full of the mockery of the rich, of the contempt of the proud.**

As they withstood the torturers, the company of martyrs said: * We serve in the forces of the King. * Though you deliver us to fire and torment, * we shall not deny the power of the Trinity.

Tone 6 **Glory be...now and ever:** Joseph asked for the body of Jesus. * He placed it in his own new tomb. * It was fitting for the Lord to come forth from the tomb * as from a bridal chamber. * You destroyed the dominion of Death. * You opened the gates of Paradise to the human race. * Glory to You, O Lord!

TROPARIA

Tone 2 The noble Joseph took down your most pure body from the Cross. * He wrapped it in a clean shroud, * and with fragrant spices laid it in burial in a new tomb. * But You arose in three days, O Lord, * bestowing great mercy upon the world.

Glory be: *Of the Saint*

Tone 2 **Now and ever:** The angel stood by the tomb and cried out to the women bringing ointment: * Ointments are for the dead, * but Christ has shown himself not subject to corruption. * So now cry out: The Lord has risen, * bestowing great mercy upon the world.

Wednesday Matins

SESSIONAL HYMN I

Tone 2 You have wrought salvation in the midst of the earth, O Christ our God. * You have stretched out your most pure hands upon the Cross. * You have gathered together all nations who cry to You: * O Lord, glory to your power!

Arise then, Lord, lift up your hand. O God, do not forget the poor!

By rising from the tomb You burst the bonds of Hades. * By destroying the condemnation of Death, O Lord, * You freed us all from the snares of the Enemy. * By revealing yourself to your apostles, * You sent them to proclaim You. * Through them, You have given peace to the universe; * for You alone are the Lord and are full of mercy.

God is to be feared in his holy place. He is the Lord, the God of Israel.

Blessed is the earth that has been watered by your blood, * O victorious athletes of the Lord, * and holy are the places that shelter your bodies. * For in the arena you have triumphed over the Enemy, * and with courage you proclaimed your faith in Christ. * Because of his goodness obtain for us * the salvation of our souls by your prayers.

Glory be...now and ever: The Virgin who gave You birth

stood beneath the Cross, * and not being able to see You suffer unjustly, * she sighed and cried out, saying: * O my Son who is beyond all suffering, how do You now suffer? * I praise and glorify your immense goodness.

SESSIONAL HYMN II

Tone 2 The blessed myrrh-bearers hurried to your tomb, O Savior, * to anoint You with myrrh as a mortal, O Master, * but the angel proclaimed joy to them: * The Lord is risen! * Announce to the apostles his fearful Resurrection from the tomb.

Glory be...now and ever: *(Repeat the above)*

Having beheld the Resurrection of Christ...

CANON

HYMN OF LIGHT

Tone 2 You, O King and Lord, * have fallen asleep * in the flesh as a mortal man, * but on the third day You arose again. * You have raised Adam * from his corruption and made Death powerless. * You are the Pasch of incorruption. * You are the salvation of the world.

Tone 2 **Glory be...now and ever:** O myrrh-bearing women, listen to the news that brings joy: * I have put Hades, that cruel tyrant, to flight; * I have made the world rise from the depths of the tomb; * hasten to my friends, the disciples, and quickly bring this good news to them. * For it is my will that the work of my hands shines with joy * because in days of old it gave birth to sorrow.

AT THE PRAISES

Tone 2 Wishing to assume Adam's poverty, O Christ our God, * You took flesh from the Virgin and came to earth. * Accepting to be nailed on the Cross, * You freed us from the slavery of the Enemy. * O Lord, glory to You! *(2 times)*

Rejoice, O nations and be glad; * for the angel sat on the stone of the grave * and gave us the good news, saying: * Christ the Savior of the world is risen from the dead. * He has filled the world with fragrant aroma. * Rejoice, O nations and be glad.

The multitude of saints prays to You, O Christ: * Have mercy on us and save us.

Tone 1 **Glory be...now and ever:** With fear, the women came to the tomb eager to anoint your body, * and when they did not find it, they looked anxiously one to the other; * for they were not aware of the Resurrection. * Then an angel appeared to them and said: * Christ is risen! He grants us his great mercy.

APOSTICHA

Tone 2 The myrrh-bearing disciples of Christ lamented with bitter tears: * How can the Redeemer die? * As they wept, an angel from the tomb cried out to them: * The great Sun who disappeared beneath the earth * now is risen as He said. * Receive the tidings of joy. * Run and proclaim to all: * Christ is risen as God from the tomb.

O Lord, you once favored your land and revived the fortunes of Jacob.

After the Sabbath had passed, * in the darkness of night, the myrrh-bearers prepared their spices, O Christ. * They came to the tomb to anoint the divine, most pure body, * and instead they learned of your Resurrection; * they hurried to proclaim to your chosen ones, * that You had proceeded from the tomb, * and they cried out: Rejoice! O Lover of Mankind.

Mercy and faithfulness have met; justice and peace have embraced.

The women disciples of the Lord * hurried to anoint with spices the God most high, * who had lain in the earth as one dead. * Instead they saw a young man standing at the right of the tomb. * His countenance flashed like lightning. * He proclaimed: Know that the Word is risen on the third day from the tomb. * Announce his Resurrection to the apostles.

Tone 5 **Glory be...now and ever:** O Lord, who clothes yourself with light as with a garment, * Joseph and Nicodemus took You down from the Cross, * and seeing You without life, without a garment, and without a grave, * in their compassion they wept and lamented: * Woe is me, most sweet Jesus. * The sun was covered with darkness * when it saw You suspended upon the Cross. * The earth quaked with fear, * and the veil of the Temple was torn in two. * I see that You willingly endured death for my sake. * How then shall I bury You, O my God? * With what linens shall I cover You? * With what hands shall I touch your most pure body? * What hymns shall I sing at your death? * Therefore, O compassionate Lord, I glorify your passion, * and I praise your burial and your resurrection, crying out: * O Lord, glory to You!

Wednesday Evening Vespers

AT PSALM 140

Tone 2 When they heard the joyful words * of the angels sitting in the tomb of the Word, * the women who ran there with good intent * realized that their purpose would be changed. * No longer would they carry myrrh. * Instead, they evangelized the apostles: * He who was hidden in the earth is risen from Hades. * They initiated the apostles into the mystery * of Him who became man for us.

Before the first light of dawn, * the myrrh-bearing women came to the tomb in fear, * bringing sweet spices for Christ, the Giver of life, * who killed Hades by being numbered among the dead. * An angel stood before them, crying: * Why do you seek the Life-giver, the Living One, among the dead? * Go and proclaim his Resurrection.

O blessed Joseph, * you carried in your arms the Word enthroned upon the Cherubim. * You bore on your shoulders the One who first clothed himself in our flesh, * and then died to give life to us who lay dead. * Once, you mourned his death; * but now, together with the honorable myrrh-bearers, * you see his Resurrection and rejoice.

Three Stichera from the Saint of the day

Tone 1 **Glory be...now and ever:** Mary Magdalene and the other Mary came to the tomb seeking the Lord * and saw an angel as radiant as light sitting upon the stone. * He said to them: Why do you seek the Living One among the dead? * He is risen as He said, * and you shall find Him in Galilee. * To Him let us bow down and sing: * O Lord, risen from the dead, glory to You!

APOSTICHA

Tone 2 Your Resurrection, O Christ our Savior, * has enlightened the whole universe; * and, through it, You call back to yourself all creation. * Almighty God, glory to You!

Their span extends through all the earth, their words to the utmost bounds of the world.

Throughout the universe, O Savior, * You have extolled

the name of your chief apostles. * They learned the ineffable secrets of heaven, * and they became a source of healing for all; * their very shadow made people whole once more. * The first performed miracles even though he was a sinner; * the second, chosen from among the Jews, * explained the divine teachings of grace. * Through their prayers, O God of tenderness, * grant your great mercy to us.

God is to be feared in his holy place. He is the Lord, the God of Israel.

Great is the glory you obtained by faith, O Saints; * for not only did you triumph over the Enemy in your sufferings, * but after death you healed the infirm and drove out evil spirits, * O physicians of souls and bodies. * Intercede before the Lord, * entreating Him to have mercy on our souls.

Tone 2 **Glory be...now and ever:** The women brought spices mixed with tears to your tomb, * but their words became full of joy * when they said: The Lord is risen!

TROPARIA

Tone 2 When You descended to death, O Immortal Life, * You destroyed the Abyss by the radiance of your divinity. * And when You raised the dead from the depths of the earth, * all the heavenly powers cried out: * O Giver of life, Christ our God, glory to You!

Glory be: *Of the Saint*

Tone 2 **Now and ever:** The angel stood by the tomb and cried out to the women bringing ointment: * Ointments are for the dead, * but Christ has shown himself not subject to corruption. * So now cry out: The Lord has risen, * bestowing great mercy upon the world.

Thursday Matins

SESSIONAL HYMN I

Tone 2 Bringing myrrh for your burial, * the women came secretly to the tomb at early dawn. * They feared the hatred of the people and the strength of the guard, * but courage conquered their weakness, * for their compassionate intentions were well pleasing to God. * They offered their cries to Him: * Arise, O God, and help us. * Redeem us for your name's sake.

Their span extends through all the earth, their words to the utmost bounds of the world.

You gave the fishermen more wisdom than the orators, * and You sent them as heralds through all the world. * Because of your ineffable love, O Christ our God, * give strength to your Church by their prayers, * and send your blessing upon your faithful, * O only Lover of Mankind and compasionate Lord.

God is to be feared in his holy place. He is the Lord, the God of Israel.

O Apostles, Prophets, and Martyrs, * holy Hierarchs and all you Just, * You have fought the good fight * and have safeguarded the faith; * because of his goodness, * obtain great mercy for our souls.

Glory be...now and ever: Because of you, O Mother of God and ever-Virgin Mary, * we have become sharers in the divine nature. * For us you have borne God who was clothed in our flesh. * Therefore, we extol you in faith as it is fitting.

SESSIONAL HYMN II

Tone 2 The women brought You myrrh, O Savior. * With yearning they sought to anoint You, O Lover of Mankind, * but an angel cried to them from the tomb: * The Lord and Giver of life is risen, * trampling down Death and Hades.

Glory be...now and ever: *(Repeat the above)*

Having beheld the Resurrection of Christ...

CANON

HYMN OF LIGHT

Tone 2 You, O King and Lord, * have fallen asleep * in the flesh as a mortal man, * but on the third day You arose again. * You have raised Adam * from his corruption and made Death powerless. * You are the Pasch of incorruption. * You are the salvation of the world.

***Tone 2* Glory be...now and ever:** O myrrh-bearing women, listen to the news that brings joy: * I have put Hades, that cruel tyrant, to flight; * I have made the world rise from the depths of the tomb; * hasten to my friends, the disciples, and quickly bring this good news to them. * For it is my will that the work of my hands shines with joy * because in days of old it gave birth to sorrow.

AT THE PRAISES

Tone 2 At your conception, O Lord God, * an angel said to her who is full of grace: Rejoice! * At your Resurrection an angel rolled away the stone * from the door of your glorious tomb. * The first angel spoke with signs of joy instead of sorrow, * and the latter brought us the good news * of a Lord who gives life instead of death. * Therefore, we shout to You, O Benefactor of all, * glory to You, O Lord! *(2 times)*

Unjustly attacked from every side, * we take refuge in You, O God of truth. * With the cry of your disciples we call out: * Save us, O Lord, for we are perishing. * We pray that You show our enemies * that You protect your people and save them from danger. * By the prayers of your apostles and in your goodness forgive our many sins. * O Master and Lord, glory to You!

Your relics are honored in every city and country, O victorious Martyrs, * for you have struggled valiantly * and received your crowns in heaven. * You are the glory of priests and kings * and the adornment of the holy churches of God.

Tone 2 **Glory be...now and ever:** Early at dawn, the myrrh-bearing women arose, * and, carrying spices, they came to the tomb of the Lord; * and not finding what they expected, * the pious women pondered the removal of the stone. * They spoke to one another, saying: * Where are the seals of the grave? * Where is the guard which Pilate sent with great care? * And behold, a radiant angel appeared and proclaimed to them: * Why do you tearfully seek the Living One who gives life to all mortal flesh? * Christ our God has risen from the dead. * He is the Almighty One * who grants to all enlightenment, eternal life, and great mercy.

APOSTICHA

Tone 2 When You rose as God, You enabled the myrrh-bearers to rejoice, saying: * Behold, I ascend to my Father. * From this time do not touch Me, * only go and say to my friends: * Behold, I go before you to Galilee. * Then after You appeared to them, * You breathed upon them, O Savior, * giving them your Holy Spirit.

O Lord, you once favored your land and revived the fortunes of Jacob.

The chosen apostles did not believe * the annoucement of Christ's resurrection from the dead. * When they heard the testimony of the myrrh-bearers, they ran to see the tomb; * they saw the shroud and cloth in the grave, * of Him who was sought but had not yet appeared; * but when they learned of his Resurrection, * they proclaimed what they had seen to the world, * declaring these things to all peoples.

Mercy and faithfulness have met; justice and peace have embraced.

The unapproachable Light has appeared to us. * On this day Christ the Lord shines forth from the tomb. * Hades is held captive, and Satan is bound. * Let the ends of the earth rejoice! Let creation dance! * Keep the feast, O Church of Christ! * In memory of the noble Joseph, * offer hymns to Him and to the myrrh-bearing women.

Tone 2 **Glory be...now and ever:** Why do you sprinkle your myrrh with tears, O women disciples? * The stone is rolled away, and the tomb is empty; * behold, Life has triumphed over Death. * The seals give brilliant witness: * that the guards of the godless have watched in vain, * that mortal nature has been saved by the flesh of God, * and that Hades is in mourning. * Hasten in joy, proclaiming to the apostles, * that Christ, the conqueror of Death, is the first-born of the dead, * He shall go before you into Galilee.

Thursday Evening Vespers

AT PSALM 140

Tone 8 O honorable myrrh-bearers, * you followed Christ's footsteps during his earthly life, * serving Him with eager hearts. * You would not leave Him even when He died. * Driven by compassion, * you came to his tomb bringing myrrh mixed with tears. * Therefore, we bless your holy memory.

The holy choir of women * yearned to see the Life who lay dead in the tomb. * They came in the night and heard from the angels: * Christ is risen as He said. * Go with haste and tell his disciples: * Cast sorrow away from your souls. * Instead of tears, receive inexpressible joy.

Today we rejoice in your memory, O myrrh-bearers. * We glorify the most gracious Lord who glorified you. * Never cease to intercede for us, O blessed ones, * that we may attain to eternal glory, * and that we may inherit the splendor of the saints; * for you have boldness before Him.

Three Stichera from the Saint of the day

Tone 2 **Glory be...now and ever:** The myrrh-bearing women, O Christ, rose up early and hastened to your tomb, * seeking to anoint your most pure body. * But when the glad tidings were brought to them by the words of the angel, * they hastened to the apostles as messengers of joy. * The Leader of our salvation has risen and conquered Death. * He grants the world eternal life and great mercy.

APOSTICHA

Tone 2 The slayers of the Just, * who had always delighted in your gifts, cried out: * Let Him be crucified! * Instead of their Benefactor, * they asked to receive a transgressor of the law. * But keeping silent, O Christ, You endured their hardness, * for You desired to suffer and to save us * because You are the Lover of Mankind.

I have lifted up my eyes to You enthroned in heaven. Behold, as the eyes of servants are on the hands of their masters, as the eyes of a maid are on the hands of her mistress, so are our eyes on the Lord our God until He has mercy on us.

Come, let us adore God the Word, * who was born of the Father before all ages * and was incarnate of the Virgin Mary; * for of his own free will He suffered the Cross * and submitted himself to burial * and arose from the dead to save me, a sinful one.

Have mercy on us, O Lord, have mercy on us; for we have been filled with shame; our soul is all too full of the mockery of the rich, of the contempt of the proud.

Since you did not love earthly delights, O Martyrs, * you were worthy of the blessings of heaven, * and now you abide with the angels. * O Lord, through their prayers, have mercy on us and save us.

Tone 6 **Glory be...now and ever:** Joseph asked for the body of Jesus. * He placed it in his own new tomb. * It was fitting for the Lord to come forth from the tomb * as from a bridal chamber. * You destroyed the dominion of Death. * You opened the gates of Paradise to the human race. * Glory to You, O Lord!

TROPARIA

Tone 2 The noble Joseph took down your most pure body from the Cross. * He wrapped it in a clean shroud, * and with fragrant spices laid it in burial in a new tomb. * But You arose in three days, O Lord, * bestowing great mercy upon the world.

Glory be: *Of the Saint*

Tone 2 **Now and ever:** The angel stood by the tomb and cried out to the women bringing ointment: * Ointments are for the dead, * but Christ has shown himself not subject to corruption. * So now cry out: The Lord has risen, * bestowing great mercy upon the world.

Friday Matins

SESSIONAL HYMN I

Tone 2 We bow before your sacred image, O gracious Lord, * and beg forgiveness for our offenses, O Christ our God; * for You, of your own free will, deigned to ascend the Cross in your human nature * to deliver from the bondage of the enemy those whom You have created. * Therefore, we gratefully cry out to You: * Through your coming to save the world, O Savior, * You have filled all with joy.

I will praise You, Lord, with all my heart; I will recount all your wonders.

You were not held by the stone which sealed your tomb; * You arose, granting the rock of faith to all. * O Lord, glory to You!

God is to be feared in his holy place. He is the Lord, the God of Israel.

When the martyrs of the Lord struggled in the arena, * the arrogance of the impious was humbled by their faith, * and when they shattered the deceit of idolatry, * they received crowns of victory from on high. * They now intercede for our souls.

Glory be...now and ever: Your virgin Mother wept bitterly to see your death on the Cross, O Christ. * She cried out: O my Son, what is this fearful mystery? * You give to all eternal life; * how then, by your own will, can You suffer the dishonor of death upon the Cross?

SESSIONAL HYMN II

Tone 2 In their fervor the women brought myrrh to your tomb, O Savior. * A radiant angel brought joy to their souls. * They proclaimed You as the God of all, crying to the apostles: * Truly the Life of all is risen from the tomb.

Glory be...now and ever: *(Repeat the above)*

Having beheld the Resurrection of Christ...

CANON

HYMN OF LIGHT

Tone 2 You, O King and Lord, * have fallen asleep * in the flesh as a mortal man, * but on the third day You arose again. * You have raised Adam * from his corruption and made Death powerless. * You are the Pasch of incorruption. * You are the salvation of the world.

Tone 2 **Glory be...now and ever:** O myrrh-bearing women, listen to the news that brings joy: * I have put Hades, that cruel tyrant, to flight; * I have made the world rise from the depths of the tomb; * hasten to my friends, the disciples, and quickly bring this good news to them. * For it is my will that the work of my hands shines with joy * because in days of old it gave birth to sorrow.

AT THE PRAISES

Tone 2 You have revealed the tree of your Cross, O Christ our God, * as the tree of life for us who believe in You. * Through it You have destroyed the power of Death; * You have given life to us who lay dead in sin. * Therefore, we cry to You: * O Lord, our defender, glory to You! *(2 times)*

All creation and everything that breathes glorifies You, O Lord; * for by the Cross You abolished Death * that You might manifest to the world your Resurrection from the dead. * For You alone are the Lover of Mankind.

Having suffered death for Christ, * O victorious Witnesses of the Lord, * in heaven you have placed your soul into the hands of God, * and your relics are carried through the whole world. * Priests and kings bow before them, * and all the nations cry out in joy: * Precious in the eyes of the Lord is the death of his friends.

Tone 1 **Glory be...now and ever:** Why have you come to the tomb, O myrrh-bearing women? * Why do you seek the

Living One among the dead? * Have faith, for the Lord is risen, said the angel.

APOSTICHA

Tone 2 The myrrh-bearing women had stood before the tomb; * they mourned for Christ when they saw the stone had suddenly been rolled away. * They were utterly confused by its removal, * but when they heard the angel's words confirming the Resurrection * of Him who was numbered among the dead for us, * the women disciples of Christ rejoiced.

O Lord, you once favored your land and revived the fortunes of Jacob.

The myrrh-bearing women disciples of Christ * fulfilled the command of the angel robed in white. * He said to them: Hades has been despoiled. * The King who died is risen to save us all. * He will provide his disciples with everlasting joy.

Mercy and faithfulness have met; justice and peace have embraced.

The women disciples of Christ, * forsaking their streams of tears, * brought the joyful message to his apostolic witnesses; * informing them of the resurrection of the Word from the tomb: * We demand that you listen to our wonderful news. * Rejoice, the end of sorrow has come!

Tone 1 **Glory be...now and ever:** With fear, the women came to the tomb eager to anoint your body, * and when they did not find it, they looked anxiously one to the other; * for they were not aware of the Resurrection. * Then an angel appeared to them and said: * Christ is risen! He grants us his great mercy.

Friday Evening Vespers

AT PSALM 140

Tone 2 Early at dawn, the myrrh-bearing women arose, * and, carrying spices, they came to the tomb of the Lord; * and not finding what they expected, * the pious women pondered the removal of the stone. * They spoke to one another, saying: * Where are the seals of the grave? * Where is the guard which Pilate sent with great care? * And behold, a radiant angel appeared and proclaimed to them: * Why do you tearfully seek the Living One who gives life to all mortal flesh? * Christ our God has risen from the dead. * He is the Almighty One * who grants to all enlightenment, eternal life, and great mercy.

Why do you sprinkle your myrrh with tears, O women disciples? * The stone is rolled away, and the tomb is empty; * behold, Life has triumphed over Death. * The seals give brilliant witness: * that the guards of the godless have watched in vain, * that mortal nature has been saved by the flesh of God, * and that Hades is in mourning. * Hasten in joy, proclaiming to the apostles, * that Christ, the conqueror of Death, is the first-born of the dead, * He shall go before you into Galilee.

The myrrh-bearing women, O Christ, rose up early and hastened to your tomb, * seeking to anoint your most pure body. * But when the glad tidings were brought to them by the words of the angel, * they hastened to the apostles as messengers of joy. * The Leader of our salvation has risen and conquered Death. * He grants the world eternal life and great mercy.

Three Stichera from the Saint of the day

Tone 6 **Glory be:** The myrrh-bearing women, O Savior, came to your grave, * and they saw that it was empty * but did not find your most pure body. * Therefore, they cried out with tears and said: * Who has robbed us of our Hope? * Who has taken away a naked and anointed corpse, * the only consolation to his Mother? * How could they bury the One who trampled down Hades? * But in your own power, O Lord, * arise after three days as You said * and grant great mercy to our souls.

Tone 2 **Now and ever:** At the coming of grace, O Virgin, * the shadow of the Law passed away. * For, as the bush, though burning, was not consumed, * You, though giving birth, still remained a virgin. * In place of the pillar of fire, the Sun of Righteousness shone forth. * Instead of Moses, Christ, the salvation of our souls, appeared.

APOSTICHA

Tone 2 Come, let us adore God the Word, * who was born of the Father before all ages * and was incarnate of the Virgin Mary; * for of his own free will He suffered the Cross * and submitted himself to burial * and arose from the dead to save me, a sinful one.

The Lord reigns, He is clothed in majesty.

Christ our Savior cancelled the decree that was written against us * by nailing it to the Cross; * and He abolished the dominion of Death. * Let us glorify his Resurrection on the third day.

For He has made the world firm, which shall not be moved.

Let us, together with the archangels, sing of Christ's Resurrection; * for He is the Redeemer and Savior of our souls. * He will come again in awesome glory and mighty power * to judge the world which He has fashioned.

Holiness befits your house, O Lord, for length of days.

Your Resurrection, O Christ our Savior, * has enlightened the whole universe; * and, through it, You call back to yourself all creation. * Almighty God, glory to You!

Tone 5 **Glory be...now and ever:** O Lord, who clothes yourself with light as with a garment, * Joseph and Nicodemus took You down from the Cross, * and seeing You without life, without a garment, and without a grave, * in their compassion they wept and lamented: * Woe is me, most sweet Jesus. * The sun was covered with darkness * when it saw You suspended upon the Cross. * The earth quaked with fear, * and the veil of the Temple was torn in two. * I see that You willingly endured death for my sake. * How then shall I bury You, O my God? * With what linens shall I cover You? * With what hands shall I touch your most pure body? * What hymns shall I sing at your death? * Therefore, O compassionate Lord, I glorify your passion, * and I praise your burial and your resurrection, crying out: * O Lord, glory to You!

TROPARIA

Tone 2 When You descended to death, O Immortal Life, * You destroyed the Abyss by the radiance of your divinity. * And when You raised the dead from the depths of the earth * all the heavenly powers cried out: * O Giver of Life, Christ our God, glory to You!

Tone 2 **Glory be:** The noble Joseph took down your most pure body from the Cross. * He wrapped it in a clean shroud, * and with fragrant spices laid it in burial in a new tomb. * But You arose in three days, O Lord, * bestowing great mercy upon the world.

Tone 2 **Now and ever:** The angel stood by the tomb and cried out to the women bringing ointment: * Ointments are for the dead, * but Christ has shown himself not subject to corruption. * So now cry out: The Lord has risen, * bestowing great mercy upon the world.

Saturday Matins

SESSIONAL HYMN I

Tone 2 You did not prevent the sealing of the stone at your tomb, * and by your Resurrection You bestowed on all the rock of fidelity. * O Lord, glory to You!

Arise then, Lord, lift up your hand. O God, do not forget the poor.

You did not leave the bosom of the Father, * yet for our salvation You accepted the tomb and the Resurrection. * O Lord, glory to You!

Glory be...now and ever: O Mother of God, the mysteries which surround you are exceedingly glorious, * and beyond the power of understanding. * For you retained the seal of purity, * and your virginity remained inviolate; * yet you are acknowledged, without doubt, * to be the Mother who gave birth to the true God. * We beg you, therefore, to entreat Him to save our souls.

SESSIONAL HYMN II

Tone 2 The choir of apostles joins the myrrh-bearing women in a song of joy; * together they celebrate the Feast * in the glory and honor of your Resurrection. * Inspired by them, we cry to You: * Grant great mercy to your people, O Lord and Lover of Mankind.

Glory be...now and ever: *(Repeat the above)*

Having beheld the Resurrection of Christ...

CANON

HYMN OF LIGHT

Tone 2 You, O King and Lord, * have fallen asleep * in the flesh as a mortal man, * but on the third day You arose again. * You have raised Adam * from his corruption and made Death powerless. * You are the Pasch of incorruption. * You are the salvation of the world.

***Tone 2* Glory be...now and ever:** O myrrh-bearing women, listen to the news that brings joy: * I have put Hades, that cruel tyrant, to flight; * I have made the world rise from the depths of the tomb; * hasten to my friends, the disciples, and quickly bring this good news to them. * For it is my will that the work of my hands shines with joy * because in days of old it gave birth to sorrow.

AT THE PRAISES

Tone 2 All creation and everything that breathes glorifies You, O Lord; * for by the Cross You abolished Death * that You might manifest to the world your Resurrection from the dead. * For You alone are the Lover of Mankind.

What do the Pharisees now say? * How was it that the guardian soldiers lost the King whom they were guarding? * Why was it that the stone could not retain the Rock of Life? * Therefore, either you must deliver to us Him who was buried * or worship with us Him who is risen and say: * Glory to your bountiful mercies, our Savior, glory to You!

Rejoice, O nations and be glad; * for the angel sat on the stone of the grave * and gave us the good news, saying: * Christ the Savior of the world is risen from the dead. * He has filled the world with fragrant aroma. * Rejoice, O nations, and be glad.

At your conception, O Lord God, * an angel said to her who is full of grace: Rejoice! * At your Resurrection an angel rolled away the stone * from the door of your glorious tomb. * The first angel spoke with signs of joy instead of sorrow, * and the latter brought us the good news * of a Lord who gives life instead of death. * Therefore, we shout to You, O Benefactor of all, * glory to You, O Lord!

Tone 1 **Glory be...now and ever:** Mary Magdalene and the other Mary came to the tomb seeking the Lord * and saw an angel as radiant as light sitting upon the stone. * He said to them: Why do you seek the Living One among the dead? * He is risen as He said, * and you shall find Him in Galilee. * To Him let us bow down and sing: * O Lord, risen from the dead, glory to You!

APOSTICHA

Tone 2 Joseph of Arimathea took You down from the Tree, * the Life of all, cold in death. * Bathing You in sweet and costly myrrh, * gently he covered You with linen so fine, * and with sorrow and tender love in his heart, * he embraced your most pure body. * Marveling at this awesome sight, * he cried to You in fear, O Christ: * Glory to your condescension, O Lover of Mankind!

O Lord, you once favored your land and revived the fortunes of Jacob.

When they placed You in the tomb, O Redeemer of all, * all the powers of Hades quaked in fear. * Broken and defeated by your death, * Hades no longer reigned supreme, * and the dead came forth alive from their tombs, * casting off the bonds of their captivity. * Adam, too, was filled with joy, * and he gratefully cried out to You, O Christ: * Glory to your condescension, O Lover of Mankind!

Mercy and faithfulness have met; justice and peace have embraced.

The powers of heaven shook with fear, * beholding your boundless long-suffering. * They saw You numbered with transgressors, * mocked as a deceiver, slain by the lawless ones, * and the stone closing your tomb * was sealed by the same hands that pierced your side. * But the angels knew your death would be our life, * and joyfully they cried to You, O Christ: * Glory to your condescension, O Lover of Mankind.

Tone 6 **Glory be...now and ever:** Joseph asked for the body of Jesus. * He place it in his own new tomb. * It was fitting for the Lord to come forth from the tomb * as from a bridal chamber. * You destroyed the dominion of Death. * You opened the gates of Paradise to the human race. * Glory to You, O Lord!

Sunday of the Paralytic

Vespers

AT PSALM 140

Tone 3 By your Cross, O Christ our Savior, * the power of Death has been vanquished, * and the deceit of the devil has been destroyed. * Therefore, the human race, saved by faith, * offers You hymns of praise forever.

O Lord, all creation has been enlightened by your Resurrection, * and Paradise has been reopened; * therefore, all creation extols You * and offers You hymns of praise forever.

I glorify the power of the Father, Son, and Holy Spirit; * and I praise the dominion of the undivided Divinity, * the consubstantial Trinity * who reigns forever and ever.

We adore your precious Cross, O Christ, * and with hymns of praise we glorify your Resurrection; * for by your wounds we have all been healed.

Let us sing the praises of the Savior, * who was incarnate of the Virgin; * for He was crucified for our sake, * and on the third day He arose from the dead, * granting us his great mercy.

Christ descended into Hades and announced to those confined there: * Take courage, for today I have conquered Death. * I am the Resurrection, the One who will set you free. * I have shattered the gates of the realm of Death.

O Christ our God, we unworthily stand in your most pure temple * and offer to You our evening hymns. * From the depths of our souls we cry out to You: * O Lover of Mankind, who has enlightened the world * by your Resurrection on the third day, * deliver your people from the hands of your enemies.

Tone 1 O ineffable goodness who created the human form, * You came to heal those who are ill. * O Christ, by your word You raised the Paralytic at the Sheep Pool; * You healed the suffering of the woman with the flow of blood; * You showed mercy to the tormented daughter of the Canaanite woman; * and You did not disdain the prayer of the centurion. * Because of this we cry out in praise; * O Almighty Lord, glory to You! *(2 times)*

The Paralytic was like an unburied dead man, * and when he saw You, O Lord, he cried out: * Have mercy on me, for my bed has become my grave. * Of what use is my life? * I have no need for the Sheep Pool, * for there is none to put me into the water. * Therefore, I come to You, O Fountain of all healing, * that with all I may cry to You: * O Lord Almighty, glory to You!

Tone 5 **Glory be:** Jesus went up to Jerusalem to the Sheep Pool * which in Hebrew was called Bethesda. * And there lay a great multitude of sick people in its five porticoes; * for the angel of the Lord went down at certain times and stirred the water, * granting healing to those who approached in faith. * The Lord saw there a man with a chronic illness, * and He asked him: Do you want to be healed? * The sick man replied: * I have no one to put me into the pool when the water is stirred. * I have spent my money on physicians * and received no help from anyone. * The Physician of soul and body said to him: * Take up your pallet and walk; * proclaim to the whole world * the greatness of my mercy and my mighty deeds.

Tone 3 **Now and ever:** O most honorable Virgin, we are filled with awe * when we consider that you gave birth to Christ who is both God and man. * O immaculate Lady, without knowing man, * you gave birth in the flesh to a Son without a human father. * This Son, from all eternity, was begotten by God the Father without a mother, * and, when He took on our human nature, * He did not undergo any change. * Nothing was added to his divine nature, nor was it divided. * The properties of both his divine and human nature remained intact. * We, therefore, entreat you, O Blessed Virgin, * to save the souls of those who, in true faith, * acknowledge you as the Mother of God.

APOSTICHA

Tone 3 O Christ, who darkened the sun by your passion * and enlightened all creation by your Resurrection, * accept our evening prayer, for You love all people.

PASCHAL HYMNS

Let God arise and let his enemies be scattered, and let those who hate Him flee from before his face.

Today the sacred Pasch is revealed to us, * holy and new Pasch, * the mystical Passover, * the venerable Passover, * the Pasch which is Christ the Redeemer, * spotless Pasch, great Pasch, * the Pasch of the faithful, * the Pasch which is the key to the gates of Paradise, * the Pasch which sanctifies all the faithful.

As smoke vanishes, so let them vanish as wax melts before the fire.

O Women, * be the heralds of good news and tell what you saw; * tell of the vision and say to Zion: * Accept the good news of joy from us, * the news that Christ has risen. * Exalt and celebrate * and rejoice, O Jerusalem, * seeing Christ the King coming from the tomb * like a bridegroom.

So let the wicked perish at the presence of God, and let the righteous ones rejoice.

The myrrh-bearing women * arrived just before the dawn * at the tomb of the Giver of Life * and found an angel seated on the stone * who spoke these words to them: * Why do you seek the Living among the dead? * Why do you mourn the Incorruptible among those subject to decay? * Go, announce the good news * to his disciples.

This is the day that the Lord has made; let us exalt and rejoice in it.

Pasch so delightful, * Pasch of the Lord is the Pasch, * most honored Pasch now dawned on us. * It is the Pasch! * Therefore, let us joyfully embrace one another. * O Passover, save us from sorrow; * for today Christ has shown forth from the tomb * as from a bridal chamber * and filled the women with joy by saying: * Announce the good news * to my apostles.

Tone 8 **Glory be:** On Solomon's porch, there lay many sick, * and in the midst of the Feast, Christ found among them * a man who had been paralyzed for thirty-eight years. * To him He called out with a Master's voice: * Do you wish to be made well? * And the Paralytic Man replied: * Lord, I have no one to put me into the pool when the water is stirred. * The Lord said to him: Take up your bed. * Behold, you have become whole; do not sin again. * Therefore, O Lord, by the prayers of the Theotokos, * send down upon us your great mercy.

Tone 5 **Now and ever:** This is the Resurrection day. * Let us be enlightened by this Feast, * and let us embrace one another. * Let us call Brethren * even those who hate us, * and in the Resurrection, * forgive everything; and let us sing: * Christ is risen from the dead! * By death He conquered Death, * and to those in the graves He granted life.

TROPARIA

Tone 3 Let the heavens rejoice, and let the earth be glad. * For the Lord has shown the might of his right hand. * By his death the Lord has conquered Death. * He has become the first-born of the dead; * He has delivered us from the depths of the Abyss * and has granted great mercy to the world.

Tone 3 **Glory be...now and ever:** We sing your praises, O Virgin: * for, as the Mother of God, you always intercede for the salvation of the human race. * It is from you that our God and your Son took flesh. * Then, by suffering the passion on the Cross, * and out of love for humanity, He delivered us from corruption.

Sunday Matins

SESSIONAL HYMN I

Tone 3 Christ is risen from the dead, * He who is the first-fruits of those that had been asleep, * the first-born of creation and the Creator of all things that were made. * By himself He renewed the nature of our corrupt race. * Therefore, O Death, you shall reign no more; * for the Lord of all nullified your power and dissolved it.

Arise then, Lord, lift up your hand. O God, do not forget the poor!

When You tasted death in the flesh, O Lord, * You took away the bitterness of death by your Resurrection, * and made the human race prevail over it, * restoring victory over the ancient curse. * Therefore, O Protector of our life, glory to You!

Glory be...now and ever: Gabriel was rapt in amazement as he beheld your virginity * and the splendor of your purity, O Mother of God; * and he cried out to you: * By what name shall I call you? * I am bewildered; I am lost! * I shall greet you as I was commanded to do: * Rejoice, O Woman Full of Grace!

SESSIONAL HYMN II

Tone 3 You have deigned to take upon yourself our entire human condition, O Lord, * and You willed to let yourself be nailed on the Cross, O God our Creator. * You have suffered in your humanity * destroying Death by your death * in order to redeem the human race. * Therefore, we sing to You as the Giver of life: * Glory to your infinite mercy, O Christ our God.

I will praise You, Lord, with all my heart; I will recount all your wonders.

Let us believers speak of divine things, * of the secret of your inscrutable crucifixion and of your ineffable Resurrection; * for today Death and Hades have been led captive, * and the human race has been invested with incorruption. * Therefore, we cry out in gratitude: * Glory to your Resurrection, O Christ!

Glory be...now and ever: The heavenly powers rejoiced with love, * and the human race was filled with emotion, * when the angel's greeting was addressed to you, O Mother of God. * Both in heaven and on earth a common feast bursts forth in brightness, * for our first father is delivered from death. * Together with the angel we also cry out: * Rejoice, O most pure Mother, O immaculate Virgin.

HYPAKOE

The brilliant angel startled the myrrh-bearing women and said: * Why do you seek the living One in the grave? * He is truly risen and has emptied the tombs. * Know, therefore, that the changeless One changed corruption to incorruption. * Say to Him: How dreadful are your works, O Lord; * for by your death You have saved the human race.

GRADUAL HYMNS

Antiphon I

You led the captives of Zion out of Babylon; * now also save me from my sinful desires. * O Word, lead me into your life.

Those who sow in tears for God in dry land * shall reap as they sing for joy, * as they gather the sheaves of eternal life.

Glory be...now and ever: From the Holy Spirit shines every perfect gift, * as from the Father and the Son; * in Him all creation lives and moves.

Antiphon II

If the Lord does not build the house of virtues, * then in vain do we labor; * but if He defends and protects our lives, * none shall prevail against our city.

The saints are truly as the fruit of your womb, * and they

have not ceased to be children of the Father, O Christ, * through the breath of the Spirit.

Glory be...now and ever: The Holy Spirit gives every creature the power to exist; * in Him resides all wisdom and holiness. * Let us adore Him with the Father and the Word, for He is God.

Antiphon III

Happy are they who fear the Lord * and who walk in the way of his commandments; * for nourishment they shall have the fruit of life.

Rejoice with gladness, O chief Shepherd, * as You behold your children's children around your table * offering branches of good deeds.

Glory be...now and ever: All the richness of glory is in the Holy Spirit. * From Him comes grace and life for all creation. * Therefore, He is praised with the Father and the Word.

PROKEIMENON

Tone 3 Proclaim to the nations: God is King. The world He made firm in its place.

v. O sing a new song to the Lord.

GOSPEL

Luke 24: 1-12

Having beheld the Resurrection of Christ, * let us adore the holy Lord Jesus * who alone is sinless. * We bow to your Cross, O Christ, * and we praise and glorify your holy Resurrection. * You are our God * and besides You we recognize no other, * and we invoke your name. * Come, all you faithful, * and let us bow to the holy Resurrection of Christ, * since, through the Cross, * joy has come to all the world. * Ever praising the Lord, * let us extol his Resurrection, * since He, having endured the Crucifixion, * has destroyed Death by his death.

(3 times)

CANON

The CANON OF THE RESURRECTION may be sung first with each Ode of the Canon; the versicle "Christ is risen from the dead" is sung with the Canon of the Resurrection.

ODE 1

Tone 1 You destroyed the boundaries of death, O im maculate Virgin, * when You gave birth to Christ, the eternal Life,* who today is risen from the tomb * and enlightens the world.

Refrain: **Most holy Mother of God, save us!**

Seeing your Son and our God risen, * O Full of Grace and immaculate One, * you rejoice together with the apostles, O Mother of God; * you were the first to receive the proclamation of salvation * as the beginning of all joy.

Tone 3 You are God glorified on high who worked miracles of old * changing the depths into dry land * and drowning the charioteers * to save the people who worshiped You, O Redeemer.

Refrain: **Glory to your holy Resurrection, O Lord!**

O only King who works wonders, * You worked miracles of old; * You went on the Cross willingly, O God of goodness, * and by death destroyed Death to give us life.

O faithful people, rejoice today in honor of the risen Christ. * Vanquished Hades promptly frees its ancient captives * who sing of God's wondrous deeds.

O Christ, who by your word and divine majesty, * once cured the Paralytic Man and made him take up his pallet, * although he had been ill for a very long time, * cure also my soul so grievously distressed.

Once in the pool at the Sheepgate * an angel descended from time to time, * healing one person at a time; * but Christ now purifies an innumerable multitude by divine baptism.

O mighty Prince of the angels on high, * leader of the heavenly servants, * protect and keep safe from all danger * the faithful gathered in your Church * to sing hymns and to praise the Lord.

Glory be: With the bodiless angels we sing without ceasing * of the three persons of the timeless God, * of the Father, the Word, and the Spirit, * to whom belongs the kingdom and undivided power.

Now and ever: O pure Virgin, grant to your faithful people, * who unceasingly venerate you in faith, * to escape all dangers that threaten them, * from invasion and civil war, * from the sword of the impious and all kinds of evil.

It is the day of Resurrection, * O people, let us be enlightened by it. * The Passover is the Lord's Passover, * since Christ, our God, has brought us from death to life * and from earth to heaven. * Therefore, we sing the hymn of victory.

ODE 3

Tone 1 I returned today to life that knows no sunset, * by the goodness of Him born of you, O immaculate Virgin; * make his glory shine to the ends of the world.

Refrain: **Most holy Mother of God, save us!**

The God whom you brought into the world in the flesh, O immaculate Virgin, * is risen from the dead as He foretold. * Dance and celebrate and extol Him as God.

Tone 3 The sterile soul who was without child * gave birth to a child of renown; * and the Mother, radiant because of her Son, sang out: * My heart is strengthened in God. * There is none holy or just besides the Lord.

Refrain: **Glory to your holy Resurrection, O Lord!**

Seeing You hanging on the Cross, the sun refused its rays, O Word; * the earth trembled everywhere; * the dead rose from the tomb * when You died, O all-powerful God.

When You entered with your soul * into the depths of the earth, O Savior, * Hades was forced to give up the souls which it held, * and they sang a hymn of thanksgiving to your power, O Lord.

For many years, my soul has cruelly suffered, O God of goodness; * cure it as You did the Paralytic * that I may walk in the ways * that You invite those who love your name.

Holy Archangel of God, * intercede together with the Powers on high * for those who sing to you in faith. * Save us, guard us, and protect us, * who are assailed by the passions of this life.

Glory be: Let us glorify God * and praise the Father, the Son, and the Holy Spirit, * glorified by all the heavenly powers, * who with fear sing to the one divinity: * Holy, holy, holy are You, O God our Savior.

Now and ever: The manner of your conception was without seed, * and your birthgiving surpassed all understanding, * an astonishing deed, a wondrous miracle, * praised by angels and glorified by mortals, * O our Lady, the immaculate Virgin Mary.

Come, let us partake of a new drink, * not miraculously produced from the barren rock, * but from the fountain of immortality, * springing up from the tomb of Christ. * In Him is our firm strength.

SESSIONAL HYMN

Tone 3 One word from the Word of the universe * gave movement to the Paralytic Man. * Out of love for us Christ appeared upon the earth, * and the sick man took up his pallet and walked, * in spite of the wicked Scribes who would not see the miracle worked by the Lord, * and in their malice they envied Him who freed our souls from chains.

Glory be...now and ever: Before the incomparable grace of your virginity, * before the beauty of divine brightness * radiating from your holiness, * Gabriel was struck with fear and cried out, O Mother of God: * What praise worthy of your holiness can I offer you? * What sublime name can I call you? * How shall I name you? * But in accordance with the command given me, I sing: * Rejoice, O full of grace!

ODE 4

Tone 1 O immaculate Virgin, * He who made Adam your first father, * was made a man from your womb, * and by his death He destroyed the death caused by sin, * and today He makes the divine brilliance of his holy Resurrection shine on you.

Refrain: **Most holy Mother of God, save us!**

The Messiah to whom you gave birth, * you behold today even more beautiful, O holy Virgin; * for He rises in glory from among the dead, * brilliant with beauty and grace and purity; * with the apostles you glorify the Lord today in joy * for the salvation of the human race.

Tone 3 Habbakuk prefigured your immaculate womb * in the overshadowed mountain. * Therefore, we sing, O Virgin: * The Lord has come from Teman, * the Holy God from the overshadowed mountain.

Refrain: **Glory to your holy Resurrection, O Lord!**

The people inflamed by envy * nailed You on the Cross, O Lord; * but You destroyed the captivity of Death, * and in your power You rose from the tomb, * raising the world with You.

O women, why do you seek to anoint with myrrh the inexhaustible perfume? * For the angel clothed in white said to the myrrh-bearers: * He is risen from the tomb, * and his sweet fragrance fills the whole world.

O Lord, You bore the image of a servant. * You appeared in your compassion beyond understanding. * O Word, You cured the man who suffered for many years * and ordered him to take up his pallet.

From time to time an angel of the Lord * came to stir up the waters of the pool of the Sheepgate. * One man recovered his health, * but now an infinite number are saved by Christ through baptism.

Great prince of angels and guide of the wandering, * Archangel of the Lord, present now with us, * carry the prayer of all to our only Lord and Creator.

Glory be: The holy Trinity is one in nature * in which we distinguish three persons: * the Father, beyond that which is, * the Son, eternal with Him, * and the Holy Spirit, the all-powerful Lord.

Now and ever: O pure Virgin, how do you nurse the eternal One? * How do you bring into the world an infant older than the first person? * How do you carry in your arms, as a Son, * the One who is carried on the shoulders of the Cherubim?

Let Habakkuk, * speaking in behalf of God, * stand with us at the divine watch; * let him show us the brilliant angel who proclaims: * Today, salvation comes to the world; * for Christ, being almighty, is risen.

ODE 5

Tone 1 Divinely illumined by the life-giving rays * of the Resurrection of your Son, * O Mother of God and Virgin immaculate, * the assembly of the faithful shines in beauty.

Refrain: **Most holy Mother of God, save us!**

O King of glory, * when You became incarnate, your mother's virginity remained, * and You did not break the seals of the tomb. * All creation rejoices when it sees your holy Resurrection.

Tone 3 O Christ, enlighten my soul and heart * with your never-setting light; * guide me to the reverence of You, O Lord, * for your commandments are the light of my eyes.

Refrain: **Glory to your holy Resurrection, O Lord!**

Lifted on the wood of the Cross, * You lifted up the whole

world with you. * By your descent to Hades, O God, * You raised up the dead from all ages.

Christ is risen as He promised. * He emptied the kingdom of Hades; * then He showed himself to the apostles, * giving them a share of the eternal joy.

A brilliant angel dressed in white * appeared to the women and said: * Do not cry, for our Life is risen, * giving life to those in the graves.

O Christ, cure my soul as You once cured the Paralytic Man, * for it is under the influence of evil and sin. * Guide me that I may walk in your paths.

O Michael, the great prince of angels, * save the people gathered in your Church today, * for they proclaim the wonders of God.

Glory be: O faithful, we see the Trinity in three persons receiving the same worship; * we proclaim the unity in nature * of the Father, the Son, and the Holy Spirit.

Now and ever: O Virgin, you conceived without seed, * and we sing of your motherhood beyond understanding * which made you the Mother of the Creator, * and we call you blessed and we extol you.

Let us rise at early dawn * and bring to our Master a hymn instead of myrrh; * and we shall see Christ, * the Sun of Righteousness * who enlightens the life of all.

ODE 6

Tone 1 O Virgin Mother of God, * those who were once subjected to death * and to the corruption of the grave, * are now raised to immortal and eternal life * by Him who was incarnate from your womb.

Refrain: **Most holy Mother of God, save us!**

O immaculate Virgin, * He who wondrously dwelt in your womb and became flesh, * descended into the depths of the earth, * and rising from the tomb, * raised with Him all human nature.

Tone 3 The abyss of passions opens before me, * as a tempest of enemies surrounding me. * Hasten to save me, O Savior God, * as You delivered the prophet from the sea monster.

Refrain: **Glory to your holy Resurrection, O Lord!**

Willingly You were lifted on the Cross; * You were buried

in the sepulcher as dead, O Christ; * You gave life to the dead in Hades; * and You rose as God all-powerful.

When Hades met You in the depths, * it was shaken and had to give up its prisoners * who never cease singing, O Savior God, * of your wondrous Resurrection.

When the disciples of the Lord * saw Christ rise from the tomb, * they worshiped the Life of the whole world with joyful hearts, * full of enthusiasm and love.

The man who for many years laid upon a bed in pain, * was cured by your word, O Source of life; * and he glorified your infinite mercy.

O Michael, the great prince of angels, * standing before the throne of the Lord, * be present also among us, * and by your intercession guide us on the paths of life.

Glory be: I sing of the Trinity in three persons; * I proclaim the unity of nature, * of the eternal Father, of the only son, and of the divine Spirit, * the Supreme God venerated by the powers of heaven.

Now and ever: He who holds the whole world in his hands * was carried in your arms, O virgin Mother; * and in his tender love He snatches us by his hands * from the influence of the Evil One who holds us captive.

You have descended into the realm of Death, O Christ, * and have broken ancient bonds which held the captive; * You arose from the tomb on the third day * like Jonah from the whale.

KONTAKION

Tone 3 With your divine protection, O Lord, * as You once raised the Paralytic, now lift up my soul * paralyzed with all kinds of sin and evil deeds of wickedness, * so that, as saved, I may cry out to You: * Glory to your might, O merciful Christ!

IKOS

O Lord Jesus, eternal with your divine Father, * You hold the whole world in your hands * and share sovereign power with the Spirit. * You appeared in the flesh curing illness and driving out passions. * You gave sight to the blind; * You raised the Paralytic by your divine word * and commanded him to walk and to take his pallet on his shoulders. * With him we celebrate and sing to You: * Glory be to your might, O merciful Christ!

ODE 7

Tone 1 O Virgin immaculate, * today your Son destroyed Death, * giving eternal life to all mortals from all ages, * for He is the God of our fathers, * and to Him alone belong blessing and glory.

***Refrain:* Most holy Mother of God, save us!**

O Full of Grace, * He who reigns over all creation * became incarnate and dwelt in your womb, * having suffered death by the Cross; * as God all-powerful He is risen, * making us rise with Him.

Tone 3 You spread dew upon the fiery furnace * and saved the children of Abraham from the flames, * You are blessed forever, Lord God of our fathers.

***Refrain:* Glory to your holy Resurrection, O Lord!**

When it saw You hanging on the Cross, * the sun held back its light, * unable to give light to the world, * when You wished to lie down, O King of all, * to enlighten the nations.

Why do you seek among the dead the One who has life? * He is risen; He is no longer in the tomb, * an angel brilliant with light once told the myrrh-bearers.

For many years a man had lain upon his bed; * by your word You cured him and cried out: * O Paralytic, rise up and take your pallet; * walk and proclaim the marvels of God.

O Michael, the archangel of the Lord, * be the guide of the faithful * gathered in your holy temple to praise God; * and by the strength of your intercession, * be their refuge against all adversity.

Glory be: O holy Trinity, save us from all danger, * the faithful who sing to You unceasingly, * for You are the Master and God of all; * and make us able to share in the inheritance of eternal good.

Now and ever: You remained a virgin when you gave birth without seed * to Him begotten by the Father before all ages; * this is a miracle which surpasses understanding * and for which we extol you.

God, who saved the three youths from the furnace, * has become man * and suffered as any mortal; * but his passion clothed his mortality * with the splendor of incorruption. * He is the only blessed One, God of our fathers, * and is worthy of all praise.

ODE 8

Tone 1 The Creator came into this world * from you, O Virgin Mother of God; * destroying the jail of Hades, * He gave resurrection to us mortals; * and we also bless Christ forever.

Refrain: **Most holy Mother of God, save us!**

Destroying all power of Death * on the day of his Resurrection, O Virgin, * your Son and the all-powerful God * made us partakers of his glory and divinity. * We also bless Christ forever.

Tone 3 The heaven of heavens, the mountains and the hills, * the oceans and all the human race * praise in hymns the One whom the angels in heaven glorify unceasingly as God, * blessing your Creator and exalting Him forever.

Refrain: **Glory to your holy Resurrection, O Lord!**

The veil was torn when You were crucified, O Savior, * and Death gave up all the mortals which it had swallowed. * Hades was stripped when it saw your descent into its depths.

O Death, where is your sting? * O Hades, where is your victory now? * You have been put to death by the risen King; * you have been brought to nothing; you reign no more; * for the mighty God has delivered your captives.

An angel appeared, saying: * O myrrh-bearers, run and hasten to the apostles; * announce that the Master is risen. * O wonder! The Lord is risen, * and with Him the dead who from the ages have fallen asleep.

The Paralytic who had lain for many years cried out: * have pity on my misery, O Redeemer. * And Christ ordered him to rise, * to take up his pallet, and to walk as he needed.

O great prince of the bodiless angels, * O leader of the powers of heaven, * with them pray for the forgiveness of our sins, * the conversion of our life, and the enjoyment of eternal happiness.

Let us bless the Lord, Father, Son and Holy Spirit.

O indivisible and three-personed Divinity which no hand has created, * O eternal Father, Son of God, and Holy Spirit,* we sing to You with one voice * a holy hymn in company with the Seraphim.

Now and ever: O Mother of God and ever-Virgin Mary, * the holy prophet Isaiah recognized in you * the book written by the hand of the Father, * the timeless Word saving from error * those who sing to you with sacred hymns.

Let us praise, bless, and worship the Lord, singing and exalting Him above all forever.

This is that chosen and holy day, * Feast of feasts, * most solemn day, * only king and lord of all Sabbaths, * on which we ever praise Christ.

OMIT MAGNIFICAT

ODE 9

Tone 1 O Virgin, with one voice we, the faithful, extol you: * Rejoice, door of the Lord; rejoice, spiritual city; * rejoice, for you made the light of your Son shine upon us * on the day of his Resurrection.

Refrain: **Most holy Mother of God, save us!**

O immaculate One, full of grace, * exalt and dance in joy, O divine door of brightness; * for Jesus rested in the tomb * and rose in glory more brilliant than the sun; * and He enlightens the whole human race.

Tone 3 The fire of the divinity was born in the womb of the Virgin. * Moses foresaw this in the bush that burnt without being consumed on Mount Sinai; * Daniel saw this in an unhewn mountain; * while Isaiah saw this in a shoot growing from the root of David.

Refrain: **Glory to your holy Resurrection, O Lord!**

When You were lifted on the Cross, O Jesus, * You lifted up all with You. * By your own will You were buried in a tomb * and raised up all the dead from their tombs. * They praise your infinite might, your ineffable power, and unconquerable majesty.

Beautiful as a bridegroom from the bridal chamber, * You rose from the grave, O Word shining with glory. * You destroyed the darkness of Hades * and freed those held captive there, * as they sing with one voice: * Glory to your Resurrection, O Lord.

The women approached the tomb, * mixing groans and tears with the spices they carried; * and they learned of the glorious Resurrection of Christ * which we, the faithful, celebrate, * exalting in the joy of our hearts.

The bodily strength listened to your command, O Christ, * and the Paralytic of long ago showed that he was ready to walk, * and he carried the pallet on which he had lain for many years; * and in his joy, O Christ, he glorified your power.

O Leader, present in a majestic way * before the great unsetting Light, * ask Him to give light to our souls * and give peace to our life which is always threatened * by the snares and menaces of the serpent.

Glory be: O Trinity, fullness of light and life, * I glorify You in piety; * O eternal Father, O Word of God, and Holy Spirit, * indivisible majesty in three persons, * divinity without confusion, * whom we glorify with the angels: * Holy, holy, holy are You, O Lord our God.

Now and ever: Your womb has become a bearer of brightness, * for from it came forth the great Sun which is Christ. * Through Him the world was illumined with joy; * through Him was driven out the darkness of sin. * Therefore, we praise as the source of all good, * the divine Spouse and all-immaculate Virgin.

Shine in splendor, * O new Jerusalem! * For the glory of the Lord * is risen upon you. * O Zion, sing with joy and rejoice! * And you, pure Mother of God, * rejoice in the Resurrection of your Son.

HYMN OF LIGHT

Tone 2 You, O King and Lord, * have fallen asleep * in the flesh as a mortal man, * but on the third day You arose again. * You have raised Adam * from his corruption and made Death powerless. * You are the Pasch of incorruption. * You are the salvation of the world.

Tone 3 **Glory be...now and ever:** The Lover of Mankind and all-compassionate Lord * came to the pool of Bethesda. * There He found a man paralyzed from his youth; * He healed his infirmity and said to him: * Take up your mat and go your way. * Walk in the path of righteousness.

AT THE PRAISES

Tone 3 Come together, all you nations, * and understand the might of this awesome mystery! * Our Savior, the Word from the beginning, * has suffered crucifixion and burial for us of his own will. * On the third day He rose again to save us all. * Let us worship Him.

The soldiers that guarded You, O Lord, * related all the wonders which had come to pass; * but the vain assembly of the Sanhedrin filled their hands with bribes, * thinking they could hide your Resurrection which is glorified through all the world. * Have mercy on us.

All creation was filled with joy * when it received the news of your Resurrection. * When Mary Magdalene went to your tomb, * she found an angel in shining garments sitting on the stone. * He said: Why do you seek the Living among the dead? * He is not here; He is risen as He said. * He goes before you to Galilee.

O Master, the Lover of Mankind, * in your light we see light. * For You have risen from the dead, * granting salvation to the human race. * Let all creation glorify You; * have mercy on us, O sinless One.

The myrrh-bearing women, O Lord, * offered You their tears as a morning praise. * Then hastening to seek your incorruptible body, * they came to your grave bearing fragrant ointments. * An angel sitting on the stone spoke to them saying: * Why do you seek the Living among the dead? * For truly He has trampled down death, * and He is risen because He is God, * granting to all of us great mercy.

The brilliant angel on the life-giving tomb * said to the myrrh-bearing women: * Truly the Savior emptied the tombs and led Hades captive. * He is risen on the third day, * for He alone is the almighty God.

Mary Magdalene arrived on the first day of the week * seeking You in the grave. * And when she did not find You, she cried out with sighs: * Woe is me, O my Savior. * How have You been stolen, O King of all? * From within the grave two angels * bearing the message of life cried out to her saying: * Woman, why are you weeping? * She answered, saying: I cry because they have removed my Lord from the grave, * and I do not know where they have taken Him. * But as she turned around and saw You, she said: * My Lord and my God, glory to You!

The soldiers enclosed Life in the tomb, * but the thief opened Paradise with his word by saying: * For my sake, You have been crucified with me * and have hung on the tree of the Cross; * You have appeared to me sitting on the throne with the Father. * You are Christ our God who gives great mercy to the world.

Tone 8 **Glory be:** O Lord, the pool did not heal the Paralytic, * but your word renewed him. * His many years of sickness could not hinder your power. * Your voice held more authority over him than his infirmity. * He threw away the burden of his sickness and carried the weight of his bed, * a testimony to your abundant compassion. * Glory to You, O Lord!

Tone 2 **Now and ever:** You are truly most blessed, O virgin Mother of God. * Through the One who was incarnate of you, * Hades was chained, Adam revived, the curse wiped out, * Eve set free, Death put to death, * and we ourselves were brought back to life. * That is why we cry out in praise: * Blessed are You, O Christ our God, * who finds in this your good pleasure; glory to You!

AFTER THE DISMISSAL

Gospel Stanza Number 3

Tone 3 **Glory be...now and ever:** The disciples were rebuked for the hardness of their hearts * because they doubted when Mary Magdalene proclaimed to them * the Resurrection of the Savior and his appearance to her. * But,when they were strengthened with miracles and wonders, * they were sent out to preach. * And when You, O Lord, ascended to your Father, the Source of all light, * the disciples preached throughout the world * verifying their words with wonders and miracles. * Therefore, we who were enlightened by them, * glorify your Resurrection from the dead, O Lover of Mankind.

Sunday Evening Vespers

AT PSALM 140

Tone 8 O wonder of wonders! * The Creator of all has appeared in the flesh; * He desired the lowliness of our nature because He is most compassionate. * He lived on earth and worked many miracles. * He healed the Paralytic, saying to him: * Stand up, take up your pallet, and sin no more.

O Savior, my Lord and my God, * You desired to raise the fallen human race, * You walked upon the earth as a man, * healing the sick through your tender compassion; * and having come to the pool at the Sheepgate, * You found the man who had been sick for thirty-eight years. * By your word alone You restored him to health.

The Pharisees were consumed with jealousy * and found fault with your deeds of mercy, * O most merciful Lord. * They became inflamed with anger * and sinned against the Law. * They sought to put You to death because of the Sabbath, * though You are the true Life; * for on the Sabbath You healed the one who had been sick * and told the Paralytic to stand up and walk.

Three Stichera from the Saint of the day

Tone 5 **Glory be...now and ever:** Near the pool at the Sheepgate lay a Paralytic, * who upon seeing You called out: * I have no one to help me into the waters when they are stirred. * Before I reach the pool, another goes before me and obtains the cure; * and so I lie here with my sickness. * Without delay, the compassionate Savior said to him: * For your sake I became incarnate; * for your sake I was clothed in the flesh; * and yet you say you have no one. * Take up your pallet and walk. * All is possible with You, O Lord; * all is obedient to you, and all submits to You. * Remember us all, and be merciful to us * because You love all people, O most holy One.

APOSTICHA

Tone 3 By your Cross, O Christ our Savior, * the power of Death has been vanquished * and the deceit of the devil has been destroyed. * Therefore, the human race, saved by faith, * offers You hymns of praise forever.

I have lifted up my eyes to You enthroned in heaven. Behold, as the eyes of servants are on the hands of their masters, as the eyes of a maid are on the hands of her mistress, so are our eyes on the Lord our God until He has mercy on us.

I have sinned greatly and offended You, O Master, * who by nature are gracious and merciful. * Like the prodigal, I repent sincerely. * Receive me, O heavenly Father, * and make me one of your servants.

Have mercy on us, O Lord, have mercy on us; for we have been filled with shame; our soul is all too full of the mockery of the rich, of the contempt of the proud.

Great is the power of your Cross, O Lord; * for though it was raised in one place, it acts throughout the world. * It made apostles of fishermen * and martyrs of the Gentiles. * We beg them to intercede for our souls.

Tone 1 **Glory be...now and ever:** O ineffable Goodness who created the human form, * You came to heal those who are ill. * O Christ, by your word You raised the Paralytic at the Sheep Pool; * You healed the suffering of the woman with the flow of blood; * You showed mercy to the tormented daughter of the Canaanite woman; * and You did not disdain the prayer of the centurion. * Because of this we cry out in praise; * O Almighty Lord, glory to You!

TROPARIA

Of the Saint

Tone 3 **Glory be...now and ever:** Let the heavens rejoice, and let the earth be glad. * For the Lord has shown the might of his right hand. * By his death the Lord has conquered Death. * He has become the first-born of the dead; * He has delivered us from the depths of the Abyss * and has granted great mercy to the world.

Monday Matins

SESSIONAL HYMN I

Tone 3 Christ is risen from the dead, * the first-fruits of them that sleep, * the first-born of all creation, * and the maker of all created things. * In his flesh He restored the human nature which had grown corrupt. * Your reign is over, O Death, * for the Master of all has made your power of no avail.

Lord, do not reprove me in your anger; punish me not in your rage.

Repent, O my soul, as a stranger upon the earth; * for the dust no longer sings in the tomb, * and there is no more redemption from sin. * Now cry out to Christ, our God: * O Lord who probes the depths of our hearts, I have sinned; * do not condemn me, but have mercy on me.

Their span extends through all the earth, their words to the utmost bounds of the world.

Your courage and your steadfastness have overcome the traps of the Enemy, * O victorious Martyrs worthy of all honor; * you have deserved unending happiness. * Now intercede with the Lord * that He may save his flock who loves Christ.

Glory be...now and ever: Gabriel was rapt in amazement as he beheld your virginity * and the splendor of your purity,

O Mother of God; * and he cried out to you: * By what name shall I call you? * I am bewildered; I am lost! * I shall greet you as I was commanded to do: * Rejoice, O Woman Full of Grace!

SESSIONAL HYMN II

Tone 3 You loosed the Paralytic's bonds on the Sabbath day, * but the Scribes were paralyzed, bound in envy's chains. * They complained: It is not lawful to heal on the Sabbath! * Our fathers kept the Sabbath rest; * will You now destroy this command? * They would not recognize You as Master of the Law * and the Savior of our souls.

Glory be...now and ever: *(Repeat the above)*

Having beheld the Resurrection of Christ...

CANON

HYMN OF LIGHT

Tone 2 You, O King and Lord, * have fallen asleep * in the flesh as a mortal man, * but on the third day You arose again. * You have raised Adam * from his corruption and made Death powerless. * You are the Pasch of incorruption. * You are the salvation of the world.

Tone 3 **Glory be...now and ever:** The Lover of Mankind and all-compassionate Lord * came to the pool of Bethesda. * There He found a man paralyzed from his youth; * He healed his infirmity and said to him: * Take up your mat and go your way. * Walk in the path of righteousness.

AT THE PRAISES

Tone 3 Come together, all you nations, * and understand the might of this awesome mystery! * Our Savior, the Word from the beginning, * has suffered crucifixion and burial for us of his own will. * On the third day He rose again to save us all. * Let us worship Him. *(2 times)*

Often when I am singing praises to You, * I find myself in a sinful condition; * and when my mouth is praising You, * my soul is thinking about vanities. * Correct me completely through penance, O Christ our God; * have mercy on me and save me.

Come, all you people, let us venerate the memory of the victorious martyrs of the Lord, * for in the presence of angels and people, * they have received the crown of victory from Christ; * and they intercede with Him for our souls.

Tone 1 **Glory be...now and ever:** The Paralytic was like an unburied dead man, * and when he saw You, O Lord, he cried out: * Have mercy on me, for my bed has become my grave. * Of what use is my life? * I have no need for the Sheep Pool, * for there is none to put me into the water. * Therefore, I come to You, O Fountain of all healing, * that with all I may cry to You: * O Lord Almighty, glory to You!

APOSTICHA

Tone 3 The leaders of the people, * blinded by malice and envy, * even though they had seen signs and wonders of power, * would not believe in You, * the only-begotten Son of God and Lord of all, * who by a word made the Paralytic whole.

I will sing forever of your love, O Lord; through all ages my mouth will proclaim your truth.

The guardians of the Law * saw the Paralytic loosed from his bonds on the Sabbath. * The Scribes cried out: * It is not lawful to heal on the Sabbath. * Healing profanes the Sabbath day.

Your love lasts forever; your truth is firmly established as the heavens.

O you guardians of the Sabbath, * do you not know Me? * I am the Lord and Master of the Sabbath. * If I loose the affliction of the Paralytic on the Sabbath, * why do you murmur against Me? * You say that it is forbidden to carry a bed on the Sabbath day.

Tone 5 **Glory be...now and ever:** Jesus went up to Jerusalem to the Sheep Pool * which in Hebrew was called Bethesda. * And there lay a great multitude of sick people in its five porticoes; * for the angel of the Lord went down at certain times and stirred the water, * granting healing to those who approached in faith. * The Lord saw there a man with a chronic illness, * and He asked him: * Do you want to be healed? * The sick man replied: * I have no one to put me into the pool when the water is stirred. * I have spent my money on physicians * and received no help from any one. * The Physician of soul and body said to him: * Take up your pallet and walk; * proclaim to the whole world * the greatness of my mercy and my mighty deeds.

Monday Evening Vespers

AT PSALM 140

Tone 1 O ineffable Goodness who created the human form, * You came to heal those who are ill. * O Christ, by your word You raised the Paralytic at the Sheep Pool; * You healed the suffering of the woman with the flow of blood; * You showed mercy to the tormented daughter of the Canaanite woman; * and You did not disdain the prayer of the centurion. * Because of this we cry out in praise; * O Almighty Lord, glory to You! *(2 times)*

The Paralytic was like an unburied dead man, * and when he saw You, O Lord, he cried out: * Have mercy on me, for my bed has become my grave. * Of what use is my life? * I have no need for the Sheep Pool, * for there is none to put me into the water. * Therefore, I come to You, O Fountain of all healing, * that with all I may cry to You: * O Lord Almighty, glory to You!

Three Stichera from the Saint of the day

Tone 5 **Glory be...now and ever:** Jesus went up to Jerusalem to the Sheep Pool * which in Hebrew was called Bethesda. * And there lay a great multitude of sick people in its five porticoes; * for the angel of the Lord went down at certain times and stirred the water, * granting healing to those who approached in faith. * The Lord saw there a man with a chronic illness, * and He asked him: * Do you want to be healed? * The sick man replied: * I have no one to put me into the pool when the water is stirred. * I have spent my money on physicians * and received no help from any one. * The Physician of soul and body said to him: * Take up your pallet and walk; * proclaim to the whole world * the greatness of my mercy and my mighty deeds.

APOSTICHA

Tone 3 O Lord, all creation has been enlightened by your Resurrection, * and Paradise has been reopened; * therefore, all creation extols You * and offers you hymns of praise forever.

I have lifted up my eyes to You enthroned in heaven. Behold, as the eyes of servants are on the hands of their masters, as the eyes of a maid are on the hands of her mistress, so are our eyes on the Lord our God until He has mercy on us.

Save me, O my Lord God, * for You are the Savior of all. * A storm of passion is tossing me about, * and the weight of transgression is sinking me. * Give me your helping hand * and lead me to the light of humility; * for You alone are merciful, and You love all people.

Have mercy on us, O Lord, have mercy on us; for we have been filled with shame; our soul is all too full of the mockery of the rich, of the contempt of the proud.

Great is the power of your martyrs, O Christ. * For, lying in their tombs, they drive out evil spirits; * and fighting in defense of godliness, * they subdued the power of the enemy by faith in the Trinity.

Tone 8 **Glory be...now and ever:** On Solomon's porch, there lay many sick, * and in the midst of the feast, Christ found among them * a man who had been paralyzed for thirty-eight years. * To him He called out with a Master's voice: * Do you wish to be made well? * And the Paralytic Man replied: * Lord, I have no one to put me into the pool when the water is stirred. * The Lord said to him: Take up your bed. * Behold, you have become whole; do not sin again. * Therefore, O Lord, by the prayers of the Theotokos, * send down upon us your great mercy.

TROPARIA

Of the Saint

Tone 3 **Glory be...now and ever:** Let the heavens rejoice, and let the earth be glad. * For the Lord has shown the might of his right hand. * By his death the Lord has conquered Death. * He has become the first-born of the dead; * He has delivered us from the depths of the Abyss * and has granted great mercy to the world.

Tuesday Matins

SESSIONAL HYMN I

Tone 3 You tasted death in the flesh, O Lord, * but You blunted its sting by your Resurrection. * You strengthened the human race against its power; * You abolished its ancient curse. * Glory to You, O Lord, * the protector of our lives.

Lord, do not reprove me in your anger; punish me not in your rage.

How long will you remain in sin, O my soul? * How long

will you scorn repentance? * Consider the nearness of judgment and cry out to the Lord: * Save me, for I have sinned, O my God.

Their span extends through all the earth, their words to the ut most bounds of the world.

By faith you shine as brilliant as the stars, * O holy Martyrs whose struggles we now praise. * Without fear you stood before the torments of the tyrants * and put an end to the blasphemies of the false gods; * you were armed only with the truth * and the invincible trophy of the Cross.

Glory be...now and ever: O Mother of God, our rampart and our strength, * the powerful helper of the whole world, * O Virgin blessed above all, * by your prayers save your servants from all dangers.

SESSIONAL HYMN II

Tone 3 You loosed the Paralytic's bonds on the Sabbath day, * but the Scribes were paralyzed, bound in envy's chains. * They complained: It is not lawful to heal on the Sabbath! * Our fathers kept the Sabbath rest; * will You now destroy this command? * They would not recognize You as Master of the Law * and the Savior of our souls.

Glory be...now and ever: *(Repeat the above)*

Having beheld the Resurrection of Christ...

CANON

HYMN OF LIGHT

Tone 2 You, O King and Lord, * have fallen asleep * in the flesh as a mortal man, * but on the third day You arose again. * You have raised Adam * from his corruption and made Death powerless. * You are the Pasch of incorruption. * You are the salvation of the world.

Tone 3 **Glory be...now and ever:** The Lover of Mankind and all-compassionate Lord * came to the pool of Bethesda. * There He found a man paralyzed from his youth; * He healed his infirmity and said to him: * Take up your mat and go your way. * Walk in the path of righteousness.

AT THE PRAISES

Tone 3 The soldiers that guarded You, O Lord, * related all the wonders which had come to pass; * but the vain assembly of the Sanhedrin filled their hands with bribes, * thinking they could hide your Resurrection which is glorified through all the world. * Have mercy on us. *(2 times)*

Collect my scattered spirit, O Lord; * remove the thorns from my heart. * Give me the repentance of Peter, * the sighs of the publican, * and the tears of the sinful woman, * so that I may cry out to You in a loud voice: * Save me, O my God, * the Lover of Mankind and the only compassionate One.

The soldiers of Christ have banished all fear * before the kings and tyrants; * with great courage they have confessed the Lord of the universe, * our King and our God; * and now they intercede for our souls.

Tone 8 **Glory be...now and ever:** O Lord, the pool did not-not heal the Paralytic, * but your word renewed him. * His many years of sickness could not hinder your power. * Your voice held more authority over him than his infirmity. * He threw away the burden of his sickness and carried the weight of his bed, * a testimony to your abundant compassion. * Glory to You, O Lord!

APOSTICHA

Tone 3 Your word has shone forth, healing paralyzed limbs, * as a life-giving strength, O my Word, through whom all things were made. * A man lay on his bed for many years; * he had no reason to hope that he would ever rise from it. * But by your command, he picked it up and went his way.

I will sing forever of your love, O Lord; through all ages my mouth will proclaim your truth.

Obeying your command, filled with almighty power, * the Paralytic was filled with joy. * He picked up his bed and walked, * bearing witness to You and crying out: * This is He who ordered me to be made whole.

Your love lasts forever; your truth is firmly established as the heavens.

The man lay paralyzed for many years, * his limbs useless from youth. * He cried: Have mercy on me, Christ the Deliverer. * I am fettered by helplessness. * You straightened his limbs, O Savior, * commanding him to pick up his mat.

Tone 5 **Glory be...now and ever:** Near the pool at the Sheepgate lay a Paralytic, * who upon seeing You called out: * I have no one to help me into the waters when they are stirred. * Before I reach the pool, another goes before me and obtains the cure; * and so I lie here with my sickness. *

Without delay, the compassionate Savior said to him: * For your sake I became incarnate; * for your sake I was clothed in the flesh; * and yet you say you have no one. * Take up your pallet and walk. * All is possible with You, O Lord; * all is obedient to you, and all submits to You. * Remember us all, and be merciful to us * because You love all people, O most holy One.

Mid-Pentecost

Vespers

AT PSALM 140

Tone 4 The midpoint of the Feast has arrived; * the days which begin with the Resurrection of the Savior * and are fulfilled in the divine Feast of Pentecost. * Truly it unites both Feasts * and draws light from their double brightness,* giving honor to the Ascension of the Lord, * which prefigures our glory. *(2 times)*

Truly Zion heard and was glad * when it received the glad tidings of the Resurrection of Christ. * Faithful children also rejoiced at beholding it. * Seeing the blood of Christ washed away by the Holy Spirit, * the Church prepares to worthily celebrate * the joyous midpoint of these two holy Feasts. *(2 times)*

The over-abundant outpouring of the divine Spirit over all is drawing near, * as it is written by the prophet Joel. * The promise of Christ, given to his disciples * after his death, burial, and resurrection, * proclaims the coming of the Comforter. *(2 times)*

Tone 6 **Glory be...now and ever:** The midweek of the festal season has arrived, O Christ, * the midpoint of your Resurrection and the coming of your Holy Spirit. * Coming together, we glorify the mystery of your miracles; * and filled with fear, we cry out to You: * Send down upon us your great mercy!

READINGS

Composite I - *See Appendix A, page 456*
Composite II - *See Appendix A, page 456*
Proverbs 9: 1 - 11

APOSTICHA

Tone 1 The middle of the fifty days is here, * wherein Christ manifested his divine power. * He healed the Paralytic, raising him from his bed by a word. * In the flesh He worked signs and wonders, * granting his people eternal life and great mercy.

Remember your people whom You chose long ago.

You came to the temple, O Wisdom of God, * in the midst of the Feast, * to teach and edify the Jews, the Scribes, and the Pharisees: * Let all who thirst come to Me and drink the water of life. * They will never thirst again. * Whoever believes in Me, streams of living water shall flow from them. * How great is your goodness and your compassion. * Glory to You, O Christ our God!

Tone 2

God is our King from time past, the Giver of help through all the land.

Jesus went up to the Temple in the middle of the Feast. * He proclaimed to the stiff-necked people: * Let all who thirst come to Me and drink. * I will give them the water of life, and they will never thirst again. * Living streams will flow from the hearts of those who believe in Me. * They will find the Light of the world.

Tone 8 **Glory be...now and ever:** While You taught the Scribes in the midst of the Feast, O Savior, * they murmured: How can this man who never studied be learned? * They would not believe that You are the Wisdom who created the world. * O Lord, glory to You!

TROPARION

Tone 8 When the Paschal Feast is half completed, * quench my thirsty soul with the waters of devotion; * for You, O Savior, have announced to all: * Let all who are thirsty come to Me and drink. * O Christ our God, Source of our life, * glory be to You! *(3 times)*

Wednesday Matins

SESSIONAL HYMN I

Tone 4 He who endowed the hearts of all with reason * stood in the midst of the Temple, * speaking truth to the lovers of falsehood. * He cried out: Why do you seek to arrest Me, the Giver of life? * He proclaimed boldly in the middle of the Feast: * Judge not by external appearance, O transgressors.

Glory be...now and ever: *(Repeat the above)*

SESSIONAL HYMN II

Tone 5 The Master of all stood in the Temple * in the middle of the great Feast. * He disputed with the Scribes and Pharisees, speaking clearly and boldly to all. * By his words we are given courage to confess Him as King and God, * full of compassion and great mercy.

Glory be...now and ever: *(Repeat the above)*

Having beheld the Resurrection of Christ...

CANON I

ODE 1

Tone 4 When Israel crossed the abyss of the Red Sea as on dry land, * in the desert they put to flight the power of Amalek, * because of the hands of Moses which were stretched out in the form of a cross.

Refrain: **Glory be to You, O Lord, glory be to You!**

The wondrous gifts of your divine incarnation which surpasses understanding * now shine on us, O Lord; * they bring forth good gifts as a source of grace and divine splendor.

O Christ, You have appeared in the middle of this resplendent feast * radiating with your divine brightness; * You yourself are the joyful feast of the people You save, * for You indeed bring salvation.

Glory be: Coming from God, O Lord, You are our wisdom, holiness, and redemption; * You bring us from earth to heaven on high * and give us the gift of your divine Spirit.

Now and ever: Your flesh has not known the corruption of the grave, O Lord; * without seed it was formed and without corruption it remained, * surpassing nature and its laws.

You walled up the sea and drowned Pharaoh and his chariots; * You saved your people by leading them across dry land, O Lord; * and You led to the mountain of holiness those who say: * Let us sing a hymn of victory to our God, for He is victorious in battle.

ODE 3

Tone 4 Your Church rejoices in You, O Christ, and cries out: * O Lord, You are my strength, my refuge, and my help.

Refrain: **Glory be to You, O Lord, glory be to You!**

You have opened the life-giving sources of water * to your Church, O merciful God, by saying: * All who thirst, come and drink in joy.

Glory be: Revealing your ascension from earth to heaven,* You have promised to send your Holy Spirit from on high .

Now and ever: The life-giving Lord who has become flesh from the Virgin * has given eternal life to all the faithful in his mercy.

My heart is made firm in the Lord; * my strength exalts in my God; * my mouth is opened before my enemies; * for your salvation makes me dance with joy.

SESSIONAL HYMN

Tone 8 When the feast was half completed, You cried out in the middle of the Temple: * All who thirst, come to Me and drink, * for whoever shall drink from this divine river * shall receive the streams of my teaching flowing from my side. * Whoever sees Me as the One sent by the divine Father * shall be glorified with Me. * Therefore we cry out to You: * Glory to You, O Christ our God, * for You have poured out on your servants * the rich streams of your love for all.

Glory be...now and ever: You poured out the stream of wisdom and life for the world; * You invited your people to drink from the rivers of salvation; * for the ones who receive your divine Law * shall extinguish the burning coals of error in themselves. * They shall never again thirst in all eternity * and shall never lack your gifts, O Lord and heavenly King. * That is why we glorify your power, O Christ our God. * We ask You to take away our sins * and to grant your servants the abundance of your great mercy.

ODE 4

Tone 4 Seeing you hanging on the cross, * You, the Sun of Justice, * the Church truly stands still in her place and cries out: * Glory to your power, O Lord.

Refrain: **Glory be to You, O Lord, glory be to You!**

By your power You have broken the gates of Death; * You have shown us the path to eternal life; * You opened its gates to the faithful who cry to You: * Glory to your power, O Lord.

In your hand You hold both the middle and the ends of the universe, * whose distant reaches You embrace in your greatness; * in the middle of the Temple, You declare, O Lord: * O friends of God, come and enjoy the heavenly good gifts.

As God You possess the power of the universe * and have destroyed the domain of Death; * O Christ, You announce the sending of the Holy Spirit * who proceeds from the almighty Father.

Refrain: **Most holy Mother of God, save us!**

Together with the eternal Word born of you, * richly pour out the grace of God * on those who praise you, O spouseless Mother; * and beseech Him without ceasing, O pure Virgin, * to forgive our sins.

In his prophetic vision, Habakkuk foresaw your coming, O Lord, * and so he declared: * The Lord is coming from Teman. * Glory to your infinite condescension, O Christ.

ODE 5

Tone 4 O Lord, You have come as the Light to this world, * the holy Light who draws from the darkness of ignorance * those who sing to You with faith.

Refrain: **Glory be to You, O Lord, glory be to You!**

Having come to the middle of this holy Feast, * let us hasten, O friends of God * to acquire also the perfection of virtues.

How holy indeed is this present solemnity! * It stands in the middle of the two great Feasts * and receives light from both of them.

Refrain: **Most holy Mother of God, save us!**

Even the archangel could not comprehend * the ineffable mystery of your immaculate birth, * O compassionate Savior born of the Virgin.

O Lord our God, give us your peace; * O Lord our God, take possession of us. * We know no other god but You, * and we call upon your name, O Lord.

ODE 6

Tone 4 Your Church cries out to You in a loud voice: * I offer You a sacrifice of praise, O Lord; * in your compassion You have purified it from the blood of demons * by the blood which flows from your side.

Refrain: **Glory be to You, O Lord, glory be to You!**

Today is the celebration of mid-Pentecost: * it is illuminated from one side by the divine splendor of the holy Pasch, * and from the other by the shining grace of the Paraclete.

You have come into the Temple, O Christ; You have spoken to the crowds assembled there, * revealing your proper majesty * and showing yourself to be the consubstantial Son of the Father.

Refrain: **Most holy Mother of God, save us!**

Be my refuge and protectress, O only Mother of God; * and in the dangers of this life, enlighten me with your divine brightness.

I am drowning in the surges of this life * as if beneath the waves of the ocean, * and as Jonah, I cry out to You, O Word: * Save my life from the Abyss, O merciful Lord.

KONTAKION

Tone 4 O Christ God, Creator and Lord of all, * when the Paschal Feast was half completed, * You told those present: Come and draw the water of immortality. * Let us, therefore, adore You and cry out with faith: * Grant us your goodness, * for You are the Source of our life.

IKOS

My soul has become sterile because of sin; * pour the streams of your blood over it and make it fertile in virtues; * for You have commanded all to come to You, O Word of God, * and to draw the waters of immortality * which cleanse the sins of those who sing of your divine and glorious Resurrection. * O God of goodness, send the strength of the Spirit, who truly descended from heaven, * upon your disciples who acknowledge your divinity, * for You are the Source of our life.

ODE 7

Tone 4 Inflamed more by their piety than by the heat of the flames, * the children of Abraham cried out in the furnace of the Persians: * Blessed are You, O Lord, in the temple of your glory.

Refrain: **Glory be to You, O Lord, glory be to you!**

By your strength, You have broken the power of Death, O

Lord, * and to the dead You have shown the way of life. * In thanksgiving they cry out: * Blessed are You, O Lord, in the temple of your glory.

The Pharisees saw You bearing our flesh, * but they did not acknowledge You as the Word of God. * However, we sing to You: * Blessed are You, O Lord, in the temple of your glory.

Refrain: **Most holy Mother of God, save us!**

Rejoice, O sanctified dwelling, O divine tabernacle of the Most High; * through you, O Mother of God, joy has been given to us and we cry out: * Blessed are you among women, O immaculate Queen.

With the help of God * the flaming furnace of the Chaldeans was covered with the dew of the Spirit, * and the youths began to sing: * Blessed are You, O God of our fathers.

ODE 8

Tone 4 Extending his hand into the pit, * Daniel closed the mouths of lions; * filled with the zeal of their faith, * the young men extinguished the power of the fire as they sang: * Bless the Lord, all you works of the Lord.

Refrain: **Glory be to You, O Lord, glory be to You!**

Coming forth from the tomb * in the beauty and brightness of your divinity, * You appeared to your apostles, O Lord, * and promised to send the power of the Spirit to those who sing: * Bless the Lord, all you works of the Lord.

As God, You put Death to death; * O Source of life, You gushed forth eternal life * which the grace of these bright days symbolizes for those who sing: * Bless the Lord, all you works of the Lord.

Let us bless the Lord, Father, Son, and Holy Spirit.

You have appeared, O Christ the Sun of Justice, * sending your apostles as rays of light to the world, * as divine bearers of the inaccessible light, * to chase away the darkness of error and to sing: * Bless the Lord, all you works of the Lord.

Now and ever: Behold, from the tribe of Judah comes the prince who will rule; * for you have given birth, O immaculate Virgin, * to the promise of old and the hope of the nations, * the Christ to whom we sing: * Bless the Lord, all you works of the Lord.

Let us praise, bless, and worship the Lord, singing and exalting Him above all forever.

The One who gloriously reigns and who is unceasingly glorified as God, * He it is that you angels in heaven must bless and praise and exalt forever.

OMIT MAGNIFICAT

ODE 9

Tone 4 Christ the cornerstone not hewn by any hand * has been hewn from you, O Virgin and untarnished mountain. * It is He who reunites the separate nations; * and so, filled with joy and gladness, we extol you, O Mother of God.

Refrain: **Glory be to You, O Lord, glory be to You!**

From Christ we have learned a new way of life; * let us strive with all our hearts to follow this * so that we may enjoy the coming of the Spirit.

The mortal nature that I bear, O Giver of life, * You have clothed with immortality; * with the grace that knows no curruption, O Savior, * You have raised my nature with You * and have led it to the Father to share in his peace.

Glory be: Having been called again to the life of heaven * by the powerful mediation of Him who humbled himself and became a servant * in order to raise us up to Him, * it is truly proper that we extol Him.

Now and ever: We the faithful, all believe * that you are the cause, the root, and the spring * from which our Source of immortality comes; * and in our hymns we praise you, * for you have brought forth the Lord and our Life.

Mothers cannot be virgins, nor virgins be mothers; * but in you, O Mother of God, * both virginity and motherhood were present. * Therefore, all the people of the earth unceasingly extol you.

CANON II

ODE 1

Tone 8 All you people, clap your hands; * Christ the Giver of life has broken the bonds of Hades, * He has raised up the dead, and by his word He healed the sick; * for He is our God and gives life to those who love his name.

Refrain: **Glory be to You, O Lord, glory be to You!**

Changing water into wine, You have worked a miracle, O

Lord, * You formerly changed the rivers of Egypt into blood;* and, as a new wonder, You have raised the dead. * Glory to your ineffable plan of salvation, O Lord; * glory to your condescension which raises us up to You.

O Lord, You are our resurrection; * You are the stream of eternal life; * You wished to know both hunger and thirst, O Savior. * Submitting to the laws of nature, You have come to Shechem * and asked the Samaritan woman to give You a drink.

You blessed the loaves and multiplied the fish, O God beyond understanding, * and You satisfied the crowds completely. * You promised the source of eternal wisdom to those who thirst; * You are our God, O Savior, who gives life to those who love your name.

Glory be: I glorify three persons sharing the same throne and the same eternity: * the Father, Son, and Holy Spirit, a unity of three persons * in the one supreme divinity.

Now and ever: In your womb only, O Mother of God, have you been able to contain your own creator. * O what a wonder! You remained a virgin while giving birth to Him. * Because He is your Son and God, * implore Him unceasingly for the sheep of your flock.

You walled up the sea and drowned Pharaoh and his chariots; * You saved your people by leading them across dry land, O Lord; * and You led to the mountain of holiness those who say: * Let us sing a hymn of victory to our God, for He is victorious in battle.

ODE 3

Tone 8 Do not judge by appearances, * said the Lord to those whom He was teaching * when He came into the Temple, as it is written, * in the middle of the Feast prescribed by the Law.

Refrain: **Glory be to You, O Lord, glory be to You!**

Do not judge by appearances: * Christ has truly come as the One foretold by the prophets; * He comes from Zion to gather the whole world.

If you do not believe in his words, * at least believe in the works of the Lord; * you shall err by rejecting the Holy One * of whom Moses spoke in the Law.

If the Messiah is to come into the world, * and if He has

already come, He is the Christ; * and you shall err by rejecting Him * of whom Moses spoke in the Law.

Glory be: Bowing before the Father, * let us praise the co-eternal Son and the Spirit of holiness, * adoring God in the one Trinity.

Now and ever: Without undergoing change, the Lord has become flesh * even though He is One of the Holy Trinity; * and the burning fire of his divinity * has not consumed the all pure womb of the Mother of God.

My heart is made firm in the Lord; * my strength exalts in my God; * my mouth is opened before my enemies; * for your salvation makes me dance with joy.

SESSIONAL HYMN

Tone 8 When the feast was half completed, You cried out in the middle of the Temple: * All who thirst, come to Me and drink, * for whoever shall drink from this divine river * shall receive the streams of my teaching flowing from my side. * Whoever sees Me as the One sent by the divine Father * shall be glorified with Me. * Therefore we cry out to You: * Glory to You, O Christ our God, * for You have poured out on your servants * the rich streams of your love for all.

Glory be...now and ever: You poured out the stream of wisdom and life for the world; * You invited your people to drink from the rivers of salvation; * for the ones who receive your divine Law * shall extinguish the burning coals of error in themselves. * They shall never again thirst in all eternity * and shall never lack your gifts, O Lord and heavenly King. * That is why we glorify your power, O Christ our God. * We ask You to take away our sins * and to grant your servants the abundance of your great mercy.

ODE 4

Tone 8 Christ, who has come among us, * is the Messiah announced by the prophets. * The works He does bear witness to this; * for He changed water into wine, * and by his word the Paralytic was healed.

Refrain: **Glory be to You, O Lord, glory be to You!**

Christ is the Messiah announced by the Scriptures. * He has come in truth, illuminating the entire universe; * and by his brilliant wonders, He shows us that He is truly the Source of life.

I have shown you only one work, * and you are already

amazed. * You practice circumcision even on the Sabbath; * why then do you reproach Me * for having healed the Paralytic by the power of my word?

I have worked numerous miracles; * for which one do you wish to stone Me? * Is it for having healed a man completely by my word? * Do not judge by appearances only.

With the help of the Holy Spirit, * Christ has worked among his divine apostles, * and relying on the prophets, * by striking signs He has led the nations to the knowledge of God.

Glory be: O indivisible Trinity * eternal Father, only Son, and Holy Spirit, * sharing the same throne and same glory in heaven, * save those who sing to your name; * O Giver of life, deliver us from all danger.

Now and ever: O divine Spouse and most pure Mother, * who contained in your womb the uncontainable God, * cease not to intercede for us * that we may be delivered from all danger; * for you are our refuge at all times.

In his prophetic vision, Habakkuk foresaw your coming, O Lord, * and so he declared: * The Lord is coming from Teman. * Glory to your infinite condescension, O Christ.

ODE 5

Tone 8 You made the apostles shine with brilliant works, * and You exalted your disciples throughout the whole world, * granting them glory, O God our Savior; * and You gave them the kingdom of heaven.

Refrain: **Glory be to You, O Lord, glory be to You!**

With their miracles and teaching * your disciples have enlightened the ends of the earth, * announcing in many ways, O Savior, the word of your kingdom.

We give glory to your majesty; * we offer You our hymns and songs, * because You have appeared on earth for us, * illuminating the world and calling the human race back to You.

Glory be: Glory to You, O holy Father, the unbegotten One; * glory to You, O only Son and Word beyond time; * glory to You, O divine Spirit who reigns with them, * and who shares the same nature as the Father and the Son.

Now and ever: Your womb, O Mother of God, has become the holy table * on which the heavenly bread, Christ our

God, now rests. * Those who eat this bread shall never die * as He who satisfied the whole world had promised.

O Lord our God, give us your peace; * O Lord our God, take possession of us. * We know no other god but You, * and we call upon your name, O Lord.

ODE 6

Tone 8 You encompass the whole world, O Jesus; * yet at the mid-point of the Feast, * You came into the Temple and taught the crowds your word of truth, * as the holy evangelist John says.

Refrain: **Glory be to You, O Lord, glory be to You!**

Opening your lips, O Lord, * You proclaimed the timeless Father and the Spirit of holiness to the world; * and You remained consubstantial with them even after your incarnation.

You fulfilled the work of the Father, * and your works confirmed your word. * You accomplished healings and miracles, O Savior, * raising up the Paralytic, purifying lepers, and resurrecting the dead.

The timeless Son has entered into time; * He has become a man and assumed our human condition. * In the middle of the Feast, He taught, saying: * Hasten and draw from the inexhaustible Source of life.

Glory be: We, the faithful, all glorify the one divinity in three persons, * indivisible and uncreated, * the Father, Son, and Holy Spirit.

Now and ever: We praise your virginity which remained after your giving birth; * we glorify you as Virgin and Mother, * O only pure and virginal Spouse; * for God has truly taken flesh in your womb to give us life.

I am drowning in the surges of this life * as if beneath the waves of the ocean, * and as Jonah, I cry out to You, O Word: * Save my life from the Abyss, O merciful Lord.

KONTAKION

Tone 4 O Christ God, Creator and Lord of all, * when the Paschal Feast was half completed, * You told those present: Come and draw the water of immortality. * Let us, therefore, adore You and cry out with faith: * Grant us your goodness, * for You are the Source of our life.

IKOS

My soul has become sterile because of sin; * pour the streams of your blood over it and make it fertile in virtues; * for You have commanded all to come to You, O Word of God, * and to draw the waters of immortality * which cleanse the sins of those who sing of your divine and glorious Resurrection. * O God of goodness, send the strength of the Spirit, who truly descended from heaven, * upon your disciples who acknowledge your divinity, * for You are the Source of our life.

ODE 7

Tone 8 You felt bodily fatigue, O Lord, * yet You give rest to all. * You felt thirst, O Source of miracles; * and asking for water, You promised us the living water of salvation.

Refrain: **Glory be to You, O Lord, Glory be to You!**

You spoke with the Samaritan woman, O Lord, * and You refuted the foolishness of the impious. * The first acknowledged You as the Messiah, * and the others did not believe that You are the Son of God.

O Source who brings forth immortality, * You promised the living water which springs up to eternal life, O Savior, * to those who receive from You the Holy Spirit * who proceeds from the eternal Father.

With five loaves You fed thousands of hungry people, * and with what was left over * they gathered enough to feed thousands more, * and thus your disciples glorified You, O Savior.

Those who eat your bread shall live forever, * and those who drink your blood shall live in You * and You shall live in them; * and You will raise them up on the last day.

O Lord, You work wonders in your plan of salvation; * by your miracles You confirm your divine power. * You dispel illnesses and raise the dead, * and to the blind You give divine brightness.

You cleansed lepers; * You raised up the lame and the Paralytic Man; * You healed the woman with the hemorrhage; * You walked on water as on dry land, * showing your glory to your disciples, O Lord.

Glory be: O Lord, we bow before your Father beyond time * and before the grace of your Holy Spirit, * whom You shared with your apostles * as You sent them to preach the good news of salvation.

Now and ever: In your womb you enclosed the boundless One, * and with your breasts you fed the Nourisher of the world; * and in your arms you carried the Creator of the world, O holy Mother of God.

With the help of God * the flaming furnace of the Chaldeans was covered with the dew of the Spirit, * and the youths began to sing: * Blessed are You, O God of our fathers.

ODE 8

Tone 8 Come, all you people and behold: * The One who is praised as the King of glory in heaven * is slandered by the crowds of the ungodly. * Seeing this, sing to the Messiah * who has spoken through the prophets of old.

Refrain: **Glory be to You, O Lord, glory be to You!**

You are truly the Christ who comes into the world; * You are the source of salvation, * and with You is the forgiveness of the sins of our fathers; * You are truly the life of the people who hope in You.

In the middle of the Feast, * the Wisdom of God comes into the Temple, as it is written, * and He begins to teach that the Messiah, the Christ, * truly is the One who gives life to the world.

On the Sabbath as on other days * Christ worked wondrous miracles, * caring for those afflicted with various illnesses; * but the Pharisees became angry with Him.

On a Sabbath day Christ healed the Paralytic Man * who had been lying on his mat for many years. * Doing this, He broke the Law and brought upon himself * the insults of those who were watching.

Did not Moses prescribe circumcision in the Law? * That is why you circumcise even on the Sabbath, * and heal the body of this man completely!

The ungrateful people who formerly dwelt in the desert * have seized their Benefactor in hatred; * filled with conceit, they wag their tongues in blasphemy.

Let us bless the Lord, Father, Son, and Holy Spirit.

The Holy Trinity is but one God, * and there is no change in either the Father or the Son * when one begets and the other is begotten; * and I glorify the triple light of the divinity forever.

Now and ever: Tell us how you gave birth to the Light * who comes forth eternally from the Father * and whom we praise with the Holy Spirit, * the One who wished to be born of your womb, * and who alone knew this throughout the ages.

Let us praise, bless, and worship the Lord, singing and exalting Him above all forever.

The One who gloriously reigns and who is unceasingly glorified as God, * He it is that you angels in heaven must bless and praise and exalt forever.

OMIT MAGNIFICAT

ODE 9

Tone 8 In the middle of the Feast of fifty days * You came into the Temple, O Savior, * and You began to teach the astonished Pharisees who said: * How does He know the Scriptures since He has never been taught?

Refrain: **Glory be to You, O Lord, glory be to You!**

Gushing forth streams of grace and salvation, * You performed wondrous signs, O Redeemer, * healing the infirmed and dispelling illnesses; * but the Pharisees became angry at seeing the miracles You accomplished.

Reproving those who accused You in the Temple, You cried out, O Redeemer: * Do not judge by appearances, but by what is right, * for the Law itself prescribes that you should circumcise a man on the Sabbath.

You granted the greatest of miracles, O Savior, * to your disciples, as You promised; * You sent them to preach your glory throughout the whole world. * They proclaimed to all people * the grace of your Incarnation and your holy Resurrection.

If you circumcise on a Sabbath day * without breaking or violating the Law, * why do you reproach Me * for having healed a man completely by my word? * Do not judge by the flesh but by the Spirit.

O Word who healed a withered hand by your word, * come and till the dried-up land of my heart; * make it bear much fruit * so that I too may offer You the fruits of repentance, O Savior.

Purifying the leprosy of my heart * and illuminating the eyes of my soul, * make me rise up, O Word of God, from this bed of grief on which I am stretched out * as the

Paralytic who was lying on his mat.

Glory be: The praise of your name is foreign to the impious, * O Father, Son, and Holy Spirit, * eternal essence, all-powerful and uncreated, * who laid the foundations of the whole world * by a sign of your divine will.

Now and ever: In your womb, O Virgin Mother of God, * you sheltered One of the Holy Trinity, Christ, the Fountain of life, * whom all creation praises and before whom the angels stand and tremble. * Intercede with Him that our souls may be saved.

Mothers cannot be virgins, nor virgins be mothers; * but in you, O Mother of God, * both virginity and motherhood were present. * Therefore, all the people of the earth unceasingly extol you.

HYMN OF LIGHT

Tone 3 You hold the inexhaustible chalice of gifts; * grant that I may draw living water for the remission of my sins * that I may be overcome by thirst for You, * O only compassionate One. *(3 times)*

AT THE PRAISES

Tone 4 The Wisdom, the Power, and the Image of the Father, * the eternal Word and Son of God, * came to the Temple in the flesh. * He taught the chosen people, ignorant and hard-hearted; * they marveled at the depth of his wisdom, saying among themselves: * How can this man know the Scriptures when He has never studied? *(2 times)*

Christ the Messiah argued with the Pharisees; * He disputed with the Scribes, crying out to them: * Do not judge by appearances, you deceitful transgressors. * I healed the Paralytic on the Sabbath. * I am the Lord of both the Sabbath and the Law. * Why do you seek to kill Me, who will give life to the dead?

The ungrateful people of Israel, the fearful transgressors, * threatened to stone Moses. * Isaiah was hewn asunder with a wooden saw; * wise Jeremiah was thrown into a filthy pit. * After all this, they raised the Lord on the cross and scoffed at Him: * Would You destroy the Temple? * Save yourself, and then we will believe in you.

Tone 4 **Glory be...now and ever:** O faithful, newly illumined by the Resurrection of Christ our Savior, * we have reached the middle of the Master's Feast. * Let us keep the commandments of God in sincerity. * Thus we shall be made worthy to celebrate his Ascension * and the coming of the Holy Spirit.

GREAT DOXOLOGY AND DISMISSAL

Wednesday Evening Vespers

AT PSALM 140

Tone 1 By your death, O Christ, You destroyed the dominion of Death. * By your glorious rising You gave life to all. * You raised the human race with yourself by your condescension. * So we sing to You in grateful praise, * celebrating the feast of your radiant Resurrection on the third day * for the midpoint of these precious days has shone for us, * O Benefactor of our souls, Jesus the Giver of life.

Before your precious Cross and passion, O almighty Christ, * You performed most glorious miracles among the peoples. * As it is written, in the midst of the Feast of the Law, You cried out: * If anyone thirsts, let him come to Me * and draw the drink of divine water and life. * I grant the water of life and power and wisdom to all; * for this I have willed to become a man, as the Lover of Mankind.

Seeing me paralyzed on the bed of my sins, * O all-merciful Christ, * You took pity on my useless limbs; * You willed to become incarnate for me, * flooding me with the great sea of Your love. * You have come to me invisibly, * raising me up as the Paralytic of old, * teaching me to walk in the ways of your commandments. * Never permit me to depart from You, O Savior, * as the people of old abandoned You, * even though they witnessed many miracles before your Passion, * O our God, who willingly suffered in the flesh for our sake.

Three Stichera from the Saint of the day

Tone 2 **Glory be...now and ever:** When You came to the Temple, O Christ, in the middle of the Feast, * You taught the people, saying: * Whoever believes in Me, even if he dies, he shall live. * The Pharisees and Sadducees and Scribes were enraged and cried: * Who is this man to utter blasphemies? * They did not understand that You are our

God, * glorified with the Father and the Spirit before the ages. Glory to You!

APOSTICHA

Tone 3 O Christ, who darkened the sun by your passion * and enlightened all creation by your Resurrection, * accept our evening prayer, for You love all people.

Through all the world their voice resounds; their message reaches to the ends of the earth.

Your teaching has gone forth to all the earth, O holy Apostles. * You have destroyed the captive power of idols * by proclaiming the knowledge of God. * This is your good work, O holy ones. * For this we praise and glorify your memory.

God is to be feared in his holy place. He is the Lord, the God of Israel.

Your martyrs, O Lord, have been confirmed by faith * and strengthened by hope. * By the love of your cross they have been spiritually fortified, * and so have overcome the anguish of suffering. * They have obtained the crowns, * and together with the angels they pray for our souls.

Tone 3 **Glory be...now and ever:** In the middle of the Feast * let us glorify Him who worked salvation in the middle of the earth. * The Life was hanging on the tree between two thieves. * He was silent with the one who blasphemed, * but the one who believed heard: * Today you will be with Me in Paradise. * He descended into the tomb, destroying Hades * and He arose on the third day, saving our souls.

TROPARIA

Of the Saint

Tone 8 **Glory be...now and ever:** When the Paschal Feast is half completed, * quench my thirsty soul with the waters of devotion; * for You, O Savior, have announced to all: * Let all who are thirsty come to Me and drink. * O Christ our God, Source of our life, * glory be to You!

Thursday Matins

SESSIONAL HYMN I

Tone 3 To lead home the entire human race, * You came to dwell among us and were nailed to the Cross, my Creator. * You chose to endure death as a man * in order to free humanity from Death as God. * Therefore, we cry to You as our life-giving Lord: * Glory to your Resurrection, O Christ.

Their span extends through all the earth; their words to the utmost bounds of the world.

You have illumined the memory of your apostles, O Lord, * and You have given them the strength to imitate your Passion, O almighty God. * They have courageously conquered the power of Satan * and received the gift of healing. * By their prayers, O Lord, grant peace to the world.

God is to feared in his holy place. He is the Lord, the God of Israel.

Strengthened with the armor of Christ, * and having put on the weapons of faith, * you confronted the legions of the Enemy and courageously overcame them. * Sustained by your hope for life, * you stood up to the trials and torments of the tyrants, * and thus you have received the crown, O victorious witnesses of Christ our God.

Glory be...now and ever: The prophets have announced, and the apostles have taught, * the martyrs have confessed, and we ourselves have believed * that you are truly the Mother of God, * and we extol your ineffable birth-giving.

SESSIONAL HYMN II

Tone 8 Standing in the middle of the Temple, O Lord, * You commanded the attention of all who came to the Feast. * They heard your divine cry: * Let all who thirst come to Me and drink. * All who drink from the river of my teachings * shall overflow with divine life. * Those who believe in Me shall be glorified with Me by the Father who sent Me. * Therefore, we cry to You: Glory to You, O Christ our God. * You have poured out on your servants the torrent of your love.

Glory be...now and ever: *(Repeat the above)*

Having beheld the Resurrection of Christ...

CÁNON

(From the Feast of Mid-Pentecost, pages 158-171)

HYMN OF LIGHT

Tone 3 You hold the inexhaustible chalice of gifts; * grant that I may draw living water for the remission of my sins * so that I may be overcome by thirst for You, * O only compassionate One. *(3 times)*

AT THE PRAISES

Tone 3 O Master, the Lover of Mankind, * in your light we see light. * For You have risen from the dead, * granting salvation to the human race. * Let all creation glorify You; * have mercy on us, O sinless One. *(2 times)*

O holy Apostles, you have kept the commandments of Christ without blemish; * what you have received as a gift, you have given as a gift, * healing the passions of our souls and bodies; * and through the favor you have with God, * intercede in our behalf that our souls may be saved.

As stars you have enlightened the whole world * even after your death, O holy Martyrs; * having fought the good fight, you are able to intercede before Christ * that He may grant great mercy to our souls.

Tone 4 **Glory be...now and ever:** Before ascending the Cross, O Lord, * You went up to the Temple in the middle of the Feast. * You taught the Jews with authority concerning the Law; * for You yourself gave the Law to Moses. * They were astounded by the boundless mystery of your wisdom, * yet they contrived malice against You in their envy, saying: * This man has never studied the Scriptures with the Scribes. * They refused to recognize You as the Savior of our souls.

APOSTICHA

Tone 2 Great are You, O our King! * Glorious is your power. * Wondrously You assumed poverty, * filling all creation with inexhaustible gifts of grace.

Remember your people whom You chose long ago.

Standing in the Temple, * in the middle of the Feast, * You quenched our thirst with streams of divine grace, * gushing from You, O compassionate One.

God is our King from time past, the Giver of help through all the land.

Wishing to save me, * You were clothed in flesh most wondrously * without seed from the Virgin. * Now from the midst of your Temple, * You have poured grace on me.

Tone 8 **Glory be...now and ever:** In the middle of the Feast, * before your Passion and glorious Resurrection, * You taught the unbelievers in the Temple, O gracious Lord. * You cried out to the Scribes and Pharisees: * Let all who thirst come to Me and drink! * From the hearts of those who believe in Me * rivers of living water, the Spirit of God, shall flow! * Your wisdom and understanding are far beyond our words. * Glory to You, our God who perfects all things!

Thursday Evening Vespers

AT PSALM 140

Tone 4 The midpoint of the Feast has arrived; * the days which begin with the Resurrection of the Savior * and are fulfilled in the divine Feast of Pentecost. * Truly it unites both Feasts * and draws light from their double brightness, * giving honor to the Ascension of the Lord * which prefigures our glory.

Truly Zion heard and was glad * when it received the glad tidings of the Resurrection of Christ. * Faithful children also rejoiced at beholding it. * Seeing the blood of Christ washed away by the Holy Spirit, * the Church prepares to worthily celebrate * the joyous midpoint of these two holy Feasts.

The over-abundant outpouring of the divine Spirit over all is drawing near, * as it is written by the prophet Joel. * The promise of Christ, given to his disciples * after his death, burial, and resurrection, * proclaims the coming of the Comforter.

Three Stichera from the Saint of the day

Tone 6 **Glory be...now and ever:** The midweek of the festal season has arrived, O Christ, * the midpoint of your Resurrection and the coming of your Holy Spirit. * Coming together, we glorify the mystery of your miracles; * and filled with fear, we cry out to You: * Send down upon us your great mercy!

APOSTICHA

Tone 3 The tree of disobedience gave the world the flower of death * while the tree of the Cross blossomed into life and immortality. * We, therefore, worship You, O crucified Christ. * Let the light of your countenance shine upon us.

Through all the world their voice resounds; their message reaches to the ends of the earth.

By your Cross, O Christ our Savior, * the power of Death has been vanquished, * and the deceit of the devil has been destroyed. * Therefore, the human race, saved by faith, * offers You hymns of praise forever.

God is to be feared in his holy place. He is the Lord, the God of Israel.

Great is the power of your Cross, O Lord, * for though it was set in one place, it acts throughout the world. * It made apostles of fishermen * and martyrs of the Gentiles. * We beg them to intercede for our souls.

Tone 8 **Glory be...now and ever:** In the middle of the Feast, * before your passion and glorious Resurrection, * You taught the unbelievers in the Temple, O gracious Lord. * You cried out to the Scribes and Pharisees: * Let all who thirst come to Me and drink! * From the hearts of those who believe in Me * rivers of living water, the Spirit of God, shall flow! * Your wisdom and understanding are far beyond our words. * Glory to You, our God who perfects all things!

TROPARIA

Of the Saint

Tone 8 **Glory be...now and ever:** When the Paschal Feast is half completed, * quench my thirsty soul with the waters of devotion; * for You, O Savior, have announced to all: * Let all who are thirsty come to Me and drink. * O Christ our God, Source of our life, * glory be to You!

Friday Matins

SESSIONAL HYMN I

Tone 3 Having chosen to suffer death on a cross, * You planted it in the middle of creation. * Your body was willingly nailed on it to save us, * and, therefore, the sun hid its rays. * Seeing this, the good thief acknowledged you as God, * and because of his faith he gained Paradise, crying to You: * Remember me, O Lord, in your kingdom.

I will praise You, Lord, with all my heart; I will recount all your wonders.

We, the faithful, discoursing on divine things, * touch a wondrous mystery: * his Crucifixion which our minds cannot comprehend, * and his Resurrection which our words cannot describe. * For today Death and Hades are despoiled; * the human race is clothed in incorruption; * and we cry in thanksgiving: * Glory to your Resurrection, O Christ!

Arise then, Lord, lift up your hand. O God, do not forget the poor!

Your courage and your steadfastness have overcome the traps of the Enemy, * O victorious Martyrs worthy of all honor. * You have deserved unending happiness; * now intercede with the Lord * that He may save his flock who loves Christ.

Glory be...now and ever: As a scepter of power, O Mother of God, * we have the Cross of your Son. * By it we humble the pride of the Enemy, * and we extol you unceasingly with all our heart.

SESSIONAL HYMN II

Tone 8 The waters of life and wisdom flow upon the world, O Savior. * You have called everyone to draw from the well of salvation. * If anyone receives your divine law, * the flames of the Deceiver will surely be quenched in him. * Those who drink of your fullness shall never thirst again, * O Master, King of heaven. * Therefore, we glorify your power, O Christ our God. * Grant us forgiveness of our sins. * Send down abundant blessings on your servants.

Glory be...now and ever...*(Repeat the above)*

Having beheld the Resurrection of Christ...

CANON

(From the Feast of Mid-Pentecost, pages 158-171)

HYMN OF LIGHT

Tone 3 You hold the inexhaustible chalice of gifts; * grant that I may draw living water for the remission of my sins * so that I may be overcome by thirst for You, * O only compassionate One. *(3 times)*

AT THE PRAISES

Tone 3 By pride I was cast out from joy, * a corpse falling into the deep, * but you did not abandon me, O Master. * Because of me, you were lifted upon the Cross. * You have saved me, carrying me to glory; * O my Redeemer, glory to You! *(2 times)*

Come together, all you nations, * and understand the might of this awesome mystery! * Our Savior, the Word from the beginning, * has suffered crucifixion and burial for us of his own will. * On the third day He rose again to save us all. * Let us worship Him.

Come, all you faithful, * let us honor the memory of the martyrs. * They became a spectacle to angels and people; * they have received crowns of victory from Christ; * and they ceaselessly pray for our souls.

Tone 8 **Glory be...now and ever:** In the middle of the Feast of the Law, * our Savior went up to the Temple. * He stood in the midst of the crowd, * teaching them with authority: * I am the Light of the world. * All who follow Me shall not walk in darkness * but shall have the light of immortal life.

APOSTICHA

Tone 2 You wished to raise me * from the death of sin * and united me to the Father, * O eternal Word and Lover of Mankind.

Remember your people whom You chose long ago.

Darkness is driven away; * for behold, the Messiah, in the midst of the Feast, * has put it to flight * with grace as bright as the morning star.

God is our King from time past, the Giver of help through all the land.

The Savior cries: Come and draw near in faith, * all those who long to drink of the living waters . * Drink grace and be filled with joy divine.

Tone 8 **Glory be...now and ever:** Let us cleanse our thoughts to the very depths * that our souls may be brilliantly illumined. * Then we shall see Christ * who by his boundless goodness taught in the Temple, * who endured the agony of the Cross and rose from the dead, * triumphing over the Enemy and saving our race. * To Him let us cry: * Glory to You, O incomprehensible Lord!

Friday Evening Vespers

AT PSALM 140

Tone 1 The Creator of all and Giver of life, * the Word co-eternal with the divine Father * who willed to take flesh from the Virgin, becoming a man, * has manifested the unspeakable teachings of wisdom to all.

In the midst of the Feast, O Christ, * You stood in the Temple, O Master of the Law, * teaching with authority and refuting the Scribes, * amazing all with the wisdom of your words and wondrous signs, * as in the past, Moses wrote of You.

The Giver of wisdom and bestower of blessings, * pouring out divine streams from the inexhaustible fountain, cried out: * Come to Me, all who thirst, and draw the water of life; * rivers of divine grace shall flow from you.

Three Stichera from the Saint of the day

Tone 1 **Glory be:** The middle of the fifty days is here * in which Christ clearly disclosed his divine power. * He made the Paralytic whole and raised him from his bed by a word; * He worked miracles in the flesh, * granting to all eternal life and great mercy.

Tone 3 **Now and ever:** O most honorable Virgin, we are filled with awe * when we consider that you gave birth to Christ who is both God and man. * O immaculate Lady, without knowing man, * you gave birth in the flesh to a Son without a human father. * This Son, from all eternity, was begotten by God the Father without a mother; * and, when He took on our human nature, * He did not undergo any change. * Nothing was added to his divine nature, nor was it divided. * The properties of both his divine and human nature remained intact. * We, therefore, entreat you, O blessed Virgin, * to save the souls of those who, in true faith, * acknowledge you as the Mother of God.

APOSTICHA

Tone 3 By your Cross, O Christ our Savior, * the power of Death has been vanquished, * and the deceit of the devil has been destroyed. * Therefore, the human race, saved by faith, * offers You hymns of praise forever.

The Lord is king, with majesty enrobed; the Lord has robed himself with might, He has girded himself with power.

O Lord, all creation has been enlightened by your Resurrection, * and Paradise has been reopened; * therefore, all creation extols You * and offers You hymns of praise forever.

The world You made firm, not to be moved; your throne has stood firm from of old.

I glorify the power of the Father, Son, and Holy Spirit; *

and I praise the dominion of the undivided Divinity, * the consubstantial Trinity * who reigns forever and ever.

Holiness is fitting to your house, O Lord, until the end of time.

O Christ, who darkened the sun by your passion * and enlightened all creation by your Resurrection, * accept our evening prayer, for You love all people.

Tone 1 **Glory be...now and ever:** You came to the Holy of Holies, O Wisdom of God, * in the middle of the Feast * to teach and edify the Scribes and the Pharisees: * Let all who thirst come to Me * and drink the water of life that they may never thirst. * Whoever believes in Me, streams of living water shall flow from them. * How great is your goodness and compassion, O Christ God. Glory to You!

TROPARIA

Of the Saint

Tone 8 **Glory be...now and ever:** When the Paschal Feast is half completed, * quench my thirsty soul with the waters of devotion; * for You, O Savior, have announced to all: * Let all who are thirsty come to Me and drink. * O Christ our God, Source of our life, * glory be to You!

Saturday Matins

SESSIONAL HYMN I

Tone 3 Christ is risen from the dead, * He who is the first-fruits of those that had been asleep, * the first-born of creation and the Creator of all things that were made. * By himself He renewed the nature of our corrupt race. * Therefore, O Death, you shall reign no more; * for the Lord of all nullified your power and dissolved it.

Arise then, Lord, lift up your hand. O God, do not forget the poor!

When You tasted death in the flesh, O Lord, * You took away the bitterness of death by your Resurrection, * and made the human race prevail over it, * restoring victory over the ancient curse. * Therefore, O Protector of our life, glory to You!

Glory be...now and ever: We praise you as the mediatrix of our salvation, O Virgin Theotokos. * For your Son, our God, who took flesh from you, * endured the passion of the

Cross, * delivering us from corruption as the Lover of Mankind.

SESSIONAL HYMN II

Tone 8 In the middle of the Feast of the Law, * my Savior went up to the Temple to teach. * He exposed the ignorance of the faithless ones. * The Lover of Mankind cried to the crowd in a mighty voice: * Let all who thirst come to Me and drink. * I promise that those who believe in Me will drink from the river of pure wisdom. * We, your people, cry to You: * Send down your most Holy Spirit upon us, O Christ our God, * and save us, for You are rich in mercy.

Glory be...now and ever: *(Repeat the above)*

Having beheld the Resurrection of Christ...

CANON

(From the Feast of Mid-Pentecost, pages 158-171)

HYMN OF LIGHT

Tone 3 You hold the inexhaustible chalice of gifts; * grant that I may draw living water for the remission of my sins * so that I may be overcome by thirst for You, * O only compassionate One. *(3 times)*

AT THE PRAISES

Tone 3 Come together, all you nations, * and understand the might of this awesome mystery! * Our Savior, the Word from the beginning, * has suffered crucifixion and burial for us of his own will. * On the third day He rose again to save us all. * Let us worship Him.

The soldiers that guarded You, O Lord, * related all the wonders which had come to pass; * but the vain assembly of the Sanhedrin filled their hands with bribes, * thinking they could hide your Resurrection which is glorified through all the world. * Have mercy on us.

All creation was filled with joy * when it received the news of your Resurrection. * When Mary Magdalene went to your tomb, * she found an angel in shining garments sitting on the stone. * He said: Why do you seek the Living among the dead? * He is not here; He is risen as He said. * He goes before you to Galilee.

O Master, the Lover of Mankind, * in your light we see light. * For You have risen from the dead, * granting salvation to the human race. * Let all creation glorify You; * have mercy on us, O sinless One.

Tone 4 **Glory be...now and ever:** O faithful, newly illumined by the Resurrection of Christ our Savior, * we have reached the middle of the Master's Feast. * Let us keep God's commandments in sincerity. * Thus we shall be made worthy to celebrate his Ascension * and to attain to the coming of the Holy Spirit.

APOSTICHA

Tone 2 The fountain, flowing with spiritual drink of wisdom, * has entered the Temple. * Shall we not drink our fill of divine teaching?

Remember your people whom You chose long ago.

Your ungrateful people * sought to kill You, O Word, * when they heard You proclaiming to the crowd * the teachings of salvation.

God is our King from time past, the Giver of help through all the land.

You came, O Creator, and stood on Zion * in the midst of your people; * You offered to them * salvation and grace.

Tone 4 **Glory be...now and ever:** Before ascending the Cross, O Lord, * You went up to the Temple in the middle of the Feast. * You taught the Jews with authority concerning the Law, * for You yourself gave the Law to Moses. * They were astounded by the boundless mystery of your wisdom, * yet they contrived malice against You in their envy, saying: * This man has never studied the Scriptures with the Scribes. * They refused to recognize You as the Savior of our souls.

Sunday of the Samaritan Woman

Vespers

AT PSALM 140

Tone 4 We never cease to adore your life-giving Cross, O Christ our God, * and we glorify your Resurrection on the third day. * For You, almighty One, have thereby restored the corrupted nature of all * and reopened the way to heaven, * since You alone are gracious and You love all people.

O Savior, You have absolved the penalty of disobedience, * committed through the tree of Eden, * by willingly being nailed to the tree of the Cross. * As almighty God, You descended into Hades * and broke asunder the bonds of death. * We, therefore, venerate your Resurrection from the dead * and joyfully cry out to You: * almighty Lord, glory to You!

O Lord, You have battered down the gates of Hades, * and by your death You have dissolved the realm of Death. * You have freed the human race from corruption, * bestowing life, incorruption, and your great mercy upon the world.

Come, all you people, * let us sing the praises of our Savior's Resurrection on the third day. * For we have thereby been delivered from the invincible bonds of Hades, * and we have received incorruption together with eternal life. * Therefore, we cry out to You * after your crucifixion, burial, and resurrection: * Save us by your Resurrection, for You love all people.

The midpoint of the Feast has arrived; * the days which begin with the Resurrection of the Savior * and are fulfilled in the divine Feast of Pentecost. * Truly it unites both Feasts * and draws light from their double brightness, * giving honor to the Ascension of the Lord, * which prefigures our glory.

Truly Zion heard and was glad * when it received the glad tidings of the Resurrection of Christ. * Faithful children also rejoiced at beholding it. * Seeing the blood of Christ washed away by the Holy Spirit, * the Church prepares to worthily celebrate * the joyous midpoint of these two holy Feasts.

The over-abundant outpouring of the divine Spirit over all is drawing near, * as it is written by the prophet Joel. * The promise of Christ, given to his disciples * after his death, burial, and resurrection, * proclaims the coming of the Comforter.

Tone 1 At the sixth hour, You came to the well, O Fountain of Wonders, * to ensnare the fruit of Eve; * for at that very hour, * she had been driven from Paradise by the guile of the serpent. * When the Samaritan woman came to draw water, * You said to her, O Savior: * Give Me water to drink, and I will give you waters of eternal life. * And the woman hastened to the city and proclaimed to the people: * Come and see Christ the Lord, the Savior of our souls.

Tone 2 When the Lord came to the well of Jacob, * the Samaritan woman entreated Him, saying: * Give me the water of faith, O Giver of life, * that I may obtain the waters of baptism, joy, and salvation. * O Lord, glory to You!

Truly, the Son, Word of God, co-eternal with the Father, * the Fountain of Wonders himself, came to the fountain, * where a woman of Samaria came to draw water. * And when the Savior saw her, He said to her: * Give Me water to drink and go call your husband. * But she addressed Him as man and not as God; * wishing to conceal the truth from Him, * she said: I have no husband. * And the Master replied: You have said the truth, that you have no husband; * for you have had five husbands, * and the one whom you now have is not your husband. * Amazed by these words, she went to the town * and proclaimed to the crowds, saying: * Come and behold Christ who grants the world great mercy.

Tone 6 **Glory be:** Jesus met the Samaritan woman at Jacob's well. * The One who covers the earth with clouds asks water of her. * O, what a wonder! * The One who rides on the Cherubim converses with an adulterous woman. * The One who suspended the earth on the waters asks for water. * The One who caused the springs of water and their lakes to overflow seeks water. * He truly desires to save this woman from the snares of the Enemy * and to fill her with living water * to extinguish the flames of her passions; * for He alone is compassionate and the Lover of Mankind.

Tone 4 **Now and ever:** O Mother of God, David, the Prophet and Forefather of Christ, foretold in song * the great things that would happen to you. * He revealed that you would be a queen, * standing at the right hand of God; * and that you would be the Mother of Life and Intercessor for the world. * He prophesied that God, in his good will toward all, * would become incarnate of you without a human father. * Thus He would restore his image within us * which had become disfigured by our passions. * He would seek out the lost sheep that was trapped in the hills; * He would lift it upon his shoulder and carry it to his Father * who would place it in the midst of his heavenly hosts. * In like manner, Christ will save the world because of his great and abundant mercy.

APOSTICHA

Tone 4 In being lifted upon the Cross, O Lord, * You abolished the curse which we had inherited from our ancestors. * By going down into Hades, * You freed from eternal captivity those imprisoned there * and granted incorruption to the human race. * We, therefore, praise your life-giving and redeeming Resurrection.

PASCHAL HYMNS

Let God arise and let his enemies be scattered, and let those who hate Him flee from before his face.

Today the sacred Pasch is revealed to us, * holy and new Pasch, * the mystical Passover, * the venerable Passover, * the Pasch which is Christ the Redeemer, * spotless Pasch, great Pasch, * the Pasch of the faithful, * the Pasch which is the key to the gates of Paradise, * the Pasch which sanctifies all the faithful.

As smoke vanishes, so let them vanish as wax melts before the fire.

O Women, * be the heralds of good news and tell what you saw; * tell of the vision and say to Zion: * Accept the good news of joy from us, * the news that Christ has risen. * Exalt and celebrate * and rejoice, O Jerusalem, * seeing Christ the King coming from the tomb * like a bridegroom.

So let the wicked perish at the presence of God, and let the righteous ones rejoice.

The myrrh-bearing women * arrived just before the dawn * at the tomb of the Giver of Life * and found an angel seated on the stone * who spoke these words to them: * Why do you seek the Living among the dead? * Why do you mourn the Incorruptible among those subject to decay? * Go, announce the good news * to his disciples.

This is the day that the Lord has made; let us exalt and rejoice in it.

Pasch so delightful, * Pasch of the Lord is the Pasch, * most honored Pasch now dawned on us. * It is the Pasch! * Therefore, let us joyfully embrace one another. * O Passover, save us from sorrow; * for today Christ has shown forth from the tomb * as from a bridal chamber * and filled the women with joy by saying: * Announce the good news * to my apostles.

Tone 8 **Glory be:** When You appeared in the flesh, O Christ God, * to accomplish your plan of salvation, * the Samaritan woman heard the word of God's love for us. * She left the well and ran to the town and said: * Come and see the One who knows the secrets of our hearts; * can this be the Christ, the Messiah whom we await, * the One who bestows great mercy?

Tone 5 **Now and ever:** This is the Resurrection Day. * Let us be enlightened by this Feast, * and let us embrace one another. * Let us call Brethren * even those who hate us, * and in the Resurrection, * forgive everything; and let us sing: * Christ is risen from the dead! * By death He conquered Death, * and to those in the graves He granted life.

TROPARIA

Tone 4 The joyful message of the Resurrection * was heard by the faithful women from the angel. * And being freed from the ancestral curse, * they boasted to the apostles: * Dead and despoiled is Death; * Christ our God is risen, * giving great mercy to the world.

Tone 8 **Glory be...now and ever:** When the Paschal Feast is half completed, * quench my thirsty soul with the waters of devotion; * for You, O Savior, have announced to all: * Let all who are thirsty come to Me and drink. * O Christ our God, Source of our life, * glory be to You!

Sunday Matins

SESSIONAL HYMN I

Tone 4 The myrrh-bearing women looked into the entrance of the tomb, * and because they could not bear the brilliance of the angel, * they trembled in astonishment and said: * Has He who opened Paradise to the thief been stolen, * or is He who proclaimed his Resurrection before his passion now risen? * Truly, Christ is risen, * granting resurrection and life to those in Hades.

Arise then, Lord, lift up your hand. O God, do not forget the poor!

You are risen, O immortal Savior, * and have raised the whole world with You. * By your power, O Christ our God, * You have crushed the dominion of Death. * You have shown your Resurrection to all, O God of mercy; * for You love us and we glorify You.

Glory be...now and ever: O Mother of God, the mystery hidden from all eternity * and unknown even to the angels, * was revealed through you to those on earth: * God took on our human nature * and united it to his divine nature in a perfect but unconfused union. * Then He willingly accepted the Cross for our sake * and thereby raised again the first created man * and saved our souls from death.

SESSIONAL HYMN II

Tone 4 Descending from his heavenly sanctuary, * Gabriel came to the stone where the Rock of life was buried; * clothed in a white garment, he cried out to the weeping women: * Put an end to your funeral hymns, * for He whom you love will always be with you. * Take courage, for He is truly risen, * He whom you seek amid your tears. * Go and announce to the apostles that the Lord is risen.

I will praise You, Lord, with all my heart; I will recount all your wonders.

You suffered crucifixion willingly, O Savior, * and mortals placed You into a new tomb, * even though You established the ends of the world with a word. * Death, our enemy, was bound and defeated through your life-giving Resurrection. * All those held captive in Hades cried out: Christ is risen; * and He shall reign forever as the Source of life.

Glory be...now and ever: Your betrothed and guardian, O Theotokos, * was amazed and perplexed when he beheld the mystery of your conception without seed. * But he recalled the rain falling on the fleece, * and the bush burning with fire but not consumed, * and the blossoming rod of Aaron; * thus he testified before the priests and cried out: * A Virgin gives birth and still remains a virgin.

HYPAKOE

The myrrh-bearing women hastened to the apostles * and related to them the account of your Resurrection, O Christ, saying: * You rose because You are God, * and You grant great mercy to the world.

GRADUAL HYMNS

Antiphon I

My sinful desires have encircled me, * from my youth they have oppresed me; * but You, O Savior, will come to aid me. * You will protect and save me.

May the enemies of Zion be confounded by the Lord; * may they be as grass which withers, * which is dried up by the fire.

Glory be...now and ever: Every spirit lives by the grace of the Holy Spirit * and is raised up in all purity; * it is mystically enlightened by the one God in three persons.

Antiphon II

From the depth of my soul I fervently cry out to You, O Lord; * let your ear be attentive to my voice, O my God.

All those who place their hope in the Lord * shall be raised above all sorrow.

Glory be...now and ever: Truly the Holy Spirit overflows with streams of grace * which water all creation and bring forth life.

Antiphon III

Let my heart rise to You, O Word, * and let not the pleasures of this world * drag me down to the wretchedness below.

As each one of us has surpassing love for his mother, * the more we should love the Lord with utmost fervor.

Glory be...now and ever: The richness of divine knowledge, contemplation, and wisdom * come from the Holy Spirit; * for in Him the Word reveals the eternal plan of the Father.

PROKEIMENON

Tone 4 Stand up and come to our help! Redeem us because of your love!

v. We heard with our own ears, O God. Our fathers have told us the story of the things You did in their days, You yourself, in days long ago.

GOSPEL

John 20: 1-10

Having beheld the Resurrection of Christ, * let us adore the holy Lord Jesus * who alone is sinless. * We bow to your Cross, O Christ, * and we praise and glorify your holy Resurrection. * You are our God * and besides You we recognize no other, * and we invoke your name. * Come, all you faithful, * and let us bow to the holy Resurrection of Christ, * since, through the Cross, * joy has come to all the world. * Ever praising the Lord, * let us extol his Resurrection, * since He, having endured the Crucifixion, * has destroyed Death by his death. *(3 times)*

CANON

The CANON OF THE RESURRECTION may be sung first with each Ode of the Canon; the versicle "Christ is risen from the dead" is sung with the Canon of the Resurrection.

ODE 1

Tone 1 You destroyed the boundaries of death, O immaculate Virgin, * when You gave birth to Christ, the eternal Life, * who today is risen from the tomb * and enlightens the whole world.

Refrain: **Most holy Mother of God, save us!**

Seeing your Son and our God risen, * O Full of Grace and immaculate One, * you rejoice together with the apostles, O Mother of God; * you were the first to receive the proclamation of salvation * as the beginning of all joy.

Tone 8 All you people, clap your hands; * Christ the Giver of life has broken the bonds of Hades; * He has raised up the dead, and by his word He healed the sick; * for He is our God and gives life to those who love his name.

Refrain: **Glory be to You, O Lord, glory be to You!**

Changing water into wine, You have worked a miracle, O Lord, * You formerly changed the rivers of Egypt into blood; * and as a new wonder, You have raised the dead. * Glory to your ineffable plan of salvation, O Lord; * glory to your condescension which raises us up to You.

O Lord, You are our resurrection; * You are the stream of eternal life; * You wished to know both hunger and thirst, O Savior. * Submitting to the laws of nature, You have come to Shechem * and asked the Samaritan woman to give You a drink.

Refrain: **Most holy Mother of God, save us!**

In your womb only, O Mother of God, have you been able to contain your own creator. * O what a wonder! You remained a virgin while giving birth to Him. * Because He is your Son and God, * implore Him unceasingly for the sheep of your flock.

Tone 4 He who struck Egypt and its tyrant and drowned them in the sea * has saved from the servitude of Pharaoh * his people who sing the victorious hymn of Moses, * for He is covered with glory.

Refrain: **Glory to your holy Resurrection, O Lord!**

The buried One is awakened, * and He awakens the human race with Him; * all creation rejoices, * and may the spiritual clouds rain down justice on this day.

O Lord, You willingly suffered crucifixion in the flesh, * and on the third day You arose from the dead, * emptying the prisons of Hades * and delivering those held captive, * for You are the Prince of life.

Having seen the resplendent angel, * the myrrh-bearing women fearfully fled from the tomb; * they hastened to the disciples to tell them of the resurrection of Christ.

O Lord, You are the living water * who built your dwelling place above the waters; * You gave the Samaritan woman the waters she asked for, * as she acknowledged your infinite mercy.

Glory be: Grant salvation to the faithful * who sincerely glorify You, O Holy Trinity, * Father, Son, and Holy Spirit; * O Creator of the world, * in your goodness grant us the forgiveness of our sins.

Now and ever: Rejoice, O throne of fire and golden candelabrum, * shining cloud and palace of the Word. * Rejoice, O mystical table * who was worthy to bear Christ, our bread of life.

It is the day of Resurrection; * O people, let us be enlightened by it. * The Passover is the Lord's Passover, * since Christ, our God, has brought us from death to life * and from earth to heaven. * Therefore, we sing the hymn of victory.

ODE 3

Tone 1 I returned today to life that knows no sunset, * by the goodness of Him born of you, O immaculate Virgin; * make his glory shine to the ends of the world.

***Refrain:* Most holy Mother of God, save us!**

The God whom you brought into the world in the flesh, O immaculate Virgin, * is risen from the dead as He foretold. * Dance and celebrate and extol Him as God.

Tone 8 Do not judge by appearances, * said the Lord to those whom He was teaching * when He came into the Temple, as it is written, * in the middle of the Feast prescribed by the Law.

***Refrain:* Glory be to You, O Lord, glory be to You!**

Do not judge by appearances: * Christ has truly come as the One foretold by the prophets; * He comes from Zion to gather the whole world.

If you do not believe in his words, * at least believe in the works of the Lord; * you shall err by rejecting the Holy One * of whom Moses spoke in the Law.

***Refrain:* Most holy Mother of God, save us!**

Without undergoing change, the Lord has become flesh * even though He is One of the Holy Trinity; * and the burning fire of his divinity * has not consumed the all pure womb of the Mother of God.

Tone 4 My heart is strengthened in the Lord * who teaches the faithful how to pray; * He weakens the weapons of war * and girds the weak with strength.

***Refrain:* Glory to your holy Resurrection, O Lord!**

You were raised on the Cross of your own will, O Word, * and the rocks were rent asunder when they saw You. * All creation trembled with fear, * and the dead came forth from the tombs as from a dream.

Seeing your soul descend into Hades, O Word, * the souls of the just escaped from the bonds which held them through the ages; * and they praised your power which surpasses every spirit.

Why all this bother? * Why do you come with myrrh, O women, seeking the Lord in the tomb? * He is risen and the world is raised with Him, * said the resplendent angel to the myrrh-bearing women.

O Prince of Life and Fountain of immortality, * You sat down at the well, * and in your goodness filled the Samaritan woman * with the waters of wisdom which she asked of you.

Glory be: Unique and supreme is the God whom we praise, * the Father, Son, and divine Spirit, * the Trinity whom the heavenly powers glorify: * Holy, holy, holy are You forever.

Now and ever: Having wondrously conceived the God of the universe in your womb, O Virgin Mother, * you gave birth in a manner that surpasses understanding, * and remained a virgin as before you gave birth.

Come, let us partake of a new drink, * not miraculously produced from the barren rock, * but from the Fountain of immortality, * springing up from the tomb of Christ. * In Him is our firm strength.

KONTAKION

Tone 4 O Christ God, Creator and Lord of all, * when the Paschal Feast was half completed, You told those present: * Come and draw the water of immortality. * Let us, therefore, adore You and cry out with faith: * Grant us your goodness, * for You are the Source of our life.

SESSIONAL HYMN

Tone 4 Let heaven rejoice and let mortals dance, * for Christ is born of the Virgin and appears in our flesh. * By his death He has delivered the human race from the corruption of the grave. * He asked the Samaritan woman for water, * and in a striking miracle He in turn offered to her * the fountain of grace and immortal life.

Glory be...now and ever: O Prince of wisdom and Master of knowledge, * in the middle of the Feast prescribed by the Law, * You sat in the Temple and taught the crowds gathered there: * Whoever are thirsty, let them come to Me; * let them drink the water that I now give; * in it everyone shall taste joy and life divine.

ODE 4

Tone 1 O immaculate Virgin, * He who made Adam your first father, * was made a man from your womb; * and by his death He destroyed the Death caused by sin; * and today He makes the divine brilliance of his holy Resurrection shine on you.

Refrain: **Most holy Mother of God, save us!**

The Messiah to whom you gave birth, * you behold today even more beautiful, O holy Virgin; * for He rises in glory from among the dead, * brilliant with beauty and grace and purity; * with the apostles, you glorify the Lord today in joy * for the salvation of the human race.

Tone 8 Christ who has come among us * is the Messiah announced by the prophets. * The works He does bear witness to this, * for He changed water into wine, * and by his word the Paralytic was healed.

Refrain: **Glory be to You, O Lord, glory be to You!**

Christ is the Messiah announced by the Scriptures. * He has come in truth, illuminating the entire universe; * and by his brilliant wonders, He shows us that He is truly the Source of life.

I have shown you only one work, * and you are already amazed. * You practice circumcision even on the Sabbath; * why then do you reproach Me * for having healed the Paralytic by the power of my word?

Refrain: **Most holy Mother of God, save us!**

O divine Spouse and most pure Mother * who contained in your womb the uncontainable God, * cease not to intercede for us * that we may be delivered from all danger, * for you are our refuge at all times.

Tone 4 I heard your voice and I was afraid; * I acknowledge your works worthy of admiration, * for the earth is filled with your praise, O Lord.

Refrain: **Glory to your holy Resurrection, O Lord!**

Let the heavens rejoice and let the earth exalt! * The Lord is risen and has appeared to all his apostles.

Your power, O Death, has been abolished by the death of Christ our God; * and as the spouses come forth from the bridal chamber, * the dead arise from the tomb, * following the risen Lord.

Why are you crying, O women? * Why do you come with myrrh looking for the immortal One? * He is risen as He promised, * said the angel to the myrrh-bearing women.

O Lord, to the woman of Samaria who asked You for water, * You gave the water of divine knowledge; * she no longer thirsts, but she praises You always.

Glory be: O Trinity and supreme God, * Father, Son, and Holy Spirit, * sharing the same power and the same eternity, * save all who praise your name.

Now and ever: Moses, the giver of the Law formerly saw

you in the burning bush, * and Daniel recognized you in the holy mountain, * O only Virgin who gave birth to God.

Let Habakkuk, * speaking in behalf of God, * stand with us at the divine watch; * let him show us the brilliant angel who proclaims: * Today, salvation comes to the world; * for Christ, being Almighty, is risen.

ODE 5

Tone 1 Divinely illumined by the life-giving rays * of the Resurrection of your Son, * O Mother of God and Virgin immaculate, * the assembly of the faithful shines in beauty.

Refrain: **Most holy Mother of God, save us!**

O King of glory, * when You became incarnate, your mother's virginity remained, * and You did not break the seals of the tomb. * All creation rejoices when it sees your holy Resurrection.

Tone 8 You made the apostles shine with brilliant works, * and You exalted your disciples throughout the whole world, * granting them glory, O God our Savior, * and You gave them the kingdom of heaven.

Refrain: **Glory be to You, O Lord, glory be to You!**

With their miracles and teaching, * your disciples have enlightened the ends of the earth, * announcing in many ways, O Savior, the word of your kingdom.

We give glory to your majesty; * we offer You our hymns and songs, * because You have appeared on earth for us, * illuminating the world and calling the human race back to You.

Refrain: **Most holy Mother of God, save us!**

Your womb, O Mother of God, has become the holy table * on which the heavenly bread, Christ our God, now rests. * Those who eat this bread shall never die * as He who satisfied the whole world had promised.

Tone 4 O Lord, let the light of your commandments shine on me, * for my spirit keeps watch before You, O Christ, and sings: * You are my God; I take refuge in You, O divine King of peace.

Refrain: **Glory to your holy Resurrection, O Lord!**

Arriving at your holy grave early in the morning, * the myrrh-bearing women saw a resplendent angel; * they were seized with fear, O Christ, * as they learned of your holy Resurrection.

Death is trampled down, Hades is imprisoned, * and the captives are delivered by the Resurrection of Christ. * Let us exalt with joy and clap our hands; * let us celebrate with gladness.

O Apostles, be jubilant together with the angels in heaven; * dance for joy, all you mortals. * Death has vanished before the risen Christ, * and Adam exalts, banishing all sadness.

O Lord and Giver of life, * You gave the Samaritan woman streams of knowledge and forgiveness; * we also praise your infinite mercy.

Glory be: Tri-personal Unity and consubstantial Trinity, * Father, Son, and Holy Spirit, * indivisible by nature, we praise You as the one and only God, * the Master, Creator, and Lord of the universe.

Now and ever: O impassable door and untilled earth, * O ark of the covenant in which the Manna was kept, * O chalice and candelabrum, O censer of the divinity; * such are the names by which we know you, O Virgin.

Let us rise at early dawn * and bring to our Master a hymn instead of myrrh; * and we shall see Christ, * the Sun of Righteousness * who enlightens the life of all.

ODE 6

Tone 1 O Virgin Mother of God, * those who were once subjected to death * and to the corruption of the grave, * are now raised to immortal and eternal life * by Him who was incarnate from your womb.

Refrain: **Most holy Mother of God, save us!**

O immaculate Virgin, * He who wondrously dwelt in your womb and became flesh, * descended into the depths of the earth, * and rising from the tomb, * raised with Him all human nature.

Tone 8 You encompass the whole world, O Jesus; * yet at the mid-point of the Feast, * You came into the Temple and taught the crowds your word of truth, * as the holy evangelist John says.

Refrain: **Glory be to You, O Lord, glory be to You!**

You fulfilled the work of the Father, * and your works confirmed your word. * You accomplished healings and miracles, O Savior, * raising up the Paralytic, purifying lepers, and resurrecting the dead.

The timeless Son has entered into time; * He has become a man and assumed our human condition. * In the middle of the Feast, He taught, saying: * Hasten and draw from the inexhaustible Source of life.

Refrain: **Most holy Mother of God, save us!**

We praise your virginity which remained after your giving birth; * we glorify you as Virgin and Mother, * O only pure and virginal Spouse, * for God has truly taken flesh in your womb to give us life.

Tone 4 May the storm not drown me, * and may the abyss not swallow me in the ocean of my passions. * For behold, I am thrown into the deep sea, * and as Jonah I cry out to You: * From the depths raise me up to You, O my God.

Refrain: **Glory to your holy Resurrection, O Lord!**

The impious ones nailed You to the Cross, * and a sword pierced your side; * the noble Joseph buried You in a new tomb, O Jesus Christ. * You resurrected in glory and raised with You all creation * who now praises your power, O Savior.

O Lord, in your power You crushed the gates and bolts of Hades; * You resurrected as God and told the myrrh-bearing women to rejoice. * They in turn announced to the disciples: * The living God is risen and has appeared to enlighten the world.

O women, why do you weep as for the dead? * And why do you bring this myrrh? * Christ is risen, said the resplendent angel; * He has left the linen shroud and the cloth. * Go quickly to his friends and announce the Resurrection!

O inexhaustible Source of life, * O Ocean of mercy and Lord of goodness, You stopped on your way and were seated at Jacob's well; * to the Samaritan woman You said: * Give me water to drink, and you shall receive streams of forgiveness.

Glory be: With the bodiless angels I praise in faith * the eternal Father, the Son who shares the same throne in heaven, * and the consubstantial Spirit, * the unique and royal majesty, * the divine Creator and the providence of the world.

Now and ever: O only Virgin who gave birth, * we praise you as the throne of the Lord, * the impassable door and unhewn mountain, * the spiritual candlestick and the room filled with light, * the tabernacle that manifests glory, * the ark of the covenant, the chalice, and the holy table.

You have descended into the realm of Death, O Christ, * and have broken ancient bonds which held the captive; * You arose from the tomb on the third day * like Jonah from the whale.

KONTAKION

Tone 8 When the Samaritan woman came to the well with faith, * she beheld You, O Water of Wisdom. * You allowed her to drink in abundance * and glorified her eternally, * for she inherited the heavenly kingdom.

IKOS

Let us worthily listen to the Gospel in which St. John clearly teaches us about the sacred mysteries which took place one time in Samaria. Speaking to a woman, the Lord asked her for water, He who formerly gathered the waters in one place, the Word of God who shares the same throne with the Father and the Spirit. For He has come to seek his fallen image, and his memory is glorified forever.

ODE 7

Tone 1 O Virgin immaculate, * today your Son destroyed Death, * giving eternal life to all mortals from all ages, * for He is the God of our fathers, * and to Him alone belong blessing and glory.

Refrain: **Most holy Mother of God, save us!**

O Full of Grace, * He who reigns over all creation * became incarnate and dwelt in your womb, * having suffered death by the Cross; * as God all-powerful He is risen, * making us rise with Him.

Tone 8 You felt bodily fatigue, O Lord, * yet You give rest to all. * You felt thirst, O Source of miracles, * and asking for water, You promised us the living water of salvation.

Refrain: **Glory be to you, O Lord, glory be to You!**

You spoke with the Samaritan woman, O Lord, * and You refuted the foolishness of the impious. * The first acknowledged You as the Messiah, * and the others did not believe that You are the Son of God.

Eating the flesh of the Lord as our bread, * and drinking the blood of his side as our wine, * in this new life in the Spirit, * let us henceforth live in the grace of God.

Refrain: **Most holy Mother of God, save us!**

In your womb you enclosed the boundless One, * and with your breasts you fed the Nourisher of the world; * and in your arms you carried the Creator of the world, O holy Mother of God.

Tone 4 Do not reject us until the end because of your holy name; * do not break your eternal covenant; * do not keep your love far away from us; * O Lord, God of our fathers, who is glorified forever.

Refrain: **Glory to your holy Resurrection, O Lord!**

At the moment of your divine Passion, O God of mercy, * according to your will You were placed among the ranks of criminals; * and when You bowed your head, O Creator, * the rocks were split in two and the earth trembled, * and the dead, who were asleep through the ages, were raised up.

Why do you seek among the dead the One who lives in eternity? * He is risen as He said; * see the empty tomb, the cloths, and the shroud. * Hasten and tell this to the apostles, * said the one who appeared as a young man to the holy women.

You are the Fountain of life, said the woman of Samaria to Christ. * My soul is always thirsty, O Word; * quench me with the grace of God * that the dryness of ignorance does not hold me in its power, * but that I may proclaim your wonders, O Lord.

Glory be: We sing to the indivisible Trinity, * consubstantial in the unity of three persons that we perceive: * The Father, Son, and Holy Spirit, * the eternal Creator of the universe, * God who is praised by the powers of heaven.

Now and ever: After your wondrous birth-giving, O holy Mother of God, * you preserved your virginity without blemish. * Thus angels and people everywhere sing to you with an incessant voice, * O tabernacle most pure in which the infinite One dwelt.

God, who saved the three youths from the furnace, * has become man * and suffered as any mortal; * but his passion clothed his mortality * with the splendor of incorruption. * He is the only blessed One, God of our fathers, * and is worthy of all praise.

ODE 8

Tone 1 The Creator came into this world * from you, O

Virgin Mother of God; * destroying the jail of Hades, * He gave resurrection to us mortals; * and we also bless Christ forever.

Refrain: **Most holy Mother of God, save us!**

Destroying all power of Death * on the day of his Resurrection, O Virgin, * your Son and the all-powerful God * made us partakers of his glory and divinity. * We also bless Christ forever.

Tone 8 Come, all you people and behold: * The One who is praised as the King of glory in heaven * is slandered by the crowds of the ungodly. * Seeing this, sing to the Messiah * who has spoken through the prophets of old.

Refrain: **Glory be to You, O Lord, glory be to You!**

You are truly the Christ who comes into the world; * You are the source of salvation, * and with You is the forgiveness of the sins of our fathers; * You are truly the life of the people who hope in You.

In the middle of the Feast, * the Wisdom of God comes into the Temple, as it is written, * and He begins to teach that the Messiah, the Christ, * truly is the One who gives life to the world.

Refrain: **Most holy Mother of God, save us!**

Tell us how you gave birth to the Light * who comes forth eternally from the Father * and whom we praise with the Holy Spirit, * the One who wished to be born of your womb, * and who alone knew this throughout the ages.

Tone 4 In your wisdom, O Lord, You gather together the universe * and the foundations of the earth; * You establish these foundations again and set them over the great waters. * That is why we sing to You in joy: * Bless the Lord, all you works of the Lord.

Refrain: **Glory to your holy Resurrection, O Lord!**

You willingly suffered death, O only immortal One; * and You crushed the bronze gates; * You took Hades captive, O heavenly King, * and freed those who had been held there through the ages * so that they may unceasingly praise the power of your goodness.

O long-suffering One, You were raised on the Cross; * the rocks were split open and the sun hid itself; * the curtain of the Temple was torn in two; * the earth shook and Hades was humiliated, * trembling because it had to give up its prisoners.

You appeared to those lying in darkness, * O unsetting Light and Life of the world; * when the just people saw You, they were jubilant and cried out: * You have come to deliver the captives by your power which we now praise.

Seated at the well at the sixth hour of the day, * You gave living water to the Samaritan woman, O Savior God, * and in your goodness, You granted her streams of knowledge. * For this reason we also sing to You: * Bless the Lord, all you works of the Lord.

Let us bless the Lord, Father, Son, and Holy Spirit.

We praise the Father who is from all eternity, * the co-eternal Son, and the Spirit of holiness, * tri-personal and unique divinity, * having neither confusion nor division, * the Creator of the world and sovereign majesty for whom we sing: * Bless the Lord, all you works of the Lord.

Now and ever: With lips purified by a burning coal, * Isaiah foretold the Fire of the divinity * who was incarnate of you, O Virgin, in a wondrous fashion. * He burned away the sins of mortals to divinize our nature in his love, * O all-pure Virgin.

Let us praise, bless, and worship the Lord, singing and exalting Him above all forever.

This is that chosen and holy day, * Feast of feasts, * most solemn day, * only king and lord of all Sabbaths, * on which we ever praise Christ.

OMIT MAGNIFICAT

ODE 9

Tone 1 O Virgin, with one voice we, the faithful, extol you: * Rejoice, door of the Lord; rejoice, spiritual city; * rejoice, for you made the light of your Son shine upon us * on the day of his Resurrection.

Refrain: **Most holy Mother of God, save us!**

O immaculate One, full of grace, * exalt and dance in joy, O divine door of brightness; * for Jesus rested in the tomb * and rose in glory more brilliant than the sun; * and He enlightens the whole human race.

Tone 8 In the middle of the Feast of fifty days * You came into the Temple, O Savior, * and You began to teach the astonished Pharisees who said: * How does He know the Scriptures since He has never been taught?

Refrain: **Glory be to you, O Lord, glory be to You!**

Gushing forth streams of grace and salvation, * You performed wondrous signs, O Redeemer, * healing the infirmed and dispelling illnesses; * but the Pharisees became angry at seeing the miracles You accomplished.

You granted the greatest of miracles, O Savior, * to your disciples, as You promised; * You sent them to preach your glory throughout the whole world. * They proclaimed to all people * the grace of your Incarnation and your holy Resurrection.

Refrain: **Most holy Mother of God, save us!**

In your womb, O Virgin Mother of God, * you sheltered One of the Holy Trinity, Christ, the Fountain of life, * whom all creation praises and before whom the angels stand and tremble. * Intercede with Him that our souls may be saved.

Tone 4 The Lord works wonders with the strength of his arm; * He overthrows the powerful from their thrones; * He raises up the humble. * He is the God of Israel, the rising Sun, and the Light from on high. * He protects us and directs our paths on the way of peace.

Refrain: **Glory to your holy Resurrection, O Lord!**

Behold Christ, the Life of all, * who of his own will is seen hanging on the Cross. * Seeing this, both the earth and the prisons of Hades trembled, * and many of the just were raised up in their bodies.

You came forth from the tomb, resplendent in beauty, * as a bridegroom coming from his bridal chamber. * O Christ, You have conquered Death; * and by your divine power You broke the tyranny and the bolts of Hades, * illuminating the world by your holy Resurrection.

Let us all together form a spiritual choir * to sing praises to the risen Lord. * Let the earth exalt and let heaven rejoice; * let the clouds rain down justice like the dew * upon us who keep this feast of Christ; * and let us celebrate in joy!

The Source of every good thing, who gives life to all the living, * and who pours out his teachings in abundance, * says to the woman of Samaria: * Give Me water to drink * that I in turn may give you the water * which will dry up the stream of your sins.

Glory be: O unique Light having no division, * such is the triple Sun of the one divinity: * the Father, Son, and Holy

Spirit, * unique Life and Creator of the universe. * Together with the angels let us, the faithful, sing to Him * with a thrice-holy and sacred song.

Now and ever: O pure Virgin and tabernacle of the Light,* enlighten the eyes of my heart * which have been blinded by the deceits of the Enemy; * and make me worthy to contemplate with a pure heart * the marvelous brightness of the brilliant Sun * who is born of your womb.

Shine in splendor, * O new Jerusalem! * For the glory of the Lord * is risen upon you. * O Zion, sing with joy and rejoice! * And you, pure Mother of God, * rejoice in the resurrection of your Son.

HYMN OF LIGHT

Tone 2 You, O King and Lord, * have fallen asleep * in the flesh as a mortal man, * but on the third day You arose again. * You have raised Adam * from his corruption * and made Death powerless. * You are the Pasch of incorruption. * You are the salvation of the world.

Tone 4 **Glory be:** Meeting a woman in a village of Samaria, O almighty Savior, * You asked her for water to drink, * even though in ancient times in the desert * You brought forth from the most hard rock * the stream from which Israel drank in abundance. * O Giver of life, You awakened faith in the heart of the Samaritan woman, * and she now tastes both joy and living water in heaven forever.

Tone 4 **Now and ever:** O Lord and Lover of Mankind, * You appeared in the Temple in the middle of the Feast and said: * All who thirst, come to Me and draw the living water; * in it you will find joy * and you shall enjoy both grace and eternal life.

AT THE PRAISES

Tone 4 You suffered death on the Cross, * and You arose from the dead. * We glorify your holy Resurrection, O almighty Lord.

By your Cross You delivered us from the ancient curse, O Christ; * by your death You have utterly destroyed the Devil * who tyrannized the human race; * by your Resurrection You have filled the whole world with joy. * Therefore, we cry out to You: * O Lord who rose from the dead, glory to You!

By your Cross lead us to your truth, O Christ our Savior; *

deliver us from the snares of the Enemy. * You are risen from the dead; * now raise us up from our fall into sin. * Stretch forth your hand to us, O Lord, * through the prayers of your saints.

O only Son and Word of God, * You were not separated from the bosom of the Father * when You came to earth out of love for us * and became a man without undergoing change. * In the flesh You suffered death on the Cross * even though You are beyond all suffering in your divinity. * You rose from the dead, granting immortality to the human race, * for You alone, O Lord, are almighty.

In your flesh You accepted death, O God our Savior, * to give us the gift of immortal life. * You dwelled in the tomb to deliver us from Hades * and made us sharers in your Resurrection. * You suffered in the flesh but were raised as God. * Therefore, we sing to You: * O Source of life, O Lord and Lover of Mankind, glory to You!

The rocks were split asunder, O Savior, * when your Cross was planted on Golgotha; * and the gate-keepers of Hades shook with fear * when your body was placed in the grave like the dead. * For You abolished the might of Death, * and in your Resurrection You granted immortality to the dead. * O Lord and Giver of life, glory to You!

Tone 3

Ride on in triumph for the cause of truth and goodness and right.

Let heaven and earth greatly rejoice today. * Christ has shone forth as a man in the flesh. * He desires to set Adam free from the curse. * He comes to Samaria and amazes everyone with his wonders. * Though He wraps the heavens in clouds, He asks a woman for water to drink. * Therefore, let us, the faithful, worship Him. * In his good will, He voluntarily emptied himself for us.

Tone 6

Your love is for justice; your hatred for evil. Therefore, God, your God, has anointed you with the oil of gladness.

The Lord spoke thus to the Samaritan woman: * If you knew the gift of God * and who it is who asks you: Give Me water to drink, * you would have asked Him, and He would give you living water * that you may never thirst again.

Tone 6 **Glory be:** Jesus, our Savior, the Fountain of life, * came to the well of Jacob the Patriarch. * He asked a

Samaritan woman for water to drink. * She told Him that Jews have no dealings with Samaritans; * but the wise Creator incited her curiosity with the sweetness of his words, * and she asked Him for the water of everlasting life. * She received his gift and announced to all: * Come and see Him who knows all secrets as God. * He has come in the flesh for the salvation of the human race.

Tone 2 **Now and ever:** You are truly most blessed, O virgin Mother of God. * Through the One who was incarnate of you, * Hades was chained, Adam revived, the curse wiped out, * Eve set free, Death put to death, * and we ourselves were brought back to life.* That is why we cry out in praise: * Blessed are You, O Christ our God, * who finds in this your good pleasure; glory to You!

AFTER THE DISMISSAL

Gospel Stanza Number 7

Tone 7 **Glory be...now and ever:** Behold the end of night and dawn of day. * Why have you stood at the grave, O Mary? * Great darkness covered your mind, so you asked the angel: * Where has Jesus been placed? * Behold the disciples who hastened to the tomb * saw a sign of his Resurrection in the coffin wrappings and the cloth * and remembered what was said about Him in the Scriptures. * Therefore, we who believe through them, * praise You, O Christ, the Giver of life.

Sunday Evening Vespers

AT PSALM 140

Tone 5 Today the Feast of mid-Pentecost appears in its grace and brightness, * and as the noon hour divides the day, * so this Feast stands in the middle of the Paschal season. * It radiates the light of the Resurrection of Christ * and reflects the signs of eternal life. * It discloses the Ascension into heaven, * and it foretells the coming of the most beloved Spirit, * the glorious feast of Pentecost. * And so it bestows upon our souls peace and great mercy.

Today we have come to the midweek of the festal season. * As a river of divine glory, * the Lord gives streams of goodness to all and calls out: * All who thirst, come to Me and drink deeply, * because I am the Fountain of compassion and the Ocean of mercy. * From Him flows forgiveness to the peoples; * He washes away sin and cleanses infirmities. * He saves those who celebrate his Resurrection, * embraces with love those who honor his glorious Ascension, * and bestows upon our souls peace and great mercy.

He stood in the center of the Temple, the infinite Lord God. * He is God in essence, yet became incarnate for our sakes, * taking upon himself the limits of the flesh, * from which the living water of his word comes to everyone, saying: * Come and purify your hearts * and quench the heat of your passions. * Let no one be deprived of drink. * The water that I give is the grace of God * by which you partake of the better and eternal life. * Whoever drinks of it will share with Me, the Creator, * the kingdom and the glory of God.

Three Stichera from the Saint of the day

Tone 8 **Glory be...now and ever:** In the middle of the Feast, * before your Passion and glorious Resurrection, * You taught the unbelievers in the Temple, O gracious Lord. * You cried out to the Scribes and Pharisees: * Let all who thirst come to Me and drink! * From the hearts of those who believe in Me, * rivers of living water, the Spirit of God, shall flow! * Your wisdom and understanding are far beyond our words. * Glory to You, our God, who perfects all things!

APOSTICHA

Tone 4 We never cease to adore your life-giving Cross, O Christ our God, * and we glorify your Resurrection on the third day. * For You, almighty One, have thereby restored the corrupted nature of all * and reopened the way to heaven, * since You alone are gracious, and You love all people.

I have lifted up my eyes to You enthroned in heaven. Behold, as the eyes of servants are on the hands of their masters, as the eyes of a maid are on the hands of her mistress, so are our eyes on the Lord our God until He has mercy on us.

With my tears I desire to wash away the mark of my sins, O Lord, * and through penance, I long to make the rest of my life pleasing to You; * but the Enemy deceives me and struggles with my soul. * Save me before I completely perish, O Lord.

Have mercy on us, O Lord, have mercy on us; for we have been filled with shame; our soul is all too full of the mockery of the rich, of the contempt of the proud.

You are glorified in the memory of your saints, O Christ God. * Through their intercessions, * send upon us great mercy.

Tone 6 **Glory be...now and ever:** The midweek of the festal season has arrived, O Christ, * the midpoint of your Resurrection and the coming of your Holy Spirit. * Coming together, we glorify the mystery of your miracles; * and filled with fear, we cry out to You: * Send down upon us your great mercy!

TROPARIA

Of the Saint

Tone 8 **Glory be...now and ever:** When the Paschal Feast is half completed, * quench my thirsty soul with the waters of devotion; * for You, O Savior, have announced to all: * Let all who are thirsty come to Me and drink. * O Christ our God, Source of our life, * glory be to You!

Monday Matins

SESSIONAL HYMN I

Tone 4 The myrrh-bearing women looked into the entrance of the tomb, * and because they could not bear the brilliance of the angel, * they trembled in astonishment and said: * Has He who opened Paradise to the thief been stolen, * or is He who proclaimed his Resurrection before his passion now risen? * Truly, Christ is risen, * granting resurrection and life to those in Hades.

Lord, do not reprove me in your anger; punish me not in your rage.

O Lord, lead my poor soul back to You, * for I have spent my whole life in sin; * receive me as the sinful woman and save me.

Their span extends through all the earth; their words to the utmost bounds of the world.

In memory of the victorious martyrs, * today the heavenly armies come to illumine the hearts of believers * and to cause grace to shine over the whole world; * through their prayers, O God all-powerful, * grant us your great mercy.

Glory be...now and ever: O virgin Mother of God, * you are the unshakable rampart of Christians; * for when we take refuge in you, * we do not risk being wounded by the Enemy. * And if we should happen to sin again, * we cry out: Rejoice, O Full of Grace; * the Lord is with you.

SESSIONAL HYMN II

Tone 8 The Word and Wisdom of the Father, * who entrusted his apostles with God's command * to proclaim his coming to the ends of the earth, * was fearfully reviled by a transgressing people. * They were seduced by demons in their wanton madness; * but He endured their insults patiently, crying out to them: * Do not judge Me rashly, O lawless ones. * Let us cry to Him: O Lover of Mankind, Christ our God, * send forgiveness of sins to those who praise your boundless glory in faith.

Glory be...now and ever: *(Repeat the above)*

Having beheld the Resurrection of Christ...

CANON

(From the Feast of Mid-Pentecost, pages 158-171)

HYMN OF LIGHT

Tone 3 You hold the inexhaustible chalice of gifts; * grant that I may draw living water for the remission of my sins * so that I may be overcome by thirst for You, * O only compassionate One. *(3 times)*

AT THE PRAISES

Tone 4 You suffered death on the Cross, * and You arose from the dead. * We glorify your holy Resurrection, O almighty Lord. *(2 times)*

I am the lost sheep of your mystical flock, * and I take refuge in You, O good Shepherd. * Have mercy on me, O God.

How could we not admire the sublime fight you have fought, O holy Martyrs? * In your bodies you were victorious over the bodiless Enemy * by professing your faith in Christ * and arming yourself with the sign of the Cross; * for this reason you have received the power to expel demons and overcome the Enemy. * Intercede unceasingly for the salvation of our souls.

Tone 8 **Glory be...now and ever:** In the middle of the Feast of the Law, * our Savior went up to the Temple. * He stood in the midst of the crowd, * teaching them with authority: * I am the Light of the world. * All who follow Me shall not walk in darkness * but shall have the light of immortal life.

APOSTICHA

Tone 2 You bowed the heavens and came down, my Savior; * You took flesh from the Virgin; * You united what was divided, * pouring forgiveness of sins over me.

Remember your people whom You chose long ago.

You wished to raise me from the death of sin * and to unite me to the Father, * O eternal Word and Lover of Mankind.

God is our King from time past, the Giver of help through all the land.

You are King of all, * great in wisdom. * Through You the Father created the world * with the Holy Spirit.

Tone 8 **Glory be...now and ever:** Let us cleanse our thoughts to the very depths * that our souls may be brilliantly illumined. * Then we shall see Christ, * who by his boundless goodness taught in the Temple, * who endured the agony of the Cross and rose from the dead, * triumphing over the Enemy and saving our race. * To Him let us cry: * Glory to You, O incomprehensible Lord!

Monday Evening Vespers

AT PSALM 140

Tone 1 The Creator of all and Giver of life, * the Word coeternal with the divine Father * who willed to take flesh from the Virgin, becoming a man, * has manifested the unspeakable teachings of wisdom to all.

In the midst of the Feast, O Christ, * You stood in the Temple, O Master of the Law, * teaching with authority and refuting the Scribes * amazing all with the wisdom of your words and wondrous signs, * as in the past, Moses wrote of You.

The Giver of wisdom and bestower of blessings, * pouring out divine streams from the inexhaustible fountain, cried out: * Come to Me, all who thirst, and draw the water of life; * rivers of divine grace shall flow from you.

Three Stichera from the Saint of the day

Tone 2 **Glory be...now and ever:** When You came to the Temple, O Christ, in the middle of the Feast, * You taught the people, saying: * Whoever believes in Me, even if he dies, he shall live. * The Pharisees and Sadducees and Scribes were enraged and cried: * Who is this man to utter blasphemies? * They did not understand that You are our God, * glorified with the Father and the Spirit before the ages. Glory to You!

APOSTICHA

Tone 4 O Savior, You have absolved the penalty of disobedience, * committed through the tree of Eden, * by willingly being nailed to the tree of the Cross. * As almighty God, You descended into Hades * and broke asunder the bonds of Death. * We, therefore, venerate your Resurrection from the dead * and joyfully cry out to You: * Almighty Lord, glory to You!

I have lifted up my eyes to You enthroned in heaven. Behold, as the eyes of servants are on the hands of their masters, as the eyes of a maid are on the hands of her mistress, so are our eyes on the Lord our God until He has mercy on us.

Who is there among the storm-tossed * who hastens to your harbor and is not saved, O Lord? * Who is ill and seeks your healing and is not cured? * O Creator of everyone and Healer of the sick, * save me before I completely perish, O Lord.

Have mercy on us, O Lord, have mercy on us; for we have been filled with shame; our soul is all too full of the mockery of the rich, of the contempt of the proud.

O God, who has accepted the long-suffering of the holy martyrs, * accept our song, O Lover of Mankind, * and grant us your great mercy through their prayers.

Tone 3 **Glory be...now and ever:** In the middle of the Feast * let us glorify Him who worked salvation in the middle of the earth. * The Life was hanging on the tree between two thieves. * He was silent with the one who blaphemed, * but the one who believed heard: * Today you will be with Me in Paradise. * He descended into the tomb, destroying Hades, * and He arose on the third day, saving our souls.

TROPARIA

Of the Saint

Tone 8 **Glory be...now and ever:** When the Paschal Feast is half completed, * quench my thirsty soul with the waters of devotion; * for You, O Savior, have announced to all: * Let all who are thirsty come to Me and drink. * O Christ our God, Source of our life, * glory be to You!

Tuesday Matins

SESSIONAL HYMN I

Tone 4 By your own will, O Savior, * You endured the Cross. * Mortals placed You in a new tomb, * though your word summoned the universe into existence. * Thus the Stranger was bound, * Death was despoiled without mercy,* and when the prisoners of Hades saw your life-bearing Resurrection * they cried out: Christ, the Giver of life, is risen! * He shall live forever!

Lord, do not reprove me in your anger; punish me not in your rage.

Consider, O my soul, how we shall appear at the judgment: * In that dread hour the judgment seat will be set up, * for the deeds of each shall be examined by an impartial Judge. * Behold, the terrible fire is ready to receive all things as an unleashed ocean. * O my soul, do penance before the end.

Their span extends through all the earth; their words to the utmost bounds of the world.

Your martyrs have adorned the Church with their blood throughout the world; * clothed with purple and fine linen, * they sing to You with their mouths, O Christ our God. * Now show compassion to this people who belong to You; * give peace to all our governments * and great mercy to our souls.

Glory be...now and ever: What an awesome mystery and unheard of wonder! * How does the Virgin bear You, the Creator of the world, * and yet remain a virgin after childbirth? * You were brought into this world by her. * Strengthen our faith and calm the nations, * and give peace to the world through your love for us.

SESSIONAL HYMN II

Tone 8 The waters of life and wisdom flow upon the world, O Savior. * You have called everyone to draw from the well of salvation. * If anyone receives your divine Law, * the flames of the Deceiver will surely be quenched in him. * Those who drink of your fullness shall never thirst again, * O

Master and King of heaven. * Therefore, we glorify your power, O Christ our God. * Grant us forgiveness of our sins. * Send down abundant blessings on your servants.

Glory be...now and ever: *(Repeat the above)*

Having beheld the Resurrection of Christ...

CANON

(From the Feast of Mid-Pentecost, pages 158-171)

HYMN OF LIGHT

Tone 3 You behold the inexhaustible chalice of gifts; * grant that I may draw living water for the remission of my sins * so that I may be overcome by thirst for You, * O only compassionate One. *(3 times)*

AT THE PRAISES

Tone 4 By your Cross You delivered us from the ancient curse, O Christ; * by your death You have utterly destroyed the Devil * who tyrannized the human race; * by your Resurrection You have filled the whole world with joy. * Therefore, we cry out to You: * O Lord who rose from the dead, glory to You! *(2 times)*

Wash me with my tears, O Savior, * for I am blemished because of my many sins. * And so I bow before You; * I have sinned, O God; have mercy on me.

O holy Martyrs, you have become citizens with the angels, * for in the arena you professed your faith in Christ; * you have despised the pleasures of this world, * holding firmly to the anchor of faith; * you have become a source of healing for the faithful. * Intercede unceasingly for the salvation of our souls.

Tone 4 **Glory be...now and ever:** Before ascending the Cross, O Lord, * You went up to the Temple in the middle of the Feast. * You taught the Jews with authority concerning the Law, * for You yourself gave the Law to Moses. * They were astounded by the boundless mystery of your wisdom, * yet they contrived malice against You in their envy: * This man has never studied the Scriptures with the Scribes. * They refused to recognize You as the Savior of our souls.

APOSTICHA

Tone 2 O my Christ, You are the beginning, the middle, and the end. * You came to the Temple * in the middle of the Feast * to flood me with forgiveness.

Remember your people whom You chose long ago.

Zion heard the divine power * of your Resurrection, O Word. * She rejoices with her children, * praising your compassion.

God is our King from time past, the Giver of help through all the land.

You shone forth, O Word, * the brightness of the Father; * but in these latter days, You came to me as a mortal. * You forgave all my sins.

Tone 8 **Glory be...now and ever:** In the middle of the Feast of the Law, * our Savior went up to the Temple. * He stood in the midst of the crowd, * teaching them with authority: * I am the Light of the world. * Those who follow Me shall not walk in darkness, * but shall have the light of immortal life.

Tuesday Evening Vespers

Final day of the Feast of Mid-Pentecost

(The text for Vespers is taken from the feastday.)

Wednesday Matins

Final day of the Feast of Mid-Pentecost

(The text for Matins is taken from the feastday.)

Wednesday Evening Vespers

AT PSALM 140

Tone 4 Christ met the Samaritan woman by the well. * Though He asked for water, He thirsted for her salvation. * He knew everything she had done. * She gave Him a drink and drew living water, the fullness of joy. * She proclaimed to all in her town: * Behold, the Messiah foretold in the Law of old * has appeared clothed in humanity. * He has unveiled all my hidden thoughts.

Behold, the anointed Messiah has appeared on earth. * The Samaritan woman proclaimed to the town: * It was written in the Law of old * that a great prophet would come, both God and man. * He knew all my deeds. * He uncovered everything hidden in the depths of my heart. * The whole town ran and saw the truth of her words. * They marveled, confirmed in faith by the sight.

Once at the sixth hour, O Master, * our first mother saw You walking in Paradise. * Now her daughter, at the same hour, sees You, O Fountain of life, * sitting at the well, asking her for water to drink. * You are the Fountain of living water. * Her thirst was quenched by drinking of your life-bearing streams. * She proclaimed to those in the town: * Come! Drink from the river of abundance.

Three Stichera from the Saint of the day

Tone 1 **Glory be...now and ever:** At the sixth hour, You came to the well, O Fountain of Wonders, * to ensnare the fruit of Eve; * for at the very hour, * she had been driven from Paradise by the guile of the serpent. * When the Samaritan woman came to draw water, * You said to her, O Savior: * Give Me water to drink, and I will give you waters of eternal life. * And the woman hastened to the city and proclaimed to the people: * Come and see Christ the Lord, the Savior of our souls.

APOSTICHA

Tone 4 O Lord, You have battered down the gates of Hades, * and by your death You have dissolved the realm of Death. * You have freed the human race from corruption, * bestowing life, incorruption, and your great mercy upon the world.

I have lifted up my eyes to You enthroned in heaven. Behold, as the eyes of servants are on the hands of their masters, as the eyes of a maid are on the hands of her mistress, so are our eyes on the Lord our God until He has mercy on us.

O Christ, You have enlightened the choir of the apostles with the Holy Spirit. * On their behalf, O God, wash away the filth of our sins * and have mercy on us.

Have mercy on us, O Lord, have mercy on us; for we have been filled with shame; our soul is all too full of the mockery of the rich, of the contempt of the proud.

O Saints who have the boldness to approach the Savior, * pray without ceasing for us sinners, * asking remission for our sins * and mercy for our souls.

Tone 2 **Glory be...now and ever:** When the Lord came to the well of Jacob, * the Samaritan woman entreated Him, saying: * Give me the water of faith, O Giver of life, * that I may obtain the waters of baptism, joy, and salvation. * O Lord, glory to You!

TROPARIA

Of the Saint

Tone 4 **Glory be...now and ever:** The joyful message of the Resurrection * was heard by the faithful women from the angel. * And being freed from the ancestral curse, * they boasted to the apostles: * Dead and despoiled is Death; * Christ our God is risen, * giving great mercy to the world.

Thursday Matins

SESSIONAL HYMN I

Tone 4 You were willingly crucified for us; * You were counted among the dead, O Giver of life. * You are risen on the third day, O Christ our God.* You demolished the dominion of Death by your power. * By your Resurrection You gave life to all in Hades. * Therefore, we all bless You and sing of your Resurrection, O immortal Lord.

Their span extends through all the earth; their words to the utmost bounds of the world.

Your apostles have shone as torches throughout the world, O Christ, * enlightening our souls with the brightness of your divine teachings. * By them You have dispelled the lies of the false gods, * brightening the world with the teachings of the faith. * By their prayers, save our souls.

God is to be feared in his holy place. He is the Lord, the God of Israel.

Armed with your Cross, O Christ our God, * your martyrs have overcome the tricks of the Enemy; * they have shone as stars leading your people. * They grant healing to those who call upon them with faith. * By their prayers, save our souls.

Glory be...now and ever: O Virgin all-immaculate, * you have given birth to the God of goodness. * Together with the apostles, implore Him unceasingly * that, before the end, * He may grant forgiveness of sins and the improvement of life * to us, the faithful, who sing to you with love; * for you alone are worthy of our hymns.

SESSIONAL HYMN II

Tone 6 You opened the fountain of your divinity * to the

Samaritan woman, O Lord. * Because of her faith, You poured upon her * rivers of divinely inspired knowledge. * Send forgiveness of sins down upon us as well, * O Lord beyond all goodness.

Glory be...now and ever: *(Repeat the above)*

Having beheld the Resurrection of Christ...

CANON

The CANON OF THE RESURRECTION may be sung first with each Ode of the Canon; the versicle "Christ is risen from the dead" is sung with the Canon of the Resurrection.

ODE 1

Tone 1 You destroyed the boundaries of death, O immaculate Virgin, * when You gave birth to Christ, the eternal Life, * who today is risen from the tomb * and enlightens the whole world.

Refrain: **Most holy Mother of God, save us!**

Seeing your Son and our God risen, * O Full of Grace and immaculate One, * you rejoice together with the apostles, O Mother of God; * you were the first to receive the proclamation of salvation * as the beginning of all joy.

Tone 4 He who struck Egypt and its tyrant and drowned them in the sea * has saved from the servitude of Pharaoh * his people who sing the victorious hymn of Moses, * for He is covered with glory.

Refrain: **Glory to your holy Resurrection, O Lord!**

The buried One is awakened, * and He awakens the human race with Him; * all creation rejoices, * and may the spiritual clouds rain down justice on this day.

O Lord, You willingly suffered crucifixion in the flesh, * and on the third day You arose from the dead, * emptying the prisons of Hades * and delivering those held captive, * for You are the Prince of life.

Having seen the resplendent angel, * the myrrh-bearing women fearfully fled from the tomb; * they hastened to the disciples to tell them of the resurrection of Christ.

O Lord, You are the living water * who built your dwelling place above the waters; * You gave the Samaritan woman the waters she asked for, * as she acknowledged your infinite mercy.

Glory be: Grant salvation to the faithful * who sincerely glorify You, O Holy Trinity, * Father, Son, and Holy Spirit; * O Creator of the world, * in your goodness grant us the forgiveness of our sins.

Now and ever: Rejoice, O throne of fire and golden candelabrum, * shining cloud and palace of the Word. * Rejoice, O mystical table * who was worthy to bear Christ, our bread of life.

It is the day of Resurrection; * O people, let us be enlightened by it. * The Passover is the Lord's Passover, * since Christ, our God, has brought us from death to life * and from earth to heaven. * Therefore, we sing the hymn of victory.

ODE 3

Tone 1 I returned today to life that knows no sunset, * by the goodness of Him born of you, O immaculate Virgin; * make his glory shine to the ends of the world.

Refrain: **Most holy Mother of God, save us!**

The God whom you brought into the world in the flesh, O immaculate Virgin, * is risen from the dead as He foretold. * Dance and celebrate and extol Him as God.

Tone 4 My heart is strengthened in the Lord * who teaches the faithful how to pray; * He weakens the weapons of war * and girds the weak with strength.

Refrain: **Glory to your holy Resurrection, O Lord!**

You were raised on the Cross of your own will, O Word, * and the rocks were rent asunder when they saw You. * All creation trembled with fear, * and the dead came forth from the tombs as from a dream.

Seeing your soul descend into Hades, O Word, * the souls of the just escaped from the bonds which held them through the ages; * and they praised your power which surpasses every spirit.

Why all this bother? * Why do you come with myrrh, O women, seeking the Lord in the tomb? * He is risen and the world is raised with Him, * said the resplendent angel to the myrrh-bearing women.

O Prince of Life and Fountain of immortality, * You sat down at the well, * and in your goodness filled the Samaritan woman * with the waters of wisdom which she asked of you.

Glory be: Unique and supreme is the God whom we praise, * the Father, Son, and divine Spirit, * the Trinity whom the heavenly powers glorify: * Holy, holy, holy are You forever.

Now and ever: Having wondrously conceived the God of the universe in your womb, O Virgin Mother, * you gave birth in a manner that surpasses understanding, * and remained a virgin as before you gave birth.

Come, let us partake of a new drink, * not miraculously produced from the barren rock, * but from the Fountain of immortality, * springing up from the tomb of Christ. * In Him is our firm strength.

SESSIONAL HYMN

Tone 4 Let heaven rejoice and let mortals dance, * for Christ is born of the Virgin and appears in our flesh. * By his death He has delivered the human race from the corruption of the grave. * He asked the Samaritan woman for water, * and in a striking miracle He in turn offered to her * the fountain of grace and immortal life. *(3 times)*

ODE 4

Tone 1 O immaculate Virgin, * He who made Adam your first father, * was made a man from your womb; * and by his death He destroyed the Death caused by sin; * and today He makes the divine brilliance of his holy Resurrection shine on you.

Refrain: **Most holy Mother of God, save us!**

The Messiah to whom you gave birth, * you behold today even more beautiful, O holy Virgin; * for He rises in glory from among the dead, * brilliant with beauty and grace and purity; * with the apostles, you glorify the Lord today in joy * for the salvation of the human race.

Tone 4 I heard your voice and I was afraid; * I acknowledge your works worthy of admiration, * for the earth is filled with your praise, O Lord.

Refrain: **Glory to your holy Resurrection, O Lord!**

Let the heavens rejoice and let the earth exalt! * The Lord is risen and has appeared to all his apostles.

Your power, O Death, has been abolished by the death of Christ our God; * and as the spouses come forth from the bridal chamber, * the dead arise from the tomb, * following the risen Lord.

Why are you crying, O women? * Why do you come with myrrh looking for the immortal One? * He is risen as He promised, * said the angel to the myrrh-bearing women.

O Lord, to the woman of Samaria who asked You for water, * You gave the water of divine knowledge; * she no longer thirsts, but she praises You always.

Glory be: O Trinity and supreme God, * Father, Son, and Holy Spirit, * sharing the same power and the same eternity, * save all who praise your name.

Now and ever: Moses, the giver of the Law formerly saw you in the burning bush, * and Daniel recognized you in the holy mountain, * O only Virgin who gave birth to God.

Let Habakkuk, * speaking in behalf of God, * stand with us at the divine watch; * let him show us the brilliant angel who proclaims: * Today, salvation comes to the world; * for Christ, being Almighty, is risen.

ODE 5

Tone 1 Divinely illumined by the life-giving rays * of the Resurrection of your Son, * O Mother of God and Virgin immaculate, * the assembly of the faithful shines in beauty.

Refrain: **Most holy Mother of God, save us!**

O King of glory, * when You became incarnate, your mother's virginity remained, * and You did not break the seals of the tomb. * All creation rejoices when it sees your holy Resurrection.

Tone 4 O Lord, let the light of your commandments shine on me, * for my spirit keeps watch before You, O Christ, and sings: * You are my God; I take refuge in You, O divine King of peace.

Refrain: **Glory to your holy Resurrection, O Lord!**

Arriving at your holy grave early in the morning, * the myrrh-bearing women saw a resplendent angel; * they were seized with fear, O Christ, * as they learned of your holy Resurrection.

Death is trampled down, Hades is imprisoned, * and the captives are delivered by the Resurrection of Christ. * Let us exalt with joy and clap our hands; * let us celebrate with gladness.

O Apostles, be jubilant together with the angels in

heaven; * dance for joy, all you mortals. * Death has vanished before the risen Christ, * and Adam exalts, banishing all sadness.

O Lord and Giver of life, * You gave the Samaritan woman streams of knowledge and forgiveness; * we also praise your infinite mercy.

Glory be: Tri-personal Unity and consubstantial Trinity, * Father, Son, and Holy Spirit, * indivisible by nature, we praise You as the one and only God, * the Master, Creator, and Lord of the universe.

Now and ever: O impassable door and untilled earth, * O ark of the covenant in which the Manna was kept, * O chalice and candelabrum, O censer of the divinity; * such are the names by which we know you, O Virgin.

Let us rise at early dawn * and bring to our Master a hymn instead of myrrh; * and we shall see Christ, * the Sun of Righteousness * who enlightens the life of all.

ODE 6

Tone 1 O Virgin Mother of God, * those who were once subjected to death * and to the corruption of the grave, * are now raised to immortal and eternal life * by Him who was incarnate from your womb.

Refrain: **Most holy Mother of God, save us!**

O immaculate Virgin, * He who wondrously dwelt in your womb and became flesh, * descended into the depths of the earth, * and rising from the tomb, * raised with Him all human nature.

Tone 4 May the storm not drown me, * and may the abyss not swallow me in the ocean of my passions. * For behold, I am thrown into the deep sea, * and as Jonah I cry out to You: * From the depths raise me up to You, O my God.

Refrain: **Glory to your holy Resurrection, O Lord!**

The impious ones nailed You to the Cross, * and a sword pierced your side; * the noble Joseph buried You in a new tomb, O Jesus Christ. * You resurrected in glory and raised with You all creation * who now praises your power, O Savior.

O Lord, in your power You crushed the gates and bolts of Hades; * You resurrected as God and told the myrrh-bearing women to rejoice. * They in turn announced to the disciples: * The living God is risen and has appeared to enlighten the world.

O women, why do you weep as for the dead? * And why do you bring this myrrh? * Christ is risen, said the resplendent angel; * He has left the linen shroud and the cloth. * Go quickly to his friends and announce the Resurrection!

O inexhaustible Source of life, * O Ocean of mercy and Lord of goodness, You stopped on your way and were seated at Jacob's well; * to the Samaritan woman You said: * Give me water to drink, and you shall receive streams of forgiveness.

Glory be: With the bodiless angels I praise in faith * the eternal Father, the Son who shares the same throne in heaven, * and the consubstantial Spirit, * the unique and royal majesty, * the divine Creator and the providence of the world.

Now and ever: O only Virgin who gave birth, * we praise you as the throne of the Lord, * the impassable door and unhewn mountain, * the spiritual candlestick and the room filled with light, * the tabernacle that manifests glory, * the ark of the covenant, the chalice, and the holy table.

You have descended into the realm of Death, O Christ, * and have broken ancient bonds which held the captive; * You arose from the tomb on the third day * like Jonah from the whale.

KONTAKION

Tone 8 When the Samaritan woman came to the well with faith, * she beheld You, O Water of Wisdom. * You allowed her to drink in abundance * and glorified her eternally, * for she inherited the heavenly kingdom.

IKOS

Let us worthily listen to the Gospel in which St. John clearly teaches us about the sacred mysteries which took place one time in Samaria. Speaking to a woman, the Lord asked her for water, He who formerly gathered the waters in one place, the Word of God who shares the same throne with the Father and the Spirit. For He has come to seek his fallen image, and his memory is glorified forever.

ODE 7

Tone 1 O Virgin immaculate, * today your Son destroyed Death, * giving eternal life to all mortals from all ages, * for

He is the God of our fathers, * and to Him alone belong blessing and glory.

Refrain: **Most holy Mother of God, save us!**

O Full of Grace, * He who reigns over all creation * became incarnate and dwelt in your womb, * having suffered death by the Cross; * as God all-powerful He is risen, * making us rise with Him.

Tone 4 Do not reject us until the end because of your holy name; * do not break your eternal covenant; * do not keep your love far away from us; * O Lord, God of our fathers, who is glorified forever.

Refrain: **Glory to your holy Resurrection, O Lord!**

At the moment of your divine Passion, O God of mercy, * according to your will You were placed among the ranks of criminals; * and when You bowed your head, O Creator, * the rocks were split in two and the earth trembled, * and the dead, who were asleep through the ages, were raised up.

Why do you seek among the dead the One who lives in eternity? * He is risen as He said; * see the empty tomb, the cloths, and the shroud. * Hasten and tell this to the apostles, * said the one who appeared as a young man to the holy women.

You are the Fountain of life, said the woman of Samaria to Christ. * My soul is always thirsty, O Word; * quench me with the grace of God * that the dryness of ignorance does not hold me in its power, * but that I may proclaim your wonders, O Lord.

Glory be: We sing to the indivisible Trinity, * consubstantial in the unity of three persons that we perceive: * The Father, Son, and Holy Spirit, * the eternal Creator of the universe, * God who is praised by the powers of heaven.

Now and ever: After your wondrous birth-giving, O holy Mother of God, * you preserved your virginity without blemish. * Thus angels and people everywhere sing to you with an incessant voice, * O tabernacle most pure in which the infinite One dwelt.

God, who saved the three youths from the furnace, * has become man * and suffered as any mortal; * but his passion clothed his mortality * with the splendor of incorruption. * He is the only blessed One, God of our fathers, * and is worthy of all praise.

ODE 8

Tone 1 The Creator came into this world * from you, O Virgin Mother of God; * destroying the jail of Hades, * He gave resurrection to us mortals; * and we also bless Christ forever.

***Refrain:* Most holy Mother of God, save us!**

Destroying all power of Death * on the day of his Resurrection, O Virgin, * your Son and the all-powerful God * made us partakers of his glory and divinity. * We also bless Christ forever.

Tone 4 In your wisdom, O Lord, You gather together the universe * and the foundations of the earth; * You establish these foundations again and set them over the great waters. * That is why we sing to You in joy: * Bless the Lord, all you works of the Lord.

***Refrain:* Glory to your holy Resurrection, O Lord!**

You willingly suffered death, O only immortal One; * and You crushed the bronze gates; * You took Hades captive, O heavenly King, * and freed those who had been held there through the ages * so that they may unceasingly praise the power of your goodness.

O long-suffering One, You were raised on the Cross; * the rocks were split open and the sun hid itself; * the curtain of the Temple was torn in two; * the earth shook and Hades was humiliated, * trembling because it had to give up its prisoners.

You appeared to those lying in darkness, * O unsetting Light and Life of the world; * when the just people saw You, they were jubilant and cried out: * You have come to deliver the captives by your power which we now praise.

Seated at the well at the sixth hour of the day, * You gave living water to the Samaritan woman, O Savior God, * and in your goodness, You granted her streams of knowledge. * For this reason we also sing to You: * Bless the Lord, all you works of the Lord.

Let us bless the Lord, Father, Son, and Holy Spirit.

We praise the Father who is from all eternity, * the coeternal Son, and the Spirit of holiness, * tri-personal and unique divinity, * having neither confusion nor division, * the Creator of the world and sovereign majesty for whom we sing: * Bless the Lord, all you works of the Lord.

Now and ever: With lips purified by a burning coal, * Isaiah foretold the Fire of the divinity * who was incarnate of you, O Virgin, in a wondrous fashion. * He burned away the sins of mortals to divinize our nature in his love, * O all-pure Virgin.

Let us praise, bless, and worship the Lord, singing and exalting Him above all forever.

This is that chosen and holy day, * Feast of feasts, * most solemn day, * only king and lord of all Sabbaths, * on which we ever praise Christ.

OMIT MAGNIFICAT

ODE 9

Tone 1 O Virgin, with one voice we, the faithful, extol you: * Rejoice, door of the Lord; rejoice, spiritual city; * rejoice, for you made the light of your Son shine upon us * on the day of his Resurrection.

Refrain: **Most holy Mother of God, save us!**

O immaculate One, full of grace, * exalt and dance in joy, O divine door of brightness; * for Jesus rested in the tomb * and rose in glory more brilliant than the sun; * and He enlightens the whole human race.

Tone 4 The Lord works wonders with the strength of his arm; * He overthrows the powerful from their thrones; * He raises up the humble. * He is the God of Israel, the rising Sun, and the Light from on high. * He protects us and directs our paths on the way of peace.

Refrain: **Glory to your holy Resurrection, O Lord!**

Behold Christ, the Life of all, * who of his own will is seen hanging on the Cross. * Seeing this, both the earth and the prisons of Hades trembled, * and many of the just were raised up in their bodies.

You came forth from the tomb, resplendent in beauty, * as a bridegroom coming from his bridal chamber. * O Christ, You have conquered Death; * and by your divine power You broke the tyranny and the bolts of Hades, * illuminating the world by your holy Resurrection.

Let us all together form a spiritual choir * to sing praises to the risen Lord. * Let the earth exalt and let heaven rejoice; * let the clouds rain down justice like the dew * upon us who keep this feast of Christ; * and let us celebrate in joy!

The Source of every good thing, who gives life to all the living, * and who pours out his teachings in abundance, * says to the woman of Samaria: * Give Me water to drink * that I in turn may give you the water * which will dry up the stream of your sins.

Glory be: O unique Light having no division, * such is the triple Sun of the one divinity: * the Father, Son, and Holy Spirit, * unique Life and Creator of the universe. * Together with the angels let us, the faithful, sing to Him * with a thrice-holy and sacred song.

Now and ever: O pure Virgin and tabernacle of the Light, * enlighten the eyes of my heart * which have been blinded by the deceits of the Enemy; * and make me worthy to contemplate with a pure heart * the marvelous brightness of the brilliant Sun * who is born of your womb.

Shine in splendor, * O new Jerusalem! * For the glory of the Lord * is risen upon you. * O Zion, sing with joy and rejoice! * And you, pure Mother of God, * rejoice in the resurrection of your Son.

HYMN OF LIGHT

Tone 2 You, O King and Lord, * have fallen asleep * in the flesh as a mortal man, * but on the third day You arose again. * You have raised Adam * from his corruption and made Death powerless. * You are the Pasch of incorruption. * You are the salvation of the world.

Glory be...now and ever: Meeting a woman in a village of Samaria, O almighty Savior, * You asked her for water to drink, * even though in ancient times in the desert * You brought forth from the most hard rock * the stream from which Israel drank in abundance. * O Giver of life, You awakened faith in the heart of the Samaritan woman, * and she now tastes both joy and living water in heaven forever.

AT THE PRAISES

Tone 4 O only Son and Word of God, * You were not separated from the bosom of the Father * when You came to earth out of love for us * and became a man without undergoing change. * In the flesh You suffered death on the Cross * even though You are beyond all suffering in your divinity. * You rose from the dead, granting immortality to the human race, * for You alone, O Lord, are almighty. *(2 times)*

Your Holy Spirit has made teachers * of your disciples who were without learning; * and by the attraction of their words resounding in every language, * they caused error to disappear, * O Christ our God all-powerful.

We admire your struggles, O holy Martyrs; * for, clothed in a mortal body, * you have driven back the invisible Enemy. * You were fearless before the threats of the tyrants; * you have undergone the worst of tortures; * and now you enjoy the glory that you deserve from Christ * who grants great mercy to our souls.

Tone 2 **Glory be...now and ever:** Truly, the Son, Word of God, co-eternal with the Father, * the Fountain of Wonders himself, came to the fountain, * where a woman of Samaria came to draw water. * And when the Savior saw her, He said to her: * Give Me water to drink and go call your husband. * But she addressed Him as man and not as God; * wishing to conceal the truth from Him, * she said: I have no husband. * And the Master replied: You have said the truth, that you have no husband; * for you have had five husbands, * and the one whom you now have is not your husband. * Amazed by these words, she went to the town * and proclaimed to the crowds, saying: * Come and behold Christ who grants the world great mercy.

APOSTICHA

Tone 4 You are the Fountain of goodness, * the Bestower of life, the Abyss of compassion. * Why do You ask the Samaritan woman: * Give Me water to drink. * Was it so that she could receive forgiveness from You? * We praise your compassion, * the goodness that saves the human race.

Ride on in triumph for the cause of truth and goodness and right.

Come, see the man sitting by the well. * Today He told me everything I have done. * He is truly the great Prophet. * He knows everything. He brings hidden things to light. * He quenches our thirst with the water of life. * We shall never thirst again, O Lover of Mankind.

Your love is for justice; your hatred for evil. Therefore God, your God, has anointed you with the oil of gladness.

The ever-flowing Fountain, the Life immortal, * the River always pure and never dry, * in his wanderings sat down near the well. * He sent his chosen disciples to buy food * while He communed with a woman, * desiring to free her from her sins, * to ensnare and enlighten the eyes of her soul.

Tone 3 **Glory be...now and ever:** Let heaven and earth greatly rejoice today. * Christ has come as a man in the flesh. * He desires to set Adam free from the curse. * He comes to Samaria to fill all with wonder. * He asks a woman for water, * though He fills the heavens with clouds. * Let all the faithful worship Him * who willingly emptied himself for us.

Thursday Evening Vespers

AT PSALM 140

Tone 4 Behold the Messiah Jesus * whose coming Moses foretold in the Law. * In his compassion, He has appeared on earth. * As a mortal He spoke with me by the well. * He is truly the Anointed One who has come into the world; * so the Samaritan woman told the people of Shechem.

From the mouth of the joyful woman * the whole town heard the news of sweet flowing water. * She hurried to lead them quickly to the well. * There they found the River of life, the Fountain of immortality, * who gives refreshment to our souls.

When the people in the town saw the Fountain * who came in the likeness of human nature, * they cried to the woman: * It is no longer because of your words that we believe. * Now we really know. * He is the eternal salvation and atonement for the world.

Three Stichera from the Saint of the day

Tone 6 **Glory be...now and ever:** Jesus met the Samaritan woman at Jacob's well. * The One who covers the earth with clouds asks water of her. * O, what a wonder! * The One who rides on the Cherubim converses with an adulterous woman. * The One who suspended the earth on the waters asks for water. * The One who caused the springs of water and their lakes to overflow seeks water. * He truly desires to save this woman from the snares of the Enemy * and to fill her with living water * to extinguish the flames of her passions; * for He alone is compassionate and the Lover of Mankind.

APOSTICHA

Tone 4 With your Cross to help us at all times, O Christ,* we destroy with ease * the snares of the Enemy.

I have lifted up my eyes to You enthroned in heaven. Behold, as the eyes of servants are on the hands of their masters, as the eyes of a maid are on the hands of her mistress, so are our eyes on the Lord our God until He has mercy on us.

In being lifted upon the Cross, O Lord, * You abolished the curse which we had inherited from our ancestors. * By going down into Hades, * You freed from eternal captivity those imprisoned there * and granted incorruption to the human race. * We, therefore, praise your life-giving and redeeming Resurrection.

Have mercy on us, O Lord, have mercy on us; for we have been filled with shame; our soul is all too full of the mockery of the rich, of the contempt of the proud.

O Martyrs of the Lord, * you are living sacrifices and spiritual offerings * and perfect incense burnt to God. * You are sheep that know God and are known to Him, * and wolves cannot break into his fold. * Pray that we may be led with you * to pasture beside the still waters.

Tone 6 **Glory be...now and ever:** The Lord spoke thus to the Samaritan woman: * If you knew the gift of God * and who it is that asks you: Give Me water to drink, * you would have asked Him, and He would give you living water * that you may never thirst again.

TROPARIA

Of the Saint

Tone 4 **Glory be...now and ever:** The joyful message of the Resurrection * was heard by the faithful women from tha Angel. * And being freed from the ancestral curse, * they boasted to the apostles: * Dead and despoiled is Death; * Christ our God is risen, * giving great mercy to the world.

Friday Matins

SESSIONAL HYMN I

Tone 4 You were nailed to the Cross, O Lord and Lover of Mankind, * to call us back from the midst of pagans. * You willingly stretched out your hands * and let your side be pierced with a lance. * Glory to You, O God of tenderness!

I will praise You, Lord, with all my heart; I will recount all your wonders.

You rose from the tomb, O immortal Savior, * raising your world by your power, O Christ our God. * You have broken in pieces the dominion of Death, * revealing the Resurrection to all. * Therefore, we all glorify You, O merciful Lover of Mankind.

God is to be feared in his holy place. He is the Lord, the God of Israel.

Your martyrs have received the crown of immortality from You * because of the struggles they have endured, O Lord. * By the strength of your arm they have conquered tyrants * and have reduced to nothing the boldness of demons. * By their prayers, O Christ our God, save our souls.

Glory be...now and ever: Seeing You raised upon the Cross, O Word of God, * your Mother cried maternally and said: * What is this strange wonder, O my Son? * How are You going down into death, * for You are the Life of the world? * But in your mercy You wish to give life to the departed.

SESSIONAL HYMN II

Tone 4 The Samaritan woman, as was her custom, * came to draw water from an earthly and perishable well. * Instead, she drew living water, * for she discovered the Well of Life. * He was resting where Jacob dug his well of old. * The noonday heat fatigued Him, * though He made the fiery sun to light the world.

Glory be...now and ever: *(Repeat the above)*

Having beheld the Resurrection of Christ...

CANON

(From Thursday, pages 216-225

HYMN OF LIGHT

Tone 2 You, O King and Lord, * have fallen asleep * in the flesh as a mortal man, * but on the third day you arose again. * You have raised Adam * from his corruption and made Death powerless. * You are the Pasch of incorruption. * You are the salvation of the world.

Glory be...now and ever: Meeting a woman in a villiage of Samaria, O almighty Savior, * You asked her for water to drink, * even though in ancient times in the desert * You brought forth from the most hard rock * the stream from which Israel drank in abundance. * O Giver of life, You awakened faith in the heart of the Samaritan woman, * and she now tastes both joy and living water in heaven forever.

AT THE PRAISES

Tone 4 To those who fear You, O Lord, * You have given the sign of your precious Cross * by which the rulers of darkness are overthrown; * and we have been restored to our first blessedness. * Therefore, we glorify your loving providence for us, * O almighty Jesus, the Savior of our souls. *(2 times)*

By your Cross lead us to your truth, O Christ our Savior; * deliver us from the snares of the Enemy. * You are risen from the dead; * now raise us up from our fall into sin. * Stretch forth your hand to us, O Lord, * through the prayers of your saints.

Precious is the death of your friends, O Lord; * by the sword, the flames, and the cold, they offered their lives * in the hope of obtaining the reward of their labors; * and their patience has merited your great mercy for them, O Savior.

Tone 6 **Glory be...now and ever:** Jesus, our Savior, the Fountain of life, * came to the well of Jacob the Patriarch. * He asked a Samaritan woman for water to drink. * She told Him that Jews have no dealings with Samaritans; * but the wise Creator incited her curiosity with the sweetness of his words, * and she asked Him for the water of everlasting life. * She received his gift and announced to all: * Come and see Him who knows all secrets as God. * He has come in the flesh for the salvation of the human race.

APOSTICHA

Tone 4 After coming to the well to draw water, * the Samaritan woman left behind her empty jar. * She ran to the town and shouted: * I have found the Fountain of bountiful life. * Come and drink from the saving stream; * refresh your hearts and wash away evil passions.

Ride on in triumph for the cause of truth and goodness and right.

You have spoken truly by saying you have no husband, * said the Savior to the Samaritan woman; * for you have had five husbands, * and he whom you now have is not your husband. * Immediately she went and cried out to the people of the town: * I have seen a man who told me everything I have ever done.

Your love is for justice; your hatred for evil. Therefore God, your God, has anointed you with the oil of gladness.

At the well of Jacob, the Samaritan woman * drew from the heavenly well another life-giving stream; * it flowed from the fountain * where she was accustomed to draw the corruptible water which came from the ground. * But it became a flowing stream in her heart, * a fountain that was previously unknown, * flowing as a fresh dew upon her burning passions.

Tone 8 **Glory be...now and ever:** When You appeared in the flesh, O Christ our God, * according to your ineffable plan of salvation, * the Samaritan woman heard your word of truth. * She left her jar at the well * and ran to tell the people of the town: * Come and see a man who knows the secrets of our hearts! * Could He not be the Christ, the awaited Messiah, * the One who possesses great mercy?

Friday Evening Vespers

AT PSALM 140

Tone 1 At the sixth hour, You came to the well, O Fountain of Wonders, * to ensnare the fruit of Eve; * for at that very hour, * she had been driven from Paradise by the guile of the serpent. * When the Samaritan woman came to draw water, * You said to her, O Savior: * Give Me water to drink, and I will give you waters of eternal life. * And the woman hastened to the city and proclaimed to the people: * Come and see Christ the Lord, the Savior of our souls.

Tone 2 When the Lord came to the well of Jacob, * the Samaritan woman entreated Him, saying: * Give me the water of faith, O Giver of life, * that I may obtain the waters of baptism, joy, and salvation. * O Lord, glory to You!

Truly, the Son, Word of God, co-eternal with the Father, * the Fountain of Wonders himself, came to the fountain, * where a woman of Samaria came to draw water. * And when the Savior saw her, He said to her: * Give Me water to drink and go call your husband. * But she addressed Him as man and not as God; * wishing to conceal the truth from Him, * she said: I have no husband. * And the Master replied: You have said the truth, that you have no husband; * for you have had five husbands, * and the one whom you now have is not your husband. * Amazed by these words, she went to the town * and proclaimed to the crowds, saying: * Come and behold Christ who grants the world great mercy.

Three Stichera from the Saint of the day

Tone 6 **Glory be:** Jesus met the Samaritan woman at Jacob's well. * The One who covers the earth with clouds asks water of her. * O, what a wonder! * The One who rides on the Cherubim converses with an adulterous woman. * The One who suspended the earth on the waters asks for water. * The One who caused the springs of water and their lakes to overflow seeks water. * He truly desires to save this woman from the snares of the Enemy * and to fill her with living water * to extinguish the flames of her passions; * for He alone is compassionate and the Lover of Mankind.

Tone 4 **Now and ever:** O Mother of God, David, the Prophet and Forefather of Christ, foretold in song * the great things that would happen to you. * He revealed that you would be a queen, * standing at the right hand of God; * and that you would be the Mother of Life and Intercessor for the world. * He prophesied that God, in his good will toward all, * would become incarnate of you without a human father. * Thus He would restore his image within us * which had become disfigured by our passions. * He would seek out the lost sheep that was trapped in the hills; * He would lift it upon his shoulder and carry it to his Father * who would place it in the midst of his heavenly hosts. * In like manner, Christ will save the world because of his great and abundant mercy.

APOSTICHA

Tone 4 We never cease to adore your life-giving Cross, O Christ our God, * and we glorify your Resurrection on the third day. * For You, almighty One, have thereby restored the corrupted nature of all * and reopened the way to heaven, * since You alone are gracious and You love all people.

The Lord reigns, He is clothed in majesty.

O Savior, You have absolved the penalty of disobedience, * committed through the tree of Eden, * by willingly being nailed to the tree of the Cross. * As almighty God, You descended into Hades * and broke asunder the bonds of Death. * We, therefore, venerate your Resurrection from the dead * and joyfully cry out to You: * Almighty Lord, glory to You!

For He has made the world firm, which shall not be moved.

O Lord, You have battered down the gates of Hades, * and by your death You have dissolved the realm of Death. * You have freed the human race from corruption, * bestowing life, incorruption, and your great mercy upon the world.

Holiness befits your house, O Lord, for length of days.

In being lifted upon the Cross, O Lord, * You abolished the curse which we had inherited from our ancestors. * By going down into Hades, * You freed from eternal captivity those imprisoned there * and granted incorruption to the human race. * We, therefore, praise your life-giving and redeeming Resurrection.

Tone 8 **Glory be...now and ever:** When You appeared in the flesh, O Christ God, * to accomplish your plan of salvation, * the Samaritan woman heard the word of God's love for us. * She left the well and ran to the town and said: * Come and see the One who knows the secrets of our hearts; * can this be the Christ, the Messiah whom we await, * the One who bestows great mercy?

TROPARIA

Of the Saint

Tone 4 **Glory be...now and ever:** The joyful message of the Resurrection * was heard by the faithful women from the Angel. * And being freed from the ancestral curse, * they boasted to the apostles: * Dead and despoiled is Death; * Christ our God is risen, * giving great mercy to the world.

Saturday Matins

SESSIONAL HYMN I

Tone 4 The myrrh-bearing women looked into the entrance of the tomb, * and because they could not bear the brilliance of the angel, * they trembled in astonishment and said: * Has He who opened Paradise to the thief been stolen, * or is He who proclaimed his Resurrection before his Passion now risen? * Truly, Christ is risen, * granting resurrection and life to those in Hades.

Glory be: You are risen, O immortal Savior, * and have

raised the whole world with You. * By your power, O Christ our God, * You have crushed the dominion of Death. * You have shown your Resurrection to all, O God of mercy, * for You love us and we glorify You.

Now and ever: O Mother of God, the mystery hidden from all eternity * and unknown even to the angels, * was revealed through you to those on earth: * God took on our human nature * and united it to his divine nature in a perfect but unconfused union. * Then, He willingly accepted the Cross for our sake * and thereby raised again the first created man * and saved our souls from death.

SESSIONAL HYMN II

Tone 4 Let heaven rejoice and celebrate. * Christ has shone forth from the Virgin. * He has revealed himself as a man to those on earth. * He has washed away everyone's corruption by his own death. * He has shown wonders to the Samaritan woman. * He has given her the well of healing waters as she asked, * for He alone is immortal.

Glory be...now and ever: *(Repeat the above)*

Having beheld the Resurrection of Christ...

CANON

(From Thursday, pages 216-225)

HYMN OF LIGHT

Tone 2 You, O King and Lord, * have fallen asleep * in the flesh as a mortal man, * but on the third day You arose again. * You have raised Adam * from his corruption and made Death powerless. * You are the Pasch of incorruption. * You are the salvation of the world.

Glory be...now and ever: Meeting a woman in a village of Samaria, O almighty Savior, * You asked her for water to drink, * even though in ancient times in the desert * You brought forth from the most hard rock * the stream from which Israel drank in abundance. * O Giver of life, You awakened faith in the heart of the Samaritan woman, * and she now tastes both joy and living water in heaven forever.

AT THE PRAISES

Tone 4 You suffered death on the Cross, * and You arose from the dead. * We glorify your holy Resurrection, O almighty Lord.

By your Cross You delivered us from the ancient curse, O Christ; * by your death You have utterly destroyed the Devil who tyrannized the human race; * by your Resurrection You have filled the whole world with joy. * Therefore, we cry out to You: * O Lord who rose from the dead, glory to You!

By your Cross lead us to your truth, O Christ our Savior; * deliver us from the snares of the Enemy. * You are risen from the dead; * now raise us up from our fall into sin. * Stretch forth your hand to us, O Lord, * through the prayers of your saints.

O only Son and Word of God, * You were not separated from the bosom of the Father * when You came to earth out of love for us * and became a man without undergoing change. * In the flesh You suffered death on the Cross * even though You are beyond all suffering in your divinity. * You rose from the dead, granting immortality to the human race, * for You alone, O Lord, are almighty.

Tone 6 **Glory be...now and ever:** Jesus, our Savior, the Fountain of life, * came to the well of Jacob the Patriarch. * He asked a Samaritan woman for water to drink. * She told Him that Jews have no dealings with Samaritans; * but the wise Creator incited her curiosity with the sweetness of his words, * and she asked Him for the water of everlasting life. * She received his gift and announced to all: * Come and see Him who knows all secrets as God. * He has come in the flesh for the salvation of the human race.

APOSTICHA

Tone 4 The woman, desiring to find relief from her many evil passions, * endured the noonday heat and came to the well. * There she met the immortal Fountain, * gushing with streams of living water. * She drank freely from the words of the Word and no longer desired the well of earthly and perishable things.

Ride on in triumph for the cause of truth and goodness and right.

Christ, the wise Creator, * ignored the customs of the Jews. * They have no dealings with Samaritans, * yet He asked the woman for a drink of water; * and by his pleasing words He led her to ask for divine water, the life-giving drink. * She drank and channeled the flood to water her town.

Your love is for justice; your hatred for evil. Therefore God, your God, has anointed you with the oil of gladness.

The Samaritan woman said to You, O Christ: * You do not even have a bucket and the well is deep. * How can You give me immortal water? * She imagined You to be merely a man, not God; * but when she drank the sweet waters of your words, * she confessed You to be both God and the Savior of all.

Tone 6 **Glory be...now and ever:** The Lord spoke thus to the Samaritan woman: * If you knew the gift of God, * and who it is that asks you: Give Me water to drink, * you would have asked Him, and He would give you living water * that you may never thirst again.

Sunday of the Man Born Blind

Vespers

AT PSALM 140

Tone 5 With your precious Cross, O Christ, * You have put the Devil to shame. * With your Resurrection You have deadened the sting of sin * and have saved us from the gates of Death. * We, therefore, glorify You, O only-begotten Son of God.

O Christ, who granted resurrection to all people, * You were led like a lamb to the slaughter. * Then the princes of Hades were struck with terror * as they saw the gates of their tearful domain being lifted up; * for Christ, the King of Glory, entered therein * and exclaimed to those in chains: Go forth from here! * and to those in darkness: Go forth into the light!

What a great wonder! * The Creator of invisible beings suffered in the flesh for the human race * and rose from the dead as immortal. * Come, therefore, all you nations and adore Him; * for through his compassion we have been freed from the snares of the Devil, * and we have learned to praise the one God in three persons.

We offer to You our evening worship, * O Light whom the darkness of night can never extinguish. * For in these latter days your radiance has appeared to the world, * shining in your flesh as light reflected from a mirror. * Your brilliance has descended even to the depths of Hades and dissolved its gloom. * O Lord, Giver of Light, glory to You; * for You have shown the radiance of your Resurrection to all the nations.

Let us glorify Christ, the Author of our salvation; * for by his resurrection from the dead, * the world has been delivered from the deception of Satan. * The choirs of angels rejoice as the treachery of evil spirits vanishes, * fallen Adam arises, and the Devil is vanquished.

Those who guarded the tomb of Christ * were told by the evil men who hired them: * Take this silver and keep silent. * Tell no one of the Resurrection of Christ; * rather tell everyone that while you were sleeping his body was stolen. * But who has ever heard of a body being stolen, * a body which had already been anointed? * Why would anyone take a body from the grave naked * and leave the burial shroud in the tomb? * Do not deceive yourselves, O people of Judea. * Study the teachings of the prophets, * and you will come to understand that Jesus Christ is almighty God * and truly the Savior of the world.

O Lord our Savior, * who subjected hell and conquered Death, * and enlightened the world through your precious Cross, * have mercy on us.

Tone 2 The man who was blind from birth asked himself: * Was I born blind because of the sin of my parents, * or am I a living sign of the unbelief of the nations? * I am not content to ask whether it is night or day; * my feet can no longer endure tripping upon the stones. * I have not seen the brightness of the sun, * nor have I seen the image and likeness of my Creator. * Yet I beseech You, O Christ our God, * to look upon me and have mercy on me. *(2 times)*

Passing by the Temple, Jesus saw a man who was blind from birth. * He had compassion on him and put mud on his eyes. * He said to him: Go to the pool of Siloam and wash. * He washed and recovered his sight; * then he rendered glory to God. * But his neighbors said to him: * Who opened your eyes which no one before could heal? * And he answered them, saying: A man called Jesus. * He told me to go and wash in the pool of Siloam, and now I see. * He is in truth Christ the Messiah, * of whom Moses wrote in the Law. * He is the Savior of our souls.

Tone 5 **Glory be:** As You walked along, O Lord, * You found a man who had been blind from birth. * In surprise, the disciples asked You: * Was it because of the sin of this man or his parents * that he was born blind, O Master? * But You, O Savior, answered them, saying: * Neither has this man sinned, nor his parents, * but that the works of God would be revealed in him. * I must accomplish the works of Him who sent Me, * which no one else can work. * As You said that, You spat on the ground * and made mud from the dust to anoint his eyes. * And You said to him: Go and wash in the pool of Siloam. * When he washed, he was healed and cried out to You: * O Lord, I believe! * And he bowed down and worshiped You. * Therefore, we also cry out to You: Have mercy on us!

Tone 5 **Now and ever:** The passing of the Israelites through the Red Sea * was already a forshadowing of the virgin-birth. * On that occasion, Moses parted the waters; * at the Incarnation, Gabriel announced the miracle of God's union with Mary. * In ancient times, the Israelites passed through the depths of the sea * without being drenched by the waters; * now the Virgin has given birth to Christ without seed. * After the Israelites passed through the sea, it remained impassable; * after the birth of Emmanuel, the immaculate Virgin remains forever incorrupt. * O God, who exists from all eternity, and yet appeared as man, * have mercy on us.

APOSTICHA

***Tone* 5** O Christ our Savior, * we lift up our voices in song to glorify You. * For, in your love for humanity, * You became incarnate without leaving heaven; * You accepted the Cross and death; * You cast down the gates of Hades; * and on the third day You arose from the dead * for the salvation of our souls.

PASCHAL HYMNS

Let God arise and let his enemies be scattered, and let those who hate Him flee from before his face.

Today the sacred Pasch is revealed to us, * holy and new Pasch, * the mystical Passover, * the venerable Passover, * the Pasch which is Christ the Redeemer, * spotless Pasch, great Pasch, * the Pasch of the faithful, * the Pasch which is the key to the gates of Paradise, * the Pasch which sanctifies all the faithful.

As smoke vanishes, so let them vanish as wax melts before the fire.

O Women, * be the heralds of good news and tell what you saw; * tell of the vision and say to Zion: * Accept the good news of joy from us, * the news that Christ has risen. * Exalt and celebrate * and rejoice, O Jerusalem, * seeing Christ the King coming from the tomb * like a bridegroom.

So let the wicked perish at the presence of God, and let the righteous ones rejoice.

The myrrh-bearing women * arrived just before the dawn * at the tomb of the Giver of Life * and found an angel seated on the stone * who spoke these words to them: * Why do you seek the Living among the dead? * Why do you mourn the Incorruptible among those subject to decay? * Go, announce the good news * to his disciples.

This is the day that the Lord has made; let us exalt and rejoice in it.

Pasch so delightful, * Pasch of the Lord is the Pasch, * most honored Pasch now dawned on us. * It is the Pasch! * Therefore, let us joyfully embrace one another. * O Passover, save us from sorrow; * for today Christ has shown forth from the tomb * as from a bridal chamber * and filled the women with joy by saying: * Announce the good news * to my apostles.

Tone 8 **Glory be:** O Christ our God, spiritual Sun of Justice, * by your pure touch, You enlightened the eyes of him * who from his mother's womb was without light. * Enlighten the eyes of our hearts * and make us children of the light and of the day, * that we may cry out to You in faith: * How great is your compassion toward us, * O Lover of Mankind, glory to You!

Tone 5 **Now and ever:** This is the Resurrection Day. * Let us be enlightened by this Feast, * and let us embrace one another. * Let us call Brethren * even those who hate us, * and in the Resurrection, * forgive everything; and let us sing: * Christ is risen from the dead! * By death He conquered Death, * and to those in the graves He granted life.

TROPARIA

Tone 5 O faithful, let us praise and adore the Word, * eternal with the Father and the Spirit, * and who was born of the Virgin for our salvation; * for He willed to be lifted upon the Cross as man and to suffer death, * and to raise the dead by his glorious Resurrection.

Tone 5 **Glory be...now and ever:** Rejoice, Virgin, impassable gateway of the Lord! * Rejoice, protective wall of those who take refuge in you! * Rejoice, peaceful haven untroubled by storms! * Rejoice, Virgin who has not known wedlock * and yet has given birth in the flesh to your Creator and God! * O Mother of God, never cease to intercede * for those who praise and worship your Son.

Sunday Matins

SESSIONAL HYMN I

Tone 5 Let us praise the honored Cross of the Lord; * let us venerate his holy burial with hymns; * let us glorify his holy Resurrection. * For He raised the dead from the graves because He is God. * He despoiled the might of Death and broke the power of Satan, * and He shed light on those who are in Hades.

Arise then, Lord, lift up your hand. O God, do not forget the poor!

You were counted among the dead, O Lord, * even though You put to death the Prince of death. * You were placed in a grave, although You emptied the graves. * On earth, the soldiers guarded the tomb, * but below, You raised the dead who from all eternity had fallen asleep. * Therefore, O Lord, the almighty and incomprehensible One, glory to You!

Glory be...now and ever: Rejoice, O holy mountain which the Lord ascended! * Rejoice, O living bush, unconsumed by the fire! * Rejoice, only bridge reaching from the world to God * and leading the dead to eternal life! * Rejoice, O pure one, free of corruption; * you gave birth without the aid of man to the Savior of the world!

SESSIONAL HYMN II

Tone 5 The transgressors of the Law, O merciful Lord, * nailed You between two thieves and pierced your side with a spear. * You submitted to burial, and You shattered the gates of Hades, * and You rose again on the third day. * Therefore, the women hastened to behold You * and told the good news of your Resurrection to the apostles. * O God most high, You are praised by the angels in heaven. * You are blessed, O Lord, glory to You!

I will praise You, Lord, with all my heart; I will recount all your wonders.

O Lord, your mystery beyond understanding is salvation for the world; * risen from the dead in a divine manner, O God, * You have raised all mortals with You. * O Lord and Giver of life, glory to You!

Glory be...now and ever: O unwedded Spouse and birth-giver of God, * you changed the sorrow of Eve into joy. * We the faithful praise and bow before you, * for you have lifted the ancient curse. * And now O most holy Virgin, all-worthy of our hymns, * intercede for our salvation.

HYPAKOE

The minds of the myrrh-bearing women were dazzled by the angelic vision, * and their souls were illumined by the divine Resurrection. * Therefore, they spoke to the apostles, saying: * Declare to the nations the Resurrection of the

Lord * who works wonders with us and bestows on us great mercy.

GRADUAL HYMNS

Antiphon I

In my sorrow I sing to You * just as David did, O Lord. * Deliver my soul from deceitful tongues.

Blessed is the life of those who dwell in the desert, * for they are carried on the wings of divine love.

Glory be...now and ever: The Holy Spirit upholds the entire universe, * both the visible and the immaterial world. * He holds all powers in himself, * for He is truly One of the Trinity.

Antiphon II

Let us go up to the mountain, O my soul, * to the place from which our help comes.

Let your right hand, O Lord, shelter me as a wing, * and preserve me from all evil deceits.

Glory be...now and ever: Let us profess the divinity of the Holy Spirit by saying: * Truly You are life and love, light and intelligence; * You are the God of goodness who reigns forever.

Antiphon III

When they said to me: Let us go into the courts of the Lord, * I offered my prayers to Him; * they were filled with joy and happiness.

In the house of David an astonishing mystery takes place, * for there a fire consumes every evil thought.

Glory be...now and ever: Truly the Holy Spirit gives life to the world, * for He fills every being with life, * as does the Father and the divine Word.

PROKEIMENON

Tone 5 Arise, then, Lord, lift up your hand! The Lord is king forever and ever.

v. I will praise You, Lord, with all my heart.

GOSPEL

John 20: 11-18

Having beheld the Resurrection of Christ, * let us adore the holy Lord Jesus * who alone is sinless. * We bow to your Cross, O Christ, * and we praise and glorify your holy Resurrection. * You are our God * and besides

You we recognize no other, * and we invoke your name. * Come, all you faithful, * and let us bow to the holy Resurrection of Christ, * since, through the Cross, * joy has come to all the world. * Ever praising the Lord, * let us extol his Resurrection, * since He, having endured the Crucifixion, * has destroyed Death by his death.

(3 times)

CANON

The CANON OF THE RESURRECTION may be sung first with each Ode of the Canon; the versicle "Christ is risen from the dead" is sung with the Canon of the Resurrection.

ODE 1

Tone 1 You destroyed the boundaries of death, O immaculate Virgin, * when You gave birth to Christ, the eternal Life, * who today is risen from the tomb * and enlightens the whole world.

Refrain: **Most holy Mother of God, save us!**

Seeing your Son and our God risen, * O Full of Grace and immaculate One, * you rejoice together with the apostles, O Mother of God; * you were the first to receive the proclamation of salvation * as the beginning of all joy.

Tone 5 Israel was able to cross as if on dry land, * the ground on which the sun has never shone, * the abyss which has never seen the sky openly. * And You, O Lord, have led them to your mountain of holiness * as they sang a hymn of victory.

Refrain: **Glory to your holy Resurrection, O Lord!**

You bore your Cross in your flesh willingly, * and You poured out life and blessings to the world, * O Lord, the only blessed One and creator of the universe. * We praise You, we bless You, and we glorify You, * as we sing a hymn of victory.

The noble Joseph placed your most pure body in a sepulcher, O long-suffering Lord, * and rolled a stone before the entrance of the tomb. * But You resurrected in glory * and raised the world with You, * and they sing a hymn of victory.

Why do you mix your tears with the myrrh that you carry, * said the resplendent angel to the women. * Christ is risen! * Go and tell the holy apostles, who are crying and lamenting bitterly, * so that they may rejoice and exalt with joy.

The Redeemer has worked marvelous wonders, * for He

healed the man born blind by making mud and saying: * Go and wash in the pool of Siloam * so that you may come to know your God who is walking on this earth; * through his goodness He now bears our flesh.

Glory be: O faithful, let us venerate the unity of three Persons; * let us glorify the Father, the Son, and the Holy Spirit, * the Creator and Redeemer of the world. * We praise the only uncreated God, and with the angels we sing: * Holy, holy, holy are You, O Lord our God.

Now and ever: In his goodness, the Lord wished to save the human race * which had fallen through the deceit of the Enemy; * He dwelt in your virginal womb, O holy Lady. * Implore Him to save the Christian people from the threat that endangers them.

Our Savior and God led the people of Israel * across the Red Sea as if on dry land * and drowned Pharaoh and his whole army. * Let us praise Him who alone is worthy of our songs, * for He is covered with glory.

ODE 3

Tone 1 I returned today to life that knows no sunset, * by the goodness of Him born of you, O immaculate Virgin; * make his glory shine to the ends of the world.

Refrain: **Most holy Mother of God, save us!**

The God whom you brought into the world in the flesh, O immaculate Virgin, * is risen from the dead as He foretold. * Dance and celebrate and extol Him as God.

Tone 5 In your power, O Lord, * strengthen my heart which has been toubled by the surges of this life, * and lead it to the harbor of peace.

Refrain: **Glory to Your holy Resurrection, O Lord!**

You strengthened our shipwrecked hearts, O long-suffering Lord, * when the whole earth was shaken * by the crucifixion You suffered in the flesh.

The noble Joseph placed You in a new tomb, O God of tenderness, * and You renew us by your Resurrection from the dead on the third day.

The angel shining with divine splendor said to the women: * Why do you seek the Lord among the dead? * He is risen as He promised.

You healed the man blind from birth, O God of mercy, * as

he came to You and glorified your marvels and your work of salvation.

Glory be: We adore You as the only God of the universe, * the three Persons whom no other has created: * the Father, the Son, and the Holy Spirit.

Now and ever: From your womb, O most holy Lady, * you gave birth as a virgin to God who is clothed in the flesh; * beseech Him to have pity on us.

O Christ, by the power of your Cross, * strengthen our hearts so that we may sing and glorify your saving Ascension.

SESSIONAL HYMN

Tone 8 The Master and Creator of the universe * met the man born blind who sighed and said: * I have never in my life seen the brilliance of the sun, * nor have I seen the brightness of the moon. * That is why I cry out to You, O Lord born of the Virgin, to enlighten the whole world: * In your mercy give light also to your servant * so that I may bow before You and say: * O Christ our God, grant me forgiveness of my sins, * for You are the One who loves all in your goodness.

ODE 4

Tone 1 O immaculate Virgin, * He who made Adam your first father, * was made a man from your womb; * and by his death He destroyed the Death caused by sin; * and today He makes the divine brilliance of his holy Resurrection shine on you.

Refrain: **Most holy Mother of God, save us!**

The Messiah to whom you gave birth, * you behold today even more beautiful, O holy Virgin; * for He rises in glory from among the dead, * brilliant with beauty and grace and purity; * with the apostles, you glorify the Lord today in joy * for the salvation of the human race.

Tone 5 O Lord, I heard your voice and I was filled with fear; * I meditated on your work of salvation, * and I glorify You, the only Lover of Mankind.

Refrain: **Glory to Your holy Resurrection, O Lord!**

Beneath a tree I discovered death; * but beneath the tree of the Cross, O Lord the Giver of life, * You gave me life again in your goodness. * That is why I glorify You, O Word.

At the time of your marvelous appearing, O Lord, * You

said to your disciples: * Go and announce my Resurrection to all nations.

To strengthen the faith in your Resurrection, O Lord, * You appeared to your friends many times; * and You filled them with joy, O Christ.

To the one who had always been blind, O Lord, * You gave sight and said to him: * Go and wash your eyes that you may see, * and that you may glorify my divinity.

Glory be: Trinity sharing the same glory and the same eternity, * divinity that cannot be divided, * in whom we see three Persons, * save the faithful who glorify You.

Now and ever: We glorify your birth-giving that surpasses nature, O most pure Virgin; * and we call you blessed, O Virgin immaculate, * for you conceived the God of the universe.

O Lord, I have heard your voice and I recognized the power of your Cross, * because through it Paradise was opened; * and I said: Glory to your power, O Lord!

ODE 5

Tone 1 Divinely illumined by the life-giving rays of the Resurrection of your Son, * O Mother of God and Virgin immaculate, * the assembly of the faithful shines in beauty.

Refrain: **Most holy Mother of God, save us!**

O King of glory, * when You became incarnate, your mother's virginity remained, * and You did not break the seals of the tomb. * All creation rejoices when it sees your holy Resurrection.

Tone 5 Come to the aid of my tormented soul * which is continually seized by the darkness of passions; * enlighten me with your rays, O Sun of justice, * so that your light may illumine my darkness.

Refrain: **Glory to your holy Resurrection, O Lord!**

You are raised upon the Cross to lift up all mortals, O God of mercy. * You crushed our enemy, the serpent, to give life to the work of your hands, * for You are the only God of the universe.

You freely suffered death and were placed in the tomb; * You emptied the kingdom of Hades, O Lord and immortal King, * and by your holy Resurrection You raised the dead with You.

You accomplished great wonders on earth, O Lord, * and You were put to death by the impious ones; * but You, O Lord, the only all-powerful One, * resurrected from the dead as You promised.

Giving sight to the one who had no earthly eyes, * You also enlightened the eyes of his heart; * and when he recognized You as his Creator, * You led him to glorify the God of love who is seen in the flesh.

Glory be: O faithful, with one heart let us glorify the triple Unity and the unique Trinity: * the Father, the Son, and the Holy Spirit, * one God and the Creator of the universe.

Now and ever: O Virgin and most pure Mother, * how did you conceive without knowing man? * How did you feed the One who feeds the world? * God alone understands this, for He is the One who caused it to be.

As we watch in the night and wait for morning, * O Lord, we cry to You: * Have mercy on us and save us, * for You are truly our God and we know no other but You.

ODE 6

Tone 1 O Virgin Mother of God, * those who were once subjected to death * and to the corruption of the grave, * are now raised to immortal and eternal life * by Him who was incarnate from your womb.

Refrain: **Most holy Mother of God, save us!**

O immaculate Virgin, * He who wondrously dwelt in your womb and became flesh, * descended into the depths of the earth, * and rising from the tomb, * raised with Him all human nature.

Tone 5 O Lord, You saved the prophet from the sea monster; * also rescue me, I beseech You, from the pit of my furious passions * so that my eyes may behold your holy temple.

Refrain: **Glory to your holy Resurrection, O Lord!**

O Lord, You were crucified between two thieves; * now deliver from the plunder of passions * those who with one voice praise your Crucifixion and holy Resurrection.

Your body was placed in the tomb, * O Christ, the Giver of life to all the dead; * but You resurrected, O Lord and Word, * and by your divine power You emptied all the graves.

After your Resurrection, O Christ, You said to your friends: * Remain in Jerusalem until you are clothed with power from on high * with an invisible protection.

You made mud and smeared it on the eyes of the man born blind; * and You let him contemplate, O Word of God, * the ineffable power by whom the world was saved.

Glory be: O unity of three Persons, * the unbegotten Father, the only Son, and the Spirit who proceeds eternally,* O unique Power of the thrice-holy Lord, * save the people who are your own.

Now and ever: Who can explain your wonders, O Virgin immaculate? * For you gave birth according to the flesh in a marvelous manner, O pure Virgin, * to the One who saves the world from all iniquity.

The abyss surrounds me completely; * the sea monster holds me as if in a tomb; * I cried to You, O Lover of Mankind, * and your right hand has saved me.

KONTAKION

Tone 5 With eyes that are spiritually blind I come to You, O Christ; * and, like the man who was blind since birth, * I cry out to You with repentance: * You are a shining Light to those who are in darkness.

IKOS

Give me to drink of your boundless wisdom and of heavenly knowledge, O Christ, for You are the light of those in darkness and the guide of those who have lost their way. Thus I will clearly recount what the Holy Book teaches in the Gospel of peace, about the miracle You performed for the blind man. He had been in darkness from his birth, and he received from You both physical and spiritual sight, and cried out in faith: For those in darkness, your light surpasses all radiance.

ODE 7

Tone 1 O Virgin immaculate, * today your Son destroyed Death, * giving eternal life to all mortals from all ages, * for He is the God of our fathers, * and to Him alone belong blessing and glory.

Refrain: **Most holy Mother of God, save us!**

O Full of Grace, * He who reigns over all creation *

became incarnate and dwelt in your womb, * having suffered death by the Cross; * as God all-powerful He is risen, * making us rise with Him.

Tone 5 The blazing flames were overcome by the prayer of the youths, * and the furnace covered with dew was the witness of this; * for it neither burned nor consumed those who praised the God of our fathers.

Refrain: **Glory to your holy Resurrection, O Lord!**

When You were raised upon the Cross, O Lord, * the sun was darkened, the earth trembled, all creation was shaken, * and the dead were raised from their tombs.

O King, when You were raised from the dead, * You also awakened the souls who were asleep; * they glorified your sovereign power * with which You broke the chains of Death.

The myrrh-bearing women hastened together early in the morning, * but when they learned of your Resurrection, O Lord, * they rejoiced with the divine apostles; * through their prayers grant us the forgiveness of our sins.

You smeared the eyes of the blind man with some mud, * and You ordered him to go to Siloam; * having washed, he recovered his sight, * and he glorified You, O Christ, the supreme King of the universe.

Glory be: Let us praise the Father without beginning, * the co-eternal Son, and the Spirit of truth: * Holy, holy, holy are You, O our God, * Creator and King of the universe.

Now and ever: You remained both virgin and holy after giving birth; * for you brought our God into the world, * and his power renews all. * Implore Him unceasingly for our salvation.

O Savior who saved the youths who sang to You in the furnace, * blessed are You, O Lord and God of our fathers.

ODE 8

Tone 1 The Creator came into this world * from you, O Virgin Mother of God; * destroying the jail of Hades, * He gave resurrection to us mortals; * and we also bless Christ forever.

Refrain: **Most holy Mother of God, save us!**

Destroying all power of Death * on the day of his Resurrection, O Virgin, * your Son and the all-powerful God * made us partakers of his glory and divinity. * We also bless Christ forever.

Tone 5 O Choir of angels and all the human race, * bless the King and Creator of the world; * praise Him, you priests, * and let the whole nation exalt Him forever.

Refrain: **Glory to your holy Resurrection, O Lord!**

O Christ and King of the universe, * when the angels saw You hanging on the Cross * and all creation trembling with fear, * they too were seized with fright and sang of your love for us.

Seeing You in the depths, Hades lamented * and hastened to give up all the dead * which it had held in its power through the ages; * and it praised your love for us, O Lord.

You performed unheard of wonders, O Christ: * You were willingly raised upon a Cross; * You were counted among the dead even though You are the conqueror of Hades; * and You freed all the captives by your mighty arm.

You gave sight to the blind man who met You, O Christ; * and You ordered Him to wash in the pool of Siloam * that he might see and announce your divinity which has appeared in the flesh for the salvation of all.

Let us bless the Lord, Father, Son, and Holy Spirit.

Indivisible Trinity and Unity beyond confusion, * O God of all and Creator of the world, * preserve from every ordeal those who praise your name * and who faithfully adore your divine majesty.

Now and ever: O most pure Virgin, full of grace, * implore your Son and our God without ceasing: * may He not be ashamed of me on the day of judgment; * rather, may He count me among the elect of his flock.

Let us praise, bless, and worship the Lord, singing and exalting Him above all forever.

The Son of God, born of the Father before all ages, * has taken flesh from the Virgin Mother in these last days. * Praise Him, you priests, * and let the whole nation exalt Him forever.

OMIT MAGNIFICAT

ODE 9

Tone 1 O Virgin, with one voice we, the faithful, extol you: * Rejoice, door of the Lord; rejoice, spiritual city; * rejoice, for you made the light of your Son shine upon us * on the day of his Resurrection.

Refrain: **Most holy Mother of God, save us!**

O immaculate One, full of grace, * exalt and dance in joy, O divine door of brightness; * for Jesus rested in the tomb * and rose in glory more brilliant than the sun; * and He enlightens the whole human race.

Tone 5 The almighty One has done wonders for you, * for you remained a virgin even after giving birth; * you gave birth without seed to your Creator. * For this reason, O Mother of God, we extol you.

Refrain: **Glory to your holy Resurrection, O Lord!**

You were nailed to the Cross, O Christ our God; * You conquered the powers of the enemies; * You wiped out the ancient curse. * For this reason, O Lord, we extol You.

O Word, when Hades saw You descend to its depths, * it was seized with fright, * and it set free all the dead * who recognized the strength of your divine power; * and joining with them, we extol You.

Seeing Him perform miracles and wondrous signs, * the people were filled with jealousy * and put to death the One who despoiled Hades by his Resurrection * and who raised all the dead by his power.

You resurrected from the dead according to your Word, * and You appeared to your disciples after your Resurrection, O Giver of life; * You performed miracles and gave sight to the blind. * With them we extol You through the ages.

Glory be: The Father is Light, the Son also is Light, and the Spirit of truth is Light; * O indivisible Light in which three flames are united, * I praise and glorify the divine King of all creation.

Now and ever: O holy Virgin, you have appeared as more spacious than the heavens; * you bore the God whom no flesh could contain; * and you gave birth to Him * for the redemption of all the faithful who extol you.

Surpassing our spirit and our understanding, * you gave birth in the world and in time to the timeless Lord; * with one voice and one heart, O Mother of God, * we the faithful extol you.

HYMN OF LIGHT

Tone 2 You, O King and Lord, * have fallen asleep * in the flesh as a mortal man, * but on the third day You arose again. * You have raised Adam * from his corruption and made Death powerless. * You are the Pasch of incorruption. * You are the salvation of the world.

Tone 5 **Glory be:** Enlighten the eyes of my soul, * blinded by the gloom of sin, O Lord. * Anoint them with humility, O compassionate One, * and wash me with tears of repentance.

Tone 5 **Now and forever:** As He went on his way, Jesus the Lord who saves us * met a man struck with blindness from his birth. * Moistening the dust of the earth with his saliva, * Christ made some mud to anoint the eyes of the Blind Man. * Then he sent him to Siloam to wash in the pool; * when he had washed, the Blind Man returned, * and he saw the brightness of your light, O Christ.

AT THE PRAISES

Tone 5 You came forth from the grave, O Lord, * which had been sealed by the transgressors of the law, * just as You were born of the Theotokos. * For the bodiless angels did not know how You were incarnate. * Likewise, the guardian soldiers did not see the moment of your Resurrection; * for these two marvels were concealed from the curious minds * but were revealed to those who worshiped the mystery in faith. * Therefore, grant joy and great mercy to us who offer You praise.

O Lord, You demolished the gates of everlasting damnation, * and You broke asunder the chains of the grave. * You rose from the tomb leaving your wrappings in the grave * in testimony of your three-day burial; * and leaving the guards watching at the tomb, * You preceded your disciples into Galilee. * Great is your mercy, O Lord whom the whole world cannot contain. * O Savior, have mercy upon us.

O Lord, who suffered for us, * the women hastened to your tomb to behold You. * When they arrived, they saw an angel sitting on the stone of the grave. * He said to them: The Lord is risen! * Go and tell the disciples that the Savior of our souls is risen from the dead.

O Lord and Savior, * You came into the midst of your disciples though the doors were closed, * just as You came out of the sealed tomb, * showing the sufferings of the flesh which You accepted; * for You submitted to suffering patiently since You are of the seed of David. * But since You are the Son of God, You saved the world. * Great is your mercy, O Lord, whom the whole world cannot contain. * O Savior, have mercy on us.

O Lord, the King of ages and Creator of all, * who accepted crucifixion and burial in the body for our sakes * to deliver us all from Hades, * You are our God, and besides You we know no other.

O Lord God, who shall proclaim your dazzling wonders, * or who shall declare your divine mysteries? * For You were willingly incarnate for our sakes, * manifesting the might of your power. * By your Cross You opened Paradise to the thief; * by your death You crushed the bars and bolts of Hades; * and by your Resurrection You enriched all creation. * Therefore, O Compassionate One, glory to You!

The myrrh-bearing women reached your tomb early in the morning, * seeking to anoint You, O immortal Word. * When they were instructed by the words of the angel, * they turned back with joy * to tell the apostles clearly that You had risen, O Life of all, * and had given the world forgiveness and great mercy.

Tone 8

Turn and show me your mercy; show justice to your friends.

In your merciful loving-kindness * You took flesh for us, O Christ our God. * You gave light to a man who, from his mother's womb, lived in darkness. * How boundless is your compassion! * You anointed his eyes with the mud your fingers had molded * and made him worthy to be flooded with light divine. * So now enlighten him, O Giver of light; * illumine our spiritual perceptions, * for You alone are the Fountain of grace.

Tone 8 **Glory be:** Who can describe your power, O Christ; * who can count the multitude of your wonders? * You appeared on earth in two natures, O compassionate One, * and thus You granted double healing to the sick. * Not only did You open the bodily eyes of the man born blind, * but You gave sight to those of his soul as well. * Therefore, He confessed You, the hidden God * who grants the world great mercy.

Tone 2 **Now and ever:** You are truly most blessed, O virgin Mother of God. * Through the One who was incarnate of you, * Hades was chained, Adam revived, the curse wiped out, * Eve set free, Death put to death, * and we ourselves were brought back to life. * That is why we cry out in praise: * Blessed are You, O Christ our God, * who finds in this your good pleasure. Glory to You!

AFTER THE DISMISSAL

Gospel Stanza Number 8

Tone 8 **Glory be...now and ever:** The warm tears of Mary were not shed in vain; * for behold, she has been worthy to hear the angels * and to behold your face, O Jesus. * But being a woman still thinking of earthly things, * she was not permitted to touch You, O Christ. * However, she was sent to proclaim to your disciples * the good news announcing your return to your heavenly inheritance. * With her, therefore, make us worthy to see You, O Lord.

Sunday Evening Vespers

AT PSALM 140

Tone 5 O Word, You are the Light that enlightens all; * O God, You are the eye of our body in this world.* We acknowledge You as the Creator of sight. * Today, from a mixture of spittle and dust, * You re-create sight for the blind man. * In times past, your fingers have created both clay and sight; * today, he receives both from You. * Until this time, the blind man was unable to see the sun. * Now he sees You, the gentle Sun and Creator of all, * who in your love has created and fashioned us.

Created with a complete human body, * the man who was blind from his mother's womb * did not know any other manner of living; * for he had always been deprived of the use of his eyes, * his feet and body stumbled over the obstacles in his path. * But thanks to You, O Lord, he was granted this treasure: * he now sees the light of the world * and proclaims You as the Lord and Master of all light * and the Creator of the entire universe.

The blind Scribes looked with suspicion * upon the blind man who was given sight * as if his eyes had not really been opened * but that he only pretended to see because of the Lord. * For they themselves preferred the darkness of the letter of the Law * to the light of Christ, our radiant Sun. * By this healing He renewed the Sabbath Feast * and enlightened the darkness of the Law, * lifting the veil to shed light upon those who had been blind, * and who now announce to the world that they see the Lord * who is the Source of our light.

Three Stichera from the Saint of the day

Tone 2 The man who was blind from birth asked himself: * Was I born blind because of the sin of my parents, * or am I a living sign of the unbelief of the nations? * I am not content to ask whether it is night or day; * my feet can no longer endure tripping upon the stones. * I have not seen the brightness of the sun, * nor have I seen the image and likeness of my Creator. * Yet I beseech You, O Christ our God, * to look upon me and have mercy on me.

APOSTICHA

Tone 5 With your precious Cross, O Christ, * You have put the Devil to shame. * With your Resurrection You have deadened the sting of sin * and have saved us from the gates of Death. * We, therefore, glorify You, O only-begotten Son of God.

I have lifted up my eyes to You enthroned in heaven. Behold, as the eyes of servants are on the hands of their masters, as the eyes of a maid are on the hands of her mistress, so are our eyes on the Lord our God until He has mercy on us.

O Lord, I have never stopped sinning; * I do not understand the need to love my neighbor. * Overcome my ignorance, O Gracious One, * and have mercy on me, * for You alone are the God of goodness.

Have mercy on us, O Lord, have mercy on us; for we have been filled with shame; our soul is all too full of the mockery of the rich, of the contempt of the proud.

You were not concerned about all these earthly matters, * and you courageously braved the tortures. * You did not sin against hope, * having confidence in God's love for all people; * and you were heirs to the kingdom of heaven, * O most praiseworthy martyrs. * Ask for peace for the world and great mercy for our souls.

Tone 2 **Glory be...now and ever:** Passing by the Temple, Jesus saw a man who was blind from birth. * He had compassion on him and put mud on his eyes. * He said to him: Go to the pool of Siloam and wash. * He washed and recovered his sight; * then he rendered glory to God. * But his neighbors said to him: * Who opened your eyes which no one before could heal? * And he answered them, saying: A man called Jesus; * He told me to go and wash in the pool of Siloam, and now I see. * He is in truth Christ the Messiah, * of whom Moses wrote in the Law. * He is the Savior of our souls.

TROPARIA

Of the Saint

Tone 5 **Glory be...now and ever:** O faithful, let us praise and adore the Word * eternal with the Father and the Spirit, * and who was born of the Virgin for our salvation; * for He willed to ascend the Cross as man and to suffer death * and to raise the dead by his glorious resurrection.

Monday Matins

SESSIONAL HYMN I

Tone 5 Let us praise the honored Cross of the Lord; * let us venerate his holy burial with hymns; * let us glorify his holy Resurrection. * For He raised the dead from the graves because He is God. * He despoiled the might of Death and broke the power of Satan, * and He shed light on those who are in Hades.

Lord, do not reprove me in your anger; punish me not in your rage.

Let us keep watch so that we may go to meet Christ; * let our vessels be filled with oil and our lamps burning brightly * that we may enter into his palace. * For when the doors shall be closed, * it is in vain that we shall cry out to God: Have mercy on us!

Their span extends through all the earth; their words to the utmost bounds of the world.

Following You, O Lord, your martyrs have drunk from the cup of your sufferings, * and they have renounced the pleasures of this life; * they have become citizens with the angels. * Through their prayers, O Lord, grant forgiveness and great mercy to our souls.

Glory be...now and ever: Together with the angels in heaven and people on earth, * we praise you in joy, O Mother of God: * Rejoice, O gate wider than the heavens! * Rejoice, O unique assistance for all people! * Rejoice, O Full of Grace who gave birth to God in the flesh!

SESSIONAL HYMN II

Tone 5 Before your Cross and Resurrection, O bountiful One, * a man blind from birth came to You in tears, crying out: * Have mercy on me, O Son of David! * Give light to my eyes that I may gaze upon You. * You anointed him with mud made from your saliva, O Word, * giving him the radiant light.

Glory be...now and ever: *(Repeat the above)*

Having beheld the Resurrection of Christ...

CANON

HYMN OF LIGHT

Tone 2 You, O King and Lord, * have fallen asleep * in the flesh as a mortal man, * but on the third day You arose again. * You have raised Adam * from his corruption and made Death powerless. * You are the Pasch of incorruption. * You are the salvation of the world.

Tone 5 **Glory be:** Enlighten the eyes of my soul, * blinded by the gloom of sin, O Lord. * Anoint them with humility, O compassionate One, * and wash me with tears of repentance.

Tone 5 **Now and ever:** As He went on his way, Jesus the Lord who saves us, * met a man struck with blindness from his birth. * Moistening the dust of the earth with his saliva, * Christ made some mud to anoint the eyes of the Blind Man. * Then he sent him to Siloam to wash in the pool; * when he had washed, the Blind Man returned, * and he saw the brightness of your light, O Christ.

AT THE PRAISES

Tone 5 You came forth from the grave, O Lord, * which had been sealed by the transgressors of the law, * just as You were born of the Theotokos. * For the bodiless angels did not know how You were incarnate. * Likewise, the guardian soldiers did not see the moment of your Resurrection; * for these two marvels were concealed from the curious minds * but were revealed to those who worshiped the mystery in faith. * Therefore, grant joy and great mercy to us who offer You praise. *(2 times)*

Woe is me, for I resemble the sterile fig tree; * I fear both the curse and the axe. * But You, the heavenly Gardener, O

Christ our God, * make my dried-up soul fertile once again. * Welcome me as the Prodigal and have mercy on me.

Blessed is the army of the King of heaven; * for even though the victorious martyrs were born on earth, * they desired no less earnestly the angelic dignity. * They despised the flesh and endured their sufferings; * thus they merited the glory of the angels. * Through their prayers, O Lord, save our souls.

Tone 2 **Glory be...now and ever:** All his life, the Blind Man's thoughts were darkened * until he cried out to You, O Lord: * Open my eyes, O Son of David and our Savior, * that with all your people I may praise your might.

APOSTICHA

Tone 5 The man who had been blind saw that those with sight were truly blind, * darkened in heart, mind, and soul; * for when they saw that he suddenly was able to see, * they interrogated him persistently: * How is it possible for you now to see the light of day? * You were blind from birth; * you sat on the roadsides and begged. * The blind man then told them who gave him sight, * and in the midst of their darkened assembly he confessed: * You are the Son, begotten of the Father before the ages, * who fashioned the lights of the universe; * and in these last days You dawned upon the world as a mortal * by the power of the Holy Spirit and from the Virgin Mary, * according to your great compassion.

Turn and show me your mercy; show justice to your friends.

The blind man walked the streets of life * like one condemned to endless labor in the pits of the earth. * His feet were bruised because he had a staff instead of eyes. * Thus he fled for refuge to the Giver of light. * He then received his sight, * and the first thing he saw was his Creator * who fashioned the human race according to his image and likeness. * He created all things: first from the dust of the earth; * and now He gives light through dust and saliva, * opening blind eyes to the sun because of his love for all.

Let my steps be guided by your promise; let no evil rule me.

When the blind man's eyes were opened, * he gazed like others upon the light of the sun. * He rejoiced in his newly-found sight. * Now he could walk the paths of life without stumbling. * He recognized the Word, equal to the Father who created all, * the morning Star and Maker of the dawn, * as the Son of God, all-radiant, * who took flesh in his unspeakable compassion. * He became human while remaining God, * assuming what He never was before, * in a union without confusion.

Tone 5 **Glory be...now and ever:** As You walked along, O Lord, * You found a man who had been blind from birth. * In surprise, the disciples asked You: * Was it because of the sin of this man or his parents * that he was born blind, O Master? * But You, O Savior, answered them, saying: * Neither has this man sinned, nor his parents, * but that the works of God would be revealed in him. * I must accomplish the works of Him who sent Me, * which no one else can work. * As You said that, You spat on the ground * and made mud from the dust to anoint his eyes. * And You said to him: Go and wash in the pool of Siloam. * When he washed, he was healed and cried out to You: * O Lord, I believe! * And he bowed down and worshiped You. * Therefore, we also cry out to You: Have mercy on us!

Monday Evening Vespers

AT PSALM 140

Tone 5 The man who had once been blind * confessed in his soul and mind, and proclaimed with his words * that his eyes had been opened through saliva and dust * by the Lord and sustainer of the universe. * He had been given his bodily sight * by none other than almighty God, * who in his exceeding goodness was clothed in our flesh. * The man who had never been able to see * argued boldly with the Scribes. * They cast him out of the synagogue; * they themselves were more blind in their souls * than he who beforehand was blind in his bodily eyes.

Behold a monument of valor! * A man once blind examines those who see and is now their judge. * When he obtained his sight by means of saliva and dust, * he perceived the Creator and Maker of all. * He recognized Him who is the Giver of light, * the Son of God and Master of the universe. * His accusers could see with earthly eyes * but were blinded by their wicked jealousy, * though the Lord multiplied miracles for all to see * by his words alone, which are wonderful in power.

When he who was blind had been given his sight, * he perceived that the Scribes had become blind. * You see no truth, but only falsehood, he said. * You accuse the Savior, and you blind yourselves. * Christ, the most sweet sun, * has risen for those held in the darkness of the Law. * He who made the Sabbath also refashioned my eyes. * He has lifted the veil that darkened me. * He has opened the eyes of the blind; * they proclaim Him to the world as the Fountain of light.

Three Stichera from the Saint of the day

Tone 5 **Glory be...now and ever:**

See page 481 for corrected text

APOSTICHA

Tone 5 With your precious Cross, O Christ, * You have put the Devil to shame. * With your Resurrection You have deadened the sting of sin * and have saved us from the gates of Death. * We, therefore, glorify You, O only-begotten Son of God.

The Lord reigns, He is clothed in majesty. Robed is the Lord, and girt about with strength.

O Christ, who granted resurrection to all people, * You were led like a lamb to the slaughter. * Then the princes of Hades were struck with terror * as they saw the gates of their tearful domain being lifted up; * for Christ, the King of Glory, entered therein * and exclaimed to those in chains: Go forth from here! * and to those in darkness: Go forth into the light!

For He has made the world firm, which shall not be moved.

What a great wonder! * The Creator of invisible beings suffered in the flesh for the human race * and rose from the dead as immortal. * Come, therefore, all you nations and adore Him; * for through his compassion we have been freed from the snares of the Devil, * and we have learned to praise the one God in three persons.

Holiness befits your house, O Lord, for length of days.

O Christ our Savior, * we lift up our voices in song to glorify You. * For, in your love for humanity, * You became incarnate without leaving heaven; * You accepted the Cross and death; * You cast down the gates of Hades; * and on the third day You arose from the dead * for the salvation of our souls.

Tone 8 **Glory be...now and ever:** O Christ our God, spiritual Sun of Justice, * by your pure touch You enlightened the eyes of him * who from his mother's womb was without light. * Enlighten the eyes of our hearts * and make us children of the light and of the day, * that we may cry out to You in faith: * How great is your compassion toward us, * O Lover of Mankind, glory to You!

TROPARIA

Of the Saint

Tone 5 **Glory be...now and ever:** O faithful, let us praise and adore the Word * eternal with the Father and the Spirit, * and who was born of the Virgin for our salvation; * for He willed to ascend the Cross as man and to suffer death * and to raise the dead by his glorious resurrection.

Tuesday Matins

SESSIONAL HYMN I

Tone 5 Let us praise the honored Cross of the Lord; * let us venerate his holy burial with hymns; * let us glorify his holy Resurrection. * For He raised the dead from the graves because He is God. * He despoiled the might of Death and broke the power of Satan, * and He shed light on those who are in Hades.

Lord, do not reprove me in your anger; punish me not in your rage.

You were counted among the dead, O Lord, * even though You put to death the Prince of death. * You were placed in a grave, although You emptied the graves. * On earth, the soldiers guarded the tomb, * but below, You raised the dead who, from all eternity, had fallen asleep. * Therefore, O Lord, the almighty and incomprehensible One, glory to You!

Their span extends through all the earth; their words to the utmost bounds of the world.

Rejoice, O holy mountain which the Lord ascended! * Rejoice, O living bush, unconsumed by the fire! * Rejoice, only bridge reaching from the world to God * and leading the dead to eternal life! * Rejoice, O pure one, free of corruption; * you gave birth without the aid of man to the Savior of the world!

SESSIONAL HYMN II

Tone 5 The Word, coeternal with the Father and the Spirit, * who clothes himself with light as his garment, * has assumed our nature in his love for us. * And as God, He has driven away the infirmities of mortals. * He has opened the eyes of one who was without light from his mother's womb.

Glory be...now and ever: *(Repeat the above)*

CANON

Having beheld the Resurrection of Christ...

HYMN OF LIGHT

Tone 2 You, O King and Lord, * have fallen asleep * in the flesh as a mortal man, * but on the third day You arose again. * You have raised Adam * from his corruption and made Death powerless. * You are the Pasch of incorruption. * You are the salvation of the World.

Tone 5 **Glory be:** Enlighten the eyes of my soul, * blinded by the gloom of sin, O Lord. * Anoint them with humility, O compassionate One, * and wash me with tears of repentance.

Tone 5 **Now and ever:** As He went on his way, Jesus, the Lord who saves us, * met a man struck with blindness from his birth. * Moistening the dust of the earth with his saliva, * Christ made some mud to anoint the eyes of the Blind Man. * Then he sent him to Siloam to wash in the pool; * when he had washed, the Blind Man returned, * and he saw the brightness of your light, O Christ.

AT THE PRAISES

Tone 5 You came forth from the grave, O Lord, * which had been sealed by the transgressors of the law, * just as You were born of the Theotokos. * For the bodiless angels did not know how You were incarnate. * Likewise, the guardian soldiers did not see the moment of your Resurrection; * for these two marvels were concealed from the curious minds * but were revealed to those who worshiped the mystery in faith. * Therefore, grant joy and great mercy to us who offer You praise.

O Lord, You demolished the gates of everlasting damnation, * and You broke asunder the chains of the grave. * You rose from the tomb leaving your wrappings in the grave * in testimony of your three-day burial; * and leaving the guards watching at the tomb, * You preceded your disciples into Galilee. * Great is your mercy, O Lord, whom the whole world cannot contain. * O Savior, have mercy upon us.

O Lord, who suffered for us, * the women hastened to your tomb to behold You. * When they arrived, they saw an angel sitting on the stone of the grave. * He said to them: The Lord is risen! * Go and tell the disciples that the Savior of our souls is risen from the dead.

O Lord and Savior, * You came into the midst of your disciples though the doors were closed, * just as You came out of the sealed tomb, * showing the sufferings of the flesh which You accepted; * for You submitted to suffering patiently since You are of the seed of David. * But since You are the Son of God, You saved the world. * Great is your mercy, O Lord, whom the whole world cannot contain. * O Savior, have mercy on us.

Tone 8 **Glory be...now and ever:** Who can describe your power, O Christ; * who can count the multitude of your wonders? * You appeared on earth in two natures, O compassionate One, * and thus You granted double healing to the sick. * Not only did You open the bodily eyes of the man born blind, * but You gave sight to those of his soul as well. * Therefore, He confessed You, the hidden God * who grants the world great mercy.

APOSTICHA

Tone 5 The guardians of the Law of Moses became blind in their minds; * for when the radiant Star of morning made himself manifest on the Sabbath * by shining upon the man born blind, * they would not admit that the Law was a shadow. * Thus they could not see the Maker of light * who by a word created the Sabbath. * On that day, through water and mud formed from saliva, * the blind man's eyes were opened. * Let us join him and confound the Pharisees' blindness; * and enlightened with a higher sight, * let us confess Christ our God.

Turn and show me your mercy; show justice to your friends.

Morning is risen for one long held in grief and darkness; *

the night of blindness is washed away in the waters. * In the pool of Siloam, the blind man receives sight by God's command. * He bears his new light to the Scribes who were lost in a fog of darkness. * He exposes the moonless night of their blindness. * He enlightens those who claim to have the light. * Cast away the blindness of the Law's old shadow! * Receive new sight from the Word! * He radiantly enlightens us who submit to Him.

Let my steps be guided by your promise; let no evil rule me.

When the blind man was illumined by the light of divine knowledge, * he mounted the bright path to heaven. * Though he had been blind in soul and body, * he met the Creator and Giver of light * who shone forth from the tomb on the third day * and by his Resurrection brightened the earth. * For mortals held fast in darkness, * the light of the new creation has dawned * through his compassion and great mercy.

Tone 8 **Glory be...now and ever:** In your merciful loving-kindness * You took flesh for us, O Christ our God. * You gave light to a man who, from his mother's womb, lived in darkness. * How boundless is your compassion! * You anointed his eyes with the mud your fingers had molded * and made him worthy to be flooded with light divine. * So now enlighten him, O Giver of light; * illumine our spiritual perceptions, * for You alone are the Fountain of grace.

Tuesday Evening Vespers

The celebrant, fully vested in bright vestments, stands before the Holy Altar and begins with: "Blessed is our God..."; immediately the Paschal Troparion is sung three times.

Christ is risen from the dead! * By death He conquered Death, * and to those in the graves He granted life.

TROPARION WITH VERSICLES

The celebrant sings the following versicles, and to each one the people respond by singing: Christ is risen...

v. Let God arise and let his enemies be scattered, * and let those who hate Him flee from before His face.

Christ is risen...

v. As smoke vanishes, so let them vanish as wax melts before the fire.

Christ is risen...

v. So let the wicked perish at the presence of God, and let the righteous ones rejoice.

Christ is risen...

v. This is the day that the Lord has made, let us exalt and rejoice in it.

Christ is risen...

v. Glory be to the Father, and to the Son, and to the Holy Spirit, now and ever and forever. Amen.

Christ is risen...

LITANY OF PEACE

AT PSALM 140

Tone 2 The man who was blind from birth asked himself: * Was I born blind because of the sin of my parents, * or am I a living sign of the unbelief of the nations? * I am not content to ask whether it is night or day; * my feet can no longer endure tripping upon the stones. * I have not seen the brightness of the sun, * nor have I seen the image and likeness of my Creator. * Yet I beseech You, O Christ our God, * to look upon me and have mercy on me.

Passing by the Temple, Jesus saw a man who was blind from birth. * He had compassion on him and put mud on his eyes. * He said to him: Go to the pool of Siloam and wash. * He washed and recovered his sight; * then he rendered glory to God. * But his neighbors said to him: * Who opened your eyes which no one before could heal? * And he answered them, saying: A man called Jesus. * He told me to go and wash in the pool of Siloam, and now I see. * He is in truth Christ the Messiah, * of whom Moses wrote in the Law. * He is the Savior of our souls.

Tone 5 As You walked along, O Lord, * You found a man who had been blind from birth. * In surprise, the disciples asked You: * Was it because of the sin of this man or his parents * that he was born blind, O Master? * But You, O Savior, answered them, saying: * Neither has this man sinned, nor his parents, * but that the works of God would be revealed in him. * I must accomplish the works of Him who sent Me, * which no one else can work. * As You said that, You spat on the ground * and made mud from the dust to anoint his eyes. * And You said to him: Go and wash in the pool of Siloam. * When he washed, he was healed and cried out to You: * O Lord, I believe! * And he bowed down and worshiped You. * Therefore, we also cry out to You: Have mercy on us!

Tone 4 The blind man imagined that his whole life was night; * he cried out to You: O Lord, open my eyes, * O Son of David, O our Savior, * that with all humanity I may praise your power.

Tone 8 O Christ our God, spiritual Sun of Justice, * by your pure touch, You enlightened the eyes of him * who from his mother's womb was without light. * Enlighten the eyes of our hearts * and make us children of the light and of the day, * that we may cry out to You in faith: * How great is your compassion toward us! * O Lover of Mankind, glory to You!

In your merciful loving-kindness * You took flesh for us, O Christ our God. * You gave light to a man who, from his mother's womb, lived in darkness. * How boundless is your compassion! * You anointed his eyes with the mud your fingers had molded * and made him worthy to be flooded with light divine. * So now enlighten him, O Giver of light; * illumine our spiritual perceptions, * for You alone are the Fountain of grace.

Tone 8 **Glory be...now and ever:** Who can describe your power, O Christ; * who can count the multitude of your wonders? * You appeared on earth in two natures, O compassionate One, * and thus You granted double healing to the sick. * Not only did You open the bodily eyes of the man born blind, * but You gave sight to those of his soul as well.* Therefore, He confessed You, the hidden God * who grants the world great mercy.

APOSTICHA

Tone 5 O Christ our Savior, * we lift up our voices in song to glorify You. * For, in your love for humanity, * You became incarnate without leaving heaven; * You accepted the Cross and death; * You cast down the gates of Hades; * and on the third day You arose from the dead * for the salvation of our souls.

PASCHAL HYMNS

It is customary in some places that the faithful come to kiss the cross during these hymns.

Let God arise and let his enemies be scattered, and let those who hate Him flee from before his face.

Today the sacred Pasch is revealed to us, * holy and new Pasch, * the mystical Passover, * the venerable Passover, * the Pasch which is Christ the Redeemer, * spotless Pasch, great Pasch, * the Pasch of the faithful, * the Pasch which is the key to the gates of Paradise, * the Pasch which sanctifies all the faithful.

As smoke vanishes, so let them vanish as wax melts before the fire.

O Women, * be the heralds of good news and tell what you saw; * tell of the vision and say to Zion: * Accept the good news of joy from us, * the news that Christ has risen. * Exalt and celebrate * and rejoice, O Jerusalem, * seeing Christ the King coming from the tomb * like a bridegroom.

So let the wicked perish at the presence of God, and let the righteous ones rejoice.

The myrrh-bearing women * arrived just before the dawn * at the tomb of the Giver of Life * and found an angel seated on the stone * who spoke these words to them: * Why do you seek the Living among the dead? * Why do you mourn the Incorruptible among those subject to decay? * Go, announce the good news * to his disciples.

This is the day that the Lord has made; let us exalt and rejoice in it.

Pasch so delightful, * Pasch of the Lord is the Pasch, * most honored Pasch now dawned on us. * It is the Pasch! * Therefore, let us joyfully embrace one another. * O Passover, save us from sorrow; * for today Christ has shown forth from the tomb * as from a bridal chamber * and filled the women with joy by saying: * Announce the good news * to my apostles.

Glory be to the Father, and to the Son, and to the Holy Spirit, now and ever and forever. Amen.

This is the Resurrection Day. * Let us be enlightened by this Feast, * and let us embrace one another. * Let us call Brethren * even those who hate us, * and in the Resurrection * forgive everything; and let us sing: * Christ is risen from the dead! * By death He conquered Death, * and to those in the graves He granted life.

TROPARIA

Of the Saint

Tone 5 O faithful, let us praise and adore the Word * eternal with the Father and the Spirit, * and who was born of the Virgin for our salvation; * for He willed to ascend the Cross as man and to suffer death * and to raise the dead by his glorious resurrection.

Tone 5 **Glory be...now and ever:** Rejoice, Virgin, impassable gateway of the Lord! * Rejoice, protective wall of those who take refuge in you! * Rejoice, peaceful haven untroubled by storms! * Rejoice, Virgin who has not known wedlock * and yet has given birth in the flesh to your Creator and God! * O Mother of God, never cease to intercede * for those who praise and worship your Son.

PASCHAL DISMISSAL

(See pages 14-15)

Wednesday Matins

The celebrant, fully vested in bright vestments, stands before the Holy Altar and begins with: "Blessed is our God..."; immediately the Paschal Troparion is sung three times.

Christ is risen from the dead! * By death He conquered Death, * and to those in the graves He granted life.

TROPARION WITH VERSICLES

The celebrant sings the following versicles, and to each one the people respond by singing: Christ is risen...

v. Let God arise and let his enemies be scattered, * and let those who hate Him flee from before His face.

Christ is risen...

v. As smoke vanishes, so let them vanish as wax melts before the fire.

Christ is risen...

v. So let the wicked perish at the presence of God, and let the righteous ones rejoice.

Christ is risen...

v. This is the day that the Lord has made, let us exalt and rejoice in it.

Christ is risen...

v. Glory be to the Father, and to the Son, and to the Holy Spirit, now and ever and forever. Amen.

Christ is risen...

SESSIONAL HYMN I

Tone 5 Let us praise the honored Cross of the Lord; * let us venerate his holy burial with hymns; * let us glorify his holy Resurrection. * For He raised the dead from the graves because He is God. * He despoiled the might of Death and broke the power of Satan, * and He shed light on those who are in Hades.

Arise, then, Lord, lift up your hand. O God do not forget the poor!

You were counted among the dead, O Lord, * even though You put to death the Prince of death. * You were placed in a grave, although You emptied the graves. * On earth, the soldiers guarded the tomb, * but below, You raised the dead who, from all eternity, had fallen asleep. * Therefore, O Lord, the almighty and incomprehensible One, glory to You!

Glory be...now and ever: Rejoice, O holy mountain which the Lord ascended! * Rejoice, O living bush, unconsumed by the fire! * Rejoice, only bridge reaching from the world to God * and leading the dead to eternal life! * Rejoice, O pure one, free of corruption; * you gave birth without the aid of man to the Savior of the world!

SESSIONAL HYMN II

Tone 5 The Word, coeternal with the Father and the Spirit, * who clothes himself with light as his garment, * has assumed our nature in his love for us. * And, as God, He has driven away the infirmities of mortals. * He has opened the eyes of one who was without light from his mother's womb.

Glory be...now and ever: *(Repeat the above)*

Having beheld the Resurrection...

CANON

The Paschal Canon, pages 3-11, the Canon of the Man Born Blind, pages 243-251, and the Canon of the Pre-Feast of the Ascension are prescribed for this day. The Paschal Canon takes precedence.

CANON FOR THE PRE-FEAST OF ASCENSION

ODE 1

Tone 1 Christ ascended to his Father in the heavens, * with his body lifting up our flesh; * let us sing to Him today a hymn of victory.

Refrain: **Glory to your holy Ascension, O Lord!**

The inspired books of Scripture * and the sayings of the prophets * are clearly fulfilled today, * for the Savior ascends with glory to the heavens after his Resurrection.

Glory be...now and ever: The earth dances mystically, * the heavens are filled with joy, * for the Ascension of Christ unites what had been separated * and breaks the barriers of enmity.

Our Savior and God led the people of Israel * across the Red Sea as if on dry land * and drowned Pharaoh and his whole army. * Let us praise Him who alone is worthy of our songs, * for He is covered with glory.

ODE 3

Tone 1 By your death, O Word, You have chained Death; * You rose from the tomb on the third day; * in glory You ascended into heaven, O Savior, * and the angels hymned your work of salvation.

Refrain: **Glory to your holy Ascension, O Lord!**

O spiritual Word, You became incarnate coming upon the earth; * You suffered the Cross and rose from the dead; * with glory You ascend to the Father of lights, * having given peace to the whole world.

Glory be...now and ever: You came upon earth to seek the lost sheep; * and having brought it back to the sheep-fold, * You ascended into heaven, O Word, * to sit gloriously at the right hand of the Father. * O Savior, glory to your goodness without end!

O Christ, by the power of your Cross, * strengthen our hearts so that we may sing and glorify * your saving Ascension.

KONTAKION

Tone 5 With eyes that are spiritually blind I come to You, O Christ; * and, like the man who was blind since birth, * I cry out to You with repentance: * You are a shining Light to those who are in darkness.

IKOS

Give me to drink of your boundless wisdom and of heavenly knowledge, O Christ, for You are the light of those in darkness and the guide of those who have lost their way. Thus I will clearly recount what the Holy Book teaches in the Gospel of peace, about the miracle You performed for the Blind Man. He had been in darkness from his birth, and he received from You both physical and spiritual sight, and cried out in faith: For those in darkness, your light surpasses all radiance.

SESSIONAL HYMN

Tone 1 O Christ, You gave sight to the man blind from birth, * and You showed your glory to the people. * You are the Light of the world, O Savior; * but through jealousy, those who were blind of heart conspired against You, * to put to death the Giver of life.

Glory be...now and ever: O Savior, You freely accepted birth in the flesh; * You appeared among us according to your good will; * You suffered in your humanity and were raised up as God; * and now You ascend into heaven in glory, * and there You have borne our human nature * which You have adorned with glory and beauty.

ODE 4

Tone 1 Our nature, once condemned by sin, * found grace, O King of all, when You assumed it. * In fear it chants your Resurrection and divine Ascension.

Refrain: **Glory to your holy Ascension, O Lord!**

The armies of angels are struck with wonder * to see You bear the human nature * and lift up the clouds, that You might ascend to the heavens.

Seeing your garments dyed with blood, O King of all, * and hearing of your Ascension, * the angelic powers worshiped in fear and in joy.

Glory be...now and ever: Let us clap our hands in honor of our God, * risen from the dead; * for He ascends into heaven, * borne by the angels as our Creator and Lord.

O Lord, I have heard your voice * and I recognized the power of your Cross, * because through it Paradise was opened; * and I said: Glory to your power, O Lord!

ODE 5

Tone 1 Christ is risen from the dead and ascends to the heavens, * delivering the human race from the curse * and honoring those who love Him * with a place with the Father in heaven.

***Refrain:* Glory to your holy Ascension, O Lord!**

By your Resurrection, O Christ, * You gave joy to your apostles; * and as You spoke with them here on earth, * You ascended to the heavens * to be with the Father whose side You never left.

Glory be...now and ever: O Christ, You fulfilled the obscure image of the Law * and the sayings of the inspired prophets, * and carried by the clouds, You arise and ascend, O Savior, to the heavens.

As we watch in the night and wait for morning, * O Lord, we cry to You: * Have mercy on us and save us, * for You are truly our God and we know no other but You.

ODE 6

Tone 1 The angels were witnesses once * when You took the form of a human, O Lover of Mankind, * and raised it up in your Ascension; * and in fear they sing your glory, O Lord.

***Refrain:* Glory to your holy Ascension, O Lord!**

The Lord of the universe ascends in glory * toward the Father in heaven, * and the entire creation celebrates the feast with joy.

Glory be...now and ever: Let every nation break out with shouts of joy, * for Christ ascends today with joy of heart * to heaven which He had never left.

The abyss surrounds me completely; * the sea monster holds me as if in a tomb; * I cried to You, O Lover of Mankind, * and your right hand has saved me.

KONTAKION

Tone 8 Although You descended into the grave, O Immortal One, * You destroyed the power of Death. * You arose again as a victor, O Christ God. * You announced to the women bearing ointment: Rejoice! * You gave peace to your apostles * and resurrection to the fallen.

IKOS

Early in the morning, before sunrise, as if it were already

day, myrrh-bearing virgins were seeking the Sun, previously descended into the grave; and they cried out one to another: Come, O friends! Let us anoint with fragrant spices the life-giving and yet already buried body of Christ who has resurrected the fallen Adam. Let us hasten, as did the Magi, and adore Christ and bring our myrrh as a gift to Him who is wrapped not in swaddling clothes but in a shroud. Let us weep and exclaim: Arise, O Master, granting resurrection to the fallen!

ODE 7

Tone 1 Having broken down the walls of enmity, O Savior, * by your passion upon the Cross * You ascended in glory to the Father, carried by the clouds.

Refrain: **Glory to your holy Ascension, O Lord!**

Seized by fear, the heavenly powers cried out in amazement: * Lift high the gates, for Christ has come; * He brings an earthly mortal body * and has destroyed the devil by his divine passion.

O Lover of Mankind, why do You wear this red garment? * To this question, Christ answers as He arrived among the heavenly powers: * It is because I have trampled the vintage in the wine-press.

Glory be:...now and ever: O Christ, we glorify in our hymns, * with one voice, your Cross and Resurrection, * and we celebrate a solemn feast in honor of your divine Ascension.

O Savior who saved the youths who sang to You in the furnace, * blessed are You, O Lord and God of our fathers.

ODE 8

Tone 1 O Light of Light, * the bright cloud lifted You up from the Mount of Olives * in view of the holy apostles who glorify You forever.

Refrain: **Glory to your holy Ascenion, O Lord!**

Clap your hands and applaud to the rhythm of our hands,* for Christ our God is risen; * He ascends to heaven from where He descended to us, * restoring in peace the ancient unity.

David said in a psalm: * Christ sits upon the Cherubim; * He is raised gloriously upon the wings of heavenly spirits, * highly glorified forever.

Glory be...now and ever: You appeared to your disciples after You arose from the tomb; * You led them to the Mount of Olives, * from where the bright cloud carried You into the heavens in glory, O Christ.

The Son of God, born of the Father before all ages, * has taken flesh from the Virgin Mother in these last days. * Praise Him, you priests, and let the whole nation exalt Him forever.

OMIT MAGNIFICAT

ODE 9

Tone 1 Today all creation celebrates a solemn feast in joy, * in honor of your divine Ascension, O Word of God; * for You have ascended to the Father, * with the human nature You assumed without change, * in a wondrous manner.

Refrain: **Glory to your holy Ascension, O Lord!**

O God our Savior, in your power You have broken the gates and bolts of Hades, * and You arose from the dead * and with glory ascended to heaven * so that the angels, seized with fright, cried out in one voice: * Lift high the gates for the entrance of our King.

Your holy apostles were amazed by your divine Ascension, * but the angels proclaimed to them: * the One whom you see ascending to heaven will return in the same way, * in glory, to judge the nations.

O Christ, just as You gave peace to your disciples * as You ascended to the heights, * shed peace upon us in abundance; * for You rule all creation in love that with one voice we may sing: * We extol You, O God our Savior.

Glory be...now and ever: O pure Virgin, you are truly the shining chariot of the spiritual Sun. * Because of you, the prisoners of darkness contemplate the revelation of the divine light, * and they glorify you, O Virgin worthy of all praise.

Surpassing our spirit and our understanding, * you gave birth in the world and in time to the timeless Lord; * with one voice and one heart, O Mother of God, * we the faithful extol you.

HYMN OF LIGHT

Tone 2 You, O King and Lord, * have fallen asleep * in the flesh as a mortal man, * but on the third day You arose again. * You have raised Adam * from his corruption and made Death powerless. * You are the Pasch of incorruption. * You are the salvation of the world. *(2 times)*

Tone 5 **Glory be...now and ever:** As He went on his way, Jesus, the Lord who saves us * met a man struck with blindness from his birth. * Moistening the dust of the earth with his saliva, * Christ made some mud to anoint the eyes of the Blind Man. * Then He sent him to Siloam to wash in the pool; * when he had washed, the Blind Man returned, * and he saw the brightness of your light, O Christ.

AT THE PRAISES

Tone 2 The man who was blind from birth asked himself: * Was I born blind because of the sin of my parents, * or am I a living sign of the unbelief of the nations? * I am not content to ask whether it is night or day; * my feet can no longer endure tripping upon the stones. * I have not seen the brightness of the sun, * nor have I seen the image and likeness of my Creator. * Yet I beseech You, O Christ our God, * to look upon me and have mercy on me.

Passing by the Temple, Jesus saw a man who was blind from birth. * He had compassion on him and put mud on his eyes. * He said to him: Go to the pool of Siloam and wash. * He washed and recovered his sight; * then he rendered glory to God. * But his neighbors said to him: * Who opened your eyes which no one before could heal? * And he answered them, saying: A man called Jesus. * He told me to go and wash in the pool of Siloam, and now I see. * He is in truth Christ the Messiah, * of whom Moses wrote in the Law. * He is the Savior of our souls.

Tone 4 The Blind Man imagined that his whole life was night; * he cried out to You: * O Lord, open my eyes, * O Son of David, O our Savior, * that with all humanity I may praise your power.

Tone 5 As You walked along, O Lord, * You found a man who had been blind from birth. * In surprise, the disciples asked You: * Was it because of the sin of this man or his parents * that he was born blind, O Master? * But You, O Savior, answered them, saying: * Neither has this man sinned, nor his parents, * but that the works of God would be revealed in him. * I must accomplish the works of Him who sent Me, * which no one else can work. * As You said that, You spat on the ground * and made mud from the dust to anoint his eyes. * And You said to him: Go and wash in the pool of Siloam. * When he washed, he was healed and cried out to You: * O Lord, I believe! * And he bowed down and worshiped You. * Therefore, we also cry out to You: Have mercy on us!

PASCHAL HYMNS

Let God arise and let his enemies be scattered, and let those who hate Him flee from before his face.

Today the sacred Pasch is revealed to us, * holy and new Pasch, * the mystical Passover, * the venerable Passover, * the Pasch which is Christ the Redeemer, * spotless Pasch, great Pasch, * the Pasch of the faithful, * the Pasch which is the key to the gates of Paradise, * the Pasch which sanctifies all the faithful.

As smoke vanishes, so let them vanish as wax melts before the fire.

O Women, * be the heralds of good news and tell what you saw; * tell of the vision and say to Zion: * Accept the good news of joy from us, * the news that Christ has risen. * Exalt and celebrate * and rejoice, O Jerusalem, * seeing Christ the King coming from the tomb * like a bridegroom.

So let the wicked perish at the presence of God, and let the righteous ones rejoice.

The myrrh-bearing women * arrived just before the dawn * at the tomb of the Giver of Life * and found an angel seated on the stone * who spoke these words to them: * Why do you seek the Living among the dead? * Why do you mourn the Incorruptible among those subject to decay? * Go, announce the good news * to his disciples.

This is the day that the Lord has made; let us exalt and rejoice in it.

Pasch so delightful, * Pasch of the Lord is the Pasch, * most honored Pasch now dawned on us. * It is the Pasch! * Therefore, let us joyfully embrace one another. * O Passover, save us from sorrow; * for today Christ has shown forth from the tomb * as from a bridal chamber * and filled the women with joy by saying: * Announce the good news * to my apostles.

Glory be to the Father, and to the Son, and to the Holy Spirit, now and ever and forever. Amen.

This is the Resurrection Day. * Let us be enlightened by this Feast, * and let us embrace one another. * Let us call

Brethren * even those who hate us, * and in the Resurrection, * forgive everything; and let us sing: * Christ is risen from the dead! * By death He conquered Death, * and to those in the graves He granted life.

GREAT DOXOLOGY

LITANY

PASCHAL DISMISSAL

(pages 14-15)

Ascension of Our Lord Jesus Christ

Vespers

AT PSALM 140

Tone 6 The Lord ascended into heaven * to send the Comforter into this world. * The heavens prepared his throne and the clouds were his ladder; * the angels marveled at the sight of a human being more exalted than themselves. * Today, the Father receives again in his bosom * the One who was in Him from all eternity, * and the Holy Spirit gives a command to all the angels: * Lift up your lintels, O you gates! * O you nations of the earth, clap your hands, * for Christ ascends to the place * where He had been from all eternity. *(2 times)*

O Lord, the Cherubim were amazed at your Ascension; * they were seized with wonder as they beheld You, O God, rising upon the clouds, * for You are the One who is seated above the clouds. * We sing a hymn of praise to You: * Glory to You for your tender mercy. *(2 times)*

O Christ, splendor and glory of the Father, * when we behold your Ascension on the holy mountain, * we sing a hymn of praise to the beauty of your countenance. * We bow down to your Passion, * we venerate your holy Resurrection, * and we glorify your noble Ascension. * O Lord, have mercy on us! *(2 times)*

O Lord and Giver of Life, * when the apostles saw You ascending upon the clouds, * a great sadness overcame them; * they shed burning tears and exclaimed: * O our Master, do not leave us orphans; * we are your servants whom You loved so tenderly. * Since You are most merciful, send down upon us your all-holy Spirit * to enlighten our souls, as You promised. *(2 times)*

After fulfilling the mystery of the plan of salvation, O Lord, * You took your apostles and went up with them to the Mount of Olives, * and there You passed beyond the firmament of heaven. * You humbled yourself and were clothed in our humanity, * and now You return to the place which You did not leave. * Send down your all-holy Spirit to enlighten our souls. *(2 times)*

Tone 6 **Glory be...now and ever:** O loving Jesus, while You lived on earth, * You were God inseparable from the

Father, * and yet You truly shared our humanity. * Ascending in glory today from the Mount of Olives, * through your great love, You lifted up our fallen nature * and enthroned it with the Father on high. * Therefore, the bodiless Powers were amazed and filled with awe * at seeing your great love for all. * Together with them, we who live on earth * glorify your condescension to us * and your ascension away from us. * Now we implore You, saying: * Through your Ascension You have filled your apostles and your Mother * with a joy that surpasses every other joy, * and through their intercession * make us worthy of the joy of your elect, * for You are rich in mercy.

READINGS

Isaiah 2: 2-3
Isaiah 62: 10-12 and 63: 1-9
Zechariah 14: 1, 4, 8-11

AT THE LITIJA

Tone 1 By going up again into heaven from which You had descended, * You did not leave us orphans, O Lord. * Show to all your people the works of your power, * that your Spirit may come down upon us * and bring peace to the world, * O Lord and Lover of Mankind.

You ascended, O Christ, to your eternal Father, * even though You were not removed from his bosom; * and the Powers could not contain their praise of the Trinity. * Even after the Incarnation * they recognize You as the only Son of the Father. * In the abundance of your goodness, have mercy on us!

Your angels, O Lord, said to the apostles: * Men of Galilee, why do you stand here looking into the sky? * Christ our God, who by leaving you ascended into heaven, * will come again in the manner by which you have seen Him leave. * Therefore, serve Him in justice and holiness.

Tone 4 When You came to the Mount of Olives, O Christ, * completing the favorable plan of your Father, * the angels in heaven were moved with wonder, * and the demons trembled beneath the earth. * The apostles were filled with both fear and joy * when You were speaking with them. * A cloud was prepared before You as an awaiting throne; * heaven opened its gates, shining with beauty; * and the earth uncovered its deep abyss * to show the fall of

Adam and his rising up to You again. * As an unseen power raised You from the earth, * You gave your blessing in a loud voice; * the cloud carried You away, and heaven opened to receive You. * Such is the great work that is beyond words, O Lord, * that You accomplished for the salvation of our souls.

You have renewed in yourself, O Lord, * the human nature which had fallen, in Adam, * into the very depths of the earth. * On this day You are raised far above * the Principalities and Powers of heaven. * Having so loved human nature, * You granted that it may be enthroned with You; * in your compassion You united it with yourself; * in union with it You have suffered; * and by your Passion You glorified it, O God, beyond all suffering. * Now the bodiless Powers are saying: * Who is this man clothed in majesty? * He is not only a man, but is indeed the God-Man, * for He possesses the appearance of both. * And the angels, arrayed in splendid garments, * encircle the apostles, saying: * As Jesus the God-Man is separated from you, * in his divine humanity He shall come again * to judge both the living and the dead; * and He grants to all the faithful * forgiveness of sins and great mercy.

When You were raised up in glory, O Christ our God, * in the sight of your disciples, * the cloud carried your body away. * The gates in heaven were opened; * the choir of angels exalted and danced with joy; * the Powers on high cried out, saying: * Lift up your lintels, O gates, * that the King of glory may enter. * As for the disciples, they were seized with fear and said: * Do not leave us, O Good Shepherd, * but send down upon us your most Holy Spirit.

Tone 4 **Glory be...now and ever:** O Lord most merciful, * after fulfilling the mystery hidden from all eternity, * You, the Creator and Master of all, * went up to the Mount of Olives with your disciples and your Mother. * For the one who, at the sight of your Passion, * had suffered more than anyone else in her motherly heart, * had more than anyone else the right to share the joy that fills us * as we witness your ascending into heaven. * We glorify your infinite mercy overflowing upon us.

APOSTICHA

Tone 2 O our God, You were born in a manner of your own choosing; * You appeared and suffered in the flesh as

You willed; * You crushed Death through your Resurrection and ascended into glory, * and You sent down the divine Spirit upon us. * Therefore, we sing a hymn of praise and glorify your divinity.

All peoples, clap your hands; cry to God with shouts of joy!

O Christ, when the Powers of heaven * beheld your Ascension from the Mount of Olives, * they wondered and exclaimed: Who is He? * And they heard the reply: He is the mighty Conqueror; * He is the mighty One in battle; * He is indeed the King of glory. * And why are his clothes crimson? * Because He comes from Bosor, which is the flesh. * As for You, O Christ, since You are God, * You are enthroned at the right hand of God the Father; * and You send down upon us the Holy Spirit * that He may enlighten us and save our souls.

God goes up with shouts of joy; the Lord goes up with trumpet blast.

O Christ, You ascended in glory * on the Mount of Olives in the presence of your disciples; * You fill all things with your divinity; * You were enthroned at the right hand of the Father * and sent down upon your disciples the Holy Spirit * who enlightens, strengthens, and saves our souls.

Tone 6 **Glory be...now and ever:** God goes up with shouts of joy, * the Lord goes up amid trumpet blast, * in order to raise up the fallen image of Adam * and to send down upon us the Holy Spirit, * the Comforter who will sanctify our souls.

TROPARION

Tone 4 You ascended in glory, O Christ our God; * You delighted the disciples with the promise of the Holy Spirit. * Through this blessing they were assured * that You are the Son of God, * the Redeemer of the world. *(3 times)*

Thursday Matins

SESSIONAL HYMN I

Tone 1 You ascended in glory, and the angels were astonished at this wonder; * the disciples were amazed at your marvelous Ascension; * and the gates opened before You, O Lord. * The Powers of heaven were also overjoyed, and they cried out: * Glory to your condescension, O Savior! * Glory to your kingdom! * Glory to your Ascension, O only Lover of Mankind!

Glory be...now and ever: *(Repeat the above)*

SESSIONAL HYMN II

Tone 3 The God who exists before all eternity * and who has mystically divinized the human nature which He assumed, * today goes up to heaven. * The angels precede Him and show to the disciples * the Lord who ascends into the clouds amid great glory, * and they then fall to the ground and say: * Glory to God who ascends into heaven!

Glory be...now and ever: *(Repeat the above)*

POLYELEOS

EXALTATION

We extol You, * O Christ the Giver of life; * and seeing You go up to heaven in your most pure body, * we praise your holy Ascension.

v. All peoples, clap your hands; cry to God with shouts of joy!

v. For the Lord, the Most High, we must fear, great king over all the earth.

v. God goes up with shouts of joy; the Lord goes up with trumpet blast.

v. O gates, lift high your heads; grow higher, ancient doors. Let Him enter, the King of glory.

v. The Lord has set his sway in heaven and his kingdom is ruling over all.

v. O God, arise above the heavens; may your glory shine on earth!

***v.* Glory be...now and ever...**

Alleluia! Alleluia! Alleluia! Glory be to You, O God! *(3 times)*

SESSIONAL HYMN

Tone 5 You descended from heaven to the earth, O Christ, * and by your Ascension You wondrously raised up the race of Adam * which had been lying in the depths of the prisons of Hades. * And having taken our nature back to heaven, * You seated it with You on the Father's throne * because of your mercy and your love for all.

Glory be...now and ever: *(Repeat the above)*

GRADUAL HYMNS

Tone 4 My sinful desires have encircled me, * from my youth they have oppressed me; * but You, O Savior, will come to aid me. * You will protect and save me.

May the enemies of Zion be confounded by the Lord; * may they be as grass which withers, * which is dried up by the fire.

Glory be...now and ever: Every spirit lives by the grace of the Holy Spirit * and is raised up in all purity; * it is mystically enlightened by the one God in three Persons.

PROKEIMENON

Tone 4 God goes up with shouts of joy; the Lord goes up with trumpet blast.

v. All peoples, clap your hands; cry to God with shouts of joy!

GOSPEL

Mark 16: 9-20

Having beheld the Resurrection...

AFTER PSALM 50

Glory be: Through the intercession of the holy apostles, O Merciful One, remit our many sins.

Now and ever: Through the intercession of the Mother of God, O Merciful One, remit our many sins.

Tone 6

Have mercy on me, God, in your kindness. In your compassion, blot out my offense.

Today the Powers on high see our nature in heaven, * and they marvel at this wondrous Ascension, * and they say to one another: * Who is this who has just arrived in heaven? * But when they recognize their own Lord, * they order the gates of heaven to be opened. * With them let us praise unceasingly * the One who shall come again from heaven in our flesh * as the judge of the universe and the almighty God.

CANON I

ODE 1

Tone 5 Our Savior and God led the people of Israel * across the Red Sea as if on dry land * and drowned Pharaoh and his whole army. * Let us praise Him who alone is worthy of our songs, * for He is covered with glory.

Refrain: **Glory to your holy Ascension, O Lord!**

All you peoples, let us praise Christ, * who is gloriously raised upon the wings of the Cherubim, * to seat us with Him at the right of the Father. * Let us sing our hymn of victory, * for He is covered with glory.

Seeing Christ, the mediator between God and mortals, * now raised on high in his flesh, * the choir of angels was seized with fear * and with one voice began to sing a hymn of victory.

God, who appeared on Mount Sinai * and gave the Law to Moses the prophet, * is now raised up bodily from the Mount of Olives. * Let us praise Him all together, * for He is covered with glory.

Glory be...now and ever: O pure Virgin and Mother of God, * intercede constantly before God who took flesh in your womb * without leaving the bosom of the Father in heaven, * that He may save from all danger * those whom He created with his own hands.

Tone 4 Enveloped by the divine cloud, * the man of unsure speech taught the Law written by God; * wiping the dust from his eyes, he saw the One-Who-Is, * and he was initiated into the knowledge of the Spirit. * Let us praise him with inspired songs.

ODE 3

Tone 5 O Christ, by the power of your Cross, * strengthen our hearts so that we may sing and glorify your saving Ascension.

Refrain: **Glory to your holy Ascension, O Lord!**

O Christ the Giver of life, * You have ascended to your Father in heaven; * and You have raised our nature with You * because of your ineffable goodness, O Lover of Mankind.

Seeing the nature of mortals raised up with You, O Savior, * the hosts of angels were astonished; * and they unceasingly sing your praises in heaven.

The choirs of angels were seized with amazement, O Christ, * when they saw You bodily raised up to heaven in glory; * and they praised your divine Ascension.

O Christ, You raised up human nature * which had been subjected to the corruption of the grave, * and You exalted it by your Ascension into heaven * where You glorify us with You.

Glory be...now and ever: O pure Virgin, intercede unceasingly * before the One who was born of your womb * for the deliverance from all error * of those who praise you as the Mother of God.

Tone 4 The shackles of a sterile womb * and the unbridled pride that filled a mother * were shattered by the prayer of Anna, the prophetess of old, * who bore a contrite and humbled heart * before the supreme and all-powerful God.

SESSIONAL HYMN

Tone 8 Riding upon the heavenly clouds, * after having brought peace to your people on earth, * You have been taken up to sit upon the divine throne * since You are consubstantial with the Father and the Spirit. * You have appeared in the flesh without change, * and You await the fulfillment of all things, * when You shall return to the earth to judge the whole world. * O just Judge, spare our souls * and grant forgiveness of sins to your servants, * O Lord and God of mercy.

Glory be...now and ever: *(Repeat the above)*

ODE 4

Tone 5 O Lord, I have heard your voice and I recognized the power of your Cross, * because through it Paradise was opened; * and I said: Glory to your power, O Lord!

Refrain: **Glory to your holy Ascension, O Lord!**

O King of angels, You ascend in glory * to send us the Paraclete from the Father; * therefore, we cry out to You: * Glory to your Ascension, O Christ!

When the Savior was bodily raised up to his Father, * the angels were seized with wonder and began to sing: * Glory to your Ascension, O Christ!

The heavenly Powers cried out one to another: * Lift up the gates for Christ our Lord; * He is the King whom we praise with one heart * together with the Father and the Spirit.

Glory be...now and ever: The Virgin gave birth without pain, * but she is both Mother and Virgin at the same time. * We sing to her with great joy: * Rejoice, O Mother of God!

Tone 4 O King of kings and only Son of the Father, *

O Word proceeding from the Father without beginning, * You send your Spirit of truth upon your apostles who sing: * Glory to your power, O Lord!

ODE 5

Tone 5 As we watch in the night and wait for morning, * O Lord, we cry to You: * Have mercy on us and save us, * for You are truly our God and we know no other but You.

Refrain: **Glory to your holy Ascension, O Lord!**

Having filled the whole world with joy, * O God of goodness and mercy, * You have ascended in your flesh * to join the Powers on high.

Seeing You raised to the heights, * the heavenly Powers were seized with fear, * and they said to one another: * Lift up the gates for the King!

Seeing the Savior exalted from earth to heaven, * the apostles were struck with fear and cried out: * Glory to You, O Lord and our King!

Glory be...now and ever: We praise you, O holy Mother of God, * a virgin even after giving birth; * for the sake of the world you truly gave birth * to the Word of God in the flesh.

Tone 4 Receive the Holy Spirit, breathing the flames of fresh dew * as a baptism that takes away sin, * O you children who are enlightened by the Church. * For today the Law comes forth from Zion; * it is the grace of the Spirit which comes in tongues of fire.

ODE 6

Tone 5 The abyss surrounds me completely; * the sea monster holds me as if in a tomb; * I cried to You, O Lover of Mankind, * and your right hand has saved me.

Refrain: **Glory to your holy Ascension, O Lord!**

The apostles exalt with joy on this day * as they see their Creator go up into the clouds; * and in the hope of the Spirit, whom they await, * they cry out in fear: * Glory to your divine Ascension!

O Lord, your angels came to your disciples and said: * You have seen Christ taken up in the flesh; * in the same way He shall come to judge the whole world.

Seeing You ascend in your body, O Lord, * the Powers of heaven cried out joyfully: * Great is your mercy, O Lord!

Glory be...now and ever: It is proper to glorify you, * O bush that burns without being consumed, * O mountain, O living ladder and gate to heaven, * O Virgin Mary, the glory of Christians.

Tone 4 O Christ, our salvation and redemption, * You have come forth in splendor from the Virgin, * to rescue us from the pit of the tomb; * as Jonah was saved from the sea monster, * the entire human race was saved after the fall of Adam.

KONTAKION

Tone 6 When You fulfilled the plan of salvation for us * and united all things on earth to those in heaven, O Christ our God, * You ascended in glory, never leaving us, but remaining ever-present. * For You proclaimed to those who love You: * I am with you and no one else has power over you.

IKOS

Leaving earthly cares to the earth and that which is waste and refuse to the dust, come, let us arise from sleep and with our eyes and hearts let us go towards higher things. Let us also lift up our thoughts and our attention from the earth to the gates of heaven, as if we were on the Mount of Olives, where we fix our eyes on the Redeemer as He is carried away to heaven. For it is there that the Lord departs for heaven; it is there also that He distributes his great gifts to the apostles, giving them strength and comforting them as a Father, guiding them as sons and saying to them: I am not separating myself from you; I shall always be with you, and no one shall ever have power over you.

ODE 7

Tone 5 O Savior who saved the youths who sang to You in the furnace, * blessed are You, O Lord and God of our fathers.

Refrain: **Glory to your holy Ascension, O Lord!**

You went up in a cloud of brightness after having saved the whole world; * blessed are You, O Lord, God of our fathers.

Having taken fallen human nature as a lost sheep upon your shoulders, * You led it to your Father, O Lord, by your divine Ascension.

Clothed in our flesh, You went up to your Father who is

also incorporeal; * blessed are You, O Lord and God of our fathers.

You have again raised our human nature * which had been put to death by sin, O God our Savior, * to present it to your Father in heaven.

Glory be...now and ever: You placed the immaculate Virgin in this world, * and You made her the Mother of God; * blessed are You, O Lord, God of our fathers.

Tone 4 The symphony of instruments was raised up to adore the lifeless golden statue; * but the bright grace of the Paraclete invites us to sing with devotion: * Blessed are You, eternal and unique Trinity!

ODE 8

Tone 5 The Son of God, born of the Father before all ages, * has taken flesh from the Virgin Mother in these last days. * Praise Him, you priests, * and let the whole nation exalt Him forever.

Refrain: **Glory to your holy Ascension, O Lord!**

Christ the Giver of life ascends in glory to heaven; * with both his natures, He is seated at the right hand of the Father. * Praise Him, you priests, * and let the whole nation exalt Him forever.

You have redeemed the work of your hands from the slavery of the false gods; * You have presented it in freedom to your Father. * O Savior, we praise and exalt You forever.

The One who descended among us * and trampled down our Enemy * now raises up our humanity by his Ascension. * Praise Him, you priests, * and let the whole nation exalt Him forever.

Glory be...now and ever: You appeared more venerable than the Cherubim, O holy Mother of God, * when you carried in your womb * the One whom they carry on their wings in heaven; * and with the bodiless angels, we mortals glorify Him forever.

Tone 4 The triple flame of the unique divinity * breaks the chains and stirs the flames with dew; * the youths sing his praises, * and every creature, the work of his hands, * blesses its only Savior and benefactor.

OMIT MAGNIFICAT

ODE 9

O my soul, extol Christ the Giver of life who ascended from earth into heaven.

The angels, seeing the Ascension of the Master, were struck with fear at how He went from earth to the heights.

(alternate before each of the following)

Tone 5 Surpassing our spirit and our understanding, * you gave birth in the world and in time to the timeless Lord; * with one voice and one heart, O Mother of God, * we the faithful extol you.

O Redeemer of the world, Christ our God, * the apostles contemplate your divine exaltation; * and in fear and in joy, they extol You.

Seeing your divinized flesh, O Christ, * the angels on high said to each other: * Truly this man is our God!

Seeing You raised upon the clouds, O Christ our God, * the choir of angels cried out: * Lift up the gates of heaven for the King of glory!

You have descended to the depths of the earth; * You have saved humanity; * and You have raised it up by your holy Ascension. * O Christ our God, we extol You!

Glory be...now and ever: Rejoice, O holy Mother of Christ our God, * for today you extol the One whom you bore * as you see Him carried by the angels from earth to heaven.

Tone 4 Rejoice, O Queen and glorious Virgin Mother! * What orator, rich in eloquence, could find the proper words * to fashion a hymn of praise worthy of you? * For every spirit shudders before the mystery of your holy birthgiving; * and we also unite our voices to glorify you.

CANON II

ODE 1

Tone 4 You have risen on the third day, even though by nature You are immortal; * You have appeared to your disciples, O Christ, * and then You returned to your Father; * You were carried upon the cloud, O Creator of the universe.

Refrain: **Glory to your holy Ascension, O Lord!**

In a psalm inspired by God, David proclaimed very clearly: * The Lord goes up to heaven amid the shouts and blasts of the trumpet * to rejoin his Father, the Giver of light.

By your suffering and Resurrection, O Lord, * You have

renewed the world which had grown old through its many sins. * And then You were taken into heaven, borne upon the cloud.

Glory be...now and ever: You have given birth to the Master of all, O most pure Queen; * He suffered of his own will and then He returned to his Father * without leaving our flesh which He had assumed.

Enveloped by the divine cloud, * the man of unsure speech taught the Law written by God; * wiping the dust from his eyes, he saw the One-Who-Is, * and he was initiated into the knowledge of the Spirit. * Let us praise him with inspired songs.

ODE 3

Tone 4 The Powers on high said to one another: * Lift up the gates of heaven. * Behold, Christ our King and our Lord has arrived, * clothed in a mortal body.

Refrain: **Glory to your holy Ascension, O Lord!**

Having come in search of fallen humanity * which had been deceived by the craftiness of the serpent, * You clothed yourself with this same human nature, * and You have taken it with You to be seated at the right hand of your Father, * amid the songs of the angels in heaven.

Earth exalts in festive joy, * and heaven also rejoices on this day: * it is the holy Ascension of the Creator of the world; * for He brings together that which had been separated.

Glory be...now and ever: Having given birth to the Conquerer of Death, * the God who alone is immortal, * O Virgin Mother most pure, * implore Him without ceasing, * that He may save me from my deadly passions.

The shackles of a sterile womb * and the unbridled pride that filled a mother * were shattered by the prayer of Anna, the prophetess of old, * who bore a contrite and humbled heart * before the supreme and all-powerful God.

SESSIONAL HYMN

Tone 8 Riding upon the heavenly clouds, * after having brought peace to your people on earth, * You have been taken up to sit upon the divine throne * since Your are consubstantial with the Father and the Spirit. * You have appeared in the flesh without change, * and You await the fulfillment of all things, * when You shall return to the earth to judge the whole world. * O just Judge, spare our souls * and grant forgiveness of sins to your servants, * O Lord and God of mercy.

Glory be...now and ever: *(Repeat the above)*

ODE 4

Tone 4 Taking with Him those whom He loved, * Jesus, the Giver of life, went up to the Mount of Olives; * and blessing them with his hands, * He was taken away by the cloud * to rejoin the fatherly bosom which He had never left.

Refrain: **Glory to your holy Ascension, O Lord!**

On this day the whole world, visible and invisible, joyfully celebrates a feast: * the angels exalt in heaven, * and the people on earth glorify the Ascension of the God of love, * who in his flesh has united himself to us.

Having demolished the dominion of Death as the immortal Lord, * You granted immortality to all people, O God who loves us. * And now You have ascended in glory, O Lord almighty, * in the sight of your holy apostles.

Glory be...now and ever: Your womb has become blessed, O most pure Virgin, * for it was worthy to shelter in a marvelous manner * the One who emptied the womb of Hades. * Pray to Him that He save those who praise his name.

O King of kings and only Son of the Father, * O Word proceeding from the Father without beginning, * You send your Spirit of truth upon your apostles who sing: * Glory to your power, O Lord!

ODE 5

Tone 4 Having conquered Death by your death, O Lord, * You took those whom You loved * and went up to the Mount of Olives; * from there You ascended to your Father in heaven, * as You were carried upon the cloud.

Refrain: **Glory to your holy Ascension, O Lord!**

Your birth and your resurrection were beyond the bounds of nature; * wondrous and equally formidable is your holy Ascension * which Elijah formerly prefigured when he was taken up in the fiery chariot * while praising You, O Lord and Giver of life.

The angels came and said to the apostles who were looking up into the sky: * Men of Galilee, why are you astonished at the Ascension of Christ, the Giver of life? * As the good and righteous Judge, * He shall come again upon the earth * to judge the whole world.

Glory be...now and ever: Christ has left you a virgin even after giving birth, O Mother of God; * and now He is raised up to his Father whom He never left, * even though He received flesh from you * and took on our soul and spirit in his ineffable goodness.

Receive the Holy Spirit, breathing the flames of fresh dew * as a baptism that takes away sin, * O you children who are enlightened by the Church. * For today the Law comes forth from Zion; * it is the grace of the Spirit which comes in tongues of fire.

ODE 6

Tone 4 The skies rain down eternal joy upon us, * for the clouds, like the Cherubim, carry Christ, * as He goes up to his Father on this day.

Refrain: **Glory to your holy Ascension, O Lord!**

You have appeared in the garment of our flesh; * You have united that which formerly had been separated, O Lover of all; * and You have gone up to the heavens in the sight of your apostles.

Why are these garments covered with red, * the garments of the One who is united to our flesh? * Thus asked the angels who saw Christ, * bearing the marks of his holy Passion.

Glory be...now and ever: O Virgin, we praise your conception and ineffable birth-giving, * which delivers us from evil and from the tomb * as well as from the dark prisons of Hades.

O Christ, our salvation and redemption, * You have come forth in splendor from the Virgin, * to rescue us from the pit of the tomb; * as Jonah was saved from the sea monster, * the entire human race was saved after the fall of Adam.

KONTAKION

Tone 6 When You fulfilled the plan of salvation for us * and united all things on earth to those in heaven, O Christ our God, * You ascended in glory, never leaving us, but remaining ever-present. * For You proclaimed to those who love You: * I am with you and no one else has power over you.

IKOS

Leaving earthly cares to the earth and that which is waste and refuse to the dust, come, let us arise from sleep and with our eyes and hearts let us go towards higher things. Let us also lift up our thoughts and our attention from the earth to the gates of heaven, as if we were on the Mount of Olives, where we fix our eyes on the Redeemer as He is carried away to heaven. For it is there that the Lord departs for heaven; it is there also that He distributes his great gifts to the apostles, giving them strength and comforting them as a Father, guiding them as sons and saying to them: I am not separating myself from you; I shall always be with you, and no one shall ever have power over you.

ODE 7

Tone 4 The bright cloud received You, O Lord, * even though You yourself are the Light, * and You were wondrously taken away from the earth. * The angels in the highest heavens sing with the apostles: * Blessed are You, O God of our Fathers!

Refrain: **Glory to your holy Ascension, O Lord!**

All you people, clap your hands, in honor of the Ascension of Christ, * and let us sing with joy: * God goes up amid shouts of joy, * the Lord amid trumpet blasts. * He is seated at the right hand of the Father, * sharing his throne for all eternity.

In days of old, Moses prophesied by singing this hymn: * May the angels of heaven bow before Christ who ascends * as before the King of the universe, * and we sing to Him: * Blessed are You, O God of our Fathers!

Glory be...now and ever: O wondrous and unheard-of marvel! * You sheltered the God whom none could contain, O Full of Grace; * for He shared the poverty of our flesh. * But today He has gone up to heaven, filled with glory, * granting life to all.

The symphony of instruments was raised up to adore the lifeless golden statue; * but the bright grace of the Paraclete invites us to sing with devotion: * Blessed are You, eternal and unique Trinity!

ODE 8

Tone 4 The angels appeared to the apostles on the day

of the Ascension and said: * Why do you stand there dumbfounded, looking up into the sky? * He who has gone up to heaven will come to the earth again * as the only judge of all humanity.

Refrain: **Glory to your holy Ascension, O Lord!**

Let us give glory to the divine majesty; * let us join our voices to praise Him; * let us sing, dance, and clap our hands, * for the Lord our God has gone from earth to heaven; * and all the angels adore Him as the Master and Creator of the world.

Our nature, which formerly had fallen, is now raised above the angels; * henceforth, it shall be seated ineffably on the divine throne. * Come, let us celebrate this feast and say: * Praise the Lord, all his works; * to Him be highest glory and praise forever.

Glory be...now and ever: Behold your Son, O Mother of God! * Having conquered Death by his Cross, * He was resurrected on the third day; * then after appearing to his disciples, * He went up to heaven again. * And we, who now bow before Him, * also praise and glorify you forever.

The triple flame of the unique divinity * breaks the chains and stirs the flames with dew; * the youths sing his praises, * and every creature, the work of his hands, * blesses its only Savior and benefactor.

OMIT MAGNIFICAT

ODE 9

O my soul, extol Christ the Giver of life who ascended from earth into heaven.

The angels, seeing the Ascension of the Master, were struck with fear at how He went from earth to the heights.

(alternate before each of the following)

Tone 4 Seeing the Ascension of the Lord, * the angels were struck with astonishment. * How is He gloriously taken from earth to heaven?

Refrain: **Glory to your holy Ascension, O Lord!**

O graciousness which surpasses understanding! * O mystery which evokes wonder! * The Master of the universe goes up from earth to heaven * and sends the Holy Spirit to his disciples * to illumine their hearts and enkindle them with his grace.

The Lord said to his disciples: * Remain in Jerusalem,

and I will send you another Paraclete * who is seated with the Father and with Me, * whom you now see raised up to heaven * and carried by a shining cloud.

The majesty which has come down from the highest heaven * and taken on the poverty of our flesh, * is now clearly raised on high * and takes our fallen nature to be seated next to the Father. * On this feast, let us all sing with one voice, * and let us clap our hands in cries of joy.

Glory be...now and ever: Christ, the Light of light, is risen from you, O all-pure One. * He has dispelled the blindness of the impious; * He has awakened those who were sleeping in the dark night. * Therefore, O Virgin worthy of our praises, * we extol you forever.

Rejoice, O Queen and glorious Virgin Mother! * What orator, rich in eloquence, could find the proper words * to fashion a hymn of praise worthy of you? * For every spirit shudders before the mystery of your holy birthgiving; * and we also unite our voices to glorify you.

HYMN OF LIGHT

Tone 2 O Christ, You were raised up to heaven in the sight of your disciples; * You again went up to share your Father's throne. * The angels who came to meet You at the heavenly gate cried out: * Open your gates and lift up your lintels * so that the King of glory may come in, * for our King comes again to the Source of light. *(3 times)*

AT THE PRAISES

Tone 1 With the angels in heaven, let us praise on earth * our God who ascends to his throne of glory, * and let us sing to Him: * Holy are You, O Father of heaven, * O co-eternal Word, and most Holy Spirit. *(2 times)*

As they gazed upon the wonder of your Ascension, O Savior, * the princes of the angels said to one another: * What is this sight that is before our eyes? * We see the form of a man, * but as God He is raised above the heavens in his body.

Seeing You ascend bodily from the Mount of Olives, O Word, * the men of Galilee heard the angels cry out to them: Why do you stand there looking up? * He shall return in his flesh * in the same way that you have seen Him taken away.

Tone 2 **Glory be...now and ever:** O our God, You were born in a manner of your own choosing; * You appeared and suffered in the flesh as You willed; * You crushed Death through your Resurrection and ascended into glory; * and You sent down the divine Spirit upon us; * therefore, we sing a hymn of praise and glorify your divinity.

Thursday Evening Vespers

AT PSALM 140

Tone 1 By going up again into heaven from which You had descended, * You did not leave us orphans, O Lord. * Show to all your people the works of your power, * that your Spirit may come down upon us * and bring peace to the world, * O Lord and Lover of Mankind.

You ascended, O Christ, to your eternal Father, * even though You were not removed from his bosom; * and the Powers could not contain their praise of the Trinity. * Even after the Incarnation, * they recognize You as the only Son of the Father. * In the abundance of your goodness, have mercy on us.

Your angels, O Lord, said to the apostles: * Men of Galilee, why do you stand here looking into the sky? * Christ our God, who by leaving you ascended into heaven, * will come again in the manner by which you have seen Him leave. * Therefore, serve Him in justice and holiness.

Three Stichera from the Saint of the day

Tone 2 **Glory be...now and ever:** O our God, You were born in a manner of your own choosing; * You appeared and suffered in the flesh as You willed; * You crushed Death through your Resurrection and ascended into glory; * and You sent down the divine Spirit upon us; * therefore, we sing a hymn of praise and glorify your divinity.

GREAT PROKEIMENON

Tone 7 But our God is in the heavens; He does whatever He wills.

- ***v.*** When Israel came forth from Egypt, Jacob's sons from an alien people.
- ***v.*** Judah became the Lord's temple, Israel became his kingdom.
- ***v.*** The sea fled at the sight; the Jordan turned back on its course.

APOSTICHA

Tone 2 He who is the fulfillment of all things * speaks to the disciples on the Mount of Olives: * My friends, the time has come for my departure. * Go and teach all nations the word you have heard Me speak. * Then He ascended in a chariot of glory, * and the apostles trembled in fear.

All peoples, clap your hands; cry to God with shouts of joy!

When your Mother and your disciples came to Bethany, O Christ, * You raised your hands to bless them; * and a cloud of light took You from their sight. * You ascended in glory to the right hand of the Father * whom we worship together with You.

God goes up with shouts of joy; the Lord goes up with trumpet blast.

Come, O faithful, let us climb the Mount of Olives; * with the apostles, let us lift our minds and hearts on high. * Let us behold the Lord as He is taken up. * Let us cry out with joy and thanksgiving: * Glory to your Ascension, O most merciful One!

Tone 6 **Glory be...now and ever:** O Christ, splendor and glory of the Father, * when we behold your Ascension on the holy mountain, * we sing a hymn of praise to the beauty of your countenance. * We bow down to your Passion, * we venerate your holy Resurrection, * and we glorify your noble Ascension. * O Lord, have mercy on us!

TROPARIA

Of the Saint

Tone 4 **Glory be...now and ever:** You ascended in glory, O Christ our God; * You delighted the disciples with the promise of the Holy Spirit. * Through this blessing they were assured * that You are the Son of God, * the Redeemer of the world.

Friday Matins

SESSIONAL HYMN I

Tone 8 You went up to the Mount of Olives, O merciful Jesus; * You ascended from the earth, taken up by a cloud of light. * The disciples beheld the fearful wonder, * while the angels on high cried out in fear. * All the hosts of heaven lifted the gates, * praising You, O King, the Creator and God of all.

Glory be...now and ever: *(Repeat the above)*

SESSIONAL HYMN II

Tone 8 Riding upon the heavenly clouds, * after having brought peace to your people on earth, * You have been taken up to sit upon the divine throne * since You are consubstantial with the Father and the Spirit. * You have appeared in the flesh without change, * and You await the fulfillment of all things, * when You shall return to the earth to judge the whole world. * O just Judge, spare our souls * and grant forgiveness of sins to your servants, * O Lord and God of mercy.

Glory be...now and ever: *(Repeat the above)*

CANON

HYMN OF LIGHT

Tone 2 O Christ, You were raised up to heaven in the sight of your disciples; * You again went up to share your Father's throne. * The angels who came to meet You at the heavenly gate cried out: * Open your gates and lift up your lintels * so that the King of glory may come in; * for our King comes again to the Source of light. *(3 times)*

APOSTICHA

Tone 2 Behold, mortal nature now ascends to heaven, * united to God almighty * in the flesh of the Word. * Truly this is an amazing wonder!

All peoples, clap your hands; cry to God with shouts of joy!

This day, bright and radiant, * now dawns in splendor. * It is the day of our Lord and Master, * for by his Ascension into heaven * all things are filled with light.

God goes up with shouts of joy; the Lord goes up with trumpet blast.

O Christ our Savior, * You sent your Spirit from on high to your disciples. * Now send down your grace * upon all your people.

Tone 5 **Glory be...now and ever:** O Lord, You did not cast aside your body at your Ascension. * The hosts of angels attending You * cried out in joy and amazement to the hosts on high: * Lift up your heads, O you gates! * Let the King of glory enter! * You have gone up to heaven, robed in your flesh; * You are borne by the chariot of the Cherubim. * O Lord, glory to You!

Friday Evening Vespers

AT PSALM 140

Tone 4 You suffered in your humanity, O Christ our God; * You rose on the third day and despoiled Death, * raising with yourself all those held fast in corruption. * You ascended to the Father, * promising to send the Paraclete to your apostles, * O almighty Jesus, the Savior of our souls.

Why do you stand gazing into heaven, * cried the angels who appeared as men * to those whom You had instructed in your mysteries. * He will come again in the same way, as He said. * He will come to judge the world. * Go, therefore, and do all that He commanded you.

After rising from the tomb, O Lord almighty, * You took your friends to the Mount of Olives. * Leading them to Bethany, You blessed them. * There you ascended, taken up by the angels, * O Jesus almighty, the Savior of our souls.

Three Stichera from the Saint of the day

Tone 6 **Glory be...now and ever:** Today the Powers on high see our nature in heaven, * and they marvel at this wondrous Ascension, * and they say to one another: * Who is this who has just arrived in heaven? * But when they recognize their own Lord, * they order the gates of heaven to be opened. * With them let us praise unceasingly * the One who shall come again from heaven in our flesh * as the judge of the universe and the almighty God.

APOSTICHA

Tone 2 Fulfilling the good will of the Father, O good One, * uniting earth with heaven, * You ascended in glory * to your eternal abode.

All peoples, clap your hands; cry to God with shouts of joy!

You went up to your Father, O bountiful One, * whom You had never left, * raising up, O Master, * the nature which had fallen.

God goes up with shouts of joy; the Lord goes up with trumpet blast.

A cloud of light lifted You to the heavens. * With fear and trembling, * all the Powers of heaven * hastened to serve your divine majesty.

Tone 7 **Glory be...now and ever:** In your mercy for us, You came to the Mount of Olives; * a cloud lifted You from before the eyes of the disciples. * They were filled with trembling as they beheld this sight * but rejoiced in expectation of the Holy Spirit. * Confirm us in Him, O Savior, and have mercy on us.

TROPARIA

Of the Saint

Tone 4 **Glory be...now and ever:** You ascended in glory, O Christ our God; * You delighted the disciples with the promise of the Holy Spirit. * Through this blessing they were assured * that You are the Son of God, * the Redeemer of the world.

Saturday Matins

SESSIONAL HYMN I

Tone 1 You ascended in glory, and the angels were astonished at this wonder; * the disciples were amazed at your marvelous Ascension; * and the gates opened before You, O Lord. * The Powers of heaven were also overjoyed, and they cried out: * Glory to your condescension, O Savior! * Glory to your kingdom! * Glory to your Ascension, O only Lover of Mankind!

Glory be...now and ever: *(Repeat the above)*

SESSIONAL HYMN II

Tone 1 You have plundered Hades, O Giver of life! * The world is enlightened by your Resurrection. * You have ascended in glory, O Savior, * holding the ransomed earth in your hands. * With the angels, we worship You and cry out: * Glory to your Ascension, O Christ! * Glory to your kingdom! * Glory to your compassion, O only Lover of Mankind!

Glory be...now and ever: *(Repeat the above)*

CANON

HYMN OF LIGHT

Tone 2 O Christ, You were raised up to heaven in the sight of your disciples; * You again went up to share your Father's throne. * The angels who came to meet You at the heavenly gate cried out: * Open your gates and lift up your lintels * so that the King of glory may come in, * for our King comes again to the Source of light. *(3 times)*

APOSTICHA

Tone 2 I will not leave you orphans; * I will remain with you always, * said the Lord to his friends. * I will send upon you the Holy Spirit.

All peoples, clap your hands; cry to God with shouts of joy!

He will come again, O men of Galilee, * in the same way as He departed. * So proclaimed the angels * to the enlightened apostles.

God goes up with shouts of joy; the Lord goes up with trumpet blast.

Your chosen disciples * descended from the Mount of Olives, * joyfully singing your praises * and glorifying your Ascension, * O Word of God and Lover of Mankind!

Tone 8 **Glory be...now and ever:** You ascended from earth to heaven in glory, * and You filled all things with your divinity. * You took your place at the right hand of the Father, * O eternal One, God the Word. * When the heavenly Powers beheld You, * they cried in fear to the apostles: * Why do you gaze upward, looking into heaven? * You see Him departing, * but He will return with glory to judge the earth. * He will render to everyone according to his works. * Let us cry out to Him: * O incomprehensible Lord, glory to You!

Sunday of the Fathers of the First Nicean Council

Vespers

AT PSALM 140

Tone 6 O Christ, You won the victory over Hades, * You ascended the Cross so that You might raise up with yourself * all those who dwelt in the darkness of death. * Almighty Savior, You are free from death * and bestow life by your divine light. * We, therefore, beseech You to have mercy on us.

Today Christ has conquered Death. * He has risen from the grave as He had foretold, * bestowing great joy upon the world. * Therefore, let us all lift up our voices and sing: * O Fount of Life, O Light whom no one can approach, * almighty Savior, have mercy on us.

O Lord, where can we sinners flee from You, * for You are present in all creation? * You are present in heaven, for it is your dwelling place. * Your power prevails in Hades where You conquered Death. * O Master, your sustaining hand touches even the depths of the sea. * Where, then, can we take refuge except in You? * We, therefore, prostrate ourselves before You and pray: * O Lord, risen from the dead, have mercy on us.

The Lord ascended into heaven * to send the Comforter into this world. * The heavens prepared his throne and the clouds were his ladder; * the angels marveled at the sight of a human being more exalted than themselves. * Today, the Father receives again in his bosom * the One who was in Him from all eternity, * and the Holy Spirit gives a command to all the angels: * Lift up your lintels, O you gates! * O you nations of the earth, clap your hands, * for Christ ascends to the place * where He had been from all eternity.

O Lord, the Cherubim were amazed at your Ascension; * they were seized with wonder as they beheld You, O God, rising upon the clouds, * for You are the One who is seated above the clouds. * We sing a hymn of praise to You: * Glory to You for your tender mercy.

O Christ, splendor and glory of the Father, * when we behold your Ascension on the holy mountain, * we sing a hymn of praise to the beauty of your countenance. * We bow down to your Passion, * we venerate your holy Resurrection, * and we glorify your noble Ascension. * O Lord, have mercy on us!

Before the morning star You were begotten of the Father; * before the ages You were conceived without a mother, * even though Arius believed You to be created, and not God.* He shamelessly confused the Creator with his creatures, * thus deserving eternal punishment. * Yet the Council of Nicea proclaimed You as the Son of God * who is enthroned with the Father and the Spirit.

Who has severed your garment, O Savior? * It was Arius who divided the Trinity * who is equal in glory and eternal majesty. * For he denied that You are one of the most Holy Trinity. * He taught the transgressing Nestorius * to say that the Virgin is not the Mother of God; * but the Council of Nicea proclaimed You as the Son of God * who is enthroned with the Father and the Spirit.

Declaring that the light could not be seen, * Arius fell into the pit of the impious ones; * his body was torn apart by the justice of God, * and he gave up his soul in a violent manner. * He was another Judas by his thoughts and deeds. * But the Council of Nicea proclaimed You as the Son of God * who is enthroned with the Father and the Spirit.

The foolish Arius divided the unity of the Holy Trinity * into three different and unequal substances. * But the God-bearing Fathers came together in Council. * Burning with the zeal of Elijah the Tishbite * and with the sword of the Holy Spirit, * they cut down these shameful blasphemies; * for they were directed by the Spirit.

Tone 6 **Glory be:** Let us honor today those mystical trumpets of the Spirit, * namely, the God-mantled Fathers, * who speaking of divine things, * sang in the midst of the Church a hymn in unison, * teaching that the Trinity is one, * not differing in substance or Godhead, * refuting Arius and defending the true faith. * They always intercede with the Lord * to have mercy on our souls.

Tone 6 **Now and ever:** Who would not bless you, most holy Virgin? * Who would not praise the most pure manner in which you gave birth? * For the only-begotten Son, who eternally proceeds from the Father, came forth from you. * He took flesh from you in a manner that is beyond understanding. * He, who by nature is God, took on our nature for our sake. * Yet He did not become divided into two persons; * rather, He remained one person with two distinct and unconfused natures. * O most pure Lady, we implore you: * Beseech your Son and God to have mercy on our souls.

Readings

Genesis 14: 14-20
Deuteronomy 1: 8-11; 15-17
Deuteronomy 10: 14-21

APOSTICHA

Tone 6 O Christ our Savior, * the angels in heaven sing the praises of your Resurrection; * make us, on earth, also worthy * to extol and glorify You with a pure heart.

The Lord reigns, He is clothed in majesty. Robed is the Lord, and girt about with strength.

Almighty God, You destroyed the brazen gates and bars of Hades * and raised up the fallen human race. * Therefore, with one accord, we cry out: * O Lord, risen from the dead, glory to you!

For He has made the world firm, which shall not be moved.

Christ willed to renew us from our corruption of old * by being nailed to a Cross and placed in a tomb. * When the women came to anoint his body, they tearfully cried out: * O, what sorrow afflicts us! * O Savior of all, how could You consent to occupy a grave? * If You truly willed this, then why did You allow your body to be stolen? * How were You removed? * What place now conceals your life-bearing body? * O Lord, appear to us as You promised * and put an end to our tears. * As they were lamenting, an angel appeared and cried out to them: * Do not weep, but tell the apostles that the Lord is risen, * granting sanctification and great mercy to the world.

Holiness befits your house, O Lord, for length of days.

O Christ, You were crucified of your own free will, * and by your burial You imprisoned Death. * As God, You rose in glory on the third day, * granting life and great mercy to the world.

Tone 4 **Glory be:** O believers, let us come together today * to celebrate in faith and true worship * the remembrance of the God-inspired Fathers * who had come together from throughout the world, * in the splendid city of Nicea. *

They rejected the doctrine of the impious Arius * and banished him from the universal Church * by a decree of the Council. * They instructed all to openly profess the Son of God, * that He is consubstantial and coeternal with the Father before eternity, * and they clearly wrote this in the Symbol of Faith. * Therefore, following their divine doctrines, * let us worship the Son in true faith, * together with the Father and the Holy Spirit, * the Trinity consubstantial in one Godhead.

Tone 4 **Now and ever:** O Lord most merciful, * after fulfilling the mystery hidden from all eternity, * You, the Creator and Master of all, * went up to the Mount of Olives with your disciples and your Mother. * For the one who, at the sight of your Passion, * had suffered more than anyone else in her motherly heart, * had more than anyone else the right to share the joy that fills us * as we witness your ascending into heaven. * We glorify your infinite mercy overflowing upon us.

TROPARIA

Tone 6 Angelic Powers descended to your grave, * and the guards fell down and appeared dead. * Mary came to the grave seeking your most pure body. * You conquered and despoiled the Abyss without being touched by it. * You, the Giver of life, met the Virgin. * O Lord, risen from the dead, glory be to You!

Tone 8 **Glory be:** O Christ our God, You are most glorified, * for You established our fathers as lights upon the earth. * Through them You led us to the true faith. * O most merciful Lord, glory to You.

Tone 4 **Now and ever:** You ascended in glory, O Christ our God; * You delighted the disciples with the promise of the Holy Spirit. * Through this blessing they were assured * that You are the Son of God, * the Redeemer of the world.

Sunday Matins

SESSIONAL HYMN I

Tone 6 When the tomb was shown to be open and Hades was lamenting, * Mary cried out to the apostles who were hiding and said: * Come out, laborers of the vineyard, and proclaim the news of the Resurrection; * for the Lord is risen, granting the world great mercy.

Arise, then, Lord, lift up your hand. O God, do not forget the poor!

Mary Magdalene stood by your tomb and wept, O Lord. * When she thought You were the gardener, she said: * Where have you hidden the eternal Life? * Where have you placed Him who sits on the throne of the Cherubim? * When she saw those guarding Him fearful and appearing as dead, she cried to them: * Give me my Lord or else cry out with me and say: * You have come forth from the tomb and raised the dead, O Lord, glory to You!

Glory be...now and ever: You called your Mother blessed, * and You willingly went to your Passion. * Your light shone from the Cross, * for You desired to go in search of Adam. * To the angels You proclaimed: Rejoice with Me, * for the lost coin has been found. * You do everything according to your wisdom; * glory to You, O Lord and God!

SESSIONAL HYMN II

Tone 6 Truly our Life was placed in the grave, * and seals were applied to the stone. * The soldiers guarded Christ as they would a sleeping king. * But, striking his enemies with blindness, the Lord rose.

I will praise You, Lord, with all my heart; I will recount all your wonders.

Through your voluntary death we have found eternal life; * for in your Resurrection, O almighty Savior, * You called all mortals back to You. * You wiped out the victory of Hades * and broke the sting of Death.

Glory be...now and ever: O Virgin and Theotokos, * pray to your Son, Christ our God, * who was willingly nailed upon the Cross and rose from the dead, * that He might save our souls.

HYPAKOE

By your voluntary and life-giving death, O Christ, * You crushed the gates of Hades and opened the Paradise of old, * because You are God. * Having risen from the dead, You redeemed our life from corruption.

GRADUAL HYMNS

Antiphon I

I lift my eyes to heaven, * to You, O Word of God. * In your mercy save me * so that I may live in You.

O Lord, have mercy on us, * for we are filled with contempt. * Restore us as your chosen vessels, O Word.

Glory be...now and ever: Truly the Holy Spirit is the cause of salvation for all; * for when He breathes on them, * He raises them from the cares of this world. * He gives them wings to carry them to heaven.

Antiphon II

Had not the Lord been with us, * none of us could stand firm in the struggle with the Enemy. * But the victors shall be exalted.

How shall I escape the enemies while I am the prey of sin? * O Word, deliver not my soul * like a bird delivered to its enemies.

Glory be...now and ever: Through the Holy Spirit everyone is divinized. * In Him is good will, understanding, peace, and blessing, * for He is equal to the Father and the Word.

Antiphon III

They who trust in the Lord are feared by their enemies * and are worthy of admiration; * for their eyes are fixed on heaven.

The party of the righteous have You as their help, O Savior; * therefore, they shall not reach out their hands to iniquity.

Glory be...now and ever: Truly the Holy Spirit has power over the whole universe. * All the heavenly hosts and all those on earth worship Him.

PROKEIMENON

Tone 6 O Lord, rouse up your might; O Lord, come to our help.

v. O Shepherd of Israel, hear us, for you lead Joseph's flock.

GOSPEL

John 21: 1-14

Having beheld the Resurrection of Christ. * let us adore the holy Lord Jesus * who alone is sinless. * We bow to your Cross, O Christ, * and we praise and glorify your holy Resurrection. * You are our God * and besides You we recognize no other, * and we invoke your name.* Come all you faithful, * and let us bow to the holy Resurrection of Christ, * since, through the Cross, joy has come to all the world. * Ever praising the Lord, let us extol his Resurrection, * since He, having endured the crucifixion, * has destroyed Death by his death.

CANON

ODE 1

Tone 6 When Israel walked upon the deep sea as upon dry land * they saw Pharaoh, their pursuer, drowning, and they exclaimed: * Let us sing a hymn of victory to God.

Refrain: **Glory to your holy Resurrection, O Lord!**

When You stretched out your hands on the Cross, O God of goodness, * You fulfilled the will of your Father. * With one heart we, therefore, sing a hymn of victory in your honor.

Filled with fright, * as a servant coming at the word of a master, Death approached You, O Master of life. * Through it You gave us resurrection and unending life.

Refrain: **Most holy Mother of God, save us!**

You have received your Creator as He himself willed, * and He took flesh ineffably in your womb without seed. * O pure Virgin, you are truly the Queen of all creation.

Tone 6 Praising the Council of the holy Fathers, O Christ, * I pray to You so that I may be able * to preserve their sacred teachings in my heart.

Refrain: **O holy Fathers, pray to God for us!**

The God-mantled Fathers gathered on this day * as bright torches flaming with light, O Christ; * they recognized You as the only Son of God, * consubstantial and coeternal with the Father.

The brilliant friends of the bridegroom * have offered jewels to your spouse, the Church, O Lord. * These jewels are their teachings of the faith, * and they have adorned the Church with beauty.

Glory be...now and ever: Vested in divinely embroidered brocades, * the holy Queen is led to the King, her Son and God, * and she prays for the salvation of our souls.

Tone 7 He drowned Pharaoh and his army in the Red Sea, * for He is the One who shattered the armies with the power of his arm. * Let us sing to Him, for He is covered with glory.

ODE 3

Tone 6 None is as holy as You, O Lord my God. * In your goodness You have exalted the strength of the faithful, * and You have established us on the unshakable rock of your name.

***Refrain:* Glory to your holy Resurrection, O Lord!**

When creation saw God crucified in the flesh, * it shuddered with fright; * but it was held secure by the hand of Him * who let himself be crucified for us.

The power of Death was shattered by death, * and henceforth it lies powerless; * for it could not bear the divine invasion of Life, * and Resurrection is granted to the whole world.

***Refrain:* Most holy Mother of God, save us!**

O pure Virgin, the wonder of your divine birthgiving surpasses the laws of nature; * for it is God himself who is ineffably conceived in your womb, * and you remain a virgin even after giving birth.

Tone 6 In his foolishness, Arius mingled movement and suffering and division into your divine generation, * but he himself was cut down by the spiritual sword.

***Refrain:* O holy Fathers, pray to God for us!**

The holy teachers, arrayed for battle like Abraham of old before the kings, * obtained the victory over your raging enemies * by the power of your arm, * O Lord of goodness.

The illustrious and first synod of your holy bishops, O Savior, * has devoutly proclaimed You as begotten before the ages, * consubstantial and eternal with the Father, and Creator of the world.

Glory be...now and ever: No word nor any mortal language can worthily praise you, O Virgin, * for it pleased Christ, the Giver of life, to be born without seed in your womb, O most pure virgin.

Tone 7 You said to your apostles, O Lord: * Remain in Jerusalem until the day when you shall be clothed with power from on high; * and I will send you another Paraclete, * the Spirit of the Father and of Me, * in whom you will be strengthened.

KONTAKION

Tone 6 When You fulfilled the plan of salvation for us * and united all things on earth to those in heaven, O Christ our God, * You ascended in glory, never leaving us, but remaining ever-present. * For You proclaimed to those who love You: * I am with you and no one else has power over you.

IKOS

Leaving earthly cares to the earth and that which is waste and refuse to the dust, come, let us arise from sleep and with our eyes and hearts let us go towards higher things. Let us also lift up our thoughts and our attention from the earth to the gates of heaven, as if we were on the Mount of Olives, where we fix our eyes on the Redeemer as He is carried away to heaven. For it is there that the Lord departs for heaven; it is there also that He distributes his great gifts to the apostles, giving them strength and comforting them as a Father, guiding them as sons and saying to them: I am not separating myself from you; I shall always be with you, and no one shall ever have power over you.

SESSIONAL HYMN

Tone 4 You have truly become the flaming torches of the truth of Christ * throughout all the earth, O blessed Fathers; * you crushed the heresies of the babbling philosophers, * and you extinguished the fiery winds of the ungodly blasphemies. * O holy Bishops of Christ, intercede for our salvation.

Glory be: Today the brilliant city of Nicea * has gathered the bishops from all over the world; * the three hundred and eighteen of them rejected the blasphemies of Arius, * who lessened One of the Holy Trinity, * the Son and Word of God; * and they affirmed the true faith.

Now and ever: O Christ, the Lover of Mankind, * You are gloriously taken up to heaven * and are seated at the right hand of the Father, * without ever having left the fatherly bosom. * You promised to send your Holy Spirit to your wise disciples; * send also your brightness upon us; * illumine our hearts and our thoughts * so that we may praise You unceasingly, O Lord.

ODE 4

Tone 6 Christ is my strength, my Lord, and my God! * This is the hymn that the holy Church sings out, * and, with a purified heart, she praises the Lord.

Refrain: **Glory to your holy Resurrection, O Lord!**

The wood of true life blossomed, O Christ, * when your

Cross was planted in the earth; * moistened by the blood and water from your most pure side, * it made life sprout up for us.

The serpent who deceived me with his tricks * shall never again propose that I become as God; * for Christ my divine Creator * has prepared the path of life for me.

Refrain: **Most holy Mother of God, save us!**

The mysteries of your divine birthgiving * are truly ineffable and beyond description * both to those in heaven and to those on earth, * O Mother of God and ever-Virgin Mary.

Tone 6 Corrupting the true faith by his arrogant spirit, * Arius was banished as a disgraceful member of the Church * by the voice of the Fathers gathered in council.

Refrain: **O holy Fathers, pray to God for us!**

The assembly of the Fathers led the battle for You, O Lord; * they routed the enemy * and proclaimed You as consubstantial with the Father and the Spirit.

By your divine humanity, * You have become the mediator between God and people; * for this reason the holy Fathers have proclaimed You, O Christ, * as the only Son who is glorified in two natures.

Glory be...now and ever: Beneath the forbidden tree, my gluttony has killed me; * but the Tree of Life who has come forth from you, O Virgin, * has raised me up and made me an inheritor of the delights of Paradise.

Tone 7 Meditating upon your final coming, O Christ, * the prophet cried out: * I have seen your power, O Lord, * for You have come to save those who are consecrated to You.

ODE 5

Tone 6 O God all-good, I beseech You: * With your divine brightness illumine the souls who love You and keep watch before You, * that they may know You, O Word of God; * for You are the true God who brings us out of the darkness of sin.

Refrain: **Glory to your holy Resurrection, O Lord!**

The Cherubim have withdrawn before me, * and henceforth, O Lord, the flaming sword shall no longer guard Eden; * for they see You, O Word of God and true God yourself, * as You open the way to Paradise for the good thief.

I no longer fear returning to the earth, O Christ our Lord; *

for even though I was abandoned, * in your great mercy, You brought me forth from the earth by your Resurrection * and raised me to the heights of immortal life.

***Refrain:* Most holy Mother of God, save us!**

In your goodness, O Queen of the universe, * save those who with all their heart recognize you as the Mother of God; * for in you we truly possess an invincible protection.

Tone 6 Truly beautiful are the feet of those who proclaim peace, * a peace that surpasses every spirit, * both of angels and of people; * this is the peace that unites the whole world and reconciles it completely.

***Refrain:* O holy Fathers, pray to God for us!**

The assembly of the Fathers has proclaimed You, O Christ, * as the Wisdom and Power of the Father * and as the Word personified. * Because of their sacred priesthood, * these holy teachers have divinely sealed this teaching.

You have allowed the Church to drink deeply * from the most pure stream of the teaching of Christ; * and now you rejoice near the restful waters with an unending joy.

Glory be...now and ever: We recognize you as the bright lampstand, O Virgin, * who makes Christ, the Sun of Justice, shine on all. * O only Mother of God, we invoke your constant protection.

Tone 7 O Lord, the Spirit of your salvation, * which formerly was received by the prophets in fear, * now creates a pure heart in your apostles * and renews in our hearts an upright spirit; * for your commandments, O Lord, bring us light and peace.

ODE 6

Tone 6 When I see the ocean of this life * swelling with the storms of temptations, * I hasten to your harbor of peace, * and I cry out to You, O God of goodness: * Rescue my life from the pit.

***Refrain:* Glory to your holy Resurrection, O Lord!**

When You were nailed to the Cross, O Lord, * You wiped out the ancient curse; * and when the sword pierced your side, * You tore up the debt of Adam and freed the whole world.

Deceived by the serpent, Adam was hurled into the pit of Hades; * but You, O compassionate God, have descended there * and have carried him upon your shoulders to the Resurrection.

Refrain: **Most holy Mother of God, save us!**

O immaculate Queen who gave birth to the Lord and Leader of all mortals, * appease the incessant surgings of my passions * and give peace to my heart.

Tone 6 The sower of dissension could not remain hidden from the ineffable justice of God, * he whose name means the quarrelsome fury; * for having imitated Judas, * he then died in the same distress.

Refrain: **O holy Fathers, pray to God for us!**

The august assembly of the holy Fathers, O Lord, * has proclaimed You as the only Son and reflection of the Father, * who makes his essence shine forth, * and as the Son who was begotten before all ages.

The well which produced the muddy and undrinkable water of godless heresies * was completely shattered; * it was carefully dug up by the prayers of the Fathers.

Glory be...now and ever: Moses, the greatest of the prophets, * showed you in advance to be the ark and golden vessel, * the holy table and the candlestand. * He prefigured in symbols, O Virgin and Mother, * the Most High taking flesh in your womb.

Tone 7 Sailing across the ocean of life and tossed about by the cares of the world, * engulfed in the midst of my sins and thrown to the monster who devours souls, * as Jonah, I cry out to You, O Christ: * Deliver me from this deadly abyss.

KONTAKION

Tone 8 The preaching of the apostles * and the decisions of the Fathers * have established the true faith of the Church * which she wears as the garment of truth * fashioned from the theology on high. * She justly governs and glorifies the great mystery of worship.

IKOS

Let us listen to the Church of God which cries out to us in a sublime proclamation: Whoever thirsts, let them come to me and drink! It is in the cup of Wisdom that I mix my wine; I have mixed it with the word of truth; and the water I pour out is not the water of strife, but that of harmony in the faith which the new Israel drinks, to whom God appeared, saying:

Look and see! I am the same, I have not changed. I am the God both before and after all time. There is no other but I. Those who drink this water will be satisfied and shall praise the great mystery of faith.

ODE 7

Tone 6 In the furnace, the angel poured out dew over the holy youths; * but at the order of God, the fire burned the Chaldeans, * and the tyrant was forced to sing: * Blessed are You, O Lord, God of our fathers!

Refrain: **Glory to your holy Resurrection, O Lord!**

Lamenting over your passion, the sun was covered with darkness at midday, * and the light was darkened over all the earth as it cried out: * Blessed are You, O Lord, God of our fathers!

At the time of your descent, O Christ, * the kingdom of the underworld was filled with light; * and our first father was filled with joy * as he danced and sang out in jubilation: * Blessed are You, O Lord, God of our fathers!

Refrain: **Most holy Mother of God, save us!**

O Virgin Mother, because of you a light is risen and illumines the whole world; * for you have given birth to the divine Creator of the universe. * Beseech Him, O all-pure Lady, to send his great mercy on us, the faithful.

Tone 6 You have prevailed over Arius * who was given over to war by his very name; * in his fury he lessened the sublimity of God, * for he refused to praise the Son and say: * Blessed are You, O Lord, God of our fathers!

Refrain: **O holy Fathers, pray to God for us!**

Imitating the son of thunder, O holy Fathers, * you have confessed that the Word is consubstantial with the Father * and shares the same throne with Him. * With your flaming mouths, you have invited us to sing: * Blessed are You, O Lord, God of our fathers!

As on the wings of the wind, O blessed Fathers, * you have come to the aid of the Word of God; * for the Holy Spirit has gathered you from the ends of the earth to sing: * Blessed are You, O Lord, God of our fathers!

Glory be...now and ever: The fire that did not consume the three youths in the furnace * was the image of your birthgiving; * for the divine fire which dwelt in your womb did not burn you, * but it enlightened all who sing: * Blessed are You, O Lord, God of our fathers!

Tone 7 In the fiery furnace, * the youths transformed the blazing flames which surrounded them into dew, * for they praised the Lord by singing: * Blessed are You, O God of our fathers!

ODE 8

Tone 6 You poured out dew upon your holy ones in the flames, * and with water You burned the sacrifice of the just ones; * for You can do all things according to your will. * O Christ, we exalt You forever.

Refrain: **Glory to your holy Resurrection, O Lord!**

The people who formerly killed the prophets * have now let themselves be overcome with envy, * and they place on the Cross the Word of God, * whom we exalt forever.

Without leaving the vault of heaven, * You descended to Hades, O Christ, * and You raised up with You * humanity which had been given over to the corruption of the grave; * this same humanity exalts You forever.

Refrain: **Most holy Mother of God, save us!**

Light of Light, the Word whom you conceived, and his glory, all please you, * for you ineffably gave birth to Him; * the Holy Spirit has made his dwelling in you. * O Virgin, we praise you forever.

Tone 6 Enflamed by the rays of your divinity, * your holy shepherds recognized You as the Creator and Lord of the universe * whom they exalt forever.

Refrain: **O holy Fathers, pray to God for us!**

The illustrious choir of the shepherds, * in their council, defined the uncreated Trinity; * and they call the faithful to sing: * It is He whom we exalt forever.

Let us bless the Lord, Father, Son, and Holy Spirit.

The honored bishops and shepherds illumine the Church of Christ; * they make it shine respendently in all places * and exalt it forever.

Now and ever: In symbols the prophets have mystically foreseen you, * the Birthgiver of the Word of God; * He took flesh and came forth from your womb in two natures; * He is the One whom we exalt forever.

Let us praise, bless, and worship the Lord, singing and exalting Him above all forever.

Tone 7 On Sinai, the bush that burned without being

consumed * revealed God to Moses * as He spoke to the one of unsure speech; * and in the furnace, the three youths, invincible in their zeal for God, * began to sing a hymn of praise: * Sing to the Lord, all you his works, and exalt Him forever.

MAGNIFICAT

ODE 9

Tone 6 For mortals it is impossible to see God * upon whom even the angels dare not gaze; * but the Word-made-flesh has been manifested to us through you, O all-pure One. * When we extol Him with the heavenly armies, * we also proclaim you blessed.

Refrain: **Glory to your holy Resurrection, O Lord!**

In You, O Word, dwelt no passions * even though in your flesh You took on our human condition; * but You delivered humanity from its passions, * and made the sufferings of each more noble by your own passion. * O our Savior, You alone are almighty and beyond all suffering.

You descended into the grave, * and in death You preserved your body from the corruption of the tomb; * your soul was not left in Hades, O Giver of life; * You awoke as from sleep, O Lord, and You raised us with You.

Refrain: **Most holy Mother of God, save us!**

Let us purify our lips, O mortals, * that we may glorify God the Father and his coeternal Son * and worship the most Holy Spirit, * the ineffable power filled with glory beyond all others. * One is the indivisible Trinity * who has power over all things.

Tone 6 The Word who is from before all ages, * and who shares the same throne and eternity with the Father in heaven, * fills you with the power of the Spirit * and unites you in council. * He makes you his companions in battle, * and now with the heavenly armies, O holy Fathers, you glorify Him forever.

Refrain: **O holy Fathers, pray to God for us!**

As wise physicians of body and soul, * you have stopped Arius and his terrible heresy; * you established the Symbol of Faith for the people, * and we, who now profess this faith, * glorify your sacred memory without ceasing.

O Light all-pure, You deliver my soul from the darkness of

passions * by the prayers of these holy bishops, O Christ; * in council they proclaimed You to be eternal and uncreated, * the Creator of the universe, * and the God who shares the same eternity with the Father.

Glory be...now and ever: O Mother of God, and Queen, * by your ineffable birthgiving which no one can comprehend, * resurrection is given to the dead; * for the Lord of life comes from you. * He is clothed in our flesh; * and dispelling the darkness of death, * He has filled the whole world with light.

Tone 7 You have conceived in all purity, * and the Word and Creator of the universe takes flesh in you, * O spouseless Mother and virginal Birthgiver of God, * the dwelling place of the One whom none could contain, * and the abode of the infinite One, your Creator. * For this, we extol you.

HYMN OF LIGHT

Tone 2 The two sons of Zebedee, with Peter, Nathaniel, and Thomas, * and two others were fishing in the Lake of Tiberias. * By the command of Christ, they cast the net on the right side * and drew out many fish. * Peter, recognizing Christ, came swimming towards Him. * This was the third appearance of the Lord after his Resurrection. * Then He shared with them bread and fish from the fire.

Tone 2 **Glory be:** Celebrating today the memory of our holy Fathers, * we beseech You through their prayers, O Master of tenderness: * Safeguard your people from all error and heresy; * and grant that we may praise your glory, O Lord: * the Father, the Word, and the Holy Spirit.

Tone 2 **Now and ever:** O Christ, You were raised up to heaven in the sight of your disciples; * You again went up to share your Father's throne. * The angels who came to meet You at the heavenly gate cried out: * Open your gates and lift up your lintels * so that the King of glory may come in, * for our King comes again to the Source of light.

AT THE PRAISES

Tone 6 Your Cross, O Lord, is Life and Resurrection to your people, * and we place our hope in it. * Therefore, we sing to You: * O our risen God, have mercy on us.

Your burial, O Master, opened Paradise to the human

race. * Delivered from Death, we now sing to You: * O our risen God, have mercy on us.

With the Father and the Spirit, * let us glorify Christ risen from the dead. * Let us cry to Him with a full voice: * You are our Life and Resurrection; have mercy on us!

You arose from the tomb on the third day, * as it was written, O Christ, * and raised our ancestors with You. * Therefore, the human race glorifies You * and praises your holy Resurrection.

Having brought together all spiritual knowledge, * and having carefully pondered all things in the Holy Spirit, * the noble Fathers composed the Symbol of Faith * in letters divinely inscribed. * They clearly proclaim the Word to be coeternal and consubstantial with the Father, * unerringly following the apostolic faith. *(2 times)*

Blessed are You, and praiseworthy, O Lord, the God of our fathers, and glorious forever is your name.

The blessed preachers of Christ received the torch of the Holy Spirit; * they spoke with divine inspiration, * using few words, but rich in meaning. * They proclaimed with boldness the doctrines of the Gospel * and the traditions of righteousness. * Clearly they have been illumined with truth from on high; * they have made firm the foundation of the faith as a strong mountain.

Summon before Me my people who made covenant with Me by sacrifice.

The chosen servants of God, * enlightened with the understanding of divine mysteries, * cast out the devouring wolves from the sheepfold of the Church. * They were faithful shepherds, * blazing with the wrath of righteous judgment, * and have slain the destroyers with the mighty sword of the Spirit.

Tone 8 **Glory be:** The choir of the holy Fathers hastened from the ends of the earth * to proclaim the unique essence and nature * of the Father, the Son, and the Holy Spirit, * and to transmit clearly the divine teaching to the Church. * Praising them in faith, we call them blessed and we sing: * Divine guard of the Lord and brilliant stars of the spiritual firmament, * unconquerable watchmen of the mystical Zion, * sweet flowers of Paradise and golden mouths of the Word, * you are the glory of Nicea and the splendor of the universe; * intercede with the Lord for our souls.

Tone 2 **Now and ever:** You are truly most blessed, O virgin Mother of God. * Through the One who was incarnate of you, * Hades was chained, Adam revived, the curse wiped out, * Eve set free, Death put to death, * and we ourselves were brought back to life. * That is why we cry out in praise: * Blessed are You, O Christ our God, * who finds in this your good pleasure; glory to You!

AFTER THE DISMISSAL

Gospel Stanza Number 10

Tone 6 **Glory be...now and ever:** After your descent into Hades, O Christ, * and your Resurrection from the dead, * the disciples grieved over your departure. * They returned to their occupations * and attended to their nets and their boats, * but their fishing was in vain. * You appeared to them since You are Lord of all; * You commanded them to cast the nets on the right side. * Immediately your word became deed. * They caught a great number of fish, * and they found an unexpected meal prepared for them on the shore, * which they immediately ate. * Now, make us worthy to enjoy this meal with them in a spiritual manner, * O Lord and Lover of Mankind.

Sunday Evening Vespers

AT PSALM 140

Tone 6 Before the morning star You were begotten of the Father; * before the ages You were conceived without a mother, * even though Arius believed You to be created, and not God.* He shamelessly confused the Creator with his creatures, * thus deserving eternal punishment. * Yet the Council of Nicea proclaimed You as the Son of God * who is enthroned with the Father and the Spirit.

Who has severed your garment, O Savior? * It was Arius who divided the Trinity * who is equal in glory and eternal majesty. * For he denied that You are one of the most Holy Trinity. * He taught the transgressing Nestorius * to say that the Virgin is not the Mother of God; * but the Council of Nicea proclaimed You as the Son of God * who is enthroned with the Father and the Spirit.

Declaring that the light could not be seen, * Arius fell into the pit of the impious ones; * his body was torn apart by the justice of God, * and he gave up his soul in a violent manner. * He was another Judas by his thoughts and deeds. * But the Council of Nicea proclaimed You as the Son of God * who is enthroned with the Father and the Spirit.

Three Stichera from the Saint of the day

Tone 6 **Glory be:** Let us honor today those mystical trumpets of the Spirit, * namely, the God-mantled Fathers, * who speaking of divine things, * sang in the midst of the Church a hymn in unison, * teaching that the Trinity is one, * not differing in substance or Godhead, * refuting Arius and defending the true faith. * They always intercede with the Lord * to have mercy on our souls.

Tone 6 **Now and ever:** O Christ, splendor and glory of the Father, * when we behold your Ascension on the holy mountain, * we sing a hymn of praise to the beauty of your countenance. * We bow down to your Passion, * we venerate your holy Resurrection, * and we glorify your noble Ascension. * O Lord, have mercy on us!

APOSTICHA

Tone 6 Having brought together all spiritual knowledge, * and having carefully pondered all things in the Holy Spirit, * the noble Fathers composed the Symbol of Faith * in letters divinely inscribed. * They clearly proclaim the Word to be coeternal and consubstantial with the Father, * unerringly following the apostolic faith.

Blessed are You, and praiseworthy, O Lord, the God of our fathers, and glorious forever is your name.

The blessed preachers of Christ received the torch of the Holy Spirit; * they spoke with divine inspiration, * using few words, but rich in meaning. * They proclaimed with boldness the doctrines of the Gospel * and the traditions of righteousness. * Clearly they have been illumined with truth from on high; * they have made firm the foundation of the faith as a strong mountain.

Summon before Me my people who made covenant with Me by sacrifice.

The chosen servants of God, * enlightened with the understanding of divine mysteries, * cast out the devouring wolves from the sheepfold of the Church. * They were faithful shepherds, * blazing with the wrath of righteous judgment, * and have slain the destroyers with the mighty sword of the Spirit.

Tone 3 **Glory be:** You were the guardians of the apostolic teachings, O holy Fathers; * and as teachers of the true faith, * you professed the holy and consubstantial Trinity. * Together in council, you rejected the blasphemy of Arius; * and with him you also refuted Macedonius * who denied the divinity of the Holy Spirit. * You condemned Nestorius, Eutyches, and Dioscorus, * together with Sabellius and Severus. * Through your prayers, preserve us from all false doctrine, * and guard our lives blamelessly in the true faith.

Tone 6 **Now and ever:** God goes up with shouts of joy, * the Lord goes up amid trumpet blast, * in order to raise up the fallen image of Adam, * and to send down upon us the Holy Spirit, * the Comforter who will sanctify our souls.

TROPARIA

Tone 8 O Christ our God, You are most glorified, * for You established our fathers as lights upon the earth. * Through them You led us to the true faith. * O most merciful Lord, glory to You.

Glory be: *Of the Saint*

Tone 4 **Now and ever:** You ascended in glory, O Christ our God; * You delighted the disciples with the promise of the Holy Spirit. * Through this blessing they were assured * that You are the Son of God, * the Redeemer of the world.

Monday Matins

SESSIONAL HYMN I

Tone 1 You ascended in glory, and the angels were astonished at this wonder; * the disciples were amazed at your marvelous Ascension, * and the gates opened before You, O Lord. * The Powers of heaven were also overjoyed and they cried out: * Glory to your condescension, O Savior! * Glory to your kingdom! * Glory to your Ascension, O only Lover of Mankind!

Glory be...now and ever: *(Repeat the above)*

SESSIONAL HYMN II

Tone 1 You have plundered Hades, O Giver of life! * The world is enlightened by your Resurrection. * You have ascended in glory, O Savior, * holding the ransomed earth in your hands. * With the angels, we worship You and cry out: *

Glory to your Ascension, O Christ! * Glory to your kingdom! * Glory to your compassion, O only Lover of Mankind!

Glory be...now and ever: *(Repeat the above)*

CANON

(From Ascension, page 283 or 289)

HYMN OF LIGHT

Tone 2 O Christ, You were raised up to heaven in the sight of your disciples; * You again went up to share your Father's throne. * The angels who came to meet You at the heavenly gate cried out: * Open your gates and lift up your lintels * so that the King of glory may come in, * for our King comes again to the Source of light. *(3 times)*

APOSTICHA

Tone 2 Let us ascend, O faithful, * to the mount of virtues * with the disciples of the Word, * that we may be made worthy * to behold the glory of Christ.

All peoples, clap your hands; cry to God with shouts of joy!

You that despise the body, * your foolish talk is now silenced. * Clearly has Christ revealed to us * that all those united in his flesh * will ascend with Him on high.

God goes up with shouts of joy; the Lord goes up with trumpet blast.

Cry out, O David! * Rejoice with the lyre! * Christ ascends in glory. * He fulfills the words of the prophets * by his mighty deeds.

Tone 2 **Glory be...now and ever:** O Christ, You ascended in glory * on the Mount of Olives in the presence of your disciples; * You fill all things with your divinity; * You were enthroned at the right hand of the Father * and sent down upon your disciples the Holy Spirit * who enlightens, strengthens, and saves our souls.

Monday Evening Vespers

AT PSALM 140

Tone 4 You suffered in your humanity, O Christ our God; * You rose on the third day and despoiled Death, * raising with yourself all those held fast in corruption. * You ascended to the Father, * promising to send the Paraclete to your apostles, * O almighty Jesus, the Savior of our souls.

Why do you stand gazing into heaven, * cried the angels who appeared as men * to those whom You had instructed in your mysteries. * He will come again in the same way, as He said. * He will come to judge the world. * Go, therefore, and do all that He commanded you.

After rising from the tomb, O Lord almighty, * You took your friends to the Mount of Olives. * Leading them to Bethany, You blessed them. * There you ascended, taken up by the angels, * O Jesus almighty, the Savior of our souls.

Three Stichera from the Saint of the day

Tone 4 **Glory be...now and ever:** When You came to the Mount of Olives, O Christ, * completing the favorable plan of your Father, * the angels in heaven were moved with wonder, * and the demons trembled beneath the earth. * The apostles were filled with both fear and joy * when You were speaking with them. * A cloud was prepared before You as an awaiting throne; * heaven opened its gates, shining with beauty; * and the earth uncovered its deep abyss * to show the fall of Adam and his rising up to You again. * As an unseen power raised You from the earth, * You gave your blessing in a loud voice; * the cloud carried You away, and heaven opened to receive You. * Such is the great work that is beyond words, O Lord, * that You accomplished for the salvation of our souls.

APOSTICHA

Tone 2 Fulfilling the good will of the Father, O good One, * uniting earth with heaven, * You ascended in glory * to your eternal abode.

All peoples, clap your hands; cry to God with shouts of joy!

You went up to your Father, O bountiful One, * whom You had never left, * raising up, O Master, * the nature which had fallen below.

God goes up with shouts of joy; the Lord goes up with trumpet blast.

A cloud of light lifted You to the heavens. * With fear and trembling, * all the Powers of heaven * hastened to serve your divine majesty.

Tone 4 **Glory be...now and ever:** You have renewed in yourself, O Lord, * the human nature which had fallen, in Adam, * into the very depths of the earth. * On this day You are raised far above * the Principalities and Powers of heaven. * Having so loved human nature, * You granted that it may be enthroned with You; * in Your compassion You united it with yourself; * in union with it You have suffered; * and by your Passion You glorified it, O God, beyond all suffering. * Now the bodiless Powers are saying: * Who is this man clothed in majesty? * He is not only a man, but is indeed the God-Man, * for He possesses the appearance of both. * And the angels arrayed in splendid garments, * encircle the apostles, saying: * As Jesus the God-Man is separated from you, * in his divine humanity He shall come again * to judge both the living and the dead; * and He grants to all the faithful * forgiveness of sins and great mercy.

TROPARIA

Of the Saint

Tone 4 **Glory be...now and ever:** You ascended in glory, O Christ our God; * You delighted the disciples with the promise of the Holy Spirit. * Through this blessing they were assured * that You are the Son of God, * the Redeemer of the world.

Tuesday Matins

SESSIONAL HYMN I

Tone 2 You descended from heaven to earth, O Christ; * from the earth You ascended to your Father on high. * Beholding your Ascension, we celebrate with the apostles * and praise your victory, O Savior.

Glory be...now and ever: *(Repeat the above)*

SESSIONAL HYMN II

Tone 3 The God who exists before all eternity * and who has mystically divinized the human nature which He assumed, * today goes up to heaven. * The angels precede Him and show to the disciples * the Lord who ascends into the clouds amid great glory, * and they then fall to the ground and say: * Glory to God who ascends into heaven!

Glory be...now and ever: *(Repeat the above)*

CANON

(From Ascension, page 283 or 289)

HYMN OF LIGHT

Tone 2 O Christ, You were raised up to heaven in the sight of your disciples; * You again went up to share your Father's throne. * The angels who came to meet you at the heavenly gate cried out: * Open your gates and lift up your lintels * so that the King of glory may come in, * for our King comes again to the Source of light. *(3 times)*

APOSTICHA

Tone 2 I will not leave you orphans; * I will remain with you always, * said the Lord to his friends. * I will send upon you the Holy Spirit.

All peoples, clap your hands; cry to God with shouts of joy!

He will come again, O men of Galilee, * in the same way as He departed. * So proclaimed the angels * to the enlightened apostles.

God goes up with shouts of joy; the Lord goes up with trumpet blast.

Your chosen disciples * descended from the Mount of Olives, * joyfully singing your praises * and glorifying your Ascension, * O Word of God and Lover of Mankind!

Tone 4 **Glory be...now and ever:** When You were raised up in glory, O Christ our God, * in the sight of your disciples, * the cloud carried your body away. * The gates in heaven were opened; * the choir of angels exalted and danced with joy; * the Powers on high cried out, saying: * Lift up your lintels, O gates, * that the King of glory may enter. * As for the disciples, they were seized with fear and said: * Do not leave us, O Good Shepherd, * but send down upon us your most Holy Spirit.

Tuesday Evening Vespers

AT PSALM 140

Tone 4 Your disciples saw You ascend above the heavens * to take your seat at the Father's right hand. * You were never separated from Him, O boundless Son. * Keeping your promise, You sent the Paraclete, * who renews the heavens and the earth, * filling your holy apostles with divine wisdom.

Wondrous is your Incarnation, O good Jesus. * You willingly endured the Cross and death, O immortal One. * You rose from the dead on the third day; * after forty days You ascended on high, * returning to heaven from which You had come down to us; * You have given peace to all those dwelling on earth, * leading us back to the Father.

Seeing You received into the cloud, O Lord, * your chosen apostles were filled with sorrow. * They cried out with bitter tears: * Do not leave us orphans, O Master! * In your compassion You loved us. * Send down to us from on high the all-merciful One, * the Holy Spirit, who will illumine our souls.

Three Stichera from the Saint of the day

Tone 5 **Glory be...now and ever:** Come, O choirs of the faithful! * Let your hearts be enlightened as befits the disciples of Christ. * Let us sing in unison a hymn on the Mount of Olives. * With the apostles, let us cry out in the psalm of David: * God goes up with shouts of joy! * The Lord goes up with trumpet blast! * He has rescued the human race from destruction and the wrath to come. * He has illumined our souls.

APOSTICHA

Tone 2 Behold, mortal nature now ascends to heaven, * united to God almighty * in the flesh of the Word. * Truly this is an amazing wonder!

All peoples, clap your hands; cry to God with shouts of joy!

This day, bright and radiant, * now dawns in splendor. * It is the day of our Lord and Master, * for by his Ascension into heaven * all things are filled with light.

God goes up with shouts of joy; the Lord goes up with trumpet blast.

O Christ our Savior, * You sent your Spirit from on high to your disciples. * Now send down your grace * upon all your people.

Tone 5 **Glory be...now and ever:** O Lord, You did not cast aside your body at your Ascension. * The hosts of angels attending You * cried out in joy and amazement to the hosts on high: * Lift up your heads, O you gates! * Let the King of glory enter! * You have gone up to heaven, robed in your flesh; * You are borne by the chariot of the Cherubim. * O Lord, glory to You!

TROPARIA

Of the Saint

Tone 4 **Glory be...now and ever:** You ascended in glory, O Christ our God; * You delighted the disciples with the promise of the Holy Spirit. * Through this blessing they were assured * that You are the Son of God, * the Redeemer of the world.

Wednesday Matins

SESSIONAL HYMN I

Tone 4 Seeing your Ascension, O Lover of Mankind, * your disciples cried out: * You are returning home to your Father; * do not leave your servants orphans, O Creator of all.

Glory be...now and ever: *(Repeat the above)*

SESSIONAL HYMN II

Tone 4 When all the heavenly Powers in battle attire * beheld the Lord of glory ascending in the flesh, * they commanded the gates of heaven to open.

Glory be...now and ever: *(Repeat the above)*

CANON

(From Ascension, page 283 or 289)

HYMN OF LIGHT

Tone 2 O Christ, You were raised up to heaven in the sight of your disciples; * You again went up to share your Father's throne. * The angels who came to meet You at the heavenly gate cried out: * Open your gates and lift up your lintels * so that the King of glory may come in, * for our King comes again to the Source of light. *(3 times)*

APOSTICHA

Tone 6 In the greatness of your compassion, O Christ, * You took flesh from the Virgin. * You willingly endured the Cross, O merciful One. * You rose from the tomb on the third day, * granting us life and resurrection.

All peoples, clap your hands; cry to God with shouts of joy!

Your disciples beheld You * ascending from earth to heaven, O Christ our God. * You promised to send them the Giver of life, * the Holy Spirit who proceeds from the Father.

God goes up with shouts of joy; the Lord goes up with trumpet blast.

O Jesus, King of all, * the hosts of angels shuddered in fear, * amazed by your wondrous Ascension. * They cried to the Powers above: * Let the heavenly gates be opened.

Tone 6 **Glory be...now and ever:** O loving Jesus, while You lived on earth, * You were God inseparable from the Father, * and yet You truly shared our humanity. * Ascending in glory today from the Mount of Olives, * through your great love, You lifted up our fallen nature * and enthroned it with the Father on high. * Therefore, the bodiless Powers were amazed and filled with awe * at seeing your great love for all. * Together with them, we who live on earth * glorify your condescenion to us * and your ascension away from us. * Now we implore You, saying: * Through your Ascension You have filled your apostles and your Mother * with a joy that surpasses every other joy; * and through their intercession * make us worthy of the joy of your elect, * for You are rich in mercy.

Wednesday Evening Vespers

AT PSALM 140

Tone 4 Having finished your work of salvation for all, O Christ, * You went up to the Mount of Olives. * From there You ascended into heaven and were borne in glory * in the presence of your disciples. * When your angels beheld this mystery, * the hosts attending You below cried out to those on high: * Open the gates, for He enters again! * He went out from here, the God and Ruler of all, * and was pleased to win the salvation of the world * in a most wondrous manner.

When the choir of apostles saw You lifted up, * they cried out: Where are You going as You leave us, O Master? * You hold the ends of the earth in your hands; * why do You abandon us? * Joyfully we have followed You, our only God. * Will You forsake us now forever? * You are our only hope; * do not leave us to suffer here as orphans! * Send us the Comforter, who proceeds from the compassionate Father, * O Savior of our souls.

Offering the most perfect blessing to your friends, * You instructed them in all your mysteries, O Master. * Behold, my beloved ones, I depart to my Father, * but I will send you another Comforter. * I will never forsake the flock I gathered; * I will never forget those whom I love. * You will be clothed with power from on high; * you will go forth, proclaiming the saving Gospel to all nations.

Three Stichera from the Saint of the day

Tone 6 **Glory be...now and ever:** God goes up with shouts of joy, * the Lord goes up with trumpet blast, * in order to raise up the fallen image of Adam * and to send down upon us the Holy Spirit, * the Comforter who will sanctify our souls.

APOSTICHA

Tone 6 You have come to the earth and raised me who had fallen; * receiving me in love, You united me to yourself. * Assuming my humanity, You exalted me in eternal glory with You. * You have raised all and crushed the One who cast me down of old. * I bless You, O Master; * I praise the unsearchable depths of your love for the human race.

All peoples, clap your hands; cry to God with shouts of joy!

Leap for joy, O Adam! Rejoice with him, O Eve! * Cast down in Paradise of old, * you were clothed in garments of corruption. * Today you receive the hope of immortality, * for your Creator has taken you back to himself. * He wondrously leads you to eternal life. * Today He lifts you on high, * restoring you to communion with the Father.

God goes up with shouts of joy; the Lord goes up with trumpet blast.

You took on my flesh and filled it with power from on high, * trampling under foot the dominion of the apostate enemy. * Now You have brought me back to the Father * from whom You were never parted. * Let us forsake worldly foolishness, O faithful; * let us glorify Him in purity of heart.

Tone 6 **Glory be...now and ever:** Today the Powers on high see our nature in heaven, * and they marvel at this wondrous Ascension, * and they say to one another: * Who is this who has just arrived in heaven? * But when they recognize their own Lord, * they order the gates of heaven to be opened. * With them let us praise unceasingly * the One who shall come again from heaven in our flesh * as the judge of the universe and the almighty God.

TROPARIA

Of the Saint

Tone 4 **Glory be...now and ever:** You ascended in glory, O Christ our God; * You delighted the disciples with the promise of the Holy Spirit. * Through this blessing they were assured * that You are the Son of God, * the Redeemer of the world.

Thursday Matins

SESSIONAL HYMN I

Tone 5 You descended from heaven to the earth, O Christ, * and by your Ascension You wondrously raised up the race of Adam * which had been lying in the depths of the prisons of Hades. * And having taken our nature back to heaven, * You seated it with You on the Father's throne, * because of your mercy and your love for all.

Glory be...now and ever: *(Repeat the above)*

SESSIONAL HYMN II

Tone 8 You went up to the Mount of Olives, O merciful Jesus; * You ascended from the earth, taken up by a cloud of light. * The disciples beheld the fearful wonder, * while the angels on high cried out in fear. * All the hosts of heaven lifed the gates, * praising You, O King, the Creator and God of all.

Glory be...now and ever: *(Repeat the above)*

CANON

(From Ascension, page 283 or 289)

HYMN OF LIGHT

Tone 2 O Christ, You were raised up to heaven in the sight of your disciples; * You again went up to share your Father's throne. * The angels who came to meet You at the heavenly gate cried out: * Open your gates and lift up your lintels * so that the King of glory may come in; * for our King comes again to the Source of light. *(3 times)*

APOSTICHA

Tone 6 You have wondrously drawn me to yourself, O Christ. * My flesh is joined to your divinity, inseparably united to You. * Two natures are joined in You without mixture, division, or change. * Glory to your awesome condescension! * Glory to your Passion, your Resurrection, and your Ascension! * You have exalted our nature * which before was cast down to the depths.

All peoples, clap your hands; cry to God with shouts of joy!

Your angels cried to the enlightened disciples, O Savior: * Why are you gazing upward, and why are your eyes filled with wonder? * He ascends in glory now as both God and man; * He shall return clothed in this same flesh, * carrying the scales of justice, * to judge all living beings in righteousness.

God goes up with shouts of joy; the Lord goes up with trumpet blast.

The choir of your apostles, filled with joy and tears, * watched your glorious Ascension, O my Savior. * They stood between heaven and earth on the mountain, * crying out to You, O Lover of Mankind: * Do not leave your servants orphans. * Send the divine Spirit to enlighten our souls.

Tone 8 **Glory be...now and ever:** You ascended from earth to heaven in glory, * and You filled all things with your divinity. * You took your place at the right hand of the Father, * O eternal One, God the Word. * When the heavenly Powers beheld You, * they cried in fear to the apostles: * Why do you gaze upward, looking into heaven? * You see Him departing, * but He will return with glory to judge the earth. * He will render to everyone according to his works. * Let us cry out to Him: * O incomprehensible Lord, glory to You!

Thursday Evening Vespers

Final day of the Feast of Ascension

(The text for Vespers is taken from the feastday)

Friday Matins

Final day of the Feast of Ascension

(The text for Matins is taken from the feastday)

Saturday of the Departed

Vespers

AT PSALM 140

Tone 6 Your martyrs did not reject You, * nor did they renounce your commandments. * Through their prayers, have mercy on us!

Your martyrs, O Christ, * have endured many sufferings for your sake * and have received their heavenly crown. * Now they intercede for our souls.

The suffering martyrs, citizens of heaven, * when taking part in the contest upon earth, * endured manifold torments. * By their intercessions and prayers, preserve us, O Lord!

Tone 8 O faithful, remembering today by name all the dead * who have lived in piety and faith, * let us sing praises to the Lord and Savior, * asking Him fervently to give them in the hour of judgment * a good defense before our God who judges the earth. * May they receive a place at his right hand in joy; * may they dwell in glory with the righteous and the saints * and be counted worthy of his heavenly kingdom.

By your own blood, O Savior, You have ransomed all people; * and by your death You have delivered us from bitter death, * granting us eternal life by your Resurrection. * Give rest then, O Lord, to all those who have fallen asleep in godliness, * whether in the wilderness or city, * on the sea or land, in every place, * both princes, priests and bishops, * monks and married people, of every age and line, * and count them worthy of your heavenly kingdom.

By your Resurrection from the dead, O Christ, * Death rules no longer over those that die in faith. * Therefore, we pray fervently: * Give rest in your courts and in the bosom of Abraham * to those servants from Adam to this present day * who have worshiped You in purity, * our departed loved ones, friends, and kin, * all who in different ways have offered faithful service to You in this life, * and now have gone to dwell with you, O God. * Count them worthy of your heavenly kingdom.

Tone 8 **Glory be:** I weep and lament * as I contemplate death, * and behold our beauty fashioned in the image of

God, * resting in the tombs, * disfigured, deprived of glory and expression. * O, what a wonder! * What is this mystery? * Why have we been delivered to corruption? * Why subjected to Death? * Indeed, as it is written, * by the command of God, * for He grants rest to the departed.

Tone 6 **Now and ever:** Who would not bless you, most holy Virgin? * Who would not praise the most pure manner in which you gave birth? * For the only-begotten Son, who eternally proceeds from the Father, came forth from you. * He took flesh from you in a manner that is beyond understanding. * He, who by nature is God, took on our nature for our sake. * Yet He did not become divided into two persons; * rather, He remained one person with two distinct and unconfused natures. * O most pure Lady, we implore you: * Beseech your Son and God to have mercy on our souls.

INSTEAD OF THE PROKEIMENON

Music for the following is found in Appendix C, page 474.

Tone 8

Alleluia! Alleluia! Alleluia!

v. Blessed are they whom You have chosen and received, O Lord.

Alleluia! Alleluia! Alleluia!

v. They are remembered from generation to generation.

Alleluia! Alleluia! Alleluia!

APOSTICHA

Tone 6 Your Cross, O Christ, has been an invincible weapon for the martyrs; * for beholding the approach of death * and forseeing the future life, * they were made strong by the hope that lies in You. * By their intercession, have mercy on us!

Their souls shall dwell with the blessed.

You have honored the work of your hands with your own image, O Savior; * You have stamped this bodily form with the likeness of your spiritual essence. * You have made me a partaker of all these blessings, O Word; * for in your sovereign power You have placed me on earth as ruler of creation. * Therefore, give rest to your servants, O God our Savior, * in the abode of the just and in the land of the living.

Blessed are they whom You have chosen and received, O Lord.

To distinguish my dignity from the rest of creation, * You planted a garden for me in Eden; * it was filled with every kind of plant. * You made me free from all sorrows and care; * and while on earth You let me share in the divine life of the angels. * Therefore give rest to your servants, O God our Savior, * in the abode of the just and in the land of the living.

Tone 6 **Glory be:** Your creating command was my origin and formation; * for You willed to fashion me, * a living creature, out of visible and invisible nature. * From the earth You formed my body and gave me a soul * by your divine and life-creating breath. * Therefore, O Christ, give rest to your servants in the place of the living, * in the abodes of the just.

Tone 6 **Now and ever:** By the prayers of her who gave birth to You, O Christ, * and of your martyrs, apostles, and prophets, * of the prelates, holy monks, the righteous ones, and all your saints, * give rest to your servants who have fallen asleep.

TROPARIA

Music for the following is found in Appendix C, pages 474-475.

Tone 8 O Creator, in the depth of your wisdom, * You lovingly govern all people * and distribute to each what is for good. * Now give rest to the souls of your servants, * for they have placed their hope in You, * our Creator, Maker, and our God.

Tone 8 **Glory be...now and ever:** We have in you, a defense and a refuge, * and an advocate acceptable to God * to whom you gave birth, O Virgin Mother of God, * the salvation of the faithful.

Saturday Matins

INSTEAD OF THE LORD GOD IS OUR LIGHT

Music for the following is found in Appendix C, page 474

Tone 8

Alleluia! Alleluia! Alleluia!

v. Blessed are they whom You have chosen and received, O Lord.

Alleluia! Alleluia! Alleluia!

v. They are remembered from generation to generation.

Alleluia! Alleluia! Alleluia!

TROPARIA

Music for the following is in Appendix C, pages 474-475.

Tone 8 O Creator, in the depth of your wisdom, * You lovingly govern all people * and distribute to each what is for good. * Now give rest to the souls of your servants, * for they have placed their hope in You, * our Creator, Maker, and our God.

Tone 8 **Glory be...now and ever:** We have in you, a defense and a refuge, * and an advocate acceptable to God * to whom you gave birth, O Virgin Mother of God, * the salvation of the faithful.

SESSIONAL HYMN I

Tone 6 As athletes have trained in the arena, * the tyrants have set themselves against the martyrs. * The choirs of angels prepare the crown of victory for them; * their wisdom astounds the kings and tyrants. * For they have conquered the devil and professed Christ. * You give them their strength, O Lord, glory to You!

God is to be feared in his holy place. He is the Lord, the God of Israel.

The saints have fought the good fight; * they have received the reward of victory from You. * They despised the judgment of the impious * and obtained the crown of immortality. * By their prayers, O our God, * grant us your great mercy.

The poor called; the Lord heard them and rescued them from all distress.

The memory of your martyrs, O Lord, * calls to mind Paradise and Eden; * for in it all creation rejoices. * Through their intercession, O Lord, * grant us your great mercy.

Glory be: In the abode of the just and in the land of the living, * place your faithful departed, O Jesus; * for You have called them from this life. * Fill them with your never-setting light, * and make them worthy of your heavenly joy.

Now and ever: You called your Mother blessed, * and You went to your Passion of your own will. * Your light shone brightly from the Cross, * for You desired to go in search of Adam. * To the angels, You announced: Rejoice with me! * For I have found the lost coin. * You created everything in wisdom. * O Lord our God, glory to You!

HYMNS FOR THE DECEASED

Music for the following is in Appendix C, pages 475-479.

Tone 5

Blessed are You, O Lord; guide me by your precepts.

The choir of saints has found the Fountain of Life * and the Gate to Paradise. * May I also find the way through repentance. * I am a lost sheep; call me back, O Savior, and save me.

Blessed are You, O Lord; guide me by your precepts.

O Lord, I am the image of your glory * which is beyond description, * even though I bear the marks of transgressions. * Have mercy on your creature. * O Master, in your compassion cleanse me. * Grant me the home I yearn for, * and again make me an inhabitant of Paradise.

Blessed are You, O Lord; guide me by your precepts.

Grant rest, O God, to your servants * and place them in Paradise * where the choirs of saints and righteous shine like stars. * O Lord, give rest to your departed servants * and remit all their transgressions.

Blessed are You, O Lord; guide me by your precepts.

In the beginning You called me from nothingness * and favored me with your divine image. * Since I transgressed your commandments, * You returned me to the earth from which I was taken. * Restore me to your likeness, * that my original beauty may be renewed in me.

Blessed are You, O Lord, guide me by your precepts.

Come to Me * all who have walked the narrow and sorrowful path, * who during life have taken upon yourselves the Cross as a yoke * and faithfully followed Me; * enjoy the honors and the heavenly crowns * which I have prepared for you.

Blessed are You, O Lord; guide me by your precepts.

O Saints, you preached the Lamb of God, * and like lambs were slain; * you were transferred to unending and everlasting life. * O Martyrs, pray fervently * that He grant us the remission of our transgressions.

Blessed are You, O Lord; guide me by your precepts.

We praise with devotion the three-fold radiance of the one Divinity * by singing aloud: * Holy are You, eternal Father, coeternal Son, and divine Spirit. * Enlighten us who faithfully serve You, * and deliver us from eternal fire.

Glory be...now and ever: Rejoice, O pure and blessed

Mother of God, * for you gave birth to God according to the flesh * for the redemption of all. * Through you, all people have found salvation. * Through you, may we also find Paradise, O Blessed One.

Alleluia! Alleluia! Alleluia! Glory be to You, O God!

LITANY OF THE DECEASED

Priest: Have mercy on us, O God, according to your great mercy, we pray You, hear us and have mercy.

R. Lord, have mercy. *(3 times)*

Let us pray for the repose of the souls of the departed servants of God, and that their every transgression, committed deliberately or through human frailty, be forgiven them.

R. Lord, have mercy. *(3 times)*

Let us also pray that the Lord God commit their souls to the place where the just repose.

R. Lord, have mercy. *(3 times)*

For the mercy of God, for the kingdom of heaven, and for the remission of their sins, let us beseech Christ, the Immortal King and our God.

R. Grant it, O Lord.

Let us pray to the Lord.

R. Lord, have mercy.

O God of spirits and of all flesh, You trampled death, and broke the power of Satan, and granted life to your world. Now grant rest, O Lord, to the souls of your departed servants, in a place of light, joy, and peace, where there is no pain, sorrow, nor mourning. As a kind and gracious God, forgive every sin committed by them in word, deed, or thought, since there is no person who exists and does not sin. You alone are without sin, your justice is everlasting justice, and your word is the truth.

For You are the resurrection, the life, and the repose of your departed servants, O Christ our God, and we glorify You together with your eternal Father, and your all-holy, gracious, and life-giving Spirit, now and ever and forever.

R. Amen.

SESSIONAL HYMN II

Music for the following is in Appendix C, pages 479-480

Tone 5 Our Savior, rest your servants with the just, * and place them in your court, as it is written. * O Savior, You love all people and are gracious; * therefore, remit all their voluntary and involuntary sins * and all those committed knowingly and unknowingly.

Tone 5 **Glory be...now and ever:** O Christ our God, through the Virgin You appeared to the world; * and through her, You have shown us to be the children of light. * Have mercy on us!

PSALM 50

CANON

ODE 1

Tone 6 When Israel walked upon the deep sea as upon dry land * they saw Pharaoh, their pursuer, drowning, and they exclaimed: * Let us sing a hymn of victory to God.

Refrain: **O Lord, rest the souls of your departed servants.**

O Master and Creator, the Lord and Judge of every person, * You hold the ends of the earth in your hands; * now give rest to all the faithful departed in You.

For all those who are departed, * of every age and situation, * of every rank and dignity, * we fervently beseech You to give salvation * to those whom You have called to yourself.

You alone have created me, O Word, with your own hand; * You have fashioned me from the earth; * by your life-giving breath You have given me a soul. * Now, O compassionate God, save those whom You have taken to yourself.

Glory be...now and ever: O most pure Virgin, refuge of the world and invincible protection, * may your intercession enkindle those * who, in the midst of their perils, * have chosen you as their unshakable rampart.

ODE 3

Tone 6 None is as holy as You, O Lord my God. * In your goodness You have exalted the strength of the faithful, * and You have established us on the unshakable rock of your name.

Refrain: **O Lord, rest the souls of your departed servants.**

Through your divine majesty, * You gather the souls of the faithful departed from the ends of the earth, * and You bring them to yourself as if carried on a cloud. * Grant rest, O Christ, to your servants whom You have brought together from all places.

You alone establish rulers and kings, judges, and magistrates; * and now as the God of all people, O Savior, * in your judgment save them from all punishment.

O Creator of the world, * grant unending joy to all whom You have taken to yourself: * virgins and elders, adults and children; * and grant them the delights of Paradise.

Glory be...now and ever: O Hope of the universe and Virgin Mother of God, * do not abandon those who unceasingly hasten to you; * but through your fervent intercession, * save from all danger those who love your name.

SESSIONAL HYMN

Tone 8 You created the world with a sign; * in your good will, O Lord, give rest to all Christians who have died in the faith: * our parents, ancestors and elders, * our brothers, sisters, and friends, * rich and poor, monks, princes, and kings. * Give them rest in the place of the just and of the saints, * O Christ our King and our God, * and forgive the sins of all your servants.

Glory be...now and ever: As the widow offered the mite in days of old, * I now offer, O Virgin, the praise which is due to you, * together with the thanksgiving for all your benefits. * For you are my help and my protection; * and without ceasing, you deliver me from all adversaries. * You save me from my oppressors as from the midst of a fiery furnace, * and with all my heart I cry out to you: * O Mother of God, come to my aid and intercede with Christ our God * that He may forgive my sins, * for you are the hope of your servants.

ODE 4

Tone 6 Christ is my strength, my Lord, and my God! * This is the hymn that the holy Church sings out, * and, with a purified heart, she praises the Lord.

Refrain: **O Lord, rest the souls of your departed servants.**

You lead your faithful flock, O Lord and Shepherd, * to green pastures near the peaceful waters; * do not deprive your servants of the joy from on high.

O Lord, with your angels in heaven, * may You now join the choirs of holy monks, bishops, and all your servants; * for they have consecrated their souls and bodies to You, O Lover of Mankind.

As the Lord of all, You alone know the way of death, * the

length of life, and the limits of every mortal; * in your supreme goodness, have mercy on your servants.

Glory be...now and ever: O most holy Virgin, you have conceived the Holy of Holies and our God; * by your divine intercession, * implore Him now to place the departed * in the abode that the saints enjoy.

ODE 5

Tone 6 O God all-good, I beseech You: * With your divine brightness illumine the souls who love You and keep watch before You, * that they may know You, O Word of God; * for You are the true God who brings us out of the darkness of sin.

Refrain: **O Lord, rest the souls of your departed servants.**

Behold the choir of martyrs, the procession of apostles and prophets, * and the multitude of the just who sing to You, O Savior, * and beseech You to save those whom You have taken from this world.

When the trumpet sounds and the tombs are opened, * and when the earth trembles in fear, * be pleased to place your faithful servants * with your flock at your right hand, O Christ.

Give rest, O Lord, to the multitude of people, * men and women, elders and children, rich and poor, * who in faith have passed from this world to You; * and in your supreme goodness, save them.

Glory be...now and ever: Every tongue and every nation, those who live and die in faith, * find their hope in you, O pure Virgin; * and we look for happiness in the world to come * because of your prayers to the Lord.

ODE 6

Tone 6 When I see the ocean of this life * swelling with the storms of temptations, * I hasten to your harbor of peace, * and I cry out to You, O God of goodness: * Rescue my life from the pit.

Refrain: **O Lord, rest the souls of your departed servants.**

Spare us, O Lord, and relent, O Savior; * show us your love and your tenderness of heart; * in your goodness, save those whom You have brought to yourself from this world.

In your goodness, do not reject those who have died suddenly: * those lost in the storms of the sea, the torrents and floods, * those who perished in the mountains or in the valleys.

O Lord, You know those who have died secretly, * on land or at sea, * and those who have fallen in war and in battle. * Accept them, O Lord, in your great mercy.

Glory be...now and ever: O immaculate Queen, * who for us mortals gave birth to the Lord who calms the seas, * calm the fire and fury of my passions, * and give rest to my heart.

KONTAKION

Tone 8 To those who have left this passing world, O immortal Savior, * give rest with the just in the abode of the elect. * If they have sinned in their life, * forgive them their faults committed willingly or unwillingly, * for You alone Lord are without sin. * We ask this through the prayers of the Mother of God who gave You birth, * and with one voice we cry out for them: Alleluia!

IKOS

You alone, who created and fashioned mortals, are immortal; for we creatures, being made from the earth, shall also return to the same earth as You, my Maker, commanded, saying to me: Because you are earth you shall also return into the earth, where all mortals shall go, singing as our funeral hymn: Alleluia!

ODE 7

Tone 6 In the furnace, the angel poured out dew over the holy youths; * but at the order of God, the fire burned the Chaldeans, * and the tyrant was forced to sing: * Blessed are You, O Lord, God of our fathers!

***Refrain:* O Lord, rest the souls of your departed servants.**

When You come with your angels to judge the universe, * and are seated upon your throne of glory, O Savior, * fill the souls of your servants with your divine joy, * so that they may sing to You: * Blessed are You, O God of our fathers!

Have mercy, O Savior, and save from eternal punishment * all those who have been devoured by wild animals, * those swallowed by the monsters of the sea, * those who have died in the mountains or caves of the earth, * together with those who have perished in natural disasters.

To those who have died by fire or the sword, * to those crushed by rocks and to the victims of thieves, * and to those who have died of hunger or disease, * now grant them a share in your joy, O Savior, * that they may piously sing to You, O God of our fathers.

Glory be...now and ever: O holy Virgin, You alone are the bridge leading mortals to God, * therefore, by your prayers, save those who left this life full of hope and love for you, * and preserve them from all danger and everlasting death.

ODE 8

Tone 6 Shudder with fright, O heavens, * and may the earth and its foundations tremble! * For behold, He who dwells in the highest heaven * is now counted among the dead * and dwells in the narrowness of the tomb. * Bless Him, O youths, and praise Him, O priests, * and let the whole nation exalt Him forever!

Refrain: **O Lord, rest the souls of your departed servants.**

Have mercy, O Lord, and grant rest to mortals of every rank * whom You have called to yourself: * Christian kings and princes, * judges and magistrates, * leaders of peoples and nations, * that we may sing to You forever.

Deliver from eternal fire, O Lover of Mankind, * the servants of your immaculate Church; * save the consecrated multitude of monks and holy priests, * and make them worthy of the glory from on high, * that we may sing to You forever.

O Christ, our Lord, * grant your salvation, mercy, and rest * to the souls of your faithful departed * in a place where they may live. * Save them from the bitter torments of Hades, * that we may sing to You forever.

Glory be...now and ever: You alone, O immaculate Virgin, * have put an end to the curse brought by Eve long ago, * and you have made life spring forth for mortals. * By your prayers now obtain eternity * for those who have left this passing life, * that we may sing to you forever.

MAGNIFICAT

ODE 9

Tone 6 Every tongue hesitates to sing your praises, * and even the highest of heavenly spirits is overwhelmed * as they sing to you, O Mother of God, * But in your goodness receive the homage of our faith * and the power of our love as it rises to you; * for you are the protectress of the Christian people, * and we extol you.

Refrain: **O Lord, rest the souls of your departed servants.**

The army of Angels intercedes with You, O God of tenderness, * together with the Cherubim and fiery Seraphim. * The Thrones, Powers, and Dominions, * the Archangels and Principalities beseech You, O almighty Lord, * to have mercy on the souls of all the departed.

Behold the procession of the inspired prophets, * the choir of the divine apostles, the patriarchs and martyrs, * the multitude of the just and all the saints, * together they all beseech You, O Lover of Mankind: * Grant salvation to all the departed souls of your faithful servants.

O Lord all-knowing, * You see and You know the multitude of mortals * and the limits of each life. * Grant forgiveness of sins and the delights of Paradise * to every faithful servant whom You have chosen in your goodness.

Glory be...now and ever: O most pure Virgin and Queen of the universe, * you are the protection of the living and the dead, * the repose, the glory, and joy of those who have the fortune to count on your help; * through your prayers save all of them.

HYMN OF LIGHT

Tone 3 O faithful, let us keep the memory of all the departed * who have finished their course and now sleep in Christ. * Let us also think about the last day * and without ceasing implore Christ * for ourselves and for all the departed.

Glory be...now and ever: O sweetness of the angels and consolation of the afflicted, * O protection of Christians and Virgin Mother of the Lord, * deliver me and save me from eternal punishment.

AT THE PRAISES

Tone 6 Fearful is the death which awaits us; * awesome is the judgment of the Master. * The unquenchable fire will be prepared, * together with the sleepless worm and the gnashing of teeth, * the outer darkness and the eternal damnation. * Therefore, let us cry out to the Savior: * Grant rest to those whom You have taken from this passing life * and give them your great mercy.

Come, all you that cling to life; * stoop down and look into the tombs and be afraid. * Behold the folly of the world! * What has become of the pampered body and rich luxuries? * Observe the destruction of life, for truly all is vanity! * Let us cry out to the Savior: * Grant rest to those whom You have taken from this passing life * and give them your great mercy.

He who formerly sat on a throne now lies in a tomb. * He who was clothed in purple disintegrates into dust. * One moment He was enthroned, and the next He was placed in the grave. * Behold the endurance of royal power. * Behold the life of mortals passes away like a dream. * Let us cry to the Savior: * Grant rest to those whom You have taken from this passing life * and give them your great mercy.

O Savior, as the Lover of Mankind, * grant rest to all those who have passed away in the hope of eternal life, * men and women together with newborn children, * of every race, condition, and state of life. * Place them in the bosom of Abraham, the place of the just, * through your great mercy.

Tone 2 **Glory be:** As a flower withers and a shadow passes * so every one will die; * but when the trumpet sounds, * the dead will rise again as in an earthquake * to meet You, O Christ our God. * Then, O Master, place in the abode of your saints * the souls of your servants * whom You have taken from us.

Tone 6 **Now and ever:** You are our God who made all things in wisdom; * You sent your prophets who foretold your coming * and your apostles who proclaimed your mighty deeds. * The first were the heralds of your advent, * while the others later illumined the nations in baptism. * From You the martyrs heard of your glory, * and now they pray fervently to You, O Master, * together with her who gave You birth, * to grant rest to the souls of the departed, * receiving us all into your kingdom. * For You endured the Cross and delivered me from condemnation, * O my Redeemer and my God.

LESSER DOXOLOGY

APOSTICHA

Tone 6 By the ineffable tenderness that You have for us, * and by the inexhaustible source of your goodness, * welcome the departed into the land of the living, O Lord, * and place them in the eternal abodes, * and assure them the enjoyment of that for which they long; * for You have poured out your blood, O Christ, * to redeem the whole world at the price of your life.

Blessed are they whom You have chosen and received, O Lord.

You accepted death to give us life; * You made the springs of life gush forth; * to the faithful You gave eternal happiness. * Now grant this to those who have fallen asleep * in the hope of resurrection. * In your goodness, wipe away their sins, * for You alone are without sin. * Show us your love so that we may praise your name, * and that, saved by You, O Christ, * we may glorify You in eternity.

They are remembered from generation to generation.

O Christ, we acknowledge your divine lordship over the living and the dead. * Grant that your faithful servants * who have returned to their only Benefactor * may share in the dwelling of the chosen * in the place of refreshment, * together with your saints in glory. * For You are the merciful God, * and in your unique goodness * You save those whom You have created in your own image.

Tone 6 **Glory be:** In days of old Adam was seized with grief * when he tasted the forbidden fruit in Eden; * for the Serpent filled it with venom, * and in this way Death entered the world, * devouring the whole human race. * But the Lord has come destroying the dragon and giving us rest. * Let us cry out: * O God our Savior, spare those whom You have taken to yourself * and give them rest with your chosen ones.

Tone 6 **Now and ever:** O most holy Virgin, you are the dwelling place of God; * you have sheltered in your womb the one person in two natures, * and without a husband you have given birth to Him. * Pray to your only Son, the first-born, * who left your virginity intact even after giving birth, * that He may grant rest to all the faithful who have fallen asleep * in the place of joy and the light that never fades.

TROPARIA

Music for the following is in Appendix C, pages 474-480.

Tone 8 O Creator, in the depth of your wisdom, * You lovingly govern all people * and distribute to each what is for good. * Now give rest to the souls of your servants, * for they have placed their hope in You, * our Creator, Maker, and our God.

Tone 8 **Glory be...now and ever:** We have in you, a defense and a refuge, * and an advocate acceptable to God * to whom you gave birth, O Virgin Mother of God, * the salvation of the faithful.

Pentecost Sunday

Vespers

AT PSALM 140

Tone 1 Behold, we celebrate today the feast of Pentecost, * the descent of the Holy Spirit, * the fulfillment of the promise and the realization of hope. * How wonderful and awesome is this great mystery! * Therefore, O Lord and Creator of all, * we cry out: Glory to You! *(2 times)*

You renewed your disciples, O Christ, * by giving them a variety of tongues * with which to proclaim that You are the immortal God, * the Word who bestows great mercy upon our souls.

The Holy Spirit provides every gift: * He inspires prophecy and perfects the priesthood; * He grants wisdom to the illiterate, * makes simple fishermen become wise theologians, * and establishes perfect order in the assembly of the Church. * Therefore, O Comforter, * equal in nature and majesty with the Father and the Son, * O Lord, glory to You!

Tone 2 We have seen the true light; * we have received the heavenly Spirit; * we have found the true faith; * and we worship the undivided Trinity; * for the Trinity has saved us. *(2 times)*

You have shown us, O Savior, * the way to salvation through the prophets; * and the grace of your Holy Spirit * has shone upon us through the apostles. * You are God from all eternity, * our God, now and forever.

O Savior of the world, * I sing a hymn of praise to You in your temple; * on my knees, I adore your invisible power, * at dawn and dusk and at noon; * indeed, at all times, I bless You, O Lord.

We your faithful people, O Lord, * prostrate our souls and bodies before You. * We sing a hymn of praise to You, the eternal Father; * and to your Son, equal to You in eternity; * and to your all-holy Spirit, coeternal with You, * the Enlightener and Sanctifier of our souls.

Let us sing a hymn of praise to the consubstantial Trinity, * Father, Son, and Holy Spirit; * for this is the command and teaching * of all prophets, apostles, and martyrs.

Tone 8 **Glory be...now and ever:** Come, all you nations of the world, * let us adore God in three holy persons, * Father, Son, and Holy Spirit — three in one. * From all eternity, the Father begets the Son, * equal to Him in eternity and majesty, * equal also to the Holy Spirit, glorified with the Son in the Father, * three persons, and yet a single power and essence and Godhead. * In deep adoration, let us cry out to God: * Holy is God who made all things through the Son * with the cooperation of the Holy Spirit. * Holy the Mighty One through whom the Father was revealed to us, * and through whom the Holy Spirit came to this world. * Holy the Immortal One, the Spirit and Comforter * who proceeds from the Father and reposes in the Son. * All-holy Trinity, glory to You!

READINGS

Numbers 11: 16-17 and 24-29
Joel 2: 23 through 3: 5
Ezekiel 36: 24-28

AT THE LITIJA

Tone 2 You have shown us, O Savior, * the way to salvation through the prophets; * and the grace of your Holy Spirit * has shone upon us through the apostles. * You are God from all eternity, * our God, now and forever.

O Savior of the world, * I sing a hymn of praise to You in your temple; * on my knees, I adore your invisible power, * at dawn and dusk and at noon; * indeed, at all times, I bless You, O Lord.

We your faithful people, O Lord, * prostrate our souls and bodies before You. * We sing a hymn of praise to You, the eternal Father; * and to your Son, equal to You in eternity; * and to your all-holy Spirit, coeternal with You, * the Enlightener and Sanctifier of our souls.

Tone 8 **Glory be...now and ever:** O Lord, when You sent down your Spirit * upon the assembled apostles, * the children of Israel were struck with awe * as they heard them speak in many tongues, * inspired by the Holy Spirit. * They knew them to be illiterate and now saw them wise, * speaking divine truths and bringing Gentiles to the faith. * Therefore, we also cry out to You: * You have appeared on earth and saved us from error; * O Lord, glory to You!

APOSTICHA

Tone 6 O Lord, the Gentiles were unaware of the power of the Holy Spirit * that had come down upon the apostles; * they thought the many tongues were an effect of drunkenness. * But we who are strengthened by them cry out ceaselessly: * O Lover of Mankind, take not your Holy Spirit away from us.

A pure heart create for me, O God; put a steadfast spirit within me.

O Lord, the descent of your Holy Spirit on your apostles * made them speak a variety of tongues. * When the unbelievers witnessed this marvel, * they took it for drunkenness, * when, in fact, it was a cause of salvation for the faithful. * We beseech You, therefore, O Lover of Mankind, * to make us worthy * of the revelation of this Spirit with us.

Do not cast me away from your presence, nor deprive me of your Holy Spirit.

Heavenly King, Comforter, * Spirit of Truth, * You are everywhere present and fill all things. * Treasury of blessings and Giver of life, * come and dwell within us, * cleanse us of all stain, * and save our souls, O gracious Lord.

Tone 8 **Glory be...now and ever:** In the days of old, pride brought confusion of tongues * to the builders of the Tower of Babel, * but now the diversity of tongues enlightened the minds * and gave knowledge for the glory of God. * Then, God punished the impious for their sin; * now, Christ enlightened fishermen through his Spirit. * Then, the confusion of tongues was for the sake of punishment; * now, there was variety so that voices could be joined in harmony* for the salvation of our souls.

TROPARION

Tone 8 Blessed are You, O Christ our God. * You filled the fishermen with wisdom, * sending down upon them the Holy Spirit. * Through them You have caught the whole world in your net. * O Lover of Mankind, glory be to You! *(3 times)*

Sunday Matins

SESSIONAL HYMN I

Tone 4 Come, O faithful, let us celebrate the feast of the Fiftieth Day: * the day which concludes the Feast of feasts; *

the day on which the pre-ordained promise is fulfilled; * the day when the Comforter descends upon the earth in tongues of fire; * the day of the disciples' enlightenment. * They are revealed as initiated into the heavenly mysteries, * for truly the light of the Comforter has illumined the world.

Glory be...now and ever: *(Repeat the above)*

SESSIONAL HYMN II

Tone 4 The fountain of the Spirit rushes down to earth, * mystically divided into flaming streams, * both refreshing and enlightening the apostles; * the fire became for them a cloud of dew, * raining enlightenment upon them. * From them we have received grace by fire and water, * for truly the light of the Comforter has illumined the world.

Glory be...now and ever: *(Repeat the above)*

POLYELEOS

EXALTATION

We extol You, * O Christ the Giver of life, * and we venerate your most Holy Spirit, * whom You sent upon your holy apostles from the Father.

v. The heavens proclaim the glory of God, and the firmament shows forth the work of his hands.

v. By his word the heavens were made, by the breath of his mouth all the stars.

v. All the earth shall remember and return to the Lord; all families of the nations worship before Him.

v. A pure heart create for me, O God; put a steadfast spirit within me.

v. Do not cast me away from your presence, nor deprive me of your Holy Spirit.

v. The Lord will give strength to his people; the Lord will bless his people with peace.

v. **Glory be...now and ever:**

Alleluia! Alleluia! Alleluia! Glory be to You, O God! *(3 times)*

SESSIONAL HYMN

Tone 8 After your resurrection from the grave, O Christ, * and your divine ascension into the highest heavens, * You made your glory descend upon the witnesses of your divinity, * and You renewed a spirit of righteousness in the hearts of your disciples. * Therefore, they have filled the world, O Savior, * with the sounds of your teaching and your work of salvation, * as a melodious harp mystically played with the divine plectrum.

Glory be...now and ever: *(Repeat the above)*

GRADUAL HYMNS

Tone 4 My sinful desires have encircled me, * from my youth they have oppressed me; * but You, O Savior, will come to aid me. * You will protect and save me.

May the enemies of Zion be confounded by the Lord; * may they be as grass which withers, * which is dried up by the fire.

Glory be...now and ever: Every spirit lives by the grace of the Holy Spirit * and is raised up in all purity; * it is mystically enlightened by the one God in three persons.

PROKEIMENON

Tone 4 Let your good Spirit guide me in ways that are level and smooth.

v. Lord, listen to my prayer; turn your ear to my appeal.

GOSPEL

John 20: 19-23

AFTER PSALM 50

Glory be: Through the intercession of the holy apostles, O Merciful One, remit our many sins.

Now and ever: Through the intercession of the Mother of God, O Merciful One, remit our many sins.

Tone 6

Have mercy on me, God, in your kindness. In your compassion, blot out my offense.

Heavenly King, Comforter, * Spirit of Truth, * You are everywhere present and fill all things. * Treasury of blessings and Giver of life, * come and dwell within us, * cleanse us of all stain, * and save our souls, O gracious Lord.

CANON I

ODE 1

Tone 7 He drowned Pharaoh and his army in the Red Sea, * for He is the One who shattered the armies with the power of his arm. * Let us sing to Him, for He is covered with glory.

Refrain: **Glory be to You, our God, glory be to You!**

As You promised your disciples in earlier days, O Christ the Lover of Mankind, * You sent your comforting Spirit; * thus You made his light shine over the world.

Glory be...now and ever: That which was formerly announced by the Law and the prophets * is fulfilled today; * for the grace of the Spirit rests on each of the faithful.

He drowned Pharaoh and his army in the Red Sea, * for He is the One who shattered the armies with the power of his arm. * Let us sing to him, for He is covered with glory.

Tone 4 Enveloped by the divine cloud, * the man of unsure speech taught the Law written by God; * wiping the dust from his eyes, he saw the One-Who-Is, * and he was initiated into the knowledge of the Spirit. * Let us praise him with inspired songs.

ODE 3

Tone 7 You said to your apostles, O Lord: * Remain in Jerusalem until the day when you shall be clothed with power from on high; * and I will send you another Paraclete, * the Spirit of the Father and of Me, * in whom you will be strengthened.

Refrain: **Glory be to You, our God, glory be to You!**

By his descent, the power of the Holy Spirit has divinely reunited in a new harmony * the tongues that were formerly divided by their evil design. * He reveals to the faithful the Trinity in whom we are strengthened.

Glory be...now and ever: You said to your apostles, O Lord: * Remain in Jerusalem until the day when you shall be clothed with power from on high; * and I will send you another Paraclete, * the Spirit of the Father and of Me, * in whom you will be strengthened.

Tone 4 The shackles of a sterile womb * and the unbridled pride that filled a mother * were shattered by the prayer of Anna, the prophetess of old, * who bore a contrite and humbled heart * before the supreme and all-powerful God.

SESSIONAL HYMN

Tone 8 The friends of the Savior were filled with joy and renewed in heart, * those who were formerly filled with fear; * for on this day the Holy Spirit descended from the heights of heaven upon the apostles. * They spoke to each person in his native tongue,* for the tongues of fire were distributed but did not consume them; * rather, they covered them with dew.

Glory be...now and ever: *(Repeat the above)*

ODE 4

Tone 7 Meditating upon your final coming, O Christ, * the prophet cried out: * I have seen your power, O Lord, * for You have come to save those who are consecrated to You.

Refrain: **Glory be to You, our God, glory be to You!**

The One who was spoken of by the prophets, * and who was formerly announced by the Law to the imperfect people, * is revealed this day as truly God and the Paraclete * to the servants and witnesses of the Word.

Glory be...now and ever: Bearing the seal of the divinity, * the Spirit was imparted to the apostles in the form of fire; * He is manifested through the gift of tongues, * for He is the divine power who comes freely from the Father.

Meditating upon your final coming, O Christ, * the prophet cried out:* I have seen your power, O Lord, * for You have come to save those who are consecrated to You.

Tone 4 O King of kings and only Son of the Father, * O Word proceeding from the Father without beginning, * You send your Spirit of truth upon your apostles who sing: * Glory to your power, O Lord!

ODE 5

Tone 7 O Lord, the Spirit of your salvation, * which formerly was received by the prophets in fear, * now creates a pure heart in your apostles * and renews in our hearts an upright spirit; * for your commandments, O Lord, bring us light and peace.

Refrain: **Glory be to You, our God, glory be to You!**

The power which descends on us is the Holy Spirit, * the goodness and wisdom of God, * the Spirit who proceeds from the Father * and is revealed by the Son to us the faithful. * He fills with holiness those in whom He dwells.

Glory be...now and ever: O Lord, the Spirit of your salvation, * which formerly was received by the prophets in fear, * now creates a pure heart in your apostles * and renews in our hearts an upright spirit; * for your commandments, O Lord, bring us light and peace.

Tone 4 Receive the Holy Spirit, breathing the flames of fresh dew * as a baptism that takes away sin, * O you children who are enlightened by the Church. * For today the Law comes forth from Zion; * it is the grace of the Spirit which comes in tongues of fire.

ODE 6

Tone 7 Sailing across the ocean of life and tossed about by the cares of the world, * engulfed in the midst of my sins and thrown to the monster who devours souls, * as Jonah, I cry out to You, O Christ: * Deliver me from this deadly abyss.

Refrain: **Glory be to You, our God, glory be to You!**

You pour out your Spirit in abundance upon all flesh, * as You had promised, O Lord; * and the universe is filled with the knowledge of You, * for the Father has begotten You as a Son, * and the Spirit proceeds from Him.

Glory be...now and ever: Sailing across the ocean of life and tossed about by the cares of the world, * engulfed in the midst of my sins and thrown to the monster who devours souls, * as Jonah, I cry out to You, O Christ: * Deliver me from this deadly abyss.

Tone 4 O Christ, our salvation and redemption, * You have come forth in splendor from the Virgin * to rescue us from the pit of the tomb; * as Jonah was saved from the sea monster, * the entire human race was saved after the fall of Adam.

KONTAKION

Tone 8 When the Most High descended and confused tongues, * He scattered the people; * but when He distributed the tongues of fire, * He called all to unity. * Therefore, with one voice, * let us praise the most Holy Spirit.

IKOS

Grant to your servants, O Jesus, a prompt and firm comfort; for our spirits are filled with sadness. Do not abandon us in our affliction and do not keep yourself far from our sorely-tried hearts, but come to us in haste. Come close to us, O Lord, who are present everywhere; in your goodness, remain united to those who love You, as You were always with your apostles, so that, united with You, we may sing and glorify your most Holy Spirit.

ODE 7

Tone 7 In the fiery furnace, * the youths transformed the blazing flames which surrounded them into dew, * for they praised the Lord by singing: * Blessed are You, O God of our fathers!

Refrain: **Glory be to You, our God, glory be to You!**

While the apostles were preaching the marvels of God, * the unbelievers took for drunkenness the power of the Spirit * who made known to us the Trinity, * the one God of our fathers!

Glory be...now and ever: According to the true faith, * we confess the indivisible nature of God the Father without beginning, * of the consubstantial Word and the Holy Spirit: * Blessed are You, O God of our fathers!

In the fiery furnace, * the youths transformed the blazing flames which surrounded them into dew, * for they praised the Lord by singing: * Blessed are You, O God of our fathers!

Tone 4 The symphony of instruments was raised up to adore the lifeless golden statue; * but the bright grace of the Paraclete invites us to sing with devotion: * Blessed are You, eternal and unique Trinity!

ODE 8

Tone 7 On Sinai, the bush that burned without being consumed, * revealed God to Moses * as He spoke to the one of unsure speech; * and in the furnace, the three youths, invincible in their zeal for God, * began to sing a hymn of praise: * Sing to the Lord, all you his works and exalt Him forever.

Refrain: **Glory be to You, our God, glory be to You!**

When the violent gust of wind bearing life descended from heaven, * the most Holy Spirit of God, in the form of tongues of fire, * breathed on the fishermen with great force; * and they began to preach the marvels of God: * Sing to the Lord, all you works of the Lord and exalt Him forever.

Let us bless the Lord, Father, Son, and Holy Spirit.

Let us approach the inviolate mountain * without fear of the terrible fire; * come, let us climb the mountain of Zion, * the city of the living God. * In joy, let us now unite ourselves with the choir of the disciples, * the bearers of the Spirit: * Sing to the Lord, all you works of the Lord and exalt Him forever.

Now and ever: On Sinai, the bush that burned without being consumed, * revealed God to Moses * as He spoke to the one of unsure speech; * and in the furnace, the three youths, invincible in their zeal for God, * began to sing a hymn of praise: * Sing to the Lord, all you his works and exalt Him forever.

Let us praise, bless and worship the Lord, singing and exalting Him above all forever.

Tone 4 The triple flame of the unique divinity * breaks the chains and stirs the flames with dew; * the youths sing his praises, * and every creature, the work of his hands, * blesses its only Savior and benefactor.

OMIT MAGNIFICAT

ODE 9

O my soul, extol the one God in three Persons.
(sung before each of the following)

Tone 7 You have conceived in all purity, * and the Word and Creator of the universe takes flesh in you, * O spouseless Mother and virginal Birthgiver of God, * the dwelling place of the One whom none could contain, * and the abode of the infinite One, your Creator. * For this, we extol you.

He who formerly was taken up in a chariot of fire, * the prophet who was filled with zeal and fervor, * prefigured the brilliant coming of the Spirit, * who descends upon the apostles this day; * and shining with the brightness of this fire, * they make the Trinity known to all.

The laws of nature are surpassed; * wonderful thing is now heard: * while the apostles resound with one voice, * by the grace of the Holy Spirit, * people, nations, and languages all understand in their own way the wonders of God, * for they have been initiated into the knowledge of the Holy Trinity.

You have conceived in all purity, * and the Word and Creator of the universe takes flesh in you, * O spouseless Mother and virginal Birthgiver of God, * the dwelling place of the One whom none could contain, * and the abode of the infinite One, your Creator. * For this, we extol you.

Tone 4 **Glory be...now and ever:** Rejoice, O Queen and glorious Virgin Mother! * What orator, rich in eloquence, could find the proper words * to fashion a hymn of praise worthy of you? * For every spirit shudders before the mystery of your holy birthgiving; * and we also unite our voices to glorify you.

CANON II

ODE 1

Tone 4 Enveloped by the divine cloud, * the man of unsure speech taught the Law written by God; * wiping the dust from his eyes, he saw the One-Who-Is, * and he was initiated into the knowledge of the Spirit. * Let us praise him with inspired songs.

***Refrain:* Glory be to You, our God, glory be to You!**

The holy and venerable mouth has said: * I am not separating myself from you, my friends. * Seated upon the throne of the Father in heaven, * I will pour out the grace of the Spirit * to enlighten those who desire it with all their heart.

Glory be...now and ever: Having ascended the mountain, * the immaculate Word fulfilled the desire of his serene heart; * for having accomplished his work, Christ rejoined his friends, * and in the form of a strong wind and tongues of fire, * He gave them the Holy Spirit as He promised.

Enveloped by the divine cloud, * the man of unsure speech taught the Law written by God; * wiping the dust from his eyes, he saw the One-Who-Is, * and he was initiated into the knowledge of the Spirit. * Let us praise him with inspired songs.

Tone 7 He drowned Pharaoh and his army in the Red Sea, * for He is the One who shattered the armies with the power of his arm. * Let us sing to Him, for He is covered with glory.

ODE 3

Tone 4 The shackles of a sterile womb * and the unbridled pride that filled a mother * were shattered by the prayer of Anna, the prophetess of old, * who bore a contrite and humbled heart * before the supreme and all-powerful God.

***Refrain:* Glory be to You, our God, glory be to You!**

Unknowable is the supreme power of God; * through Him the uneducated men became the teachers, * and by their word they confounded the wise ones in their error; * they rescued the uncultured people from their dark night * by the illumination of the Holy Spirit.

Glory be...now and ever: He proceeds from the unbegotten Light, * the eternal Light who shines as a thousand lights; * He is the One whose flaming word revealed to the people of Zion * the consubstantial splendor inherited from the Father through the Son.

The shackles of a sterile womb * and the unbridled pride that filled a mother * were shattered by the prayer of Anna, the prophetess of old, * who bore a contrite and humbled heart * before the supreme and all-powerful God.

Tone 7 You said to your apostles, O Lord: * Remain in Jerusalem until the day when you shall be clothed with power from on high; * and I will send you another Paraclete, * the Spirit of the Father and of Me, * in whom you will be strengthened.

SESSIONAL HYMN

Tone 8 The friends of the Savior were filled with joy and renewed in heart, * those who were formerly filled with fear; * for on this day the Holy Spirit descended from the heights of heaven upon the apostles. * They spoke to each person in his native tongue, * for the tongues of fire were distributed but did not consume them; * rather, they covered them with dew.

Glory be...now and ever: *(Repeat the above)*

ODE 4

Tone 4 O King of kings and only Son of the Father, * O Word proceeding from the Father without beginning, * You send your Spirit of truth upon your apostles who sing: * Glory to your power, O Lord!

Refrain: **Glory be to You, our God, glory be to You!**

Having prepared the bath of regeneration for my fallen nature by your word, * You have washed me, O Word of God, * in the flowing stream of your pierced side; * and You have signed me with the fervor of the Spirit.

Every creature bends the knee before the Paraclete, * and before the One who is begotten of the Father as the consubstantial Son; * in three Persons we recognize only one substance * which neither time nor space can contain. * The grace of the Spirit has shone as light.

Glory be...now and ever: Give homage to the sovereign power of God, * all you that venerate the substance of the divine brightness; * for Christ our benefactor works wonders and illumines us for our salvation, * filling us with the grace of the Spirit.

O King of kings and only Son of the Father, * O Word proceeding from the Father without beginning, * You send your Spirit of truth upon your apostles who sing: * Glory to your power, O Lord!

Tone 7 Meditating upon your final coming, O Christ, * the prophet cried out: * I have seen your power, O Lord, * for You have come to save those who are consecrated to You.

ODE 5

Tone 4 Receive the Holy Spirit, breathing the flames of fresh dew * as a baptism that takes away sin, * O you children who are enlightened by the Church. * For today the Law comes forth from Zion; * it is the grace of the Spirit which comes in tongues of fire.

Refrain: **Glory be to You, our God, glory be to You!**

The sovereign Spirit descends from the Father freely and willingly; * He gives the apostles the knowledge of languages. * And sharing the image and power of the Father, * He confirms the life-giving power of the Savior.

Glory be...now and ever: Not long ago the sovereign Word purified souls from sin * and made his immaculate dwelling with his apostles; * and now the consubstantial Spirit dwells there, * filling them with light.

Receive the Holy Spirit, breathing the flames of fresh dew * as a baptism that takes away sin, * O you children who are enlightened by the Church. * For today the Law comes forth from Zion; * it is the grace of the Spirit which comes in tongues of fire.

Tone 7 O Lord, the Spirit of your salvation, * which formerly was received by the prophets in fear, * now creates a pure heart in your apostles * and renews in our hearts an upright spirit; * for your commandments, O Lord, bring us light and peace.

ODE 6

Tone 4 O Christ, our salvation and redemption, * You have come forth in splendor from the Virgin * to rescue us from the pit of the tomb; * as Jonah was saved from the sea monster, * the entire human race was saved after the fall of Adam.

***Refrain:* Glory be to You, our God, glory be to You!**

Eternally renew in our hearts the Spirit of righteousness to which we aspire; * for He proceeds from the Father without being separated from Him, * and his burning fire purifies the stains of our hearts and spirits.

Glory be...now and ever: You filled the vain assembly of people with confusion, * and by the fire of your breath You offered the treasure * which the apostles dwelling in Zion so desired; * for they were awaiting the coming of the Holy Spirit, * the imprint of the Word who was begotten of the Father.

O Christ, our salvation and redemption, * You have come forth in splendor from the Virgin * to rescue us from the pit of the tomb; * as Jonah was saved from the sea monster, * the entire human race was saved after the fall of Adam.

Tone 7 Sailing across the ocean of life and tossed about by the cares of the world, * engulfed in the midst of my sins and thrown to the monster who devours souls, * as Jonah, I cry out to You, O Christ: * Deliver me from this deadly abyss.

KONTAKION

Tone 8 When the Most High descended and confused tongues, * He scattered the people; * but when He distributed the tongues of fire, * He called all to unity. * Therefore, with one voice, * let us praise the most Holy Spirit.

IKOS

Grant to your servants, O Jesus, a prompt and firm comfort; for our spirits are filled with sadness. Do not abandon us in our affliction and do not keep yourself far from our sorely-tried hearts, but come to us in haste. Come close to us, O Lord, who are present everywhere; in your goodness, remain united to those who love You, as You were always with your apostles, so that, united with you, we may sing and glorify your most Holy Spirit.

ODE 7

Tone 4 The symphony of instruments was raised up to adore the lifeless golden statue; * but the bright grace of the Paraclete invites us to sing with devotion: * Blessed are You, eternal and unique Trinity!

***Refrain:* Glory be to You, our God, glory be to you!**

When they heard the apostles speaking in the language

of each one, * those who had not recognized the voice of the prophets * said that this was drunkenness due to wine. * But in fervor and in faith we cry out: * Blessed are You, O Creator of the universe!

Joel, the prophet and the seer, * made the inspired oracle of the Word resound as he said: * I will pour out my Spirit on those who sing: * Blessed are You, O Divinity of triple brightness!

Glory be...now and ever: The third hour was filled with grace and joy * as it revealed the one substance of the divinity * shared in three persons; * and we sing on this unique and sovereign day: * Blessed are You, Father, Son, and Holy Spirit!

The symphony of instruments was raised up to adore the lifeless golden statue; * but the bright grace of the Paraclete invites us to sing with devotion: * Blessed are You, eternal and unique Trinity!

Tone 7 In the fiery furnace, * the youths transformed the blazing flames which surrounded them into dew, * for they praised the Lord by singing: * Blessed are You, O God of our fathers!

ODE 8

Tone 4 The triple flame of the unique divinity * breaks the chains and stirs the flames with dew; * the youths sing his praises, * and every creature, the work of his hands, * blesses its only Savior and benefactor.

Refrain: **Glory be to You, our God, glory be to You!**

In memory of the words of salvation, * learned from the Father and taught to the apostles, * Christ sends the Spirit in the form of tongues of fire; * and creation, transformed by your presence, sings to You: * Blessed are You, O Lord!

Let us bless the Lord, Father, Son, and Holy Spirit.

Having come freely to save us, * You have given to your apostles the eternal Light and Source of brightness * as a breath worthy of adoration; * now give to your faithful this same Spirit.

Now and ever: The mouths of the inspired prophets have sung * of your coming in the flesh, O King, * and You send the Spirit who proceeds from the paternal bosom, * sharing your creative power and your eternal rule; * for all the faithful, this is a marvel of the incarnation.

Let us praise, bless, and worship the Lord, singing and exalting Him above all forever.

The triple flame of the unique divinity * breaks the chains and stirs the flames with dew; * the youths sing his praises, * and every creature, the work of his hands, * blesses its only Savior and benefactor.

Tone 7 On Sinai, the bush that burned without being consumed, * revealed God to Moses * as He spoke to the one of unsure speech; * and in the furnace, the three youths, invincible in their zeal for God, * began to sing a hymn of praise: * Sing to the Lord, all you his works and exalt Him forever.

OMIT MAGNIFICAT

ODE 9

O my soul, extol the one God in three Persons.
(sung before each of the following)

Tone 4 Rejoice, O Queen and glorious Virgin Mother! * What orator, rich in eloquence, could find the proper words * to fashion a hymn of praise worthy of you? * For every spirit shudders before the mystery of your holy birthgiving; * and we also unite our voices to glorify you.

I wish to praise the virginal source of Life, * who alone has hidden in her womb, * the Word who heals the human race, * and who now from the right hand of the Father, * sends us the grace of the Holy Spirit.

We, upon whom the divine grace has breathed, * shining with light and transformed, * marvelously transfigured and contemplating the Wisdom of the indivisble Trinity, * we now glorify its triple brightness.

Rejoice, O Queen and glorious Virgin Mother! * What orator, rich in eloquence, could find the proper words * to fashion a hymn of praise worthy of you? * For every spirit shudders before the mystery of your holy birthgiving; * and we also unite our voices to glorify you.

Tone 7 **Glory be...now and ever:** You have conceived in all purity, * and the Word and Creator of the universe takes flesh in you, * O spouseless Mother and virginal Birthgiver of God, * the dwelling place of the One whom none could contain, * and the abode of the infinite One, your Creator. * For this, we extol you.

HYMN OF LIGHT

Tone 3 O most Holy Spirit, who proceeds from the Father through the Son, * and who has now descended upon the uneducated disciples, * save and sanctify all those who recognize You as God. *(2 times)*

Glory be...now and ever: The Father is light and the Word is light; * the Holy Spirit also is light! * He is sent upon the apostles in the form of tongues of fire, * and through Him the whole world receives the light of baptism * to adore the Holy Trinity.

AT THE PRAISES

Tone 4 All the peoples have seen wonders today * in the city of David, * when the Holy Spirit descended in tongues of fire, * as told by the God-inspired Luke, who said: * The disciples of Christ were gathered together; * there was a sound like a mighty wind, * and it filled the whole house where they were sitting. * And they began to speak in foreign tongues, * teaching the doctrine of the Holy Trinity. *(2 times)*

The Holy Spirit was, is, and always will be * without beginning and without end, * but always one with the Father and the Son. * He is Life and Giver of Life; * He is Light and Giver of Light, * good by nature and source of goodness. * It is through Him that the Father is known and the Son glorified; * and all people have come to know the one power, and the one substance, * and the same adoration of the Holy Trinity. *(2 times)*

The Holy Spirit is Light and Life, * the Living Spring mystically gushing forth, * the Spirit of Wisdom and Spirit of Knowledge, * good, upright, and understanding, * majestic, and purifying from sin. * He is God and deifies us; * Fire proceeding from fire, * speaking, acting, and distributing gifts. * It is through Him that all the prophets and the apostles of God * have received the crown, together with the martyrs. * A strange report to hear and strange to see: * the fire is divided for the sharing of gifts. *(2 times)*

Tone 6 **Glory be...now and ever:** Heavenly King, Comforter, * Spirit of Truth, * You are everywhere present and fill all things. * Treasury of blessings and Giver of life, * come and dwell within us, * cleanse us of all stain, * and save our souls, O gracious Lord.

Sunday Evening Vespers

LITANY OF PEACE

Deacon: In peace let us pray to the Lord.

R. Lord, have mercy. *(after each petition)*

For peace from on high and for the salvation of our souls, let us pray to the Lord.

For peace in the whole world, the well-being of the holy Churches of God and for the union of all, let us pray to the Lord.

For the people here present who are awaiting the grace of the Holy Spirit, let us pray to the Lord.

For those who bow their knees and hearts before the Lord, let us pray to the Lord.

That the Holy Spirit may strengthen us in the performance of what pleases Him, let us pray to the Lord.

That the Holy Spirit may send down upon us the riches of his mercy, let us pray to the Lord.

That He may accept the bending of our knees as incense before Him, let us pray to the Lord.

For all those who need his help, let us pray to the Lord.

That we be delivered from all affliction, wrath, and need, let us pray to the Lord.

Protect us, save us, and have mercy on us, O God, by your grace.

Remembering our most holy, most pure, most blessed and glorious Lady, the Mother of God and ever-Virgin Mary with all the saints, let us commend ourselves and one another, and our whole life, to Christ our God.

R. To You, O Lord.

Priest: For to You is due all glory, honor, and worship, Father, Son, and Holy Spirit, now and ever and forever.

R. Amen.

AT PSALM 140

Tone 4 All the peoples have seen wonders today * in the city of David, * when the Holy Spirit descended in tongues of fire, * as told by the God-inspired Luke, who said: * The disciples of Christ were gathered together; * there was a sound like a mighty wind, * and it filled the whole house where they were sitting. * And they began to speak in foreign tongues, * teaching the doctrine of the Holy Trinity. *(2 times)*

The Holy Spirit was, is, and always will be * without beginning and without end, * but always one with the Father and the Son. * He is Life and Giver of Life; * He is Light and Giver of Light, * good by nature and source of goodness. * It is through Him that the Father is known and the Son glorified; * and all people have come to know the one power, and the one substance, * and the same adoration of the Holy Trinity. *(2 times)*

The Holy Spirit is Light and Life, * the Living Spring mystically gushing forth, * the Spirit of Wisdom and Spirit of Knowledge, * good, upright, and understanding, * majestic, and purifying from sin. * He is God and deifies us; * Fire proceeding from fire, * speaking, acting, and distributing gifts. * It is through Him that all the prophets and the apostles of God * have received the crown, together with the martyrs. * A strange report to hear and strange to see: * the fire is divided for the sharing of gifts. *(2 times)*

Tone 6 **Glory be...now and ever:** Heavenly King, Comforter, * Spirit of Truth, * You are everywhere present and fill all things. * Treasury of blessings and Giver of life, * come and dwell within us, * cleanse us of all stain, * and save our souls, O gracious Lord.

GREAT PROKEIMENON

Tone 7 What God is great as our God? You are the God who works wonders!

v. You showed your power among the peoples.

v. I said: This is what causes my grief; that the way of the Most High has changed.

v. I remember the deeds of the Lord. I remember your wonders of old.

FIRST KNEELING PRAYER

Priest: Again and again on bended knees let us pray to the Lord.

R. Lord, have mercy.

Priest: O Lord, most pure, incorruptible, without beginning, invisible, incomprehensible, unsearchable, unchangeable, unsurpassable, immeasurable, and forebearing: You alone have immortality; You live in unapproachable light; You made heaven and earth and the sea and all things created in them. You grant to all their requests even before they ask. We pray to You, and we beseech You, O Master who loves all people, the Father of our Lord, God, and Savior, Jesus Christ. For our sake and for the sake of our salvation, He came down from heaven and was incarnate of the Holy Spirit and Mary, the ever-Virgin and the most glorious Godbearer. At first He taught us with words which were then later confirmed through deeds when He endured the saving passion, giving us, your humble, sinful, and unworthy servants, the example of offering supplications to You, with necks bowed and on bended knees, for our sins and for the people's acts done in ignorance.

Hear us on whatever day we call upon You, for You alone are most merciful and the Lover of Humankind! However, especially hear us on this present day of Pentecost on which, after our Lord Jesus Christ had ascended into heaven and was seated at your right hand, O God and Father, He sent down the Holy Spirit upon his holy disciples and apostles. The Holy Spirit came upon each of them, and filling all of them with his inexhaustible grace, they spoke of your grandeur in various tongues, and they prophesied.

Now, therefore, hear us who are praying to You, and remember us, lowly and condemned as we are, and return our souls from the captivity of sin, for we have your loving-kindness interceding for us. Accept us who fall down before You, calling out: We have sinned! To You we have been committed from birth. From our mother's womb, You are our God! But because we have spent our days in vain endeavors, we have been stripped of your help, having been deprived of every defense. But trusting in your generosities, we cry out: Do not remember the sins of our youth and of our ignorance, and cleanse us of our secret sins; and do not reject us when we become elderly, when our strength weakens.

Do not forsake us, and do not return us to the earth before You have made us worthy to return to You, and until You have prepared us, making us acceptable through grace. Appraise our iniquities by your generosities. Against the multitude of our transgressions, place the abyss of your generosities. O Lord, look down from the heights of your holiness upon your people here present who are waiting for abundant mercies from You. Visit us with your goodness. Deliver us from the assaults of the Devil. Organize our life around your holy and sacred commandments. Assign to your people an angel, a faithful guardian. Gather all of us into your kingdom. Grant forgiveness to those who put their trust in You; pardon them and us from sins. Purify us by the operation of your Holy Spirit. Abolish the schemes of the Enemy plotted against us.

Blessed are You, O Lord, Almighty Master, who illuminates the day with the light of the sun and brightens the night with glowing flashes of light, and who has enabled us to pass through the length of the day and to draw near to the beginning of the night. Hear our petitions and those of all your people; and having forgiven all of our voluntary and involuntary sins, accept our evening prayers, and send down the multitude of your mercies and your generosities upon your inheritance. Encompass us with your holy angels. Arm us with the armor of your righteousness. Surround us with your truth. Support us with your power. Deliver us from every assault and from every treacherous plot laid by the Adversary.

And grant to us, through the prayers of the most holy Godbearer and of all the saints who have been well-pleasing to You from the beginning of time, that this present evening and the approaching night and all the days of our lives may be perfect, holy, peaceful, without sin, without temptation, and without idle dreams.

For it is You who shows mercy to us and saves us, O Lord our God, and we render glory to You, Father, Son, and Holy Spirit, now and ever and forever.

R. Amen.

LITANY OF SUPPLICATION

The deacon stands in his usual place and intones the Litany. If there is no deacon, the priest intones the Litany.

Deacon: Let us all say with our whole soul and with our whole mind, let us say.

R. Lord, have mercy.

O Lord Almighty, God of our fathers, we pray You, hear and have mercy.

R. Lord, have mercy.

Have mercy on us, O God, according to your great mercy; we pray You, hear and have mercy.

R. Lord, have mercy. *(3)*

We also pray for our holy ecumenical Pontiff *(name),* the Pope of Rome, and for our most reverend Archbishop and Metropolitan *(name)*, for our God-loving Bishop *(name)*, for those who serve and have served in this holy Church, for our spiritual guides, and for all our brothers and sisters in Christ.

R. Lord, have mercy. *(3)*

We also pray for our civil authorities and for all in the service of our country.

R. Lord, have mercy. *(3)*

We also pray for the people here present who await your great and abundant mercy, for those who showed us mercy, and for all Christians of the true faith.

R. Lord, have mercy. *(3)*

Priest: For You are a merciful and gracious God, and we give glory to You, Father, Son, and Holy Spirit, now and ever and forever.

R. Amen.

SECOND KNEELING PRAYER

Priest: Again and again on bended knees let us pray to the Lord.

R. Lord, have mercy.

Priest: O Lord Jesus Christ, our God, You bestowed your peace upon us and You granted us the gift of the Most Holy Spirit. And, while still yet being present with us in this life, You continue to bestow upon the faithful this inheritance that can never be taken away. On this day, in a vivid manner, You sent down this grace upon your disciples and apostles, confirming their lips with fiery tongues so that, through them, we and the whole human race have received the knowledge of God through our own ears in our own language. We have been enlightened by the light of the Spirit and have been delivered from error, as though from darkness, by the distribution of visible and fiery tongues. Through this mysterious action, we have thereby been taught faith in You; and having been illuminated, we bless You, together with the Father and the Holy Spirit, as one Divinity and Power and Authority.

You are also the Splendor of the Father, the unchangeable and immutable Image of his essence and his nature, and the Source of wisdom and grace. Open my sinful lips and teach me the manner in which and for what needs I should pray. For You know the great multitude of my sins, but their enormity can be vanquished by your loving-kindness. For behold, I stand before You with fear, and I cast the despair of my soul into the depth of your mercy. Guide my life along your ways, for You govern all creation by a word with the ineffable power of your wisdom; show me the way in which I should walk, O tranquil Haven of those who are turbulently perplexed. Grant the Spirit of your wisdom to my deliberations, giving the Spirit of understanding to my ignorance. With the Spirit of your fear, overshadow my deeds and renew a steadfast spirit deeply within me. And with your Sovereign Spirit, stabilize the indecisiveness of my thoughts, in order that being guided every day by your gracious Spirit toward those things that are profitable for me, I may be deemed worthy to fulfill your commandments. Let me be constantly aware of your coming in glory when You will judge our deeds. Protect me from the corrupting pleasures of this world; strengthen me with the desire to strive for the treasures of the world to come.

For You have said, O Master, that whatever anyone asks for in your name, it will be received without hindrance from your Father, the coeternal God. Therefore, on this feast of the descent of your Holy Spirit, I, a sinner, also entreat your goodness so that You would grant me whatever I have asked that is for salvation. Indeed, O Lord, You are the bounteous Giver of all benefits; and You are a gracious provider who gives most abundantly those things for which we ask. You are the Compassionate One and the Merciful One who sinlessly became a partaker of our flesh; and unto those who bend their knees to You, who became the purifier of our sins, You extend your infinite loving-kindness.

O Lord, grant then your generosities to your people. Hear us from your holy heaven. Sanctify us by the power of your saving right hand. Cover us beneath the shelter of your wings, and do not despise the works of your hand. We have transgressed against You alone; against You only have we sinned, but only You do we worship. We do not know how to worship a strange god; neither do we stretch out our hands, O Master, to any other god. Pardon our transgressions and accept our prayers that we offer on bended knees. Extend the hand of your help to all of us. Accept the prayer of all as if it were pleasant incense, acceptable before your most gracious kingdom.

Lord, O Lord, who delivers us from every arrow that flies by day, deliver us from all things that walk in darkness. Accept the lifting up of our hands as an evening sacrifice. Deem us also worthy to pass blamelessly through the course of the night, untempted by evil things; and deliver us from every disturbance and apprehension that comes to us from the Devil. Grant compunction to our souls, and grant that we may meditate upon the trial at your fearsome and righteous judgment. Nail the fear of You to our flesh, and mortify all of our earthy body members so that during the quietness of sleep we may be enlightened with the vision of your judgments. Remove from us also every unseemly dream and detrimental carnal passion. Then raise us up again at the time for prayer, fortified in the faith and advancing in your commandments.

Through the benevolence and the goodness of your only-begotten Son, with whom You are blessed, together with your all-holy, gracious, and life-creating Spirit, now and ever and forever.

R. Amen.

HYMN OF GLORIFICATION

THIRD KNEELING PRAYER

Priest: Again and again on bended knees let us pray to the Lord.

R. Lord, have mercy.

Priest: O ever-flowing, living, and enlightening Source; O creative Power, co-eternal with the Father, who most marvelously fulfilled the entire plan concerning our salvation; O Christ our God, who shattered the indissoluble bonds of Death and the bolts of Hades: You trampled upon a multitude of the evil spirits, offering yourself for us as a blameless Victim and giving your most pure Body, untouched and unapproachable by any sin, as a sacrfice. And, through this awesome and inscrutable sacred sacrifice, You have given us eternal life.

For by descending into Hades and smashing the eternal gates, and having shown the way to heaven to those who were sitting in darkness, You ensnared the Prince of evil and the snake of the Abyss with divinely-wise enticements. And You bound him with the chains of gloom by your immeasurable power, and You shackled him in Tartarus, the deepest infernal region of Hades, and through your might confined him to the unquenchable fire and the eternal darkness. Thus, O greatly-eminent Wisdom of the Father, You manifested yourself as the great Helper of the misfortunate, and You enlightened those who were sitting in darkness and in the shadow of death.

You, O Lord of everlasting glory and beloved Son of the most high Father; O everlasting Light of the everlasting Light; O Sun of righteousness: hear us who are praying to You and grant repose to the souls of your servants, our ancestors, our brothers and sisters who have already departed; to all of our relatives; and to all true members of the Faith, for whom we now make a remembrance. For the authority of all things is with You; and in your hand, You control all the ends of the earth.

O almighty Master, the God of our ancestors and the Lord of mercy; O Creator of the race of mortals and of the immortals, and of all human nature — that which is still presently structured in the body and that which is, likewise, already released therefrom; O Creator of life and of its termination, of that life of being transferred into another world: You measure out the years for the living, and You appoint the time of death. You lead people down into Hades, binding them in impotency, and afterwards You raise them up, releasing them in power. You order present necessities and expediently secure those needed for the future. To those who have been wounded by the sting of death, You make them glad with the hope of resurrection.

You indeed are the Master of all, O God our Savior, the Hope of all those at the ends of the earth and of those far away at sea. On this last and great salvific day of the feast of Holy Pentecost, You showed us the mystery of the Holy Trinity, consubstantial and coeternal, without division or confusion, and You also showed us the descent and arrival of your holy and life-creating Spirit being poured out in the form of fiery tongues on your holy apostles, appointing them to be the proclaimers of the Good News of our faith, and showing them to be confessors and preachers of the true, divine teaching.

Also, on this salvific feast on which everything was totally accomplished, You deigned, therefore, to accept supplications in behalf of those who are imprisoned in Hades; and to those being held in bondage, You promised great hopes for their release from the grievous bonds constraining them by sending down your consolation.

Hear us, your humble servants, beseeching You, and grant repose to the souls of your servants who have already departed into a place of light and a place of refreshment and peace from which all illness, sorrow, and sighing have been taken away. Commit their souls to the places of the just, and make them worthy of peace and of repose. For the dead cannot praise You, O Lord, nor do those in Hades venture to offer confession to You. But we, the living, do bless You, and we do pray and offer You supplications and sacrifices for their souls.

O great and eternal God, who is holy and loves all people; who has deigned us worthy at this hour to stand before your unapproachable glory so that we might sing and praise your wonders; cleanse us, your unworthy servants, and grant us grace in order that with contrite hearts, we may without presumption offer to You the thrice-holy hymn of glorification and thanksgiving for your great gifts that You have created for us and always produce for us.

Remember, O Lord, our weakness, and do not destroy us for our transgressions; but because of our humility, show us your great mercy, in order that fleeing from the darkness of sinfulness, we may walk in the day of righteousness; and having been clothed with the armor of light, remaining unhindered by any spiteful intrigue of the Evil One, we may with confidence extol You in all things as the only true God who loves all.

For yours is indeed the great and veritable mystery, O Master and Author of all — the temporary dissolution of your creatures, and, thereafter, their reintegration and repose for all ages. In all things, we acknowledge your grace: for our entrance into this world and for our leaving it; likewise, for our hopes of resurrection unto an imperishable life, which You pledged by your unfailing promises, that we would receive in the future at your Second-coming. You are the Beginning of our resurrection and the One who loves all people; the impartial Judge of all who have lived, and the Master and Lord of recompense.

You incorporated yourself to us in the very same flesh and blood by your extreme condescension for our sake. Because of your compassionate generosity, You accepted our passions and through them, by voluntarily enduring temptation, You became for us who are tempted the Helper that You yourself promised to become. Therefore, through this action, You have given us the example of controlling our passions.

Accept, then, O Master, our entreaties and supplications, and grant repose to all the fathers, mothers, children, brothers, and sisters of each of us; to our relatives; to all the people in our country; and to all those souls who have already departed in the hope of resurrection and of eternal life.

Inscribe their names in the Book of Life, committing their spirits to the bosom of Abraham, Isaac, and Jacob in the land of the living, in the heavenly kingdom, in the paradise of delights. With your radiant angels, guide all of them into your holy dwelling place. Together with them, also raise up our bodies on the day that You have appointed according to your holy and unfailing vows. Therefore, O Lord, there is no death for your servants when we depart from the body and return to You, our God, passing over from things that are most sorrowful unto things that are most wholesome and delightful, and into repose and joyfulness.

If we have in any least way sinned against You, be merciful to us and also to them, because there is no one who is pure from stain before You, even if his life be for but a single day: You alone, O Jesus Christ our Lord, while on earth manifested yourself to be sinless. Through You, we all trust in obtaining mercy and the remission of sins.

For this reason, because You are a gracious and loving God, pardon, remit, and forgive both us and them for having fallen into sin, both voluntary and through human frailty; those committed willfully or through ignorance; those that are evident and those that are unnoticed; those committed whether in deed, or through thought, or by word, or whether in any of our conversations and emotions.

To all those departed who have preceded us, grant freedom and pardon; and bless us who are still here present, granting to us and to all your people a gracious and joyful end to our lives. Extend to us your mercy and your profound love at your fearsome and dreadful coming in glory, making us worthy of your kingdom.

O great and most high God, You alone have immortality; You live in unapproachable light; You created all things in wisdom, dividing the light from the darkness and placing the sun to rule the day and the moon and the stars to rule the night. You have deemed us sinners worthy on this present day to come before your sight in confession and to offer You our evening prayers. O Lord, who loves all people, let our prayer be directed like incense before You and accept it as a fragrant aroma. Grant that we may spend this present evening and the approaching night in peace. Clothe us with the armor of light; deliver us from the fears of the night and from all things that walk in darkness. And grant that the sleep You have given to refresh us from our fatigue might be free from every evil.

Indeed, O Master of all and gracious Provider, may we be moved to compunction on our beds and remember your most holy name throughout the night; and being illuminated by the contemplation of your commandments, may we rise up with joyfulness of soul to glorify with praise your goodness, offering prayers and supplications to your loving-kindness for our sins as well as for those of all your people whom You, through the prayers of the most holy Godbearer, visit with mercy.

For You are the repose of our souls and bodies, and we render glory to You, Father, Son, and Holy Spirit, now and ever and forever.

R. Amen.

APOSTICHA

Tone 3 Truly the tongues have become a clear sign for all; * for the people, from whom Christ came in the flesh, * were divided by lack of faith. * They fell from the divine grace and divine light * which we the Gentiles have attained. * For we are strengthened by the words of the disciples, * who proclaim the glory of God, the Benefactor of all, * with whom we bend our hearts as well as our knees, * and worship the Holy Spirit in faith, * being strengthened by the Savior of our souls.

A pure heart create for me, O God; put a steadfast spirit within me.

The comforting Spirit has now been poured out on all

flesh, * for beginning with the rank of the apostles, * He extended grace through the communion of believers. * He confirmed the truth of his presence * by the distribution of fiery tongues to the disciples * for the praise and glory of God. * With the spiritual light that enlightens our hearts, * and strengthened in the faith by the Holy Spirit, * let us beseech Him to save our souls.

Do not cast me away from your presence, nor deprive me of your Holy Spirit.

The apostles of Christ have been clothed with power from on high; * for the Comforter has renewed them, * and in them renewed the knowledge of the new mysteries * which they proclaimed to us in songs and resounding words, * teaching us to worship the one God in three persons, * the all-bountiful and eternal One. * Therefore, in the light of their teachings, * let us worship the Father, Son, and Holy Spirit, * beseeching them to save our souls.

Tone 8 **Glory be...now and ever:** Come, all you nations of the world, * let us adore God in three holy persons, * Father, Son, and Holy Spirit — three in one. * From all eternity, the Father begets the Son, * equal to Him in eternity and majesty, * equal also to the Holy Spirit, glorified with the Son in the Father, * three persons, and yet a single power and essence and Godhead. * In deep adoration, let us cry out to God: * Holy is God who made all things through the Son * with the cooperation of the Holy Spirit. * Holy the Mighty One through whom the Father was revealed to us, * and through whom the Holy Spirit came to this world. * Holy the Immortal One, the Spirit and Comforter * who proceeds from the Father and reposes in the Son. * All-holy Trinity, glory to You!

TROPARION

Tone 8 Blessed are You, O Christ our God. * You filled the fishermen with wisdom, * sending down upon them the Holy Spirit. * Through them You have caught the whole world in your net. * O Lover of Mankind, glory be to You!

(1 time)

DISMISSAL FOR PENTECOST EVENING VESPERS

(see Appendix, page 455)

Monday Matins

SESSIONAL HYMN I

Tone 4 Come, O faithful, let us celebrate the feast of the Fiftieth Day: * the day which concludes the Feast of feasts; * the day on which the pre-ordained promise is fulfilled; * the day when the Comforter descends upon the earth in tongues of fire; * the day of the disciples' enlightenment. * They are revealed as initiated into the heavenly mysteries, * for truly the light of the Comforter has illumined the world.

Glory be...now and ever: *(Repeat the above)*

SESSIONAL HYMN II

Tone 4 The fountain of the Spirit rushes down to earth, * mystically divided into flaming streams, * both refreshing and enlightening the apostles; * the fire became for them a cloud of dew, * raining enlightenment upon them. * From them we have received grace by fire and water, * for truly the light of the Comforter has illumined the world.

Glory be...now and ever: *(Repeat the above)*

CANON

(From the Feast)

AFTER ODE 3

SESSIONAL HYMN

Tone 8 The most Holy Spirit who has descended today * upon the apostles in the form of fire, * fills the assembly of the nations with astonishment. * For as they spoke with their tongues afire, * each person heard the language of his own country. * To the unbelievers, this miracle seemed like drunkenness, * but to the faithful this was a sign of their salvation. * Therefore, we glorify your power, O Christ our God, * and we your servants beseech You: * Grant us the abundance of forgiveness for our sins.

Glory be...now and ever: *(Repeat the above)*

HYMN OF LIGHT

Tone 3 O most Holy Spirit, who proceeds from the Father through the Son, * and who has now descended upon the uneducated disciples, * save and sanctify all those who recognize You as God. *(2 times)*

Glory be...now and ever: The Father is light and the Word is light, * the Holy Spirit also is light! * He is sent upon the apostles in the form of tongues of fire, * and through Him the whole world receives the light of baptism * to adore the Holy Trinity.

AT THE PRAISES

Tone 2 You have shown us, O Savior, * the way to salvation through the prophets; * and the grace of your Holy Spirit * has shone upon us through the apostles. * You are God from all eternity, * our God, now and forever. *(2 times)*

O Savior of the world, * I sing a hymn of praise to You in your temple; * on my knees, I adore your invisible power, * at dawn and dusk and at noon; * indeed, at all times, I bless You, O Lord.

We your faithful people, O Lord, * prostrate our souls and bodies before You. * We sing a hymn of praise to You, the eternal Father; * and to your Son, equal to You in eternity; * and to your all-holy Spirit, coeternal with You, * the Enlightener and Sanctifier of our souls.

Tone 8 **Glory be...now and ever:** In the days of old, pride brought confusion of tongues * to the builders of the Tower of Babel, * but now the diversity of tongues enlightened the minds * and gave knowledge for the glory of God. * Then, God punished the impious for their sin; * now, Christ enlightened fishermen through his Spirit. * Then, the confusion of tongues was for the sake of punishment; * now, there was variety so that voices could be joined in harmony * for the salvation of our souls.

Monday Evening Vespers

AT PSALM 140

Tone 1 Now the tongues of fire begin a new way of speech; * now God's mighty works are revealed, * that all on earth may believe. * This is truly the sign * that salvation has come to all peoples.

You have sent power to your disciples from on high, O Christ. * You have sent the Holy Spirit, and all things are fulfilled. * You have revealed yourself to us as the Truth. * Those who hope in You, O Good One, * shall never be confounded.

You have fulfilled your promise. * You have sent your Comforter to the world in fiery tongues. * With holy fire He melts the sins of all. * He dwells within all of us who seek Him in purity of heart.

Three Stichera from the Saint of the day

Tone 1 **Glory be...now and ever:** Behold, we celebrate today the feast of Pentecost, * the descent of the Holy Spirit, * the fulfillment of the promise and the realization of hope. * How wonderful and awesome is this great mystery! * Therefore, O Lord and Creator of all, * we cry out: Glory to You!

APOSTICHA

Tone 2 By a mighty work, O Lord, * You have kept your promise, * sending to your disciples * your divine and Holy Spirit to enlighten them.

A pure heart create for me, O God; put a steadfast spirit within me.

Suddenly from heaven * the wisdom and power of the holy Comforter * revealed all the apostles to be wise theologians.

Do not cast me away from your presence, nor deprive me of your Holy Spirit.

The children of foreigners listened with amazement; * each heard the apostles speaking his own language. * Now all nations glorify the Trinity.

Tone 1 **Glory be...now and ever:** You renewed your disciples, O Christ, * by giving them a variety of tongues * with which to proclaim that You are the immortal God, * the Word who bestows great mercy upon our souls.

TROPARIA

Of the Saint

Tone 8 **Glory be...now and ever:** Blessed are You, O Christ our God. * You filled the fishermen with wisdom, * sending down upon them the Holy Spirit. * Through them You have caught the whole world in your net. * O Lover of Mankind, glory be to You!

Tuesday Matins

SESSIONAL HYMN I

Tone 1 I praise and glorify the Holy Spirit; * I venerate Him with the Father and the Son. * He has filled the apostles of Christ with wisdom, * enlightening them to proclaim throughout all the world * one Godhead divided in three persons.

Glory be...now and ever: *(Repeat the above)*

SESSIONAL HYMN II

Tone 1 The grace of the Spirit has enlightened the apostles of Christ; * He has fearfully come down from heaven and set them on fire. * He has revealed them as stars and heralds of the Trinity, * one power and one lordship, * whom we glorify in faith.

Glory be...now and ever: *(Repeat the above)*

CANON

HYMN OF LIGHT

Tone 3 O most Holy Spirit, who proceeds from the Father through the Son, * and who has now descended upon the uneducated disciples, * save and sanctify all those who recognize You as God. *(2 times)*

Glory be...now and ever: The Father is light and the Word is light; * the Holy Spirit also is light! * He is sent upon the apostles in the form of tongues of fire, * and through Him the whole world receives the light of baptism * to adore the Holy Trinity.

APOSTICHA

Tone 2 Your apostles, O Word, * received the very essence of the Holy Spirit. * He enlightens the mind with royal splendor.

A pure heart create for me, O God; put a steadfast spirit within me.

The tongues as of fire appeared from on high, * dividing and descending upon the apostles, * to enlighten without consuming them.

Do not cast me away from your presence, nor deprive me of your Holy Spirit.

Come down to us from on high, O gracious Comforter, *

as You came to the apostles, * to sanctify and to save * those who confess You as God.

Tone 1 **Glory be...now and ever:** The Holy Spirit provides every gift: * He inspires prophecy and perfects the priesthood; * He grants wisdom to the illiterate, * makes simple fishermen become wise theologians, * and establishes perfect order in the assembly of the Church. * Therefore, O Comforter, * equal in nature and majesty with the Father and the Son, * O Lord, glory to You!

Tuesday Evening Vespers

AT PSALM 140

Tone 1 As You, with the Son and the Spirit, * adorned the heavens with fiery lights to shine on the earth, * so now You have confirmed your household with heavenly speech; * through tongues of fire your glory is proclaimed to all the earth.

When the disciples of Christ had assembled in Zion, * the all-holy Spirit appeared as fire; * He came to rest on them, fulfilling the promise. * They were enlightened by the fiery breath * and learned the mystery of the Trinity.

The Holy Spirit has come, perfecting God's plan; * the Creator renews the creature. * He is a sword of heavenly steel, * by which the disciples crush all wicked powers. * They have vanquished the sword of the Evil One, * for the salvation of our souls.

Three Stichera from the Saint of the day

Tone 2 **Glory be...now and ever:** We have seen the true light; * we have received the heavenly Spirit; * we have found the true faith; * and we worship the undivided Trinity; * for the Trinity has saved us.

APOSTICHA

Tone 4 Today the power of your Holy Spirit * has enlightened your apostles, O Lord; * You have made them wise in divine knowledge; * You have filled them with your blessed teachings. * Therefore, we glorify your saving plan, * O almighty Jesus, the Savior of our souls.

A pure heart create for me, O God; put a steadfast spirit within me.

Today your Spirit, equal in essence to You, * is sent forth from the Father, O all-powerful Master. * He is distributed in fiery tongues; * He enables your apostles to declare your wonders. * Therefore, we glorify your saving plan, * O almighty Jesus, the Savior of our souls.

Do not cast me away from your presence, nor deprive me of your Holy Spirit.

Today You have poured out the grace of your comforting Spirit, O Savior; * You have enabled mortal nature to proclaim You as You are, O Word; * You have instructed us to worship the undivided Trinity. * Therefore, we glorify your saving plan, * O almighty Jesus, the Savior of our souls.

Tone 2 **Glory be...now and ever:** You have shown us, O Savior, * the way to salvation through the prophets; * and the grace of your Holy Spirit * has shone upon us through the apostles. * You are God from all eternity, * our God, now and forever.

TROPARIA

Of the Saint

Tone 8 **Glory be:...now and ever:** Blessed are You, O Christ our God. * You filled the fishermen with wisdom, * sending down upon them the Holy Spirit. * Through them You have caught the whole world in your net. * O Lover of Mankind, glory be to You!

Wednesday Matins

SESSIONAL HYMN I

Tone 4 When the Holy Spirit came willingly to your apostles, O Christ, * He opened their mouths to speak * and united diverse languages of different people * into a harmonious confession of faith * in the uncreated Trinity. * We beg You, O good Lover of Mankind: * May He come to dwell in us as well.

Glory be...now and ever: *(Repeat the above)*

SESSIONAL HYMN II

Tone 8 The most Holy Spirit who has descended today * upon the apostles in the form of fire, * fills the assembly of the nations with astonishment. * For as they spoke with their tongues afire, * each person heard the language of his own country. * To the unbelievers, this miracle seemed like drunkenness, * but to the faithful this was a sign of their salvation. * Therefore, we glorify your power, O Christ our God, * and we your servants beseech You: * Grant us the abundance of forgiveness for our sins.

Glory be...now and ever: *(Repeat the above)*

CANON

HYMN OF LIGHT

Tone 3 O most Holy Spirit, who proceeds from the Father through the Son, * and who has now descended upon the uneducated disciples, * save and sanctify all those who recognize You as God. *(2 times)*

Glory be...now and ever: The Father is light and the Word is light; * the Holy Spirit also is light! * He is sent upon the apostles in the form of tongues of fire, * and through Him the whole world receives the light of baptism * to adore the Holy Trinity.

APOSTICHA

Tone 6 The all-holy Spirit has come on earth in tongues of fire. * He is the Light proceeding from the Light without beginning. * He consumes the sins of those * who faithfully worship three Persons in one Godhead.

A pure heart create for me, O God; put a steadfast spirit within me.

Renew us through your all-holy Spirit, O God, * the same Spirit You sent to your apostles of old. * Strengthen your inheritance again, we beg You, * that your saving will may be accomplished in the world.

Do not cast me away from your presence, nor deprive me of your Holy Spirit.

We profess our faith in the Holy Spirit. * We cry out: Do not forsake us, O Comforter! * Grant salvation to all. * Sanctify us who sing to You.

Tone 2 **Glory be...now and ever:** O Savior of the world, * I sing a hymn of praise to You in your temple; * on my knees, I adore your invisible power, * at dawn and dusk and at noon; * indeed, at all times, I bless You, O Lord.

Wednesday Evening Vespers

AT PSALM 140

Tone 1 Moses saw the One-Who-Is on the fiery mountain; * but now the Spirit has come down upon the wise apostles. * They also see God in the form of fire; * this clearly proves that in both covenants the same God speaks * through identical operations of his nature.

The divine preachers destroyed the babbling of the godless orators, * consuming their vanity by the fire of the Spirit. * He came down to baptize them with fiery tongues. * Through them we have been enlightened in the saving waters, * and in faith we confess that the Comforter is God.

Long ago You created your flaming bodiless angels, * filling them with the fire of the Spirit; * but now You have wondrously communed with material creatures. * They offer worship to You through creation, O my God, * and they sing: Wonderful are your works, O Lover of Mankind.

Three Stichera from the Saint of the day

Tone 2 **Glory be...now and ever:** We your faithful people, O Lord, * prostrate our souls and bodies before You. * We sing a hymn of praise to You, the eternal Father; * and to your Son, equal to You in eternity; * and to your all-holy Spirit, coeternal with You, * the Enlightener and Sanctifier of our souls.

APOSTICHA

Tone 4 O Holy Spirit, with the Father and the Word, * You are equal in power, majesty, and dominion. * Co-creating, ever-existing, all-good, and ruling all things, * You have filled the disciples of the Word with wisdom. * In a multitude of languages * they proclaim God's mighty works to the nations, * together with the teachings of the Trinity.

A pure heart create for me, O God; put a steadfast spirit within me.

The assembly of nations was made fruitful in the Spirit, * but the unbelievers were darkened by the drunkenness of ignorance. * When they witnessed the miracle of tongues, * they said that your disciples were drunk. * They were deceived by a worse drunkenness, * while we, who have received the saving knowledge of You through your elect, * proclaim your wonders, O our God.

Do not cast me away from your presence, nor deprive me of your Holy Spirit.

The eternal fountain, forever flowing, * the river streaming with the living waters of unutterable goodness, * dividing, as is his nature, into channels of grace, * has watered my soul. * He will deliver me from the flaming furnace of passions, * from fearful temptations, * and from the fires of damnation.

Tone 2 **Glory be...now and ever:** Let us sing a hymn of praise to the consubstantial Trinity, * Father, Son, and Holy Spirit; * for this is the command and teaching * of all prophets, apostles, and martyrs.

TROPARIA

Of the Saint

Tone 8 **Glory be...now and ever:** Blessed are You, O Christ our God. * You filled the fishermen with wisdom, * sending down upon them the Holy Spirit. * Through them You have caught the whole world in your net. * O Lover of Mankind, glory be to You!

Thursday Matins

SESSIONAL HYMN I

Tone 1 Behold, the oracles of the prophets are fulfilled! * He who disclosed himself dimly to them * now plainly reveals himself as God the Paraclete! * He is fully poured out upon the apostles. * Through them the faithful have come to worship * the uncreated Trinity.

Glory be...now and ever: *(Repeat the above)*

SESSIONAL HYMN II

Tone 5 You have filled your apostles with the light of the Spirit, O Savior; * He has made them as the sun at dawn, * for they have burned the fog of error from the face of the earth. * They have illumined the souls of the faithful, * teaching them to adore your Father and the most-holy Spirit, * who sanctifies those who worship You.

Glory be...now and ever: *(Repeat the above)*

CANON

HYMN OF LIGHT

Tone 3 O most Holy Spirit, who proceeds from the Father through the Son, * and who has now descended upon the uneducated disciples, * save and sanctify all those who recognize You as God. *(2 times)*

Glory be...now and ever: The Father is light and the Word is light; * the Holy Spirit also is light! * He is sent upon the apostles in the form of tongues of fire, * and through Him the whole world receives the light of baptism * to adore the Holy Trinity.

APOSTICHA

Tone 4 The descent of the Spirit enlightens the apostles. * Tongues of fire settled on each of them. * He revealed them as preachers of truth; * they proclaimed the Trinity to all, * the Godhead united in essence. * Therefore, all the peoples were amazed, seeing unlettered fishermen * proclaim clearly the unutterable mysteries.

A pure heart create for me, O God; put a steadfast spirit within me.

As the apostles sat in the upper room, * a mighty wind shook the house. * The apostles received the power of the Holy Spirit. * Tongues of fire settled on each of them. * They addressed the people, clearly proclaiming new teachings to them. * They verified the grace-filled news: * Christ, who had voluntarily suffered, is truly God!

Do not cast me away from your presence, nor deprive me of your Holy Spirit.

Just as You sent your Holy Spirit to your apostles, O Lord, * send down divine grace upon us today, we beseech You. * Enlighten our hearts with the unfading light of his coming, * that we may all send up fitting praise to You, * singing the thrice-holy hymn with ceaseless voices * to the Trinity, one in essence and undivided.

Tone 2 **Glory be...now and ever:** You have shown us, O Savior, * the way to salvation through the prophets; * and the grace of your Holy Spirit * has shone upon us through the apostles. * You are God from all eternity, * our God, now and forever.

Thursday Evening Vespers

AT PSALM 140

Tone 4 The Holy Spirit, the Giver of grace * has come down upon the earth, * not as in the days of old, * through the shadow of the Law or the dawn of the prophets; * but now He has been given to us in person, * through the mediation of Christ. * Let us cleanse our hearts by the practice of virtue * that we may receive his illumination, * for He enlightens us in a holy mystery.

Do not take the Holy Spirit from us, O Lover of Mankind, * but make us worthy to receive your grace. * May we be citizens of your kingdom in mind and heart. * Bestow your eternal communion upon your inheritance. * Make us temples and abodes of the heavenly Comforter, * O Jesus our God and the Savior of our souls.

Let us sing fervently to the Holy Spirit; * He is the sanctification of all. * Let us cry to Him in faith: * You came into the world by the good will of the Father; * do not depart from us. * We worship your divinity. * Show us to be temples of your wondrous goodness. * Sanctify all who sing to You in faith.

Three Stichera from the Saint of the day

Tone 7 **Glory be...now and ever:** Having received the Paraclete from the Father, * the Comforter, the Spirit of Truth, * who has come to dwell on earth today, * let us in faith worship Christ our God.

APOSTICHA

Tone 1 The Holy Spirit proceeds from the Father; * He is worshiped in the Son. * He brings strength and sustains the life of all; * He lives forever, saving those who sing to Him: * O holy Comforter, hasten to bring peace to the world.

A pure heart create for me, O God; put a steadfast spirit within me.

The Holy Spirit, the fountain of all goodness, * truly has been poured out to the ends of the earth, * bestowing heavenly grace upon the apostles, * filling them with divine goodness. * Therefore, let us cry out to Him: * O holy Comforter, hasten to bring peace to the world.

Do not cast me away from your presence, nor deprive me of your Holy Spirit.

God the Holy Spirit has been revealed to us. * He is of the same essence and majesty with the Father and the Word. * He is the all-perfect Light, * shining from the exalted Father who has no beginning. * He proceeds to earth through the Son. * Therefore, let us cry out to Him: * O holy Comforter, hasten to bring peace to the world.

Tone 8 **Glory be...now and ever:** O Lord, when You sent down your Spirit * upon the assembled apostles, * the children of Israel were struck with awe * as they heard them speak in many tongues, * inspired by the Holy Spirit. * They knew them to be illiterate and now saw them wise, * speaking divine truths and bringing Gentiles to the faith. * Therefore, we also cry out to You: * You have appeared on earth and saved us from error; * O Lord, glory to You!

TROPARIA

Of the Saint

Tone 8 **Glory be...now and ever:** Blessed are You, O Christ our God. * You filled the fishermen with wisdom, * sending down upon them the Holy Spirit. * Through them You have caught the whole world in your net. * O Lover of Mankind, glory be to You!

Friday Matins

SESSIONAL HYMN I

Tone 8 After rising from the dead and ascending into heaven, * You sent down your glory upon your disciples. * You renewed in the Spirit those who had seen You as God in the flesh. * They became musical instruments, echoing clearly for all * the melody of the saving Gospel You proclaimed.

Glory be...now and ever: *(Repeat the above)*

SESSIONAL HYMN II

Tone 8 Your beloved ones were filled with your joy, O Savior; * they who once had been fearful, receive courage; * for today, when the Holy Spirit descended from heaven, * one spoke in one language to the people, and one in another. * Tongues having the appearance of fire, * divided and rested on the disciples' heads, * not burning them, but accomplishing another of God's mighty wonders!

Glory be...now and ever: *(Repeat the above)*

CANON

HYMN OF LIGHT

Tone 3 O most Holy Spirit, who proceeds from the Father through the Son, * and who has now descended upon the uneducated disciples, * save and sanctify all those who recognize You as God. *(2 times)*

Glory be...now and ever: The Father is light and the Word is light, * the Holy Spirit also is light! * He is sent upon the apostles in the form of tongues of fire, * and through Him the whole world receives the light of baptism * to adore the Holy Trinity.

APOSTICHA

Tone 1 Elijah, filled with zeal in days of old, * was carried to glory in a chariot of fire. * Now the apostles are enlightened in Zion * by the breath of God on high. * Through this, the universe is illumined.

A pure heart create for me, O God; put a steadfast spirit within me.

Through the tongues of fire, * the apostles became participants in Christ's divine plan. * They enlightened all nations * to faithfully worship one God in three Persons: * Father, Son, and Holy Spirit.

Do not cast me away from your presence, nor deprive me of your Holy Spirit.

O Zion, holy mother of all Churches, * in you the comforting Spirit, in the form of fire, * fearfully descended upon the apostles. * Rejoice, celebrating with us the feast of Pentecost, * the day long-awaited by the universe.

Tone 6 **Glory be...now and ever:** Heavenly King, Comforter, * Spirit of Truth, * You are everywhere present and fill all things. * Treasury of blessings and Giver of life, * come and dwell within us, * cleanse us of all stain, * and save our souls, O gracious Lord.

Friday Evening Vespers

Final day of the Feast of Pentecost

(The text for Vespers is taken from the feastday.)

Saturday Matins

Final day of the Feast of Pentecost

(The text for Matins is taken from the feastday.)

Sunday of All Saints

Vespers

AT PSALM 140

Tone 8 O Christ, during this spiritual service * we sing to You these evening prayers, * commemorating the mercy You have shown us * by your Resurrection.

O Lord, O Lord, do not cast us away from your face; * but in your kindness have mercy on us * through your Resurrection.

Rejoice, O holy Zion, * the Mother of Churches and the dwelling place of God; * for you were the first to receive the forgiveness of sins * through the Resurrection.

Christ the Word was begotten by God the Father before all ages; * yet in these latter times, * He freely willed to take flesh from the Virgin who did not know man. * By his death on the Cross and his Resurrection, * He saved the human race from the ancient curse of death.

O Christ, we glorify your Resurrection; * for by rising from the dead * You freed the race of Adam from the sufferings of Hades, * and as God you granted eternal life * and great mercy to the world.

Glory to You, O Christ our Savior, * the only-begotten Son of God; * for You were nailed to the Cross * and then arose from the dead on the third day.

Tone 6 Through faithfulness the disciples of the Lord * became instruments of the Spirit * and were scattered to the ends of the earth * to proclaim his sacred word and the doctrine of truth. * From these roots, an army of martyrs blossomed forth * by the grace of the Divine Gardener. * By their numberless torments and by fire, * they imitated the holy passion of Christ, * and now they intercede for our souls.

Inflamed by the love of the Lord, * the venerable martyrs of Christ despised the fire; * and being consumed as living coals, * they burned the dried grass of the arrogance of error; * they bridled the mouths of the beasts by their prayers; * and by their beheading, they severed the hosts of the enemy. * Having courageously shed their blood, * they watered the Church with the seed of their faith.

Truly the heroic martyrs have wrestled with beasts * and were torn apart by their claws; * they fell under the edge of the sword * and were mutilated and tortured; * they were thrown into fire and burned alive, * dismembered and pierced with swords. * All this they bore courageously, * seeing in advance what was to come: * the unfading crowns and the glory of Christ. * And now they intercede for our souls.

Let us celebrate with songs of praise * the deeds of the holy people over all the earth, * honoring them, as it is fitting: * the Apostles and Martyrs, * the Bishops and Holy Women. * While living on earth, they joined with the heavenly spirits, * and by the grace of Christ, * they received immortality through their sufferings. * They shine as bright stars for us, * and now they intercede for our souls.

Tone 6 **Glory be:** You are pillars of the Church * and the fulfillment of the Gospel, * O divine ranks of Martyrs. * By your deeds you have fulfilled the words of the Savior; * for through you the gates of Hades, * once opened against the Church, have now been closed; * and through the shedding of your blood * you dried up the sacrifices poured out for the idols. * And having built up the faith of believers through your martyrdom, * you filled the heavenly spirits with admiration. * You stand before Christ, wearing your crowns; * intercede with Him for our souls.

Tone 8 **Now and ever:** In his love for the human race, * the King of heaven appeared on earth and dwelt among us. * For He took flesh from the pure Virgin, * and, being thus incarnate, He came forth from her. * The only Son of God remained one person, * but He now possessed two natures. * For this reason, we profess that He is truly perfect God and perfect man. * Therefore, we beseech you, O Virgin Mother; * implore Christ, whom we proclaim as God, * to have mercy on our souls.

READINGS

Isaiah 43: 9-14
Wisdom 3: 1-9
Wisdom 5: 15 through 6:3

AT THE LITIJA

Tone 1 With unity of faith, * let us celebrate a solemn feast of all those * who from the ages have found grace before God. * Let us remember all the Saints: * the Patriarchs, Prophets, and Apostles of Christ, * the Martyrs, and the Ascetics of all ages; * they intercede unceasingly for the peace of the world * and for the salvation of our souls.

Come, O faithful, let us celebrate, * with psalms and hymns and spiritual songs, * the glorious memory of all the Saints: * the Baptist of the Lord, the Apostles and Prophets, * the Martyrs, the Bishops, and the Doctors of the Church, * the Blessed ones, the Ascetics, and all the Just, * together with all the Holy Women. * Let us venerate their blessed memory, * and together, let us all sing: * O Christ our God and Supreme Goodness, * through their prayers grant peace to your Church, * victory over the Enemy, * and salvation for our souls.

Come, let us celebrate the memory of the Saints, * in the joy of the Holy Spirit; * for the day of their feast has arrived, * filling us with divine gifts. * With purified conscience, let us cry out with joy * and let us sing in their honor: * Rejoice, O choir of Prophets who announce the coming of Christ, * and who clearly see that which is far away. * Rejoice, O Apostles of the Lord, * fishermen who gather the whole world in your nets. * Rejoice, O company of Martyrs, * gathered from all the world in the same profession of faith; * for this you suffered punishments and tortures * before receiving the crown of victory. * Rejoice, O multitude of Holy Fathers; * by your ascetic effort you subdued the body * and put to death the passions of the flesh. * You have been carried in spirit, on the wings of divine love, to heaven * where you enjoy the eternal blessings * with the angels whose joy you share. * Therefore, O Apostles, Prophets, and Martyrs, * together with the Ascetics, * intercede with the One who crowned you in heaven, * and pray unceasingly to Him * that He may deliver from the Enemy * all those who, with faith and love, * celebrate your holy memory.

Tone 5 **Glory be:** O faithful, today let us hasten to the feast * for a spiritual banquet has been prepared; * the mystical cup has been filled with the food of joy. * It is the virtue of the Martyrs from throughout the world * who offered themselves valiantly to God * through the torments they suffered in their bodies; * and as a spiritual sacrifice, * they offered the flower of their youthful years: * their heads were cut off, and their hands were severed, * their members were mutilated and wrenched apart. * And together, all these holy ones * shared in the sufferings of Christ. * But in exchange for their miseries, * You have given them crowns in heaven, O Lord; * and now in your love for us, * grant that we may imitate their virtues.

Tone 5 **Now and ever:** O most pure Virgin, * you are the temple, the gate, the palace, and the throne of the King. * Christ, our Redeemer and Lord, * appeared through you to those who slumbered in darkness. * For He, as the Sun of Righteousness, * wished to enlighten those whom He created with his own hands * according to his own image. * Therefore, O Lady, whom we always praise in song, * we beseech you to intercede with Christ for the salvation of our souls; * for, as his mother, you can approach Him with the greatest confidence.

APOSTICHA

Tone 8 O Jesus, You descended from heaven * so that You might ascend the Cross. * O immortal Life, You came to die. * You are the true light to those who live in darkness, * and You are the resurrection of the fallen. * Therefore, O Savior of all, we glorify You.

The Lord reigns, He is clothed in majesty. Robed is the Lord, and girt about with strength.

Let us glorify Christ, the Savior of our souls * who arose from the dead. * For He took upon himself a soul and a body, * and during his passion He separated the one from the other. * His pure soul went down to conquer Hades * while his holy body lay uncorrupted in the grave.

For He has made the world firm, which shall not be moved.

O Christ, we glorify your Resurrection with psalms and hymns. * For by your victory over Death * You delivered us from the sufferings of Hades, * and as God You granted us eternal life and great mercy.

Holiness befits your house, O Lord, for length of days.

O Lord of all, Creator of heaven and earth, * You are above all understanding. * Through your passion on the Cross * You freed us from the sufferings of Hades. * And, after condescending to be buried, * You arose in glory; * and with your mighty arm You also raised up Adam. * O most merciful Lord, we glorify You, * for by your Resurrection on the third day * You granted us remission of sins and eternal life.

Tone 6 **Glory be:** Come, O faithful, let us exalt with joy: * let us celebrate in faith on this day * the feast of all the Saints; * and let us venerate their glorious memory, saying: * Rejoice, Apostles, Prophets, and Martyrs, * O Bishops, O Just and Blessed Ones, * together with the ranks of the Holy Women. * Intercede with Christ for us, * that He may grant peace to the world * and great mercy to our souls.

Tone 6 **Now and ever:** Christ the Lord, our Creator and Redeemer, * came forth from your womb, O most pure Virgin. * He clothed himself in our human flesh * to set us free from the original curse of Adam. * Therefore, O Mary, we praise you, without ceasing, * as the true Virgin Mother of God, * and we sing with the angels: * Rejoice, O Lady, advocate, protector, and salvation of our souls.

TROPARIA

Tone 8 You descended from on high, O merciful Lord. * You accepted the grave for three days * to deliver us from our passions. * O Lord, our Resurrection and our Life, glory be to You!

Tone 4 **Glory be:** Your Church throughout the world, O Lord, * is clothed with the blood of your martyrs * as with fine linens and purple robes; * and so the Church cries out to You, O Christ our God: * Send down your goodness upon your people; * grant peace to your Church and great mercy to our souls.

Tone 4 **Now and ever:** O Mother of God, the mystery hidden from all eternity * and unknown even to the angels, * was revealed through you to those on earth: * God took on our human nature * and united it to his divine nature in a perfect but unconfused union. * Then, He willingly accepted the Cross for our sake * and thereby raised again the first created man, * and saved our souls from death.

Sunday Matins

SESSIONAL HYMN I

Tone 8 You have risen from the dead, O Life of all, * and a resplendent angel said to the women: * Dry your tears and proclaim the good news to the apostles, * and cry out in praise that Christ the Lord is risen, * and as God, He was pleased to save the human race

Arise then, Lord, lift up your hand. O God, do not forget the poor!

Mortals have sealed your tomb, * O Savior, * but angels rolled the stone away from your grave; * and the women witnessed your Resurrection from the dead. * They proclaimed to your disciples in Zion * that You arose and broke asunder the bonds of death, O Life of all. * O Lord, glory to You!

Glory be...now and ever: You were born of the Virgin and for us You endured the Cross; * by your death You conquered Death and You revealed the Resurrection to us. * Do not disdain those whom You have formed with your own hand; * but show us your love, O God of tenderness. * Hear the prayer of the one who gave You birth, O Savior, * and save the people who hope in You.

SESSIONAL HYMN II

Tone 8 Clothed in a brilliant garment and shining brightly as light, * Gabriel came to the tomb of Christ and rolled back the stone. * A great fear seized the soldiers, and the guards seemed as dead; * for the seals of the tomb no longer had meaning. * The impious ones were put to shame, * for they knew that Christ had risen.

I will praise You, Lord, with all my heart; I will recount all your wonders.

You truly rose from the tomb, * and, as it is written, You commanded the holy women * to preach the Resurrection to the apostles. * As for Peter, he hastened to the tomb; * and when he saw the light in the grave he was seized with fear. * Then he saw the linen cloth lying there without the body. * He believed and cried out: Glory to You, O Christ our God; * for You have saved us all, O our Savior, * who yet remains in truth the radiance of the Father.

Glory be...now and ever: In you, O Woman full of grace, * the angelic choirs and the human race, all creation rejoices. * O sanctified Temple, mystical Paradise, and glory of virgins, * He, who is our God from before all ages, * took flesh from you and became a child. * He made your womb a throne and greater than the heavens. * In you, O Woman full of grace, all creation rejoices. * Glory be to you!

HYPAKOE

The myrrh-bearing women came to the tomb of the Giver

of life, * seeking among the dead the Lord who is deathless. * When they received the good news from the angels, * they preached to the apostles that the Lord is risen, * granting great mercy to the world.

GRADUAL HYMNS

Antiphon I

From my youth the Enemy has tempted me, * and he has consumed me with a love for pleasure. * But I place my hope in You, O Savior, * that I may obtain the victory over him.

The enemies of Zion * shall be like grass which is uprooted; * for Christ shall destroy them with the sword of suffering.

Glory be...now and ever: Truly in the Holy Spirit all shall live, * for He is the Light of Light and a great God. * Let us, therefore, praise Him * with the Father and the Word.

Antiphon II

O all-compassionate One, * let my heart be humbled in fear of You, * and may it never fall into pride.

Those who trust in the Lord * shall not fear when God shall come again * to judge all with tormenting fire.

Glory be...now and ever: By the Holy Spirit * every holy person shall prophesy and perform heavenly wonders. * They shall sing to the one God in three persons; * the Godhead, although one, shines with a triple flame.

Antiphon III

I have cried to You, O Lord. * Listen and turn your ear towards me when I cry out. * Purify me before You take me from the earth.

Truly all shall return and disappear in their mother, the earth, * to receive either honors or punishments * as reward for what they have done in their lifetime.

Glory be...now and ever: Through the Holy Spirit is made known to us * the one God who is thrice-holy: * the eternal Father, and the Son before all ages, * and the consubstantial Spirit who proceeds from the Father.

PROKEIMENON

Tone 8 The Lord will reign forever, Zion's God, from age to age.

v. My soul, give praise to the Lord! I will praise the Lord all my days.

GOSPEL

Matthew 28: 16-20

CANON

ODE 1

Tone 8 Pharaoh was drowned at the head of his chariots * when, of old, Moses struck the sea with his staff in the form of a cross * and split it in two; * but it saved Israel who was able to flee as if on dry land, * as they sang a hymn to the Lord.

Refrain: **Glory to your holy Resurrection, O Lord!**

How can we not admire the all-powerful divinity of Christ, * who by his passion has poured out on all of us, * the holy and eternal life, * without undergoing change or corruption; * for this life flows from his side and springs forth from the life-giving grave.

With what majesty has the angel appeared to the women now! * Bearing brilliant signs of his bodiless purity, * and by the brightness of his face announcing the radiance of the Resurrection, he cries out: * The Lord is risen!

Refrain: **Most holy Mother of God, save us!**

From age to age, all have called you glorious, O Mary, Mother of God; * for in your womb you welcomed the Word of God while remaining a virgin. * And after God, you are our only support; * for this reason we sing to you with all our heart.

Refrain: **Glory to your holy Resurrection, O Lord!**

The doors of affliction have become attentive, * and the jail-keepers of Hades have trembled * when they saw descending into their depths * the One who transcends the nature of all.

The angels were astonished to see, sitting on the throne of the Father, * the human nature which had fallen * and was enclosed in the darkest depths.

Refrain: **Most holy Mother of God, save us!**

We praise you, O holy Mother of God, * for in a marvelous manner you have given birth to the eternal and divine Word * who has taken flesh in your womb.

The Virgin has given birth to You, O Christ, * yet You are the life-bearing vine, * distilling the sweetness of salvation for the world.

***Refrain:* All you Saints, pray to God for us!**

Praising the multitude of the saints, * by their prayers, I beseech You to enlighten my spirit with your light; * for You are the inaccessible brightness who dispels the darkness of error by your rays, * O Word of God and Giver of Light.

Exalted on the tree of the Cross, O Lord, * You led the heritage of the nations to your name; * You beamed with the brilliance of the Holy Trinity * and banished error far from us, * by the ministry of your apostles, O Savior.

Obeying your command, O Lord, * your holy apostles have wisely left all the things of this life; * they have made the world resplendent with the light of your grace, * and they have gloriously announced the good news of your salvation.

Taking up their cross in joy and following You * to imitate your passion, O Lord, * with courage, the martyrs have rejected the threats of tyrants; * without trembling, they faced the sword and fire, * hunger, torments, and death.

Glory be...now and ever: Young virgins have shown steadfast courage * as they bore the burdens of martyrdom without bending; * and according to the word of David, * they were led after you, O holy Virgin, to your Son, * into the palace of the great King.

I will open my mouth; it will be filled by the Holy Spirit, * and I will offer praise to the Queen Mother. * I will celebrate in joy; * in my rejoicing I will sing of these wonders.

ODE 3

Tone 8 In the beginning, by your intelligence, You made the skies firm; * and You founded the earth on the waters. * Now make me firm on the rock of your commandments, O Christ; * for none is holy as You, O only Lover of Mankind.

***Refrain:* Glory to your holy Resurrection, O Lord!**

The saving suffering of your flesh, O Christ, * has justified Adam who was condemned for having tasted the bitterness of sin; * for though You were not guilty, * You suffered the ordeal of death, O sinless Lord.

The light of the Resurrection has shown upon all * who lay in the darkness and shadow of death; * for by his divinity, Jesus, my God, * has bound up the Prince of evil and plundered his booty.

***Refrain:* Most holy Mother of God, save us!**

You have appeared as higher than the Cherubim and Seraphim, O Mother of God; * for you alone, O pure Virgin, have received in your womb * the God whom none could contain. * And with our incessant hymns, * we the faithful proclaim you blessed.

***Refrain:* Glory to your holy Resurrection, O Lord!**

When I formerly transgressed the commandments of the Creator, * You dispelled me from Paradise, O Lord; * but by taking the form of a slave You taught me to obey, * and by your Cross You have taken me back in your love.

In wisdom You have made everything, O Lord: * in your foreknowledge You created the universe; * in your intelligence You created the inferno below; * and in your condescension, O Word, You deigned to raise the one whom You created in your image.

***Refrain:* Most holy Mother of God, save us!**

By your prayers, come to our aid, O most pure Virgin, * and divert the dangers which surround us.

You are the release of Eve, the mother of the living, * O Mother of God, * for you brought into the world the Author of life.

***Refrain:* All you Saints, pray to God for us!**

In their wisdom, the bishops and pastors, * who are clothed with the dignity of the priesthood, * have adorned their leadership with divine teaching * with which the Word has richly endowed them.

Resplendent with the brightness of beauty, * and shining as unerring stars, * you have made the Church of Christ * a star-filled heaven on earth * by the diversity of your holy lives.

These blessed ones, who have been faithful to your law * and who shine with many virtues, * have filled the heavenly abodes with joy; * now the many mansions of your Father's house welcomes them, O Lord.

Glory be...now and ever: From your virginal womb, O Mother of God, * you have given birth, for us, * to the divine Word who is born of God; * He is the object of the holy desire of pure and wise virgins * who form the royal procession with you.

O living and self-contained fountain! O Mother of God! *

Strengthen those who sing to you, * the choir which has assembled in spirit for the praise of your glory. * Make it worthy of the crown of victory.

SESSIONAL HYMN

Tone 8 Celebrating the memory of all the saints: * the forefathers, fathers, and patriarchs; * the apostles, martyrs, and bishops; * the prophets, just ones, ascetics, and the blessed; * and all those whose names are written in the book of life, * we invoke their universal protection. * And we beseech You, O Christ our God, * through their prayers, grant peace to the world, * so that all together we may sing to You: * O Lover of Mankind, You are truly the Lord God glorified in the council of the saints, * and You glorify their sacred memory.

Tone 8 **Glory be...now and ever:** Let us glorify the tabernacle and the heavenly gate, * the most holy mountain and the shining cloud, * the heavenly ladder and the mystical paradise, * the deliverance of Eve and the precious and great treasure of the universe. * For through her, salvation came to the world, * and the ancient debt was forgiven. * Therefore, we cry out to her: * Intercede with your Son and God to grant forgiveness of sins * to those who bow in true worship to your most holy birth-giving.

ODE 4

Tone 8 You are my strength and my power, O Lord; * You are my God and my joy. * Without leaving the bosom of the Father, You have visited our poverty. * With the prophet Habakkuk, I also cry out to You: * Glory to your power, O only Lover of Mankind!

Refrain: **Glory to your holy Resurrection, O Lord!**

You have loved me without measure, * even though I was your enemy; * You have descended upon the earth, O compassionate Savior, * to humble yourself, in a manner beyond expression, * without disdaining my extreme poverty. * By your immaculate glory, * You have glorified the one who was formerly despised.

Who would not be struck with wonder, O Lord, * in seeing You destroy Death by your Passion, * and destroying corruption by your Cross, * and emptying the treasures of Hades by your death? * Such is the work of your divine power, * O Lover of Mankind who was nailed to the Cross.

Refrain: **Most holy Mother of God, save us!**

You are the glory of believers and their advocate; * you are the refuge, the rampart, and the haven of Christians; * you bring their prayers to your Son; * and you save from all danger the faithful who recognize you as the Mother of God.

Refrain: **Glory to your holy Resurrection, O Lord!**

The impious ones have nailed You to the Cross, O Lover of Mankind; * and thus in your mercy, You save those who glorify your Passion.

Risen from the tomb, You raised with You all the dead in Hades; * in your mercy, You illumine those who glorify your Resurrection.

Refrain: **Most holy Mother of God, save us!**

You made the life-giving cluster sprout forth, * the One who gives life to the Word, * for you are the untilled earth. * O Mother of God, save all who praise your name.

All of us who have received his light, * recognize in you, O all-holy Lady and ever-virgin Mother of our God, * the Sun of Justice who has come forth from your womb.

Refrain: **All you Saints, pray to God for us!**

Assembled by your love, your saints rejoice in You; * with a pure and joyous heart, they dance with the angels of heaven eternally before You, * the Lord and God of the universe.

O glorious bishop-martyrs, * you have embraced the crown of victory, * raising to a new brightness * the anointing you have received earlier in the priesthood; * and now bearing the double crown, * you exalt with Christ in an eternal joy.

You have submitted every care of the flesh to the spirit, * O God-bearing fathers, * overcoming its uncontrollable forces by prayer and fasting; * and now shining brightly because of the absence of passions, * you have received the reward of your labors.

O witnesses of Christ, the first martyr, * you have endured tortures with nobility and courage, * as if, in combat, you were strangers to your bodies; * and now as inheritors of the kingdom, * you are a source of healing for the faithful.

Glory be...now and ever: O divine spouse, you became the Mother of our God; * for us you conceived in the flesh * the Word who was begotten before the ages. * The women who also lead a holy life * and are adorned with all kinds of virtues, * find restoration in you for the fault of the mother of the living.

Jesus, the true God, who sits in glory upon the divine throne, * now appears riding on a swift cloud; * and with his pure hand He saves those who cry: * Glory to your power, O Christ.

ODE 5

Tone 8 Why have You rejected me far from your face, O inaccessible Light? * I am miserable indeed! * The outer darkness has surrounded me; * bring me back, I beseech You, and direct my steps towards the light of your law.

Refrain: **Glory to your holy Resurrection, O Lord!**

Before your sufferings, O Savior, * You were willingly clothed in a cloak of mockery by the soldiers * to cover the nakedness of our first father; * and naked, You were nailed to the Cross, * setting aside your tunic, the symbol of death.

From the corruption of the tomb, O Christ, * You have refashioned my fallen nature by your Resurrection; * You have adorned me with eternal youth, * making me again in the image of the King, * shining with eternal brightness.

Refrain: **Most holy Mother of God, save us!**

Having the assurance of a Mother before her Son, * O Virgin all-holy, we pray to you: * Do not withhold your protection from the Christian people, * for you are our only intercessor before Christ, our Master and Lord.

Refrain: **Glory to your holy Resurrection, O Lord!**

Lead us, O Christ, by the power of your Cross, * for it is You that we adore in it; * O Lover of Mankind, give us peace!

Direct our lives, O God of goodness, * for we sing the praises of your Resurrection; * O Lover of Mankind, give us peace!

Refrain: **Most holy Mother of God, save us!**

Appease the unleashed surges of the storms of my passions, * for you gave birth to our God, * the Lord who leads us over the stormy waters.

The choir of angels in heaven and mortals on earth * adore the One to whom you gave birth, O Mother of God and Virgin most pure.

Refrain: **All you Saints, pray to God for us!**

As the divine prophets, * you were given to contemplate

in advance * the future goods and the objects of your aspiration; * and in the courage of your heart, * you were purified by a holy life; * O God-bearing holy fathers, * you were illumined by the strength of the Spirit.

The choir of saints now shines with divine gifts: * the just ones from before the Law, * the patriarchs, prophets, apostles, and martyrs, * the ascetics, teachers, bishop-martyrs, and the blessed.

On this day, we see the assembled multitude of your saints * shine with brightness in the light of your infinite grace, O Savior; * we unceasingly praise, O Lover of Mankind, * the divine treasure of your rich benefits.

Glory be...now and ever: The holy women who cherish the wondrous miracles of your Son, * despise the goods of this life, O all-holy Lady, * that in love they may be joined to his unique beauty * in the rays of his divine light.

All nations marveled at your divine glory, * for you, O Virgin who has not known wedlock, * carried within your womb the God of all, * the Eternal Son to whom you gave birth; * He grants salvation to all who sing your praises.

ODE 6

Tone 8 Grant me forgiveness, O Savior, * despite the number of my sins; * rescue me from the pit of evil, I pray You; * to You I cry out, O God of my salvation: * Save me, O Lord!

Refrain: **Glory to your holy Resurrection, O Lord!**

Beneath the tree, the Prince of evil crushed me to the ground; * but on the tree of the Cross, O Christ, * You have delivered yourself to the jeers of all. * For by your power You have laid the Evil One low, * and You have raised up fallen humanity.

Rising from the tomb, You had mercy on ancient Zion, * and in your love, You have renewed her by your divine blood, O Christ; * and in her You shall reign throughout all ages.

Refrain: **Most holy Mother of God, save us!**

By your prayers, O holy Mother of God, * may we be delivered from our sins * that we may obtain, O immaculate Virgin, * the divine illumination of the Son of God * who was marvelously incarnate in your womb.

Refrain: **Glory to your holy Resurrection, O Lord!**

Stretching your hands upon the Cross, * You healed the

hand of our first father * which had greedily grasped from the forbidden tree. * In his place You tasted the bitter gall, O Christ all-powerful, * and You saved those who glorify the sufferings of your Passion.

The Redeemer has tasted death * to crush the kingdom of the dead and its ancient condemnation; * having descended among the captives of Hades, * by his power He has risen and saved those who praise his divine Resurrection.

Refrain: **Most holy Mother of God, save us!**

We the faithful praise you, O Virgin Mother, * as the ark and temple of God, * his nuptial chamber and the gate to heaven.

O Mary, the divine spouse, * your Son, before whom the idols have disappeared, * is adored as God with the Father and the Holy Spirit.

Refrain: **All you Saints, pray to God for us!**

The saints have acknowledged You, O Christ, as the precious and chosen stone, * as the cornerstone of Zion; * and on this unshakable rock * they have established the building of their chosen stones.

The drops of your blood, O my God, * together with the water that flowed from your side, * have brought forth a new world; * and they have gathered around You * the divine assembly of all your saints.

In faith we praise the divine assembly of martyrs, * shining with grace and splendor in their crimsoned robes * and in the purple blood of their severe struggles.

Glory be...now and ever: All together we praise you as truly the Mother of God; * because of you, feminine nature has once again been strengthened. * You have struggled valiantly for Christ, * and you are known for all your virtues.

Celebrating this divine and holy feast of the Mother of God, * come, O faithful, let us clap our hands * and glorify the God to whom she gave birth.

KONTAKION

Tone 8 To You, O Lord, Author of all creation, * the universe offers the God-bearing martyrs as the first-fruit of nature. * Through their prayers and the intercession of the Mother of God * preserve your Church, your dwelling place, in perfect peace, * O most merciful One.

IKOS

Those who have borne witness over all the earth * have now become citizens of heaven; * having imitated the Passion of Christ, * they deliver us from our passions. * They are reunited today in the world beyond, * and they show how the Church of the first-born bear the mark of the heavenly assembly. * To Christ, they say: You are my God. * Through the one who gave You birth, O Lord, * preserve me, O God of mercy.

ODE 7

Tone 8 The condescension of God disrupted the fire in Babylon in days of old; * therefore, the youths danced for You * in the furnace as if in a flower-filled meadow; * and they sang: * Blessed are You, O God of our fathers!

Refrain: **Glory be to your holy Resurrection, O Lord!**

The glorious humiliation and the divine treasure of your humble heart, O Christ, * struck the angels with astonishment, * when they saw You nailed to the Cross * to save all those who sing in faith: * Blessed are You, O God of our fathers!

When You descended into the caverns of Hades, O God, * they were filled with light and the dismal darkness disappeared; * the captives, who for ages had been in chains, arose and began to sing: * Blessed are You, O God of our fathers!

Refrain: **O Most Holy Trinity, our God, glory be to You!**

Speaking of You, we praise You according to the true faith, O God. * For You are the Lord of the universe, * the Father of the only Son, Jesus Christ, * and the Father from whom the only consubstantial Spirit proceeds; * and He is coeternal with You.

In accordance with the prophecy of David, * You accomplished our salvation in the middle of the earth. * Raised upon the cross, You drew to yourself * all those who sing to You in faith: * Blessed are You, O God of our fathers!

Rising from the tomb as if from sleep, * You saved the human race from death; * through your apostles who proclaimed the Resurrection, * You led all creation to faith. * Blessed are You, O God of our fathers!

Refrain: **Most holy Mother of God, save us!**

You have appeared from the womb of the Virgin, * clothed

in our flesh for our salvation, * and we, who recognize her as the Mother of God, * now sing in thanksgiving: * Blessed are You, O God of our fathers!

O blessed Virgin, You are truly the branch that blossomed from the root of Jesse, * and you gave birth to the salvation of the faithful * who now sing to your Son: * Blessed are You, O God of fathers!

***Refrain:* All you saints, pray to God for us!**

With an unceasing voice, the multitude of saints * praises the One who rests among the saints; * they now rejoice with heavenly delight, * and they joyfully dance as they sing: * Blessed are You, O God of our fathers!

Shining with the divine splendor of the triple light of the Sun, * the multitude of saints sings to the eternal Father * with his Son and Holy Spirit, * one God in three Persons.

When You shall come in your glory at the divine council, O Lord, * and distribute to each the crown that has been merited, * grant that we may sing to You on that day: * Blessed are You, O God of our fathers!

In joy let us praise the divine assembly of all the saints, * gathered from all places and from all ranks, * from all peoples and all ways of life. * Let us join our voices with theirs that we may sing: * Blessed are You, O God of our fathers!

Glory be...now and ever: All young people, form a divine choir * around the immaculate Virgin, Mary the holy Mother of God, * and with a full voice sing out: * Rejoice, O sealed Fountain from which the source of joy flows abundantly.

The three youths courageously walked about in the flaming furnace, * preferring to worship the Creator rather than created things, * and they sang out in joy: * Blessed are You and praised above all, O Lord God of our fathers!

ODE 8

Tone 8 In his fury the tyrant of the Chaldeans * had the furnace heated seven times more than usual * for the faithful ones of the Lord; * but when he saw them saved by a stronger power, he cried out: * O Youths, bless your Creator and Redeemer; * and praise Him, you priests; * let the entire nation exalt Him forever!

***Refrain:* Glory to your holy Resurrection, O Lord!**

The divine power of Jesus has made his light shine upon

us; * for when He tasted death on the Cross for all of us, * He broke the bonds of Hades. * O Youths, bless Him unceasingly; * and praise Him, you priests; * let the entire nation exalt Him forever!

The crucified One is awakened and the arrogance of Hades is abolished; * fallen and broken humanity is raised up; * Death is banished and immortality flourishes; * life has once again claimed its rights over mortals. * O Youths, bless the Lord; * and praise Him, you priests; * let the entire nation exalt Him forever!

Refrain: **O Most Holy Trinity, our God, glory be to You!**

As a triple flame, * the Divinity shines with a single light * of the one nature shared in three persons: * the Father who engenders eternally, * the consubstantial Son, and the Spirit who reigns with Him. * O Youths, bless the Lord; * and praise Him, you priests; * let the entire nation exalt Him forever!

Refrain: **Glory to your holy Resurrection, O Lord!**

From his Cross, the Lord stretched his hands towards me, * inviting me to warm my nakedness through his self-abasement. * Praise Him, all you works of the Lord, and exalt Him forever!

The Lord has raised me from the deepest depths of Hades * to which I had descended * and has glorified me on the throne of the Father. * Praise Him, all you works of the Lord, and exalt Him forever!

Refrain: **Most holy Mother of God, save us!**

O pure Virgin, extinguish the enticing and flaming arrows * which the Enemy has hurled against us; * and we shall praise you through all the ages.

O Virgin, you gave birth in a marvelous manner * to God the Word, our Creator and Savior; * and we shall praise you through all the ages.

Refrain: **All you Saints, pray to God for us!**

Apostles, prophets, and martyrs, * divine assembly of holy bishops, * choir of the just, teachers, and blessed ones, * together with the holy myrrh-bearers, * exalt with joy and sing: * O Youths, bless the Lord; * and praise Him, you priests; * let the entire nation exalt Him forever!

All you saints who rejoice with a splendor that surpasses every spirit, * the psalmist calls you gods * because you dwell close to God * and receive the deifying rays from his light; * and shining with his unequaled glory, * you exalt Christ forever!

Let us bless the Lord, Father, Son, and Holy Spirit.

You, the saints, have appeared as many-rayed stars; * you brighten the sky of the Church by your diverse gifts and varied graces; * with justice and chastity, courage and intelligence, you sing: * Praise the Lord, you priests; * let the entire nation exalt Him forever!

Now and ever: You, the wise virgins, whom Christ has made perfect through the Spirit, * in joy you now encircle the Mother of God and immaculate Virgin, * whose divine birth-giving has saved us * from the condemnation merited by Eve; * and now, gathered in one choir, you sing: * Blessed is the fruit of her womb forever!

Let us praise, bless, and worship the Lord, singing and exalting Him above all forever.

The three youths in the furnace were saved by the offspring of the Theotokos. * He who was foretold has been born on earth, * and He joins together all creation to sing: * All you works of the Lord, bless the Lord * and praise Him above all forever!

MAGNIFICAT

ODE 9

Tone 8 Heaven was seized with stupor, and the ends of the earth were struck with astonishment * as God revealed himself clothed in our flesh; * and your womb has become more spacious than the heavens. * O Mother of God, the assembly of angels and people extol you.

Refrain: **Glory to your holy Resurrection, O Lord!**

Even though your divine nature is without beginning, * You assumed our nature in yourself, O Word of God; * You suffered in your human nature, * but as God You remain beyond all suffering. * In both your natures, without division or confusion, we extol You.

O God most high, who has descended among your servants, * on earth You called God your Father in heaven; * and risen from the tomb, You deigned to reveal as the Father of the human race, * the One who is by nature Lord and God; * with Him, all of us join in a chorus, and we extol You.

Refrain: **Most holy Mother of God, save us!**

O Virgin, you have appeared as the Mother of God, * for you gave birth bodily in a marvelous manner to the Word all-good * whom the Father has uttered from his bosom before all ages, for He is good; * and even though He bears the garment of the flesh, * we know Him as the transcendent One.

Refrain: **Glory to your holy Resurrection, O Lord!**

By nature You are the Son of God, * conceived in the womb of the Mother of God * and made flesh to save us; * seeing You suffer on the Cross in your humanity, * and in your divinity beyond all suffering, we extol You.

The dismal darkness has disappeared; * Christ, the Sun of Justice, is risen from Hades, * enlightening the world with the light of his divinity. * He is the heavenly man and the God who descended to the earth, * and in his two natures, we extol Him.

Refrain: **Most holy Mother of God, save us!**

Your joy-filled and exalted memory * is a source of healing for all who come to you, * and in faith recognize you as the Mother of God.

With psalms we praise you, O Full of Grace, * and we unceasingly sing to you: * Rejoice, for you have made joy and happiness * spring forth as a fountain for all.

Refrain: **All you Saints, pray to God for us!**

Armed with faith, hope, and love, * in joy the chosen ones have courageously endured * the threats of tyrants, their tortures and torments; * they are witnesses to the truth, * rich in Christ and victorious in combat.

Let us celebrate, as it is fitting, * this haven of salvation, the baptizer of Christ, * the apostles, prophets, and martyrs, * the bishops, ascetics, and teachers, * the patriarchs, and holy women, * the just ones, and all the saints.

Tested in the flames of temptations * and not enticed by their pleasures, * you now rejoice before the luminous throne of the Lord, * O illustrious Saints who shine in heaven * with that true light that has neither shadow nor reflection.

Glory be...now and ever: In you, those separated have been united; * through you, people have become citizens with the angels in heaven; * with them, the choir of all the saints bears witness * and celebrates your divine birth-giving, O Mother of God, in eternal canticles.

Let everyone on earth dance for joy in spirit. * Let the heavenly ranks celebrate in honor of the sacred feast. * O Mother of God, let them cry out: * Rejoice, ever-blessed Theotokos and pure ever-virgin.

HYMN OF LIGHT

Tone 1 O faithful, let us gather with the disciples on the mountain in Galilee * to behold Christ as He says to them: * I have received all power over all things on high and those below. * Let us learn how He taught them to baptize all nations * in the name of the Father, and of the Son, and of the Holy Spirit, * and how He promised his disciples * to be present with them to the end of the world.

Glory be: With our hymns, let us crown the Baptizer and Forerunner, * the apostles, prophets, and martyrs, * the hierarchs and the just ones, * the ascetics and bishop-martyrs, * the women companions of Christ and the just ones of all the ages, * together with the choir of angels, as it is fitting; * let us beseech them that we may attain the same glory before Christ our Savior.

Now and ever: O most pure Virgin, * He who is glorified by the angels as God, * without leaving the bosom of the Father, * has descended from heaven and is united to us below; * and you have obtained salvation for us * when, surpassing all human nature, * you gave birth to Him from your chaste womb. * Intercede with Him in our behalf * that He may grant us forgiveness of our sins.

AT THE PRAISES

Tone 8 O Lord, though You stood in judgment before the throne of Pilate, * You did not vacate your heavenly throne where You sit with the Father. * You arose from the dead, * releasing the world from the bondage of the Enemy; * for You are compassionate and the Lover of Mankind.

You gave us your Cross, O Lord, as a weapon against Satan * who fears and trembles since he is unable to behold its power; * for it raised the dead and triumphed over Death. * Therefore, we worship your burial and your holy Resurrection.

You were placed in a grave like the dead, O Lord; * the soldiers guarded You as a slumbering King; * and as a Treasure of life, they sealed You. * But You arose and granted incorruptibility to our souls.

The angel proclaimed your Resurrection, O Lord, * and filled the guards with fear; * but to the women he cried out, saying: * Why do you seek the Living among the dead? * Truly He is risen as God * and grants life to the whole world.

You suffered on the Cross * although You were beyond suffering in your divinity; * You accepted burial for three days * that You might set us free from the bondage of the Enemy * and grant us life through your Resurrection, * O Christ, the Lover of Mankind.

Tone 4 The Lord has filled with his favor * his saints who live on the earth. * In their flesh, they have taken on the marks of his Passion * which have become their adornment, * shining brightly with the divine beauty. * With our hymns we also praise them * as flowers that cannot wither, and as spiritual holocausts, * and as the star-filled sky of the Church.

The just call and the Lord hears and rescues them in all their distress.

Receive our praise in sacred hymns, * as citizens and inheritors of the kingdom on high and the new Paradise, * with the prophets and divine apostles, * the blessed ones and teachers, * the bishops and the just ones from all ages,* the holy women and the martyrs who have struggled in the arena, * those who have lived their lives in asceticism, * the multitude of the just and the saints.

Blessed be the Lord, God of Israel, who alone works wonders.

By the splendor of their virtues, * the holy martyrs have transformed the earth into a new heaven; * they have imitated the sufferings and death of Christ * on the path that leads to eternal life; * by grace they have washed us of our deadly passions, * and throughout all the world, * their singular courage in battle merits our songs of praise.

Tone 1 **Glory be:** The Lord appeared to his disciples * as they were going to the mountain to witness his Ascension from here below, * and they bowed down and worshiped Him. * They learned about the power given to Him in every place. * They were sent to all people under heaven * to preach his Resurrection from the dead * and his return from earth to heaven. * He promised that He would be with them forever; * his word is true, for He is Christ our God * and the Savior of our souls.

Tone 2 **Now and ever:** You are truly most blessed, O virgin Mother of God. * Through the One who was incarnate of you, * Hades was chained, Adam revived, the curse wiped out, * Eve set free, Death put to death, * and we ourselves were brought back to life. * That is why we cry out in praise: * Blessed are You, O Christ our God, * who finds in this your good pleasure; glory to You!

AFTER THE DISMISSAL

Gospel Stanza Number 1

Tone 1 **Glory be...now and ever:** The Lord appeared to his disciples * as they were going to the mountain to witness his ascension from here below, * and they bowed down and worshiped Him. * They learned about the power given to Him in every place. * They were sent to all people under heaven * to preach his Resurrection from the dead * and his return from earth to heaven. * He promised that He would be with them forever; * his word is true, for He is Christ our God and the Savior of our souls.

The Office of Matins

The priest, vested in the epitrachilion, incenses the Holy Table, icon screen, the whole church, and the people. The deacon precedes him with a lighted candle. The priest then stands before the Holy Table with the censer. The deacon stands before the closed Royal Doors.

The priest makes the sign of the cross with the censer and intones:

Priest: Glory to the holy, consubstantial, life-creating and undivided Trinity, always, now and ever and forever.

Response: Amen.

If a Celebrant is not present:

Leader: Through the prayers of our holy Fathers, O Lord Jesus Christ, our God, have mercy on us.

Response: Amen.

From Easter until the Wednesday before Ascension we sing three times:

Christ is risen from the dead! By death He conquered Death; and to those in the graves He granted life.

Glory to God in the highest,
and to his people on earth, his peace and good will. *(3 times)*

O Lord, You shall open my lips,
and my mouth will declare your praise. *(2 times)*

PSALMS OF MATINS

PSALM 3

How many are my foes, O Lord!
How many are rising up against me!
How many are saying about me:
There is no help for him in God.

But You, Lord, are a shield about me,
my glory, who lift up my head.
I cry aloud to the Lord.
He answers from his holy mountain.

I lie down to rest and I sleep.
  I wake, for the Lord upholds me.
I will not fear even thousands of people
  who are ranged on every side against me.

Arise, Lord; save me, my God,
  You who strike all my foes on the mouth,
  You who break the teeth of the wicked!
O Lord of salvation,
  bless your people.

I lie down to rest and I sleep.
  I wake, for the Lord upholds me.

PSALM 37

O Lord, do not rebuke me in your anger;
  do not punish me, Lord, in your rage.
Your arrows have sunk deep in me;
  your hand has come down upon me.
Through your anger all my body is sick:
  through my sin, there is no health in my limbs.

My guilt towers higher than my head;
  it is a weight too heavy to bear.
My wounds are foul and festering,
  the result of my own folly.
I am bowed and brought to my knees.
  I go mourning all the day long.

All my frame burns with fever;
  all my body is sick.
Spent and utterly crushed,
  I cry aloud in anguish of heart.

O Lord, You know all my longing:
  my groans are not hidden from You.
My heart throbs, my strength is spent;
  the very light has gone from my eyes.

My friends avoid me like a leper;
  those closest to me stand afar off.
Those who plot against my life lay snares;
  those who seek my ruin speak of harm,
  planning treachery all the day long.

But I am like the deaf who cannot hear,
like the dumb unable to speak.
I am like one who hears nothing
in whose mouth is no defense.

I count on You, O Lord:
it is You, Lord God, who will answer.
I pray: Do not let them mock me,
those who triumph if my foot should slip.

For I am on the point of falling
and my pain is always before me.
I confess that I am guilty
and my sin fills me with dismay.

My wanton enemies are numberless
and my lying foes are many.
They repay me evil for good
and attack me for seeking what is right.

O Lord, do not forsake me!
My God, do not stay afar off!
Make haste and come to my help,
O Lord, my God, my Savior!

O Lord, do not forsake me!
My God, do not stay afar off!
Make haste and come to my help,
O Lord, my God, my Savior!

PSALM 62

O God, You are my God, for You I long;
for You my soul is thirsting.
My body pines for You
like a dry, weary land without water.
So I gaze on You in the sanctuary
to see your strength and your glory.

For your love is better than life,
my lips will speak your praise.
So I will bless You all my life,
in your name I will lift up my hands.
My soul shall be filled as with a banquet,
my mouth shall praise You with joy.

On my bed I remember You.
  On You I muse through the night
For You have been my help;
  in the shadow of your wings I rejoice.
My soul clings to You;
  your right hand holds me fast.

Those who seek to destroy my life
  shall go down to the depths of the earth.
They shall be put into the power of the sword
  and left as the prey of the jackals.
But the king shall rejoice in God;
  all that swear by him shall be blessed
  for the mouth of liars shall be silenced.

On You I muse through the night
  for You have been my help;
  in the shadow of your wings I rejoice.
My soul clings to You;
  your right hand holds me fast.

Glory be to the Father, and to the Son,
and to the Holy Spirit,
  now and ever and forever. Amen.

And then, three times with a bow each time:

Alleluia! Alleluia! Alleluia!
  Glory be to You, O God!

The priest goes in front of the Royal Doors and reads the Prayers of Matins, found on pages 447-451. The deacon returns to the altar. The people continue:

PSALM 87

Lord my God, I call for help by day;
  I cry at night before You.
Let my prayer come into your presence.
  O turn your ear to my cry.

For my soul is filled with evils;
  my life is on the brink of the grave.
I am reckoned as one in the tomb:
  I have reached the end of my strength.

Like one alone among the dead;
  like the slain lying in their graves;
Like those You remember no more,
  cut off, as they are, from your hand.

You have laid me in the depths of the tomb,
  in places that are dark, in the depths.
Your anger weighs down upon me:
  I am drowned beneath your waves.

You have taken away my friends
  and made me hateful in their sight.
Imprisoned, I cannot escape;
  my eyes are sunken with grief.

I call to You, Lord, all the day long;
  to You I stretch out my hands.
Will You work your wonders for the dead?
  Will the shades stand and praise You?

Will your love be told in the grave
  or your faithfulness among the dead?
Will your wonders be known in the dark
  or your justice in the land of oblivion?

As for me, Lord, I call to You for help:
  in the morning my prayer comes before You.
Lord, why do You reject me?
  Why do You hide your face?

Wretched, close to death from my youth,
  I have borne your trials; I am numb.
Your fury has swept down upon me;
  your terrors have utterly destroyed me.

They surround me all the day like a flood,
  they assail me all together.
Friend and neighbor You have taken away;
  my one companion is darkness.

Lord my God, I call for help by day;
  I cry at night before You.
Let my prayer come into your presence.
  O turn your ear to my cry.

PSALM 102

My soul, give thanks to the Lord,
  all my being, bless his holy name.
My soul, give thanks to the Lord
  and never forget all his blessings.

It is He who forgives all your guilt,
  who heals every one of your ills,
Who redeems your life from the grave,
  who crowns you with love and compassion,
Who fills your life with good things,
  renewing your youth like an eagle's.

The Lord does deeds of justice,
  gives judgment for all who are oppressed.
He made known his ways to Moses
  and his deeds to Israel's children.

The Lord is compassion and love,
  slow to anger and rich in mercy.
His wrath will come to an end;
  He will not be angry forever.
He does not treat us according to our sins
  nor repay us according to our faults.

For as the heavens are high above the earth
  so strong is his love for those who fear Him.
As far as the east is from the west
  so far does He remove our sins.

As a father has compassion on his children,
  the Lord has pity on those who fear Him;
For He knows of what we are made,
  He remembers that we are dust.

As for mortals, their days are like grass;
  they flower like the flower of the field;
The wind blows and they are gone
  and their place never sees them again.

But the love of the Lord is everlasting
  upon those who hold Him in fear;
His justice reaches out to children's children
  when they keep his covenant in truth,
  when they keep his will in their mind.

The Lord has set his sway in heaven
  and his kingdom is ruling over all.
Give thanks to the Lord, all his angels,
  mighty in power, fulfilling his word,
  who heed the voice of his word.

Give thanks to the Lord, all his hosts,
  his servants who do his will.

Give thanks to the Lord, all his works,
in every place where He rules.
My soul, give thanks to the Lord!

In every place where He rules,
my soul, give thanks to the Lord!

PSALM 142

Lord, listen to my prayer:
turn your ear to my appeal.
You are faithful, You are just; give answer.
Do not call your servant to judgment
for no one is just in your sight.

The enemy pursues my soul;
he has crushed my life to the ground;
He has made me dwell in darkness
like the dead, long forgotten.
Therefore my spirit fails;
my heart is numb within me.

I remember the days that are past:
I ponder all your works.
I muse on what your hand has wrought
and to You I stretch out my hands.
Like a parched land my soul thirsts for You.

Lord, make haste and answer;
for my spirit fails within me.
Do not hide your face
lest I become like those in the grave.

In the morning let me know your love
for I put my trust in You.
Make me know the way I should walk;
to You I lift up my soul.

Rescue me, Lord, from my enemies;
I have fled to You for refuge.
Teach me to do your will
for You, O Lord, are my God.
Let your good Spirit guide me
in ways that are level and smooth.

For your name's sake, Lord, save my life;
in your justice save my soul from distress.
In your love make an end of my foes;
destroy all those who oppress me
for I am your servant, O Lord.

You are faithful, You are just; give answer.
Do not call your servant to judgment.
You are faithful, You are just; give answer.
Do not call your servant to judgment.

Let your good Spirit guide me
in ways that are level and smooth.

Glory be to the Father, and to the Son,
and to the Holy Spirit,
now and ever and forever. Amen.

And then, three times with a bow each time:

Alleluia! Alleluia! Alleluia!
Glory be to You, O God!

LITANY OF PEACE

The priest returns to the altar, and the deacon returns to the ambon for the following Litany. If there is no deacon, the priest intones the Litany before the Royal Doors.

Deacon: In peace, let us pray to the Lord.

R. Lord, have mercy. *(and after each petition)*

For peace from on high and for the salvation of our souls, let us pray to the Lord.

For peace in the whole world, for the well-being of the holy Churches of God and for the union of all, let us pray to the Lord.

For this holy Church and for all who enter it with faith, reverence, and the fear of God, let us pray to the Lord.

For our holy ecumenical Pontiff *(name)*, the Pope of Rome, let us pray to the Lord.

For our most reverend Archbishop and Metropolitan *(name)*, for our God-loving Bishop *(name)*, for the venerable priesthood, the diaconate in Christ, and all the clergy and the people, let us pray to the Lord.

For our civil authorities and all in the service of our country, let us pray to the Lord.

For this city, *(OR: for this village, OR: for this holy monastery)*, for every city and countryside, and for those living within them in faith, let us pray to the Lord.

For seasonable weather, for an abundance of the fruits of

the earth, and for peaceful times, let us pray to the Lord.

For those who travel by sea, air, and land; for the sick, the suffering, the captive, and for their safety and salvation, let us pray to the Lord.

That we be delivered from all affliction, wrath, and need, let us pray to the Lord.

Protect us, save us, have mercy on us and preserve us, O God, by your grace.

Remembering our most holy, most pure, most blessed and glorious Lady, the Mother of God and ever-Virgin Mary with all the saints, let us commend ourselves and one another, and our whole life, to Christ our God.

R. To You, O Lord.

The priest prays the following prayer quietly now or it may be taken with the Prayers of Light.

Priest: We thank You, Lord our God, for You have wakened us from our sleep, and have filled our lips with praise that we might worship You and call upon your holy name. We beg of your compassion that You have always shown towards us, hear us now and send help to those who stand before your holy glory awaiting your abundant mercy. O Lord, grant that those who serve You in fear and love may praise your ineffable goodness.

And then, aloud:

For to You is due all glory, honor, and worship, Father, Son, and Holy Spirit, now and ever and forever.

R. Amen.

GOD THE LORD

"God the Lord" is sung in the tone of the Troparion that follows it. The deacon remains at the ambon and chants the verses. If there is no deacon, the priest remains at the Royal Doors and chants the verses.

God the Lord has revealed himself to us, blessed is He who comes in the name of the Lord.

v. Give thanks to the Lord, for He is good; for his love endures forever.

v. They encircled me, compassed me about; in the Lord's name I crushed them.

v. I shall not die, I shall live and recount the deeds of the Lord.

v. The stone which the builders rejected has become the cornerstone. This is the work of the Lord, a marvel in our eyes.

TROPARIA

Then the Troparia are sung as prescribed by the Typikon. The deacon returns to the altar.

KATHISMATA

The Kathismata of the Psalter are read as prescribed. After each Kathisma, we say:

Glory be to the Father, and to the Son, and to the Holy Spirit, now and ever and forever. Amen.

And then, three times with a bow each time:

Alleluia, alleluia, alleluia; glory be to You, O God!

SMALL LITANY

Deacon: Again and again, in peace, let us pray to the Lord.

R. Lord, have mercy.

Protect us, save us, have mercy on us, and preserve us, O God, by your grace.

R. Lord, have mercy.

Remembering our most holy, most pure, most blessed and glorious Lady, the Mother of God and ever-Virgin Mary with all the saints, let us commend ouselves and one another, and our whole life, to Christ our God.

R. To You, O Lord.

SESSIONAL HYMNS

The prescribed Sessional Hymns are sung after the Litany and before the next section of the Psalter. The priest concludes by saying this Doxology aloud:

Priest: For yours is the might, and yours is the kingdom, and the power and the glory, Father, Son, and Holy Spirit, now and ever and forever.

R. Amen.

Either the Second, Third or Fourth Prayer of Light may be substituted for the Doxology to conclude the Kathisma; see pages 447-448.

SESSIONAL HYMNS

The second Kathisma is read in the same way as the first. After the second Kathisma, the deacon says the Small Litany (refer above) and the priest concludes with the following Doxology:

Priest: For You, O God, are gracious and You love mankind, and we glorify You, Father, Son, and Holy Spirit, now and ever and forever.

R. Amen.

Either the Second, Third or Fourth Prayer of Light may be substituted for the Doxology to conclude the Kathisma; see pages 447-448.

The prescribed Sessional Hymns are sung after the Litany. If there is no Gospel, then continue with Psalm 50 on page 427 or The Hymn of Resurrection, also on page 426, from Easter until Wednesday before Ascension.

POLYELEOS

Before the Polyeleos, the priest vests in the phelonion. The deacon (or priest) opens the Royal Doors, and when the Polyeleos is chanted, the priest takes the icon of the feast from the Holy Table, and preceded by the deacon with incense, processes through the Royal Doors and places the icon on the tetrapod, incensing it three times at the four sides. When it is a feast with a Polyeleos, the priest sings the Festal Exaltation after which there is a short litany and a Sessional Hymn for the feast.

PSALMS 134 and 135

Praise the name of the Lord
praise Him, servants of the Lord.
Alleluia! Alleluia! Alleluia!

Who stand in the house of the Lord,
in the courts of the house of our God.
Alleluia! Alleluia! Alleluia!

Lord, your name stands forever,
unforgotten from age to age.
Alleluia! Alleluia! Alleluia!

From Zion may the Lord be blessed,
He who dwells in Jerusalem.
Alleluia! Alleluia! Alleluia!

O give thanks to the Lord for He is good,
for his love endures forever.
Alleluia! Alleluia! Alleluia!

Who fixed the earth firmly on the seas,
for his love endures forever.
Alleluia! Alleluia! Alleluia!

He snatched us away from our foes,
for his love endures forever.
Alleluia! Alleluia! Alleluia!

To the God of heaven give thanks,
for his love endures forever.
Alleluia! Alleluia! Alleluia!

EXALTATION

(From the Feast)

EXCERPT FROM PSALM 119

On all Sundays including those during the Paschal cycle, when the Polyeleos is not taken, the following verses from Psalm 119 are taken.

They are happy whose life is blameless,
who follow God's law.

They are happy who do his will,
seeking Him with all their hearts,
who never do anything evil
but walk in his ways.

HOSTS OF ANGELS

Blessed are You, O Lord, teach me your commandments.

The hosts of angels were amazed and dazzled when they beheld You, O Savior, among the dead destroying the power of Death, raising up Adam with You and releasing all the souls from Hades.

Blessed are You, O Lord, teach me your commandments.

The radiant angel standing by the grave cried out to the ointment-bearing women: Why do you lament and mingle your tears with the spices? Look upon the grave and rejoice, for the Savior is risen from the dead.

Blessed are You, O Lord, teach me your commandments.

The ointment-bearing women hastened very early to your grave. But the angel stood by them and said: The time for lamenting is no more. Do not cry, but go and announce the Resurrection to the disciples.

Blessed are You, O Lord, teach me your commandments.

O Savior, the ointment-bearing women came to your grave with ointments, and they heard the angel say to them: Why are you seeking the Living One among the dead? Indeed, He is God. He is risen from the dead.

Glory be to the Father and to the Son and to the Holy Spirit.

We worship the Father and his Son and his Holy Spirit, the Holy Trinity, One in essence, and we cry out with the Seraphim: Holy, holy, holy are You, O Lord.

Now and ever and forever. Amen.

O Virgin, you bore the Giver of life. You redeemed Adam from his sin and granted joy to Eve instead of sadness. For He who is both God and Man was incarnate of you, and He has restored life to those who had strayed away from it.

And then, three times with a bow each time:

Alleluia! Alleluia! Alleluia!
Glory be to You, O God!

HYPAKOE AND GRADUAL HYMNS

(from the Tone of the week)

The Royal Doors are opened and the priest prepares for the Prokeimenon and Gospel.

GRADUAL HYMNS

(for Feasts)

Tone 4

My sinful desires have encircled me,
from my youth they have oppressed me;
but You, O Savior, will come to aid me.
You will protect and save me.

May the enemies of Zion be confounded by the Lord;
may they be as grass which withers,
which is dried up by the fire.

Glory be... now and ever:

Every spirit lives by the grace of the Holy Spirit,
and is raised up in all purity;
it is mystically enlightened by the one God in three Persons.

PROKEIMENON

(Of Feast or Sunday)

Deacon: Let us be attentive!

Priest: Peace † be with all!

Deacon: Wisdom! Be attentive!

Prokeimenon

GOSPEL

The deacon incenses as usual before the reading of the Gospel.

Deacon: Let us pray to the Lord.

R. Lord, have mercy.

Priest: For You are holy, O our God, and You dwell in the holy place, and to You we give glory, Father, Son, and Holy Spirit, now and ever and forever.

R. Amen.

Deacon: Let everything that lives and that breathes give praise to the Lord.

R. Let everything that lives and that breathes give praise to the Lord.

***v.* Praise God in his holy place, praise Him in his mighty heavens.**

Let everything that lives and that breathes give praise to the Lord.

Deacon: Wisdom, let us stand and listen to a reading of the Holy Gospel.

Priest: Peace † be with all!

R. And with your spirit.

Priest: A reading of the Holy Gospel according to St. (**N.**).

R. Glory be to You, O Lord; glory be to You!

Deacon: Let us be attentive!

On Sundays, one of eleven Gospels is read. Check the Gospel Book for the proper Gospel for a given Sunday. The priest reads the Gospel. Even when a deacon is present, the priest reads the Gospel at Matins.

After reading the Gospel, the priest closes the Gospel Book, kisses it and takes it to the center of the Church to place it upon the tetrapod. The faithful then approach to kiss the Gospel Book during Psalm 50 (and icon, if it is a feast). The Gospel Book remains on the tetrapod until the Great Doxology.

HYMN OF THE RESURRECTION

This is chanted on all Sundays, on the feast of the Exaltation of the Cross, and daily from Easter to the Ascension. It is omitted if a feast of the Lord falls on a Sunday.

Having beheld the Resurrection of Christ. * let us adore the holy Lord Jesus * who alone is sinless. * We

bow to your Cross, O Christ, * and we praise and glorify your holy Resurrection. * You are our God * and besides You we recognize no other, * and we invoke your name.* Come all you faithful, * and let us bow to the holy Resurrection of Christ, * since, through the Cross, joy has come to all the world. * Ever praising the Lord, let us extol his Resurrection, * since He, having endured the crucifixion, * has destroyed Death by his death.
(3 times)

PSALM 50

While Psalm 50 is chanted, the faithful come forward to venerate the Holy Gospel Book. The priest anoints the faithful on every Sunday. If there was Litija, the blessed bread is distributed at this time also. When the anointing is completed, the priest returns to the altar, and after the Royal Doors have been closed, takes off the phelonion.

Have mercy on me, God, in your kindness.
In your compassion blot out my offense.
O wash me more and more from my guilt
and cleanse me from my sin.

My offenses truly I know them;
my sin is always before me.
Against You, You alone, have I sinned;
what is evil in your sight I have done.

That You may be justified when You give sentence
and be without reproach when You judge.
O see, in guilt I was born,
a sinner was I conceived.

Indeed, You love truth in the heart;
then in the secret of my heart teach me wisdom.
O purify me, then I shall be clean;
O wash me, I shall be whiter than snow.

Make me hear rejoicing and gladness,
that the bones You have crushed may thrill.
From my sins turn away your face
and blot out all my guilt.

A pure heart create for me, O God,
put a steadfast spirit within me,
Do not cast me away from your presence,
nor deprive me of your holy spirit.

Give me again the joy of your help;
with a spirit of fervor sustain me,
That I may teach transgressors your ways
and sinners may return to You.

O rescue me, God, my helper,
and my tongue shall ring out your goodness.
O Lord, open my lips
and my mouth shall declare your praise.

For in sacrifice You take no delight,
burnt offering from me You would refuse,
My sacrifice, a contrite spirit.
A humbled, contrite heart You will not spurn.

In your goodness, show favor to Zion:
rebuild the walls of Jerusalem.
Then You will be pleased with lawful sacrifice,
burnt offerings wholly consumed,
then You will be offered young bulls on your altar.

Stichera at Psalm 50 are now sung.

On Sundays, chant the following. If a feastday of the Lord falls on a Sunday, take those of the feast.

Glory be to the Father, and to the Son, and to the Holy Spirit.

Through the intercession of the holy apostles, O Merciful One, remit our many sins.

Now and ever and forever. Amen.

Through the intercession of the Mother of God, O Merciful One, remit our many sins.

Tone 6

Have mercy on me, God, in your kindness. In your compassion, blot out my offense.

Jesus is risen from the tomb, * as He foretold, * and granted us everlasting life * and great mercy.

The priest prays the following prayer quietly now or it may be taken with the Prayers of Light. Throughout the year this prayer may be said as a conclusion to Psalm 50; outside of Great Lent it may be introduced by "Let us pray to the Lord," with the response "Lord, have mercy."

Priest: O Lord our God, You have given us forgiveness through repentance, and as a model of knowledge and confession of sins, You have revealed to us the repentance of the prophet David that led to pardon. Master, have mercy on us who have fallen into so many and so great sins. Have mercy in your kindness, and in your compassion blot out our offenses, for against You have we sinned, O Lord, who know the hidden depths of our hearts, and who alone have the power to forgive sins. A pure heart You have created for us; You have sustained us with a spirit of fervor and have given us the joy of your help. Do not cast us away from your presence, but in your goodness and love for all, grant that we may offer a sacrifice of righteousness and oblation on your holy altar until our last breath.

And then, aloud:

Through the mercies and goodness and love of your only-begotten Son, with whom You are blessed, together with your good and life-creating Spirit, now and ever and forever.

R. Amen.

The Royal Doors are now closed.

CANON

The priest closes the Royal Doors, takes off the phelonion and goes behind the altar during the Canon. On Sundays, the Canon of the Resurrection; of the Cross and Resurrection; and of the Mother of God are prescribed.

In the ordinary time of the year, one variable Ode may be taken with Ode Nine, or the Canon may be taken according to the custom of the community. After the Third Ode, the deacon takes the Small Litany:

SMALL LITANY

Deacon: Again and again, in peace let us pray to the Lord.

R. Lord, have mercy.

Protect us, save us, have mercy on us, and preserve us, O God, by your grace.

R. Lord, have mercy.

Remembering our most holy, most pure, most blessed and glorious Lady, the Mother of God and ever-virgin Mary with all the saints, let us commend ourselves and one another, and our whole life to Christ our God.

R. To You, O Lord.

The priest prays the following prayer quietly now or it may be taken with the Prayers of Light.

Priest: Treasury of all good, ever-flowing spring, Holy Father, Wonder-worker, all-powerful Ruler of all: we worship

You and beg of your mercy and compassion, help and support in our lowliness. Lord, remember those who pray to You, and let our morning prayer rise like incense before You. Grant that no one of us may be put to shame, but surround us with your mercy. Lord, remember those who keep watch and sing of your glory, and that of your only-begotten Son and our God, and of your Holy Spirit. Be their help and support and accept their prayers upon your heavenly spiritual altar.

And then, aloud:

For You are our God, and to You we give glory, to the Father, and to the Son, and to the Holy Spirit, now and ever, and forever.

R. Amen.

After the Sixth Ode, the deacon again takes the Small Litany.

The priest prays the following prayer quietly now or it may be taken with the Prayers of Light.

Priest: We give thanks to You, O Lord and God of our salvation. You have done everything that is good for our lives, and we look always to You, Savior and Benefactor of our souls. For You have given us rest in that part of the night which has passed, and now have raised us from our sleep to worship your honored name. Therefore, O Lord, we pray: give us the grace and strength to be found worthy to sing praise always, and to pray constantly, and to work for our own salvation in fear and trembling, with the help of your Christ. O Lord, remember those who pray to You in the night. Hear them and have mercy on them and crush under their feet invisible and malicious enemies.

And then, aloud:

For You are the King of peace, and the Savior of our souls, and we give thanks to You, Father, Son, and Holy Spirit, now and ever and forever.

R. Amen.

KONTAKION AND IKOS

MAGNIFICAT

At the end of the Eighth Ode, the priest (or deacon) comes with the censer before the icon of the Mother of God on the icon screen. Incensing her icon, he intones:

Deacon: Let us greatly extol the Theotokos and the Mother of Light in hymns!

Then he incenses the whole Church as usual, beginning with the Holy Table, while the people respond with "My soul magnifies the Lord..."

On certain holy days the Magnificat is not sung. In place of "Let us greatly extol..." the priest sings the proper exaltation for the feast. The people respond with the irmos of the Ninth Ode.

My soul magnifies the Lord, and my spirit rejoices in God, my Savior.

Refrain: More honorable than the Cherubim, and beyond compare more glorious than the Seraphim, who, a virgin, gave birth to God the Word; you, truly the Mother of God, we magnify!

Because He has regarded the humility of his handmaid, for behold, from henceforth all generations shall call me blessed.

Because He who is mighty has done great things for me, and holy is his name, and his love is from generation to generation to those who fear Him.

He has shown might in his arm; He has scattered the proud in the conceit of their heart.

He has put down the mighty from their seat and has exalted the humble; He has filled the hungry with good things, and the rich He has sent away empty.

He has received Israel his servant, being mindful of his love, as He spoke to our Fathers: to Abraham and to his seed forever.

HYMN OF ZECHARIAH
Father of the Forerunner

On Sundays and feastdays the Prayer of Zechariah is usually not taken, and we go directly to the Canon.

Blessed be the Lord, the God of Israel;
He has come to his people and set them free.
He has raised up for us a mighty Savior,
born of the house of his servant David.
Through his holy prophets He promised of old
that He would save us from our enemies,
from the hands of all who hate us.
He promised to show mercy to our fathers
and to remember his holy covenant.

For 8 Stichera:
This was the oath He swore to our Father Abraham:
to set us free from the hands of our enemies,
free to worship Him without fear.

For 7 Stichera:
Holy and righteous in his sight
all the days of our life.

For 6 Stichera:
You, my child, shall be called the prophet of the Most High,
for you will go before the Lord to prepare his way.

For 5 Stichera:
To give his people knowledge of salvation
by the forgiveness of their sins,
in the tender compassion of our God.

For 4 Stichera:
The dawn from on high shall break upon us,
to shine on those who dwell in darkness
and the shadow of death.

For 3 Stichera:
And to guide our feet
into the way of peace.

Glory be...Now and ever:

After the Ninth Ode, we sing
(except on pre-festive and post-festive days):

It is truly proper to glorify you, who have borne God, the ever-blessed, immaculate, and the Mother of our God. More honorable than the Cherubim, and beyond compare more glorious than the Seraphim, who, a virgin, gave birth to God the Word; you, truly the Mother of God, we magnify!

SMALL LITANY

Deacon: Again and again, in peace let us pray to the Lord.

R. Lord, have mercy.

Protect us, save us, have mercy on us, and preserve us, O God, by your grace.

R. Lord, have mercy.

Remembering our most holy, most pure, most blessed and glorious Lady, the Mother of God and ever-virgin Mary with all the saints, let us commend ourselves and one another, and our whole life to Christ our God.

R. To You, O Lord.

The priest prays the following prayer quietly now or it may be taken with the Prayers of Light.

Priest: O God, our God, who have placed all spiritual and intellectual powers under your will, we pray and beg You, accept these hymns of praise which we offer to You according to our ability together with all your creatures. Give us in exchange the riches of your goodness, for before You all beings in the heavens, or on earth and under the earth bend their knees, and everything that lives or that breathes gives praise to your glory beyond reach, for You are the one true God, full of mercy.

And then, aloud:

For all the heavenly powers praise You, and we give glory to You, to the Father, and to the Son, and to the Holy Spirit, now and ever and forever.

R. Amen.

HOLY IS THE LORD

Priest: Holy is the Lord our God!

R. Holy is the Lord our God!

Priest: Exalt the Lord our God! Bow before his footstool, for He is holy.

R. Holy is the Lord our God!

HYMN OF LIGHT

(Corresponding to the Sunday Resurrectional Gospel and/or the Feast)

PSALMS OF PRAISE

If there is a saint with the Great Doxology, we begin:

Let everything that lives and that breathes
give praise to the Lord.
Praise the Lord from the heavens,
praise Him in the heights.
To You is due a hymn, O God!

Praise Him, all his angels,
praise Him, all his host.
To You is due a hymn, O God!

*(and then continue at the * below)*

On other days, we begin:

PSALM 148

Praise the Lord from the heavens,
praise Him in the heights.
Praise Him, all his angels,
praise Him, all his host.

*Praise Him, sun and moon,
praise Him, shining stars.
Praise Him, highest heavens
and the waters above the heavens.

Let them praise the name of the Lord,
He commanded: they were made.
He fixed them forever,
gave a law which shall not pass away.

Praise the Lord from the earth,
sea creatures and all oceans,
fire and hail, snow and mist,
stormy winds that obey his word;

all mountains and hills,
all fruit trees and cedars,
beasts, wild and tame,
reptiles and birds on the wing;

all earth's kings and peoples,
earth's princes and rulers;
young men and maidens,
old men together with children.
Let them praise the name of the Lord
for He alone is exalted.
The splendor of his name
reaches beyond heaven and earth.

He exalts the strength of his people,
He is the praise of all his saints,
of the children of Israel,
of the people to whom He comes close.

PSALM 149

Sing a new song to the Lord,
his praise in the assembly of the faithful.
Let Israel rejoice in its Maker,
let Zion's sons exalt in their king.
Let them praise his name with dancing
and make music with timbrel and harp.

For the Lord takes delight in his people.
He crowns the poor with salvation.
Let the faithful rejoice in their glory,
shout for joy and take their rest.
Let the praise of God be on their lips
and a two-edged sword in their hand,

to deal out vengeance to the nations
and punishment on all the peoples;
to bind their kings in chains
and their nobles in fetters of iron.

For 6 Stichera:
To carry out the sentence pre-ordained:
this honor is for all his faithful.

PSALM 150

For 5 Stichera:
Praise God in his holy place,
praise Him in his mighty heavens.

For 4 Stichera:
Praise Him for his powerful deeds,
praise his surpassing greatness.

For 3 Stichera:
O praise Him with sound of trumpet,
praise Him with lute and harp.

For 2 Stichera:
Praise Him with timbrel and dance,
praise Him with strings and pipes.

For 1 Sticheron:
O praise Him with resounding cymbals,
praise Him with clashing of cymbals.
Let everything that lives and that breathes
give praise to the Lord.

Extra Stichs for use on Sundays when there are eight stichera:

Arise, then, Lord, lift up your hand!
O God, do not forget the poor!

I will praise You, Lord, with all my heart;
I will recount all your wonders.

If it is a feast, the "Glory be...now and ever" is from the feast. On other days, the following:

Glory be: *Of the Sunday Gospel*

Tone 2

Now and ever: You are truly most blessed, O virgin Mother of God. * Through the One who was incarnate of you, * Hades was chained, Adam revived, the curse wiped out, * Eve set free, Death put to death, * and we ourselves were brought back to life. * That is why we cry out in praise: * Blessed are You, O Christ our God, * who finds in this your good pleasure. Glory to You!

On days of Lesser Doxology, see page 441

THE GREAT DOXOLOGY

During the Psalms of Praise, the priest vests in the phelonion. At the "Glory be..." of the Psalms of Praise, the deacon (or priest) opens the Royal Doors. After the last sticheron, the priest stands before the Holy Table, facing East, raises his hands and intones:

Priest: Glory to You who show us the light!

And the people continue the Doxology. At "Holy God" the priest takes the Gospel Book from the tetrapod and processes with it through the Royal Doors and replaces it on the Holy Table.

Glory to God in the highest,
and to his people on earth, peace and good will.

Lord God, heavenly King, Almighty God and Father,
with the Lord Jesus Christ, only Son of the
Father, and the Holy Spirit.

We praise You, we bless You, we worship You,
we glorify You, we thank You for your great glory.

Lord God, Lamb of God, Son of the Father,
You take away the sin of the world, have mercy on us.

You take away the sins of the world,
hear our prayer.

You are seated at the right hand of the Father,
have mercy on us.

For You alone are holy, You alone are the Lord,
Jesus Christ,
for the glory of God the Father. Amen.

I will bless You day after day,
and praise your name forever.

Count us worthy, O Lord,
of passing this day without sin.

Blessed are You, O Lord, God of our Fathers,
and praised and glorified is your name forever. Amen.

Let your mercy, O Lord, be upon us
because we have set our hope in You.

Blessed are You, O Lord,
teach me your commandments.

Blessed are You, O Master,
make me understand your commandments.

Blessed are You, O Holy One,
enlighten me with your laws.

O Lord, You have been our refuge
from one generation to the next.

I said: Lord, have mercy on me,
heal my soul, for I have sinned against You.

O Lord, I have fled to You,
teach me to do your will,
for You, O Lord, are my God.

In You is the source of life
and in your light we see light.

Keep on loving those who know You.

Holy God, Holy and Mighty, Holy and Immortal,
have mercy on us. *(three times)*

Glory be to the Father, and to the Son, and to the Holy Spirit, now and ever and forever. Amen.
Holy and Immortal, have mercy on us.

Holy God, Holy and Mighty, Holy and Immortal,
have mercy on us.

TROPARION OF THE DAY

If there is a feast of the Lord on Sunday, now sing the Troparion of the feast. On regular Sundays, the Troparion indicated below are sung for the proper tone.

The priest remains at the altar and the doors remain open until the end of Matins. If there is a deacon, he intones the following litany at the ambon. The priest intones it from the altar.

For Tones 1, 3, 5, 7:

Tone 2 Today salvation has come to the world. * Let us sing to Him who is risen from the tomb, * the Author of Life who has crushed Death by his death * and bestowed on us victory and great mercy.

For Tones 2, 4, 6, 8:

Tone 2 You came forth from death, destroying the eternal bonds of Hades, O Lord. * You broke the curse of Death * and thus delivered us from the snares of the Evil One. * Then You appeared to your apostles and sent them forth to preach, * and through them You have bestowed your peace upon all the world, * for You alone are rich in mercy.

LITANY

Deacon: Let us complete our morning prayer to the Lord.

R. Lord, have mercy.

Protect us, save us, have mercy on us and preserve us, O God, by your grace.

R. Lord, have mercy.

That this whole day may be perfect, holy, peaceful, and without sin, let us beseech the Lord.

R. Grant it, O Lord. *(and after each following petition)*

For an angel of peace, a faithful guide, a guardian of our souls and bodies, let us beseech the Lord.

For the pardon and remission of our sins and offenses, let us beseech the Lord.

For what is good and beneficial to our souls, and for the peace of the whole world, let us beseech the Lord.

That we may spend the rest of our life in peace and repentance, let us beseech the Lord.

For a Christian, painless, unashamed, peaceful end of our life, and for a good account before the fearsome judgment-seat of Christ, let us beseech the Lord.

Remembering our most holy, most pure, most blessed and glorious Lady, the Mother of God and ever-Virgin Mary with all the saints, let us commend ourselves and one another, and our whole life, to Christ our God.

R. To You, O Lord.

The priest prays the following prayer quietly now or it may be taken with the Prayers of Light.

Priest: God of our Fathers, we praise You, we glorify You, we bless You, we thank You, for You have made the shadow of night pass and have shown us again the light of day. We beg You in your goodness and in your great mercy, cleanse our sins and hear our prayer, for we take refuge in You, O merciful and all-powerful God. Make the true Sun of righteousness shine in our hearts, enlighten our minds, and watch over all our senses, that we may live decently like people of the daytime, so that walking in your commandments, we may come to eternal life, and may be made worthy of the enjoyment of your light beyond reach, for You are the source of life.

And then, aloud:

For You are a God of mercy and kindness and love, and we glorify You, Father, Son, and Holy Spirit, now and ever and forever.

R. Amen.

Priest: Peace † be with all!

R. And with your spirit.

Deacon: Bow your heads to the Lord.

R. To You, O Lord.

The priest prays quietly:

Priest: Holy Lord, You live on high and yet stoop to look down upon earth, and with your divine eyes You see all creatures. Before You we bow down in spirit and body, and we pray You, O Holy of holies, stretch forth your invisible hand from your holy dwelling and bless us. If we have sinned in any way, either deliberately or through human frailty, forgive us, for You are good; You give us earthly and heavenly blessings, and You alone love all.

And then, aloud:

For it is You alone who have mercy and save us, and we glorify You, Father, Son, and Holy Spirit, now and ever and forever.

R. Amen.

DISMISSAL

Deacon: Wisdom!

R. Give the blessing!

Priest: Blessed is the One-Who-Is, blessed is Christ our God, always, now and ever and forever.

R. Amen. O God, strengthen the true faith, forever and ever.

If the First Hour or the Divine Liturgy follows, it begins at this point.

Priest: O most holy Mother of God, save us!

R. More honorable than the Cherubim and beyond compare more glorious than the Seraphim, who, a virgin, gave birth to God the Word; you, truly the Mother of God, we magnify.

****

From Easter until the Wednesday before Ascension we say:

R. Shine in splendor, O new Jerusalem; for the glory of the Lord is risen upon you. O Zion, sing with joy and rejoice. And you, pure Mother of God, rejoice in the resurrection of your Son.

Priest: Glory be to You, O Christ, our God, our hope; glory be to You!

R. Christ is risen from the dead! By death He conquered Death, and to those in the graves He granted life. Lord, have mercy. Lord, have mercy. Lord, have mercy. Give the blessing!

Priest: May Christ our true God, risen from the dead,
(***Bright Week only:*** by death conquering Death and granting life to those in the graves,)
have mercy on us and save us through the prayers of His most pure Mother; through the might of the precious and life-giving Cross; through the prayers of the holy, glorious, and praiseworthy apostles;
of Saint *(name)* patron*(ess)* of this holy church;
and of Saint *(name)* whose feast we commemorate today,
and through the prayers of all the Saints; for He is gracious and loves mankind.

R. Amen.

****

Priest: Glory be to You, O Christ, our God, our hope; glory be to You!

R. Glory be to the Father, and to the Son, and to the Holy Spirit, now and ever and forever. Amen. Lord, have mercy. Lord, have mercy. Lord, have mercy. Give the blessing!

Priest: May Christ our true God, have mercy on us and save us through the prayers of His most pure Mother; through the prayers of
Saint *(name)* patron*(ess)* of this holy church,
and of Saint *(name)* whose feast we commemorate today,
and through the prayers of all the Saints; for He is gracious and loves mankind.

R. Amen.

LESSER DOXOLOGY

The priest now comes before the Royal Doors, raises his hands, and says:

Priest: Glory to You who show us the light!

And the priest remains before the Royal Doors as the Doxology is sung by the congregation:

Glory to God in the highest,
and to his people on earth, peace and good will.

Lord God, heavenly King, Almighty God and Father,
with the Lord Jesus Christ, only Son of the
Father, and the Holy Spirit.

We praise You, we bless You, we worship You,
we glorify You, we thank You for your great glory.

Lord God, Lamb of God, Son of the Father,
You take away the sin of the world, have mercy on us.

You take away the sins of the world,
hear our prayer.

You are seated at the right hand of the Father,
have mercy on us.

For You alone are holy, You alone are the Lord,
Jesus Christ,
for the glory of God the Father. Amen.

I will bless You day after day,
and praise your name forever.

O Lord, You have been our refuge
from one generation to the next.

I said: Lord, have mercy on me,
heal my soul, for I have sinned against You.

O Lord, I have fled to You,
teach me to do your will,
for You, O Lord, are my God.

In You is the source of life
and in your light we see light.

Keep on loving those who know You,
count us worthy, O Lord, of passing this day
without sin.

Blessed are You, O Lord, God of our Fathers,
and praised and glorified is your name forever. Amen.

Let your mercy, O Lord, be upon us
because we have set our hope in You.

Blessed are You, O Lord,
teach me your commandments.

Blessed are You, O Master,
make me understand your commandments.

Blessed are You, O Holy One,
enlighten me with your laws.

O Lord, your mercy endures forever;
do not despise the work of your hands.

It is proper to praise You,
and hymns belong to You.

Glory belongs to You, Father, Son, and Holy Spirit,
now and ever and forever. Amen.

Then the priest returns to the altar. The deacon says the following litany at the ambon. If there is no deacon, the priest remains at the Royal Doors for this litany.

LITANY

Deacon: Let us complete our morning prayer to the Lord.

R. Lord, have mercy.

Protect us, save us, have mercy on us and preserve us, O God, by your grace.

R. Lord, have mercy.

That this whole day may be perfect, holy, peaceful, and without sin, let us beseech the Lord.

R. Grant it, O Lord. *(and after each following petition)*

For an angel of peace, a faithful guide, a guardian of our souls and bodies, let us beseech the Lord.

For the pardon and remission of our sins and offenses, let us beseech the Lord.

For what is good and beneficial to our souls, and for the peace of the whole world, let us beseech the Lord.

That we may spend the rest of our life in peace and repentance, let us beseech the Lord.

For a Christian, painless, unashamed, peaceful end of our life, and for a good account before the fearsome judgment-seat of Christ, let us beseech the Lord.

Remembering our most holy, most pure, most blessed and

glorious Lady, the Mother of God and ever-Virgin Mary with all the saints, let us commend ourselves and one another, and our whole life, to Christ our God.

R. To You, O Lord.

The priest prays the following prayer quietly now or it may be taken with the Prayers of Light.

Priest: God of our Fathers, we praise You, we glorify You, we bless You, we thank You, for You have made the shadow of night pass and have shown us again the light of day. We beg You in your goodness and in your great mercy, cleanse our sins and hear our prayer, for we take refuge in You, O merciful and all-powerful God. Make the true Sun of righteousness shine in our hearts, enlighten our minds, and watch over all our senses, that we may live decently like people of the daytime, so that walking in your commandments, we may come to eternal life, and may be made worthy of the enjoyment of your light beyond reach, for You are the source of life.

And then, aloud:

For You are a God of mercy and kindness and love, and we glorify You, Father, Son, and Holy Spirit, now and ever and forever.

R. Amen.

Priest: Peace † be with all!

R. And with your spirit.

Deacon: Bow your heads to the Lord.

R. To You, O Lord.

The priest prays quietly:

Priest: Holy Lord, You live on high and yet stoop to look down upon earth, and with your divine eyes You see all creatures. Before You we bow down in spirit and body, and we pray You, O Holy of holies, stretch forth your invisible hand from your holy dwelling and bless us. If we have sinned in any way, either deliberately or through human frailty, forgive us, for You are good; You give us earthly and heavenly blessings, and You alone love all.

And then, aloud:

For it is You alone who have mercy and save us, and we glorify You, Father, Son, and Holy Spirit, now and ever and forever.

R. Amen.

APOSTICHA

Then:

It is good to give thanks to the Lord,
and to make music to your name, O Most High,
to proclaim your love in the morning
and your truth in the watches of the night.

Holy God, Holy and Mighty, Holy and Immortal, have mercy on us. *(3 times)*

Glory be to the Father, and to the Son, and to the Holy Spirit, now and ever and forever. Amen.

O Most Holy Trinity, have mercy on us; O Lord, cleanse us of our sins; O Master, forgive our transgressions; O Holy One, come to us and heal our infirmities for Your name's sake.

Lord, have mercy. *(3 times)*

Glory be to the Father, and to the Son, and to the Holy Spirit, now and ever and forever. Amen.

Our Father, Who art in heaven, hallowed be Thy name. Thy kingdom come, Thy will be done on earth as it is in heaven. Give us this day our daily bread, and forgive us our trespasses as we forgive those who trespass against us, and lead us not into temptation, but deliver us from evil.

Priest: For Thine is the kingdom and the power and the glory, Father, Son, and Holy Spirit, now and ever and forever.

R. Amen.

TROPARION OF THE DAY

Glory be...now and ever: *The prescribed Theotokion.*

The deacon says the following litany from the ambon:

LITANY

Deacon: Have mercy on us, O God, according to Your great mercy; we pray You, hear us and have mercy.

R. Lord, have mercy. *(3 times)*

We also pray for our holy ecumenical Pontiff *(name)*, the Pope of Rome, and for our most reverend Archbishop and Metropolitan *(name)*, for our God-loving Bishop *(name)*, for those who serve and have served in this holy Church, for our spiritual guides, and for all our brothers and sisters in Christ.

R. Lord, have mercy. *(3 times)*

We also pray for our civil authorities and for all in the service of our country.

R. Lord, have mercy. *(3 times)*

We also pray for the people here present who await Your great and abundant mercy, for those who showed us mercy, and for all Christians of the true faith.

R. Lord, have mercy. *(3 times)*

Priest: For You are a merciful and gracious God, and we give glory to You, Father, Son, and Holy Spirit, now and ever and forever.

R. Amen.

DISMISSAL

Deacon: Wisdom!

R. Give the blessing!

Priest: Blessed is the One-Who-Is, blessed is Christ our God, always, now and ever and forever.

R. Amen. O God, strengthen the true faith, forever and ever.

If the First Hour or the Divine Liturgy follows, it begins at this point.

Priest: O most holy Mother of God, save us!

R. More honorable than the Cherubim and beyond compare more glorious than the Seraphim, who, a virgin, gave birth to God the Word; you, truly the Mother of God, we magnify.

****

From Easter until the Wednesday before Ascension we say:

R. Shine in splendor, O new Jerusalem; for the glory of the Lord is risen upon you. O Zion, sing with joy and rejoice. And you, pure Mother of God, rejoice in the resurrection of your Son.

Priest: Glory be to You, O Christ, our God, our hope; glory be to You!

R. Christ is risen from the dead! By death He conquered Death, and to those in the graves He granted life. Lord, have mercy. Lord, have mercy. Lord, have mercy. Give the blessing!

Priest: May Christ our true God, risen from the dead,
(***Bright Week only:*** by death conquering Death and granting life to those in the graves,)
have mercy on us and save us through the prayers of His most pure Mother; through the might of the precious and life-giving Cross; through the prayers of the holy, glorious, and praiseworthy apostles;

of Saint *(name)* patron*(ess)* of this holy church;
and of Saint *(name)* whose feast we commemorate today,
and through the prayers of all the Saints; for He is gracious and loves mankind.

R. Amen.

****

Priest: Glory be to You, O Christ, our God, our hope; glory be to You!

R. Glory be to the Father, and to the Son, and to the Holy Spirit, now and ever and forever. Amen. Lord, have mercy. Lord, have mercy. Lord, have mercy. Give the blessing!

Priest: May Christ our true God, have mercy on us and save us through the prayers of His most pure Mother; through the prayers of
Saint *(name)* patron*(ess)* of this holy church,
and of Saint *(name)* whose feast we commemorate today,
and of all the Saints; for He is gracious and loves mankind.

R. Amen.

PRAYERS OF MATINS

The following three prayers are recited during Psalms 87, 102, and 142 of the Six Psalms

FIRST PRAYER: *Prayer of the 1st Antiphon*

We thank You, Lord our God, for You have wakened us from our sleep, and have filled our lips with praise that we might worship You and call upon your holy name. We beg of your compassion that You have always shown towards us, hear us now and send help to those who stand before your holy glory awaiting your abundant mercy. O Lord, grant that those who serve You in fear and love may praise your ineffable goodness.

For to You is due all glory, honor, and worship, Father, Son, and Holy Spirit, now and ever and forever. Amen.

SECOND PRAYER: *Prayer of the 2nd Antiphon. This prayer may be read after one of the kathismata.*

From the depths of night our soul longs for You, our God, for your commandments are a light upon the earth. Give us understanding that we may be perfected in righteousness and holiness in fear of You, for it is You whom we glorify as our true God. Turn your ear and hear us. O Lord, remember each one present and praying with us by their own name, and save them by your might. Bless your people and sanctify your inheritance. Give peace to your world, to your churches, to the priests, and to all your people.

For blessed and glorified is your most honored and sublime name, Father, Son, and Holy Spirit, now and ever and forever. Amen.

THIRD PRAYER: *Prayer of the 3rd Antiphon. This prayer may be read after one of the kathismata.*

From the depths of night our soul longs for You, our God, for your commandments are a light upon the earth. Teach us, O God, your righteousness, your statutes, and your decrees. Enlighten the eyes of our minds, lest we fall asleep in sin until death. Cast out all darkness from our hearts, favor us with the Sun of righteousness, and keep our lives from danger by the seal of your Holy Spirit. Direct our steps along the road of peace. Grant that we may see the dawn and the whole day in joy, and that we may offer You our morning prayers.

For Yours is the power, and Yours is the kingdom and the might and the glory, Father, Son, and Holy Spirit, now and ever and forever. Amen.

FOURTH PRAYER: *Prayer of the 4th Antiphon. This prayer may be read after one of the kathismata.*

Lord God, holy and incomprehensible, You told the light to shine out of darkness; You have given us rest in the sleep of night; and You have raised us to glorify and praise your goodness. We beg of your mercy, accept us who now worship You and thank You with all our strength, and grant all that we ask for our salvation. Reveal us to be children of light and heirs of your eternal good gifts. In the abundance of your mercy, Lord, remember all your people who invoke your love for mankind and aid those here present and who pray with us and those traveling abroad in every place of your kingdom. Be greatly merciful to all, that we may persevere always in confidence, being saved in soul and body.

We glorify your magnificent and blessed name, Father, Son, and Holy Spirit, now and ever and forever. Amen.

FIFTH PRAYER: *Prayer of the 5th Antiphon*

Treasury of all good, ever-flowing spring, Holy Father, Wonder-worker, all-powerful Ruler of all: we worship You and beg of your mercy and compassion, help and support in our lowliness. Lord, remember those who pray to You, and let our morning prayer rise like incense before You. Grant that no one of us may be put to shame, but surround us with your mercy. Lord, remember those who keep watch and sing of your glory, and that of your only-begotten Son and our God, and of your Holy Spirit. Be their help and support and accept their prayers upon your heavenly spiritual altar.

For You are our God, and to You we give glory, to the Father, and to the Son, and to the Holy Spirit, now and ever, and forever. Amen.

SIXTH PRAYER: *Prayer of the 6th Antiphon*

We give thanks to You, O Lord and God of our salvation. You have done everything that is good for our lives, and we look always to You, Savior and Benefactor of our souls. For You have given us rest in that part of the night which has passed, and now have raised us from our sleep to worship your honored name. Therefore, O Lord, we pray: give us the grace and strength to be found worthy to sing praise always, and to pray constantly, and to work for our own salvation in fear and trembling, with the help of your Christ. O Lord, remember those who pray to You in the night. Hear them and have mercy on them and crush under their feet invisible and malicious enemies.

For You are the King of peace, and the Savior of our souls, and we give thanks to You, Father, Son, and Holy Spirit, now and ever and forever. Amen.

SEVENTH PRAYER: *Prayer of the 7th Antiphon. This prayer may be read after one of the kathismata.*

God and Father of our Lord Jesus Christ, You have raised us from our sleep and gathered us for this time of prayer. Give us grace that we may open our lips in praise. Accept the thanksgiving we offer with all our strength. Teach us your decrees, for we do not know how to pray as we should, unless You guide us by your Holy Spirit. Therefore, we pray, that if until now we have sinned in any way, in word, or deed, or thought, voluntarily or involuntarily, remit, pardon and forgive us; for if You, O Lord, should mark our guilt, Lord, who would survive? For with You is found redemption. You alone are holy and a helper and the stronghold of our lives, and our praise is for You forever.

Blessed and glorified be the power of your reign, Father, Son, and Holy Spirit, now and ever and forever. Amen.

EIGHTH PRAYER: *Prayer of the 8th Antiphon. This prayer was said with the Eighth Ode.*

Lord our God, You have shaken from us the laziness of sleep; You have called us to be holy, to lift up our hands in the night, and to confess You for your just decrees. Receive our prayers, our petitions, our confessions of faith, and our nighttime worship. Bestow on us, O Lord, an invincible faith, a confident hope, and a love without pretense. Bless our comings and our goings, our deeds and works, our words and desires. Grant that we may come to the beginning of the day praising, glorifying, and blessing the goodness of your inexpressible generosity.

For blessed is your all-holy name, and glorified is your kingdom, Father, Son, and Holy Spirit, now and ever and forever. Amen.

NINTH PRAYER: *Prayer of Psalm 50*

O Lord our God, You have given us forgiveness through repentance, and as a model of knowledge and confession of sins, You have revealed to us the repentance of the prophet David that led to pardon. Master, have mercy on us who have fallen into so many and so great sins. Have mercy in your kindness, and in your compassion blot out our offenses, for against You have we sinned, O Lord, who know the hidden depths of our hearts, and who alone have the power to forgive sins. A pure heart You have created for us; You have sustained us with a spirit of fervor and have given us the joy of your help. Do not cast us away from your presence, but in your goodness and love for all, grant that we may offer a sacrifice of righteousness and oblation on your holy altar until our last breath.

Through the mercies and goodness and love of your only-begotten Son, with whom You are blessed, together with your good and life-creating Spirit, now and ever and forever. Amen.

TENTH PRAYER: *Prayer of the Psalms of Praise*

O God, our God, who have placed all spiritual and intellectual powers under your will, we pray and beg You, accept these hymns of praise which we offer to You according to our ability together with all your creatures. Give us in exchange the riches of your goodness, for before You all beings in the heavens, or on earth and under the earth bend their knees, and everything that lives or that breathes gives praise to your glory beyond reach, for You are the one true God, full of mercy.

For all the heavenly powers praise You, and we give glory to You, to the Father, and to the Son, and to the Holy Spirit, now and ever and forever. Amen.

ELEVENTH PRAYER: *Prayer of Dismissal*

God of our Fathers, we praise You, we glorify You, we bless You, we thank You, for You have made the shadow of night pass and have shown us again the light of day. We beg You in your goodness and in your great mercy, cleanse our sins and hear our prayer, for we take refuge in You, O merciful and all-powerful God. Make the true Sun of righteousness shine in our hearts, enlighten our minds, and watch over all our senses, that we may live decently like people of the daytime, so that walking in your commandments, we may come to eternal life, and may be made worthy of the enjoyment of your light beyond reach, for You are the source of life.

For You are a God of mercy and kindness and love, and we glorify You, Father, Son, and Holy Spirit, now and ever and forever. Amen.

Hours for Bright Week

The following is used for all Hours on Resurrection Day and during all of Bright Week.

Priest: Blessed is our God, always, now and ever and forever.

Response: Amen.

If a Celebrant is not present:

Leader: Through the prayers of our holy fathers, O Lord Jesus Christ, our God, have mercy on us.

Response: Amen.

Christ is risen from the dead! By death He conquered Death, and to those in the graves He granted life. *(3 times)*

Having beheld the Resurrection of Christ, * let us adore the holy Lord Jesus * who alone is sinless. * We bow to your Cross, O Christ, * and we praise and glorify your holy Resurrection. * You are our God * and besides You we recognize no other, * and we invoke your name. * Come, all you faithful, * and let us bow to the holy Resurrection of Christ, * since, through the Cross, joy has come to all the world. * Ever praising the Lord, * let us extol his Resurrection, * since He, having endured the crucifixion, * has destroyed Death by his death.

HYPAKOE

Tone 8 The women with Mary, before the dawn, * found the stone rolled away from the tomb, * and they heard the angel say: * Why do you seek among the dead, as a mortal, the One who abides in everlasting light? * Behold the linens of burial. * Go in haste and proclaim to the world * that, having conquered Death, the Lord is risen; * for He is the Son of God, the Savior of mankind.

KONTAKION

Tone 8 Although You descended into the grave, O Immortal One, * You destroyed the power of Death. * You arose again as a victor, O Christ God. * You announced to the women bearing ointment: Rejoice! * You gave peace to your apostles* and resurrection to the fallen.

TROPARIA

Tone 8 Being God, You were present in the tomb with your body,* and yet in Hades with your soul, * in Paradise with the thief, * and on the throne, O Christ, with the Father and the Holy Spirit, * filling all things but encompassed by none.

Glory be: O Christ, You are the source of our resurrection, * and your tomb has been revealed as a giver of life * more splendid than Paradise and more radiant than any royal chamber.

Now and ever: Rejoice, O most holy and divine dwelling of the Most High, * for through you, O Mother of God, * joy has been given to all those who cry out: * Blessed are you among women, O Lady most pure!

Lord, have mercy. *(40 times)*

Glory be to the Father, and to the Son, and to the Holy Spirit, now and ever and forever. Amen.

More honorable than the Cherubim, and beyond compare more glorious than the Seraphim, who, a virgin, gave birth to God the Word, you, truly the Mother of God, we magnify.

In the name of the Lord, Father give the blessing!

Priest: Through the prayers of our holy fathers, O Lord Jesus Christ our God, have mercy on us.

R. Amen.

Christ is risen from the dead! By death He conquered Death, and to those in the graves He granted life. *(3 times).*

Glory be to the Father, and to the Son, and to the Holy Spirit, now and ever and forever. Amen. Lord, have mercy. Lord, have mercy. Lord, have mercy. Give the blessing!

Priest: May Christ our true God, risen from the dead, by death conquering Death and granting life to all in the graves, have mercy on us and save us through the prayers of his most pure Mother and all the saints, for He is gracious and loves mankind.

R. Amen.

DISMISSALS

PENTECOST SEASON

May Christ our true God, risen from the dead, (*Bright Week only: by death conquering Death and granting life to those in the graves,)* have mercy on us and save us through the prayers of his most holy Mother; through the might of the precious and life-giving Cross (*only on Wednesdays and Fridays)*; through the prayers of the holy, glorious, and praiseworthy apostles; of Saint **(name)** patron*(ess)* of this church; and of Saint **(name)** whose feast we commemorate today, and through the prayers of all the saints; for He is gracious and loves mankind.

THOMAS SUNDAY

May Christ our true God, who for our salvation came to his disciples, even though the doors were closed, and confirmed Thomas in his faith, have mercy on us and save us through the prayers of his most holy Mother; through the prayers of the holy, glorious, and praiseworthy apostles; through the prayers of our holy fathers; and through the prayers of all the saints; for He is gracious and loves mankind.

ASCENSION

May Christ our true God, who for our salvation ascended from us to heaven and sits at the right hand of God and Father, have mercy on us and save us through the prayers of his most holy Mother; through the might of the precious and life-giving Cross; through the prayers of the holy, glorious, and praiseworthy apostles; through the prayers of our holy fathers; and through the prayers of all the saints; for He is gracious and loves mankind.

PENTECOST

May Christ our true God, who for our salvation sent the all-holy Spirit from heaven in the appearance of tongues of fire upon his holy disciples and apostles, have mercy on us and save us through the prayers of his most holy Mother; through the prayers of the holy, glorious, and praiseworthy apostles; and through the prayers of all the saints; for He is gracious and loves mankind.

PENTECOST EVENING VESPERS

May He who emptied himself and came forth from the bosom of God the Father, and descended from heaven upon the earth, and took upon himself our entire nature and rendered it divine, and after that ascended again into heaven and sits at the right hand of God the Father, who also sent down upon his holy disciples and apostles the divine and Holy Spirit who is equal in substance, in power, in glory, and in eternity, who enlightened the apostles by the Holy Spirit and through them the whole world, may the same Christ our true God have mercy on us and save us through the prayers of his most holy Mother; through the might of the precious and life-giving Cross; through the prayers of the holy, glorious, and praiseworthy apostles, heralds of the divinity and bearers of the Spirit; and through the prayers of all the saints, for He is gracious and loves mankind.

APPENDIX A
Composite Readings for Mid-Pentecost

MICAH

For from Zion shall go forth instruction, and the word of the Lord from Jerusalem. He shall judge between many peoples and impose terms on strong and distant nations; for all the peoples walk each in the name of its god, but we will walk in the name of the Lord, our God, forever and ever. Hear, O mountains, the plea of the Lord; pay attention, O foundations of the earth! For the Lord has a plea against his people, and He enters into trial with Israel. O my people, what have I done to you, or how have I wearied you? Answer Me! For I brought you up from the land of Egypt, from the place of slavery I released you; and I sent before you Moses, Aaron, and Miriam. My people, remember what Moab's King Balak planned, and how Balaam, the son of Beor, answered him from Shittim to Gilgal, that you may know the just deeds of the Lord. You have been told, O people, what is good, and what the Lord requires of you: Only to do right and to love goodness, and to walk humbly with your God, for now his greatness shall reach to the ends of the earth.

ISAIAH

All you who are thirsty, come to the water! You who have no money, come, receive grain and eat; come, without paying and without cost, drink wine and milk! With joy you will draw water at the fountain of salvation and say on that day: Give thanks to the Lord, acclaim his name; among the nations make known his deeds; proclaim how exalted is his name. Why spend your money for what is not bread; your wages for what fails to satisfy? Heed me, and you shall eat well; you shall delight in rich fare. Come to me heedfully; listen, that you may have life. I will renew with you the everlasting covenant, the benefits assured to David.

Seek the Lord while He may be found; call Him while He is near. Let the scoundrel forsake his way, and the wicked one his thoughts. Let all turn to the Lord for mercy; to our God who is generous in forgiving. For my thoughts are not your thoughts, nor are your ways my ways, says the Lord. As high as the heavens are above the earth, so high are my ways above your ways and my thoughts above your thoughts. For just as from the heavens the rain and snow come down and do not return there till they have watered the earth, making it fertile and fruitful, giving seed to those who sow and bread to those who eat, so shall my word be that goes forth from my mouth. It shall not return to Me void, but shall do my will, achieving the end for which I sent it. Yes, in joy you shall depart; in peace you shall be brought back; mountains and hills shall break out in song before you, and all the trees of the countryside shall clap their hands. In place of the thornbush, the cypress shall grow; instead of nettles, the myrtle. This shall be to the Lord's renown, an everlasting imperishable sign.

APPENDIX B
Music for the Paschal Canon

TROPARION -*Tone 2*

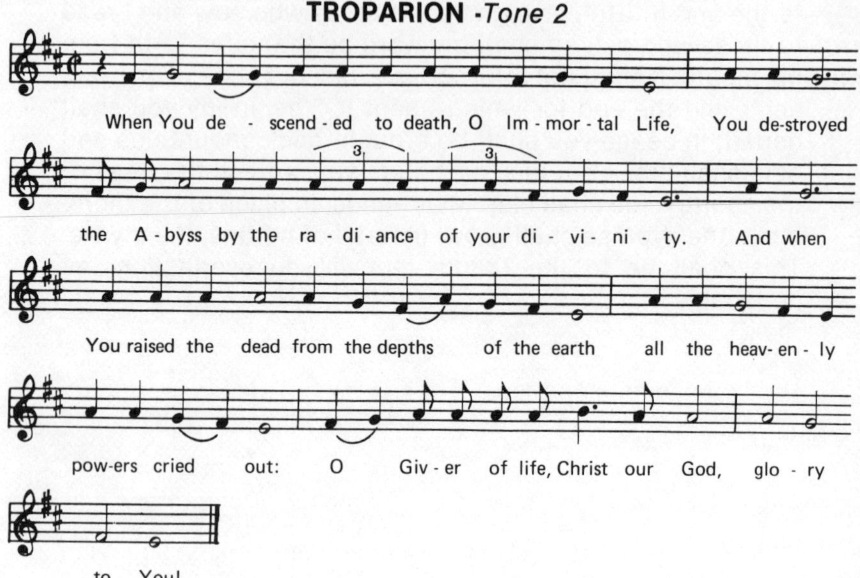
When You de - scend - ed to death, O Im - mor - tal Life, You de-stroyed
the A - byss by the ra - di - ance of your di - vi - ni - ty. And when
You raised the dead from the depths of the earth all the heav- en - ly
pow-ers cried out: O Giv - er of life, Christ our God, glo - ry
to You!

TROPARION - *Tone 6*

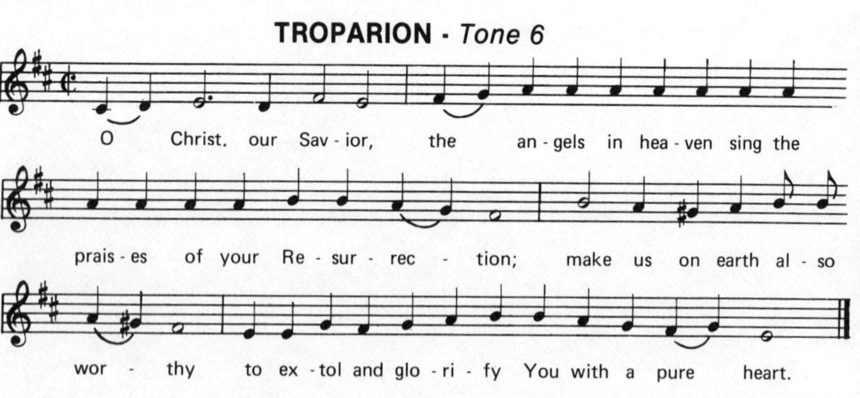
O Christ, our Sav - ior, the an - gels in hea - ven sing the
prais - es of your Re - sur - rec - tion; make us on earth al - so
wor - thy to ex - tol and glo - ri - fy You with a pure heart.

TROPARION - *Special Tone 5*

Christ is ri - sen from the dead. By death He con-quered Death,
and to those in the graves He grant - ed life.

TROPARION WITH VERSICLES

Let God a-rise and let His en- e-mies be scat-tered, and let those

who hate Him flee from be-fore His face.

Troparion: Christ is risen from the dead...

As smoke van - ish - es, so let them van - ish as wax melts be-fore a fire.

Troparion: Christ is risen from the dead...

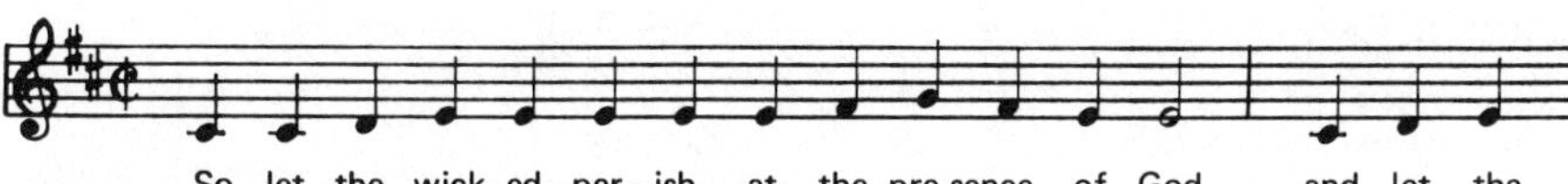

So let the wick-ed per - ish at the pre-sence of God, and let the

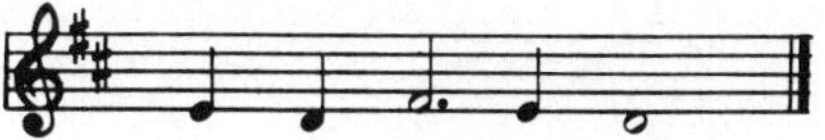

right - eous ones re - joice.

Troparion: Christ is risen from the dead...

This is the day that the Lord has made; let us ex - ult and re-joice in it.

Troparion: Christ is risen from the dead...

Glo - ry be to the Fa - ther, and to the Son, and to the Ho - ly Spir - it,

now and e - ver and for - e - ver. A - men.

Troparion: Christ is risen from the dead...

RESURRECTION CANON
ODE 1
It is the day of Re - sur - rec - tion. O Peo - ple, let us be
en - light - ened by it. The Pass - o - ver is the Lord's Pass - o - ver,
since Christ, our God, has brought us from death to life and from earth
to hea - ven. There - fore, we sing the hymn of vic - tor - y.
Refrain:
Christ is ri - sen from the dead.
Let us cleanse our sen - ses that we may see the ri - sen Christ
in the glo - ry of His re - sur - rec - tion and clear - ly hear Him
greet - ing us: Re - joice! —as we sing the hymn of vic - tor - y.
Refrain: Christ is risen from the dead.
Let the hea - vens pro - per - ly re - joice, and let the earth be glad,
and let the whole vis - i - ble and in - vi - si - ble world cel - e - brate;
for Christ, our e - ver - last - ing joy, is ri - sen.
Refrain: Christ is risen from the dead.

Katavasia: It is the day of Resurrection...

ODE 3

Come, let us par - take of a new drink, not mir - a - cu - lous - ly
pro-duced from the bar - ren rock, but from the Foun-tain of Im-mor-tal- i - ty,
spring-ing up from the tomb of Christ. In Him is our firm strength.
Refrain: Christ is risen from the dead.
To - day all things are filled with light — earth and hea - ven and the world
be - neath. Then let all cre - a - tion cel - e - brate the re - sur - rec - tion
of Christ. In Him is the firm foun-da - tion of all things.
Refrain: Christ is risen from the dead.
I was bur - ied yes - ter - day with You, O Christ; but to - day I rise,
re - sur - rect - ed with You. Yes - ter - day I cru - ci - fied my - self with You,
O Sav - ior. Now glor - i - fy me with You in your king-dom.
Refrain: Christ is risen from the dead.

Katavasia: Come, let us partake of a new drink...

HYPAKOE
The wo - men with Mar - y be - fore the dawn, found the stone
rolled a - way from the tomb, and they heard the An - gel say:
Why do you seek a - mong the dead, as a mor - tal, the One who a - bides
in e - ver - last - ing light? Be - hold the lin - ens of bur - i - al.
Go in haste and pro-claim to the world that, hav - ing con-quered
Death, the Lord is ri - sen; for He is the Son of God, the Sav-ior of man-kind.
ODE 4
Let Ha - bak - kuk, speak-ing in be-half of God, stand with us
at the di-vine watch; let him show us the bril - liant An - gel who pro-claims:
To-day, sal - va - tion comes to the world; for Christ, be-ing Al-migh- ty, is ri - sen.
Refrain: Christ is risen from the dead.
Christ had ap-peared as a man when He was born of the Vir-gin.
As a mor-tal, He was called Lamb . Be - ing un - de - filed and with-out
3

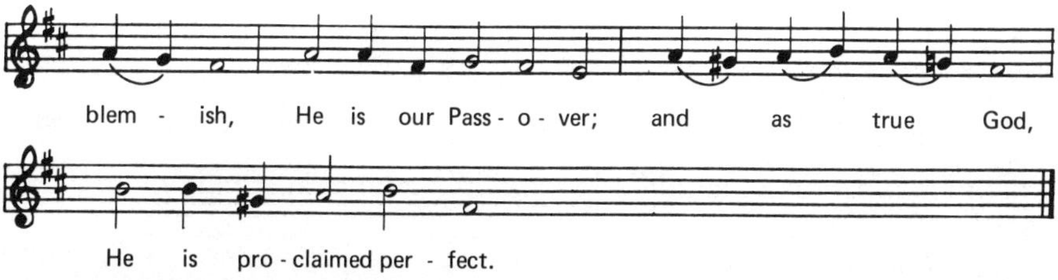

blem - ish, He is our Pass - o - ver; and as true God,
He is pro - claimed per - fect.

Refrain: Christ is risen from the dead.

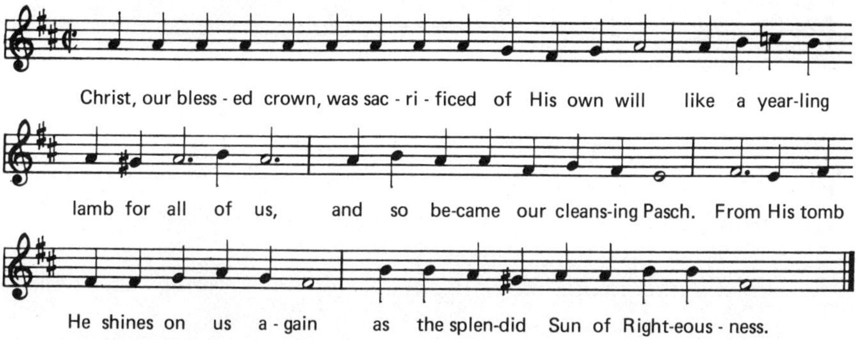

Christ, our bless - ed crown, was sac - ri - ficed of His own will like a year-ling
lamb for all of us, and so be-came our cleans-ing Pasch. From His tomb
He shines on us a - gain as the splen-did Sun of Right-eous - ness.

Refrain: Christ is risen from the dead.

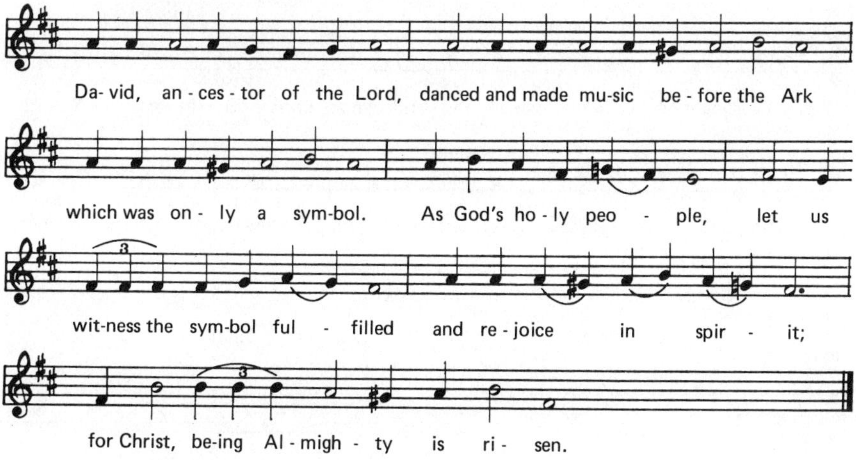

Da- vid, an - ces - tor of the Lord, danced and made mu-sic be - fore the Ark
which was on - ly a sym-bol. As God's ho - ly peo - ple, let us
wit-ness the sym-bol ful - filled and re - joice in spir - it;
for Christ, be-ing Al - migh - ty is ri - sen.

Refrain: Christ is risen from the dead.

Katavasia: Let Habakkuk, speaking in behalf...

ODE 5

Let us rise at ear - ly dawn and bring to our Mas-ter a hymn in -

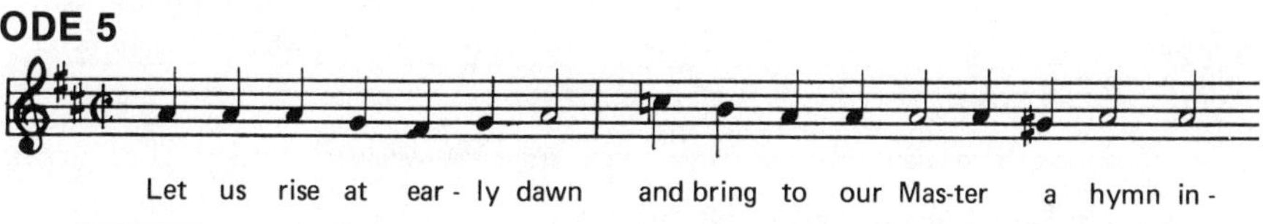

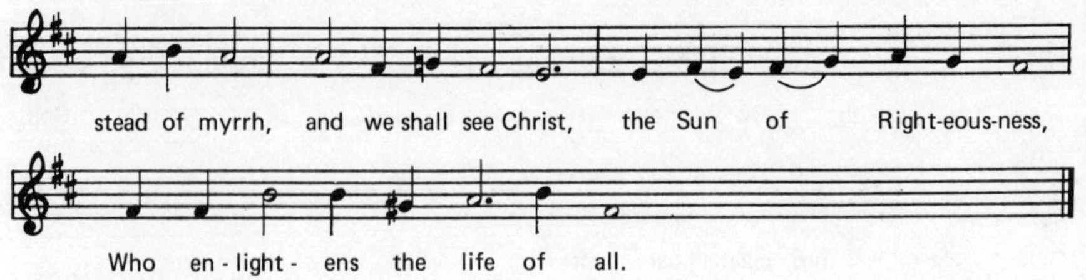
stead of myrrh, and we shall see Christ, the Sun of Right-eous-ness,
Who en - light - ens the life of all.

Refrain: Christ is risen from the dead.

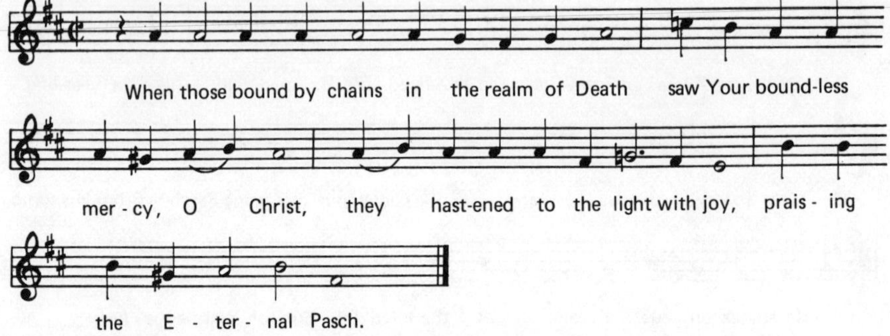
When those bound by chains in the realm of Death saw Your bound-less
mer - cy, O Christ, they hast-ened to the light with joy, prais - ing
the E - ter - nal Pasch.

Refrain: Christ is risen from the dead.

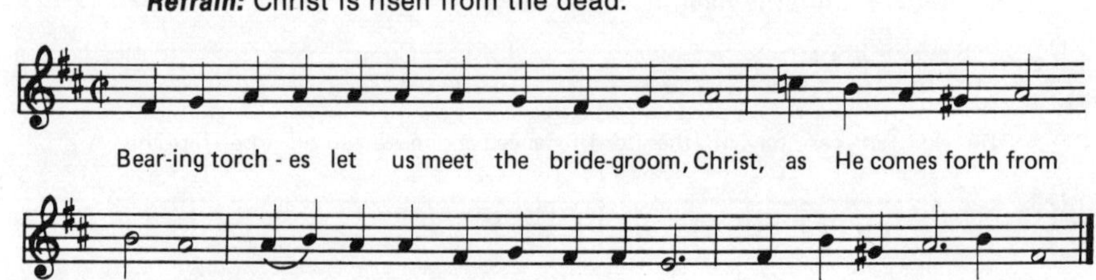
Bear-ing torch - es let us meet the bride-groom, Christ, as He comes forth from
His tomb; and let us greet, with joy-ful song, the sav - ing Pasch of God.

Refrain: Christ is risen from the dead.

Katavasia: Let us rise at early dawn...

ODE 6

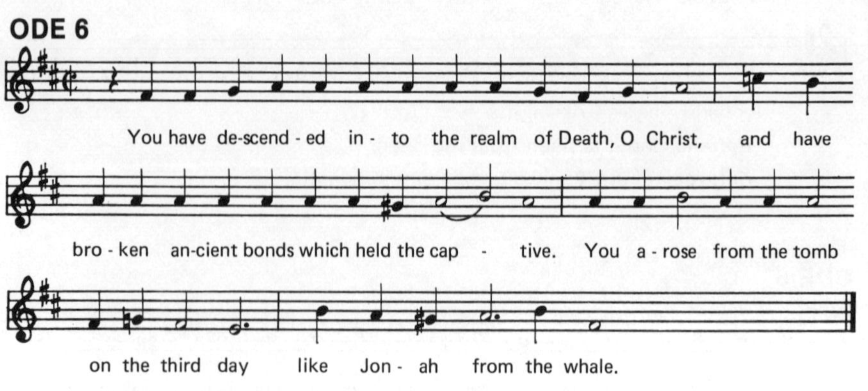
You have de-scend - ed in - to the realm of Death, O Christ, and have
bro - ken an-cient bonds which held the cap - tive. You a - rose from the tomb
on the third day like Jon - ah from the whale.

Refrain: Christ is risen from the dead.

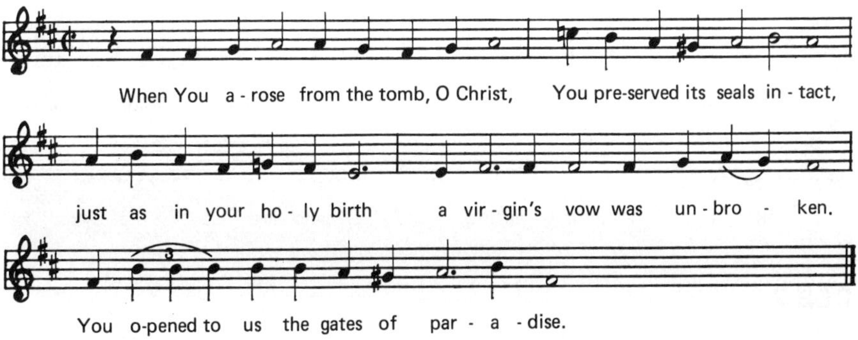

When You a - rose from the tomb, O Christ, You pre-served its seals in - tact,
just as in your ho - ly birth a vir - gin's vow was un - bro - ken.
3
You o-pened to us the gates of par - a - dise.

Refrain: Christ is risen from the dead

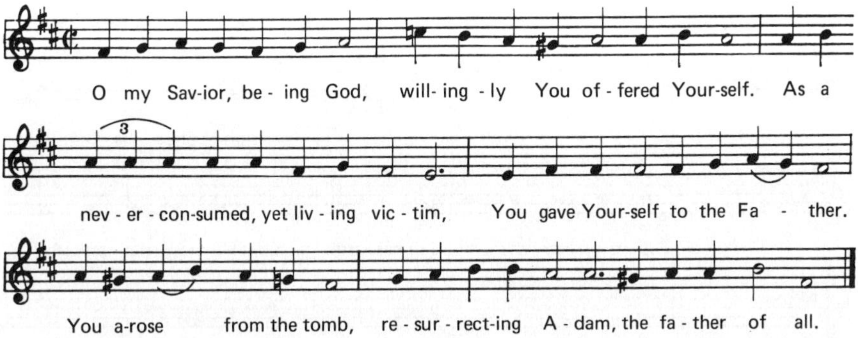

O my Sav-ior, be - ing God, will- ing - ly You of - fered Your-self. As a
3
nev - er - con-sumed, yet liv - ing vic - tim, You gave Your-self to the Fa - ther.
You a-rose from the tomb, re - sur - rect-ing A - dam, the fa - ther of all.

Refrain: Christ is risen from the dead.
Katavasia: You have descended in the realm...

KONTAKION - *Tone 8*

Al-though You descend - ed in - to the grave, O Im - mor - tal One,
You destroyed the power of Death. You a - rose a - gain as a vic - tor, O
Christ, God. You announced to the wo-men bear- ing oint - ment: Re - joice!
You gave peace to your a - pos - tles and re - sur - rec-tion to the fall - en.

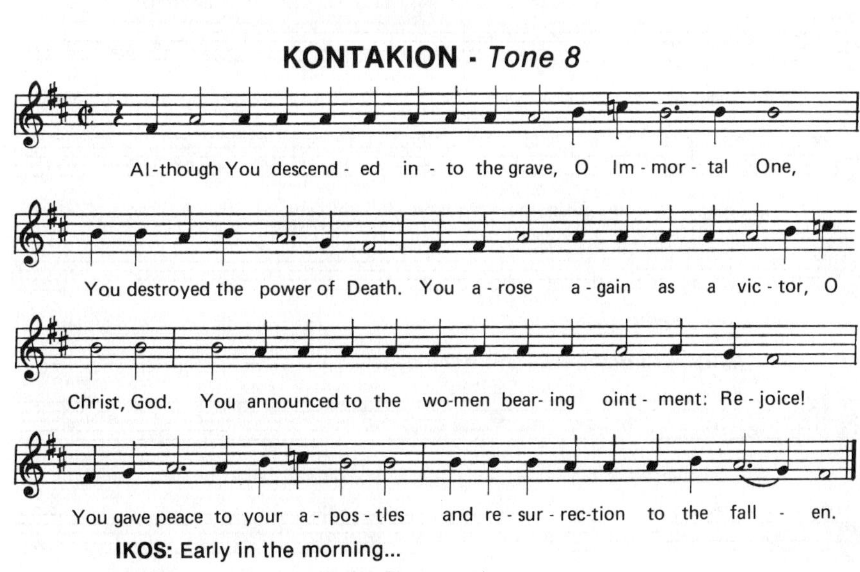

IKOS: Early in the morning...
HYMN: Having beheld the Resurrection...

Je - sus is ri - sen from the tomb, as He fore - told, and grant -
ed us e - ver-last - ing life and great mer - - - cy.

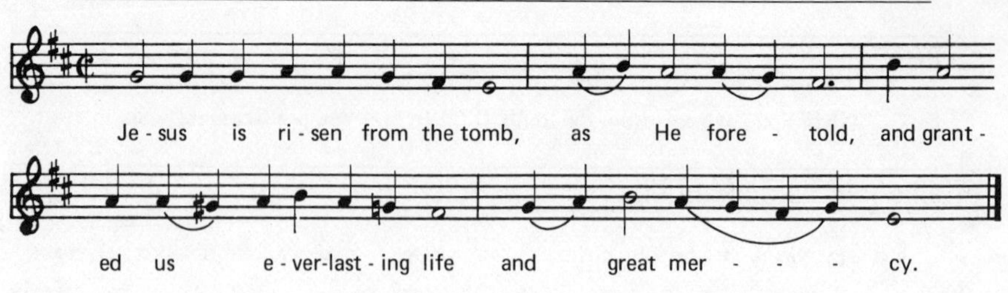

ODE 7

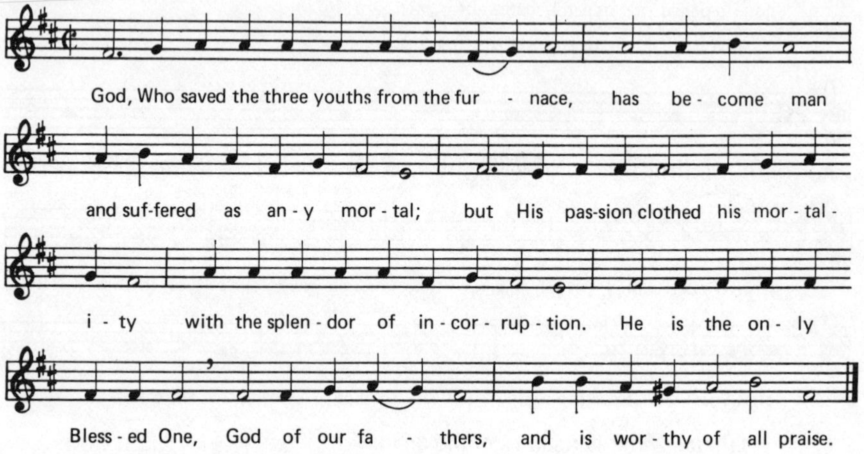

God, Who saved the three youths from the fur - nace, has be - come man
and suf-fered as an - y mor - tal; but His pas-sion clothed his mor - tal -
i - ty with the splen - dor of in - cor - rup - tion. He is the on - ly
Bless - ed One, God of our fa - thers, and is wor - thy of all praise.

Refrain: Christ is risen from the dead.

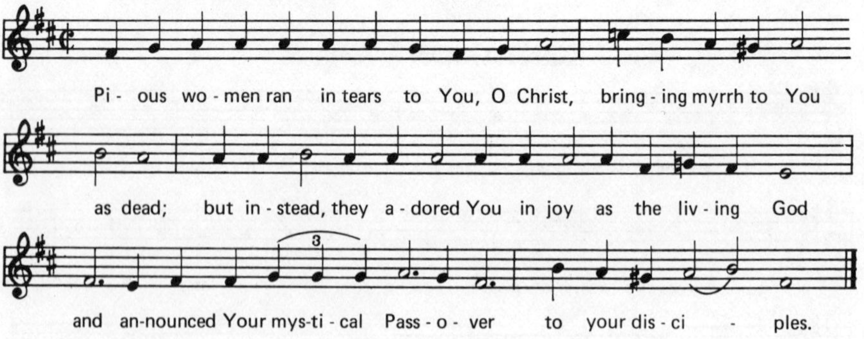

Pi - ous wo - men ran in tears to You, O Christ, bring - ing myrrh to You
as dead; but in - stead, they a - dored You in joy as the liv - ing God
3
and an-nounced Your mys-ti - cal Pass - o - ver to your dis - ci - ples.

Refrain: Christ is risen from the dead.

3
We cel - e - brate the vic - tor - y o - ver Death, the de-struc - tion of
the deep a - byss, and the birth of a new e - ter - nal life. With joy,

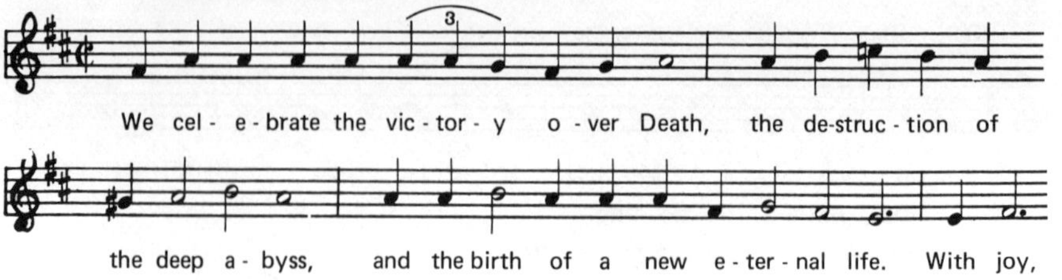

we praise the Au-thor of all things, the on - ly Bless - ed One, God
of our fa - thers, for He is wor - thy of all praise.
Refrain: Christ is risen from the dead.
This most splen-did and sav - ing night is sac - red and all-worth - y
of sol - em - ni - ty. It her - alds the bright day of re - sur - rec - tion
on which the E-ter - nal Light in the flesh, has shown forth from the tomb to all.
Refrain: Christ is risen from the dead.
Katavasia: God, who saved the three youths...
ODE 8
This is that cho - sen and ho - ly day, feast of feasts, most sol-emn day,
on - ly king and lord of all Sab-baths, on which we e - ver praise Christ.
Refrain: Christ is risen from the dead.
Come, on this glo - rious day of re - sur - rec - tion, and par-take
of the fruit of the new vine, the di - vine joy of Christ's king - dom,
e - ver prais - ing Him, our God.
Refrain: Christ is risen from the dead.

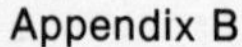

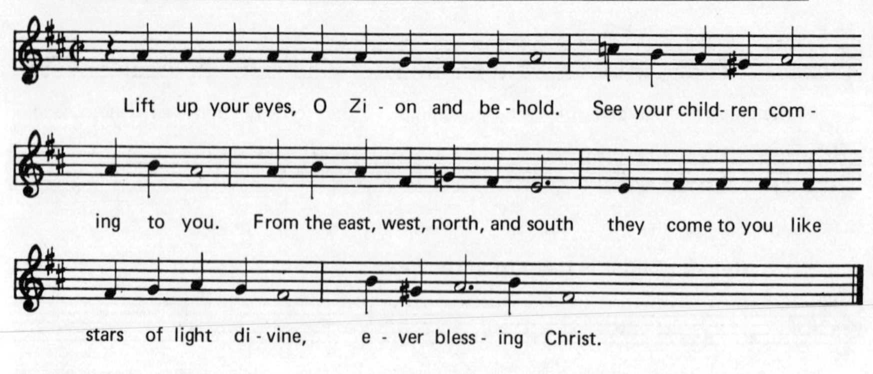
Lift up your eyes, O Zi - on and be - hold. See your child - ren com -
ing to you. From the east, west, north, and south they come to you like
stars of light di - vine, e - ver bless - ing Christ.

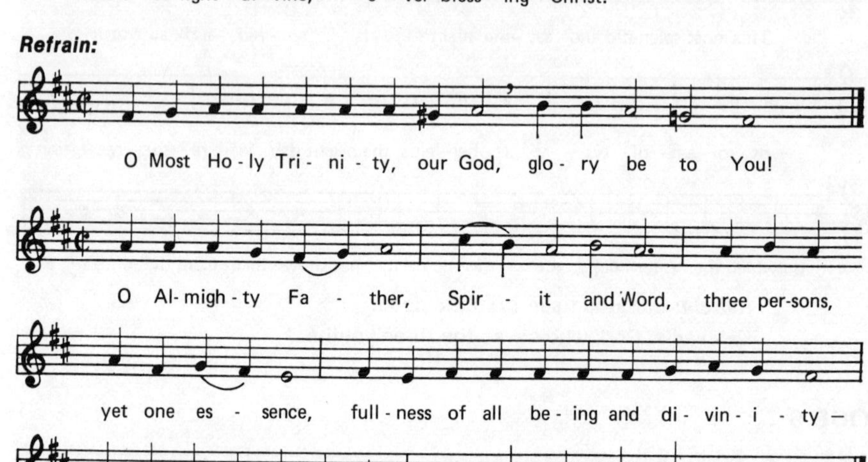
Refrain:
O Most Ho - ly Tri - ni - ty, our God, glo - ry be to You!
O Al - migh - ty Fa - ther, Spir - it and Word, three per - sons,
yet one es - sence, full - ness of all be - ing and di - vin - i - ty —
we have been bap - tized in You, and e - ver bless You.

Refrain: O Most Holy Trinity, our God, glory be to You!

Katavasia: This is that chosen and holy day...

ODE 9

Priest:

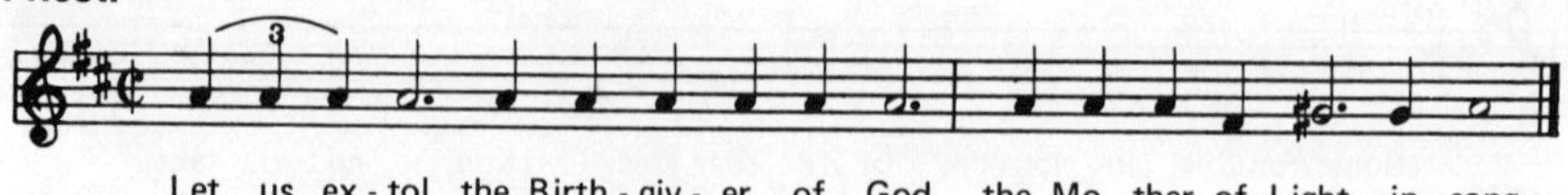
Let us ex - tol the Birth - giv - er of God, the Mo - ther of Light, in song.

The an - gel ex - claimed to her, full of grace: Re - joice,
O Pure Vir - gin; a - gain I say, re - joice! Your Son is

ri - sen from the grave on the third day and has raised the dead.
Let all na - tions re - joice.
Shine in splen - dor, O new Je - ru - sa - lem! For the glo - ry
of the Lord is ri - sen up - on you. O Zi - on sing with joy
and re-joice! And you pure Mo-ther of God, re - joice in the re - sur -
rec - tion of your Son.

Refrain: Christ is risen from the dead.

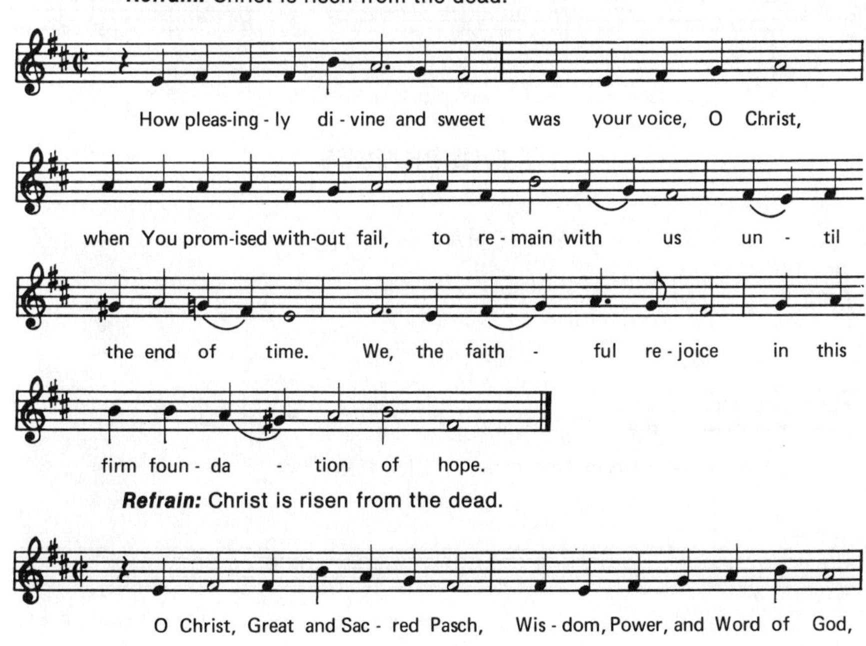
How pleas-ing - ly di - vine and sweet was your voice, O Christ,
when You prom-ised with-out fail, to re - main with us un - til
the end of time. We, the faith - ful re - joice in this
firm foun - da - tion of hope.
Refrain: Christ is risen from the dead.
O Christ, Great and Sac - red Pasch, Wis - dom, Power, and Word of God,

grant that we be with You in your king - dom , on the nev-er - end - ing day.

Refrain: Christ is risen from the dead.

Katavasia: Shine in splendor...

HYMN OF LIGHT

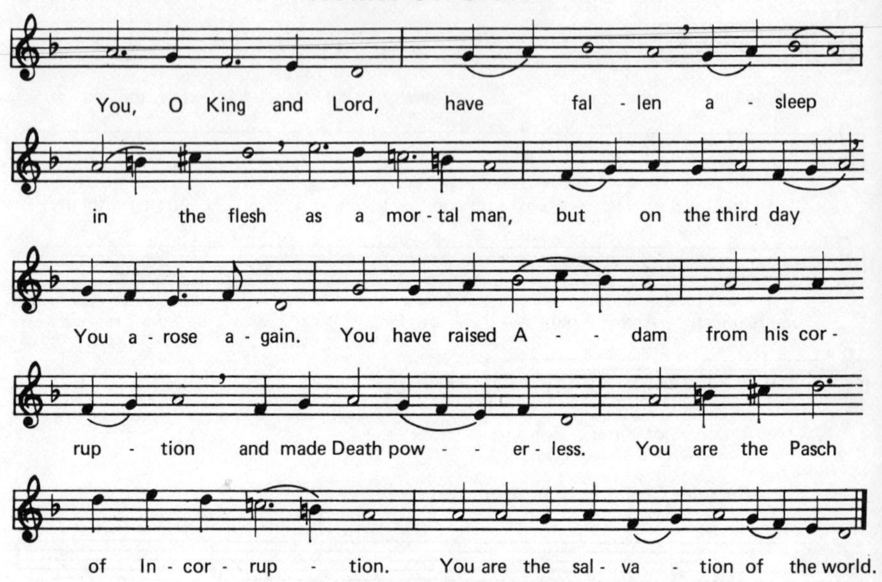
You, O King and Lord, have fal - len a - sleep
in the flesh as a mor - tal man, but on the third day
You a - rose a - gain. You have raised A - - dam from his cor -
rup - tion and made Death pow - - er - less. You are the Pasch
of In - cor - rup - tion. You are the sal - va - tion of the world.

AT THE PRAISES

PASCHAL HYMNS

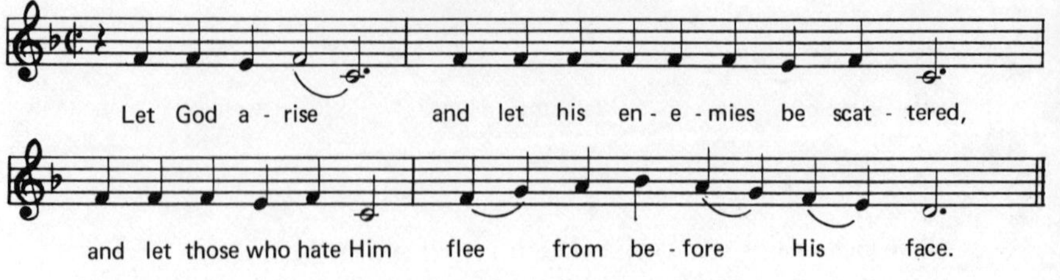
Let God a - rise and let his en - e - mies be scat - tered,
and let those who hate Him flee from be - fore His face.

To - day the sac - red Pasch is re - vealed to us, ho - ly and new Pasch,

the mys - ti - cal Pass - o - ver, the ven - er - a - ble Pass - o - ver, the Pasch
which is Christ the Re - deem - er, spot - less Pasch, great Pasch,
the Pasch of the faith - ful, the Pasch which is the key to the gates of
Par - a - dise, the Pasch which sanc-ti-fies all the faith - ful.
As smoke van - ish - es, so let them van - ish as wax
melts be - fore a fire.
O Wo - men, be the her - alds of good news and tell what you saw;
tell of the vi - sion and say to Zi - on: Ac - cept the good news of joy
from us, the news that Christ has ri - sen. Ex - ult and cel - e - brate
and re-joice, O Je - ru - sa - lem, see - ing Christ the King coming from the tomb
like a bride - groom.

So let the wick-ed per-ish at the pre-sence of God and let the
right-eous ones re- joice.
The myrrh - bear-ing wo - men ar-rived just be-fore the dawn
at the tomb of the Giv-er of Life and found an An-gel seat-ed on
the stone who spoke these words to them: Why do you seek the liv - ing
a-mong the dead? Why do you mourn the In-cor-rup-ti-ble a-mong
those sub-ject to de-cay? Go, an-nounce the good news
to His Dis- ci - ples.
This is the day that the Lord has made; let us ex-ult and re-joice in it.
Pasch so de-light-ful, Pasch of the Lord is the Pasch — most hon-ored
Pasch now dawned on us. It is the Pasch! There-fore, let us joy-ful-

ly em - brace one an - oth - er. O Pass - o - ver, save us from sor-row;
for to - day Christ has shown forth from the tomb as from a bri - dal
cham - ber and filled the wo - men with joy by say - ing: An -
nounce the good news to My A - pos - tles.
Glo - ry be to the Fa - ther, and to the Son, and to the Ho - ly Spir - it,
now and e - ver and for - e - ver. A - men.
This is the Re - sur -rec - tion Day. Let us be en-light- ened by this Feast
and let us em-brace one an - oth - er. Let us call "Bre - - thren"
e - ven those who hate us, and in the Re - sur - rec - tion
for - give ev - ery-thing; and let us sing: Christ is ri - sen
from the dead. By death He con-quered Death, and to
those in the graves He grant - ed life.

APPENDIX C
Music for Saturday of the Departed

INSTEAD OF THE PROKEIMENON

Tone 6

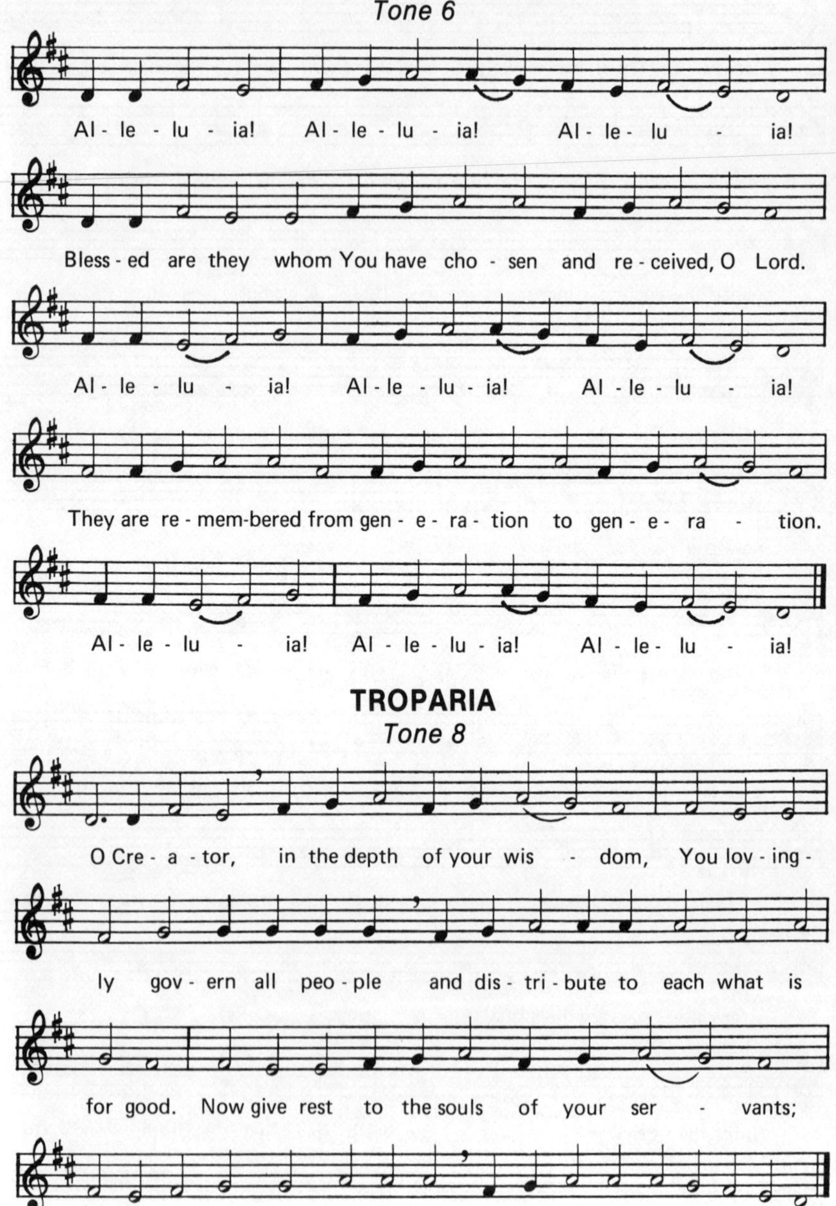
Al - le - lu - ia! Al - le - lu - ia! Al - le - lu - ia!
Bless - ed are they whom You have cho - sen and re - ceived, O Lord.
Al - le - lu - ia! Al - le - lu - ia! Al - le - lu - ia!
They are re - mem-bered from gen - e - ra - tion to gen - e - ra - tion.
Al - le - lu - ia! Al - le - lu - ia! Al - le - lu - ia!
TROPARIA
Tone 8
O Cre - a - tor, in the depth of your wis - dom, You lov - ing -
ly gov - ern all peo - ple and dis - tri - bute to each what is
for good. Now give rest to the souls of your ser - vants;
for they have placed their hope in You, our Cre - a -tor, Mak-er and our God.

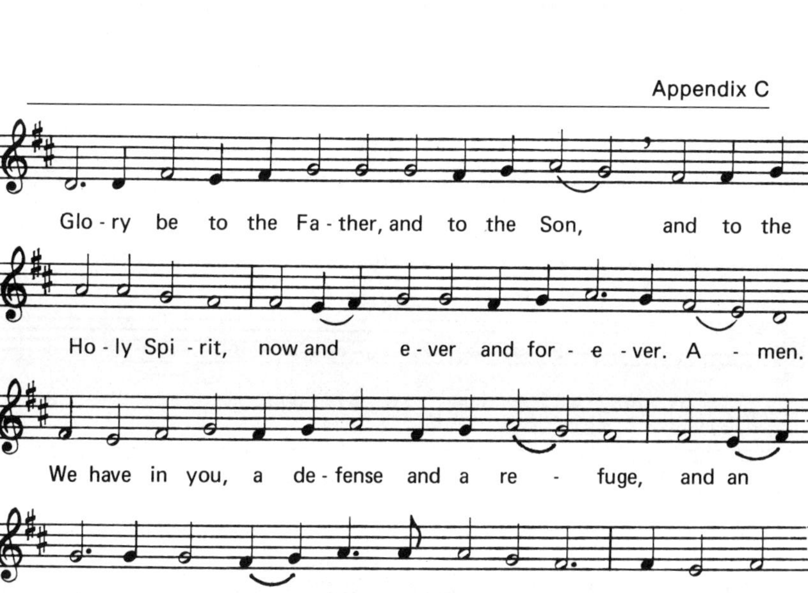
Glo - ry be to the Fa - ther, and to the Son, and to the
Ho - ly Spi - rit, now and e - ver and for - e - ver. A - men.
We have in you, a de - fense and a re - fuge, and an
ad - vo - cate ac - cept - a - ble to God to whom you

gave birth, O Vir - gin Mo - ther of God, the sal - va - tion

of the faith - ful.

HYMNS FOR THE DECEASED

Tone 5

Refrain:

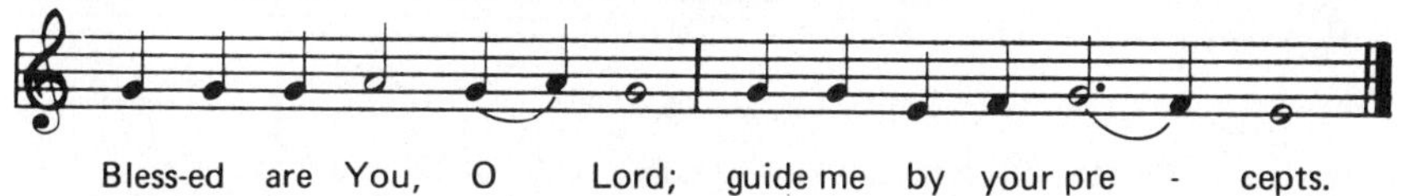
Bless-ed are You, O Lord; guide me by your pre - cepts.

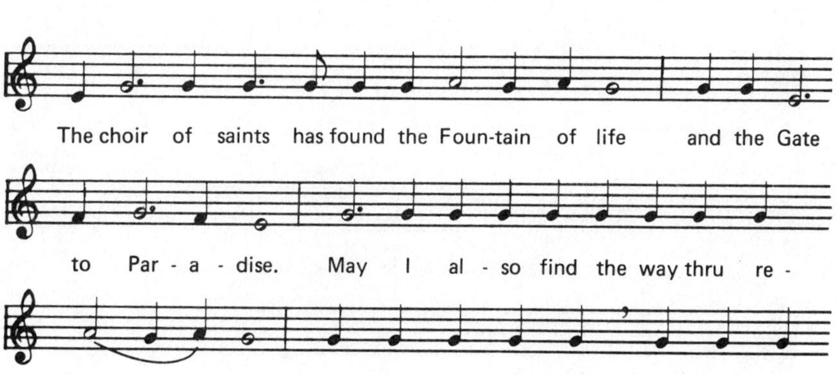
The choir of saints has found the Foun-tain of life and the Gate
to Par - a - dise. May I al - so find the way thru re -
pen - - tance. I am a lost sheep; call me back,

O Sa - vior, and save me.
Refrain: Blessed are You, O Lord; guide me by your precepts.
O Lord, I am the i - mage of your glo - - ry
which is be - yond de - scrip - tion, e - ven though I bear the
marks of trans-gres - - sions. Have mer- cy on your crea - ture.
O Mas - ter, in your com-pas-sion cleanse me. Grant me
the home I yearn for, and a - gain make me an in -
hab - i - tant of par - a - dise.
Refrain: Blessed are You, O Lord; guide me by your precepts.
Grant rest, O God, to your ser - - vants, and place them in
par - a - dise, where the choirs of saints and right-eous shine like stars.
O Lord, give rest to your de - part - ed ser - vants,

and re - mit all their trans - gres - sions.
Refrain: Blessed are You, O Lord; guide me by your precepts.
In the be - gin - ning You called me from noth - ing - ness
and fav - ored me with your di - vine i - mage. Since I trans -
gressed your com-mand - - ments, You re - turned me to the earth from
which I was tak - en. Re-store me to your like - - ness,
that my o - ri - gin - al beau - ty may be re - newed in me.
Refrain: Blessed are You, O Lord; guide me by your precepts.
Come to Me, all who have walked the nar - row and sor -
row - ful path, who dur - ing life have tak - en up - on your - selves the
Cross as a yoke and faith- ful - ly fol - lowed Me; en - joy the
hon-ors and the heav- en - ly crowns which I have pre - pared for you.
Refrain: Blessed are You, O Lord; guide me by your precepts.

O Saints, you preached the Lamb of God and like lambs were slain;

you were trans-ferred to un- end - ing and e - ver - last - ing life.

O Mar - tyrs, pray fer - vent - ly that He grant us the re- mis -

sion of our trans - gres - sions.

Refrain: Blessed are You, O Lord; guide me by your precepts.

We praise with de - vo -tion the three-fold ra - di -ance of one Di -

vi - ni - ty by sing - ing a - loud: Ho - ly are You, e -

ter - nal Fa - ther, co - e - ter - nal Son and di - vine Spir - it.

En-light - en us who faith- ful - ly serve You and de- liv - er us

from e - ter - nal fire.

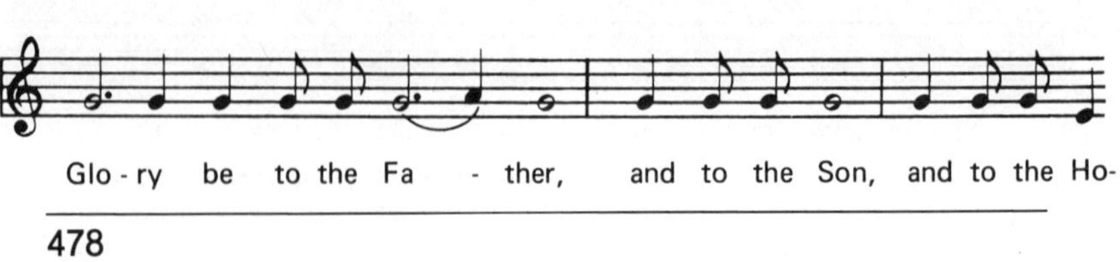
Glo - ry be to the Fa - ther, and to the Son, and to the Ho-

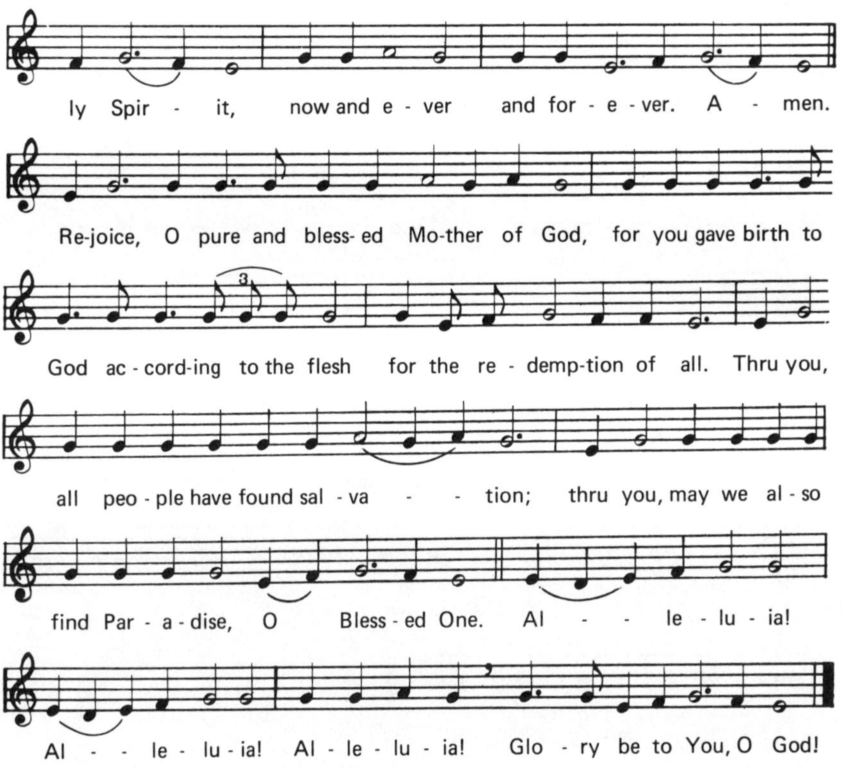

ly Spir - it, now and e - ver and for - e - ver. A - men.
Re-joice, O pure and bless- ed Mo-ther of God, for you gave birth to
God ac - cord-ing to the flesh for the re - demp-tion of all. Thru you,
all peo - ple have found sal - va - - tion; thru you, may we al - so
find Par - a - dise, O Bless - ed One. Al - - le - lu - ia!
Al - - le - lu - ia! Al - le - lu - ia! Glo - ry be to You, O God!

SESSIONAL HYMN II

Tone 5

Our Sav-ior, rest your ser - vants with the just, and place them in
your court as it is writ - ten. O Sav - ior, You love all peo - ple
and are gra - cious; there - fore, re - mit all their vol - un -
tar - y and in - vol - un - tar - y sins and all those com - mit -

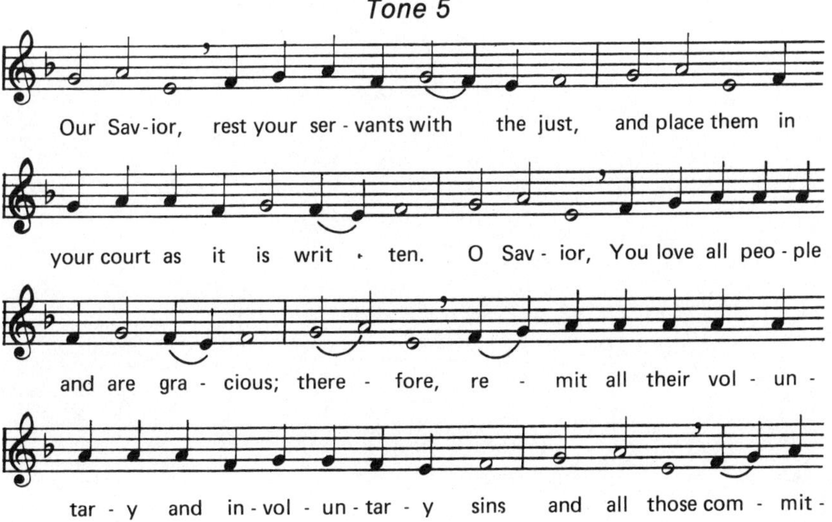

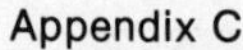

ted know-ing - ly and un - know - ing - ly.
Glo - ry be to the Fa - ther, and to the Son, and to the Ho - ly
Spir - - it, now and e - ver and for - e - - ver. A - - - men.
O Christ our God, thru the Vir - gin You ap - peared to the world;
and through her, You have shown us to be the chil - dren of light;
have mer - cy on us.

Glory be...now and ever: *(Repeat the above)*

CORRECTION FOR PAGE 260

Tone 5 **Glory be...now and ever:** As You walked along, O Lord, * You found a man who had been blind from birth. * In surprise, the disciples asked You: * Was it because of the sin of this man or his parents * that he was born blind, O Master? * But You, O Savior, answered them, saying: * Neither has this man sinned, nor his parents, * but that the works of God would be revealed in him. * I must accomplish the works of Him who sent Me, * which no one else can work. * As You said that, You spat on the ground * and made mud from the dust to anoint his eyes. * And You said to him: Go and wash in the pool of Siloam. * When he washed, he was healed and cried out to You: * O Lord, I believe! * And he bowed down and worshiped You. * Therefore, we also cry out to You: Have mercy on us!